CALIFORNIA CRIMINAL LAW

by

CHARLES W. FRICKE, LL.M., J.D., LL.D.

Judge of the Superior Court of Los Angeles County, California; formerly Assistant District Attorney of Los Angeles County, California; Professor of Criminal Law and Procedure at Loyola College. Author of: California Criminal Law; California Criminal Evidence; California Criminal Procedure; Peace Officers' Manual; Law of Criminal Arrest; Criminal Investigation, Planning and Trying Cases.

———

SEVENTH EDITION
Revised and Enlarged
1959

———

Published by
O. W. SMITH
Law Book Seller and Publisher
122 South Broadway
Los Angeles 12, California

Printed in the United States of America
during Month of May
Nineteen Hundred Fifty-Nine

PREFACE—SEVENTH EDITION

Changes in the statutory law and substantial changes in the application of the law by the decisions of our appellate courts call for another edition. As in former editions it has been the effort of the author to state the law as declared by the decisions on appeal by the courts of this State and the Supreme Court of the United States in its interpretation and application of the law of California and a few decisions of the courts of sister states which may be suggestive. Where there appeared to be a trend of decision toward a change or modification of it appeared that judicial decision, and, in a few nstances, where there should be such a change the author has taken the liberty of making suggestions.

The value of this work, especially to the student and the young lawyer will be greatly increased if he familiarizes himself with the arrangement of the work and the categories under which the various subjects and sub-topics are presented. In research the reader should also consult the author's other works—California Criminal Procedure and California Criminal Evidence—which will frequently be found to further cover matters related to the substantive law of crimes and will be found of value at the trial.

CHAS. W. FRICKE

TABLE OF CONTENTS

vii

viii

CHAPTER I.

CALIFORNIA CRIMINAL LAW

Law Is Wholly Statutory

While many of those offenses which were crimes at common law have been made, usually with some changes, crimes in California, the substantive criminal law of this state is entirely statutory and no act or omission is criminal or punishable as such unless, at the time of such act or omission, there be in force a valid statute or ordinance declaring the act therein defined to be punishable as a crime and prescribing a penalty for its violation. (Penal Code, secs. 6, 15; People v. Whipple, 100 Cal. App. 261; People v. Roland, 134 Cal. App. 675, 680; People v. Weitzel, 201 Cal. 116, 601.)

What Are Not Defenses

Similarly no excuse or justification will afford a defense to a person charged with a crime unless such defense is based on statute or ordinance. (People v. Whipple, 100 Cal. App. 261.) The so-called defenses of the "unwritten law" or "the law of necessity" have no standing in this state. (People v. Young, 70 Cal. app. 2d 28.) And, if a person is guilty of the offense with which he is charged it is no defense that he could have been prosecuted for an offense other than that with which he was charged and which might carry a lesser penalty (People v. Moulton, 116 Cal. 552; People v. Todd, 9 Cal. App. 2d 237) or that he was singled out for prosecution for an offense when there were others equally guilty who were not prosecuted (People v. Darcy, 59 Cal. App. 2d 342; People v. Oreck, 74 Cal. App. 2d 215; People v. Hess, 104 Cal. App. 2d 642, or that the penalty for the offense with which he is charged is greater than that of another offense of a more serious or aggravated character (People v. Carillo, 66 Cal. App. 146; People v. Mills, 74 Cal. App. 353) or that some other person has been convicted of the same crime (People v. Johnson, 47 Cal. 122). Other examples of untenable defenses are referred to in the discussion of the various offenses.

Construction of Penal Statutes

"The rule of the common law, that penal statutes are to be strictly construed, has no application to this code. All its provisions are to be construed according to the fair import of their terms, with a view to effect its objects and to promote justice." (Penal Code, sec. 4; People v. Fowler, 88 Cal. 136, 139.)

Repeal or Amendment of Penal Statutes

It is the general rule that the repeal or repeal by amend ment of a penal statute after the commission of a crime but before the imposition or execution of the sentence will preclude prosecution and punishment under the repealed statute but in California, unless the intent to bar prosecution and punishment is expressly declared in the amending or repealing statute, where a person has committed a crime, the law violated and the penalties continue in effect as to the crime committed even though such law is amended or repealed after the crime was committed. (Sec. 9608. Government Code, formerly Political Code, sec. 329; People v. McNulty, 93 Cal. 427; People v. Davis, 67 Cal. App. 210; People v. Pratt, 67 Cal. App. 606; People v. Edwards, 72 Cal. App. 102; People v. Righthouse, 10 Cal. 2d 86; People v. Barton, 48 Cal. App. 2d 365; People v. Tisdale, 57 Cal. 104; People v. Newell, 192 Cal. 659; People v. Williams, 24 Cal. App. 646, 650; People v. Lindsay, 75 Cal. App. 115; People v. King, 136 Cal. App. 717; In re Crane, 4 Cal. App. 2d 265; People v. McCord, 72 Cal. App. 2d 223; People v. Grosofsky, 73 Cal. App. 2nd 15.) While section 9608 of the Government Code refers to cases prosecuted by indictment or information the word "information," as used, includes a complaint (Sekt. v. Justice's Court, 26 Cal. 2d 297, 303).

Effect of Section or Chapter Titles

The head notes or black letter headings of sections of the codes in 1872 or chapter headings, forming a part of the statute when enacted, are to be given effect in interpreting such statute and, if such head note or title is of narrower scope than the section would be without such heading or title, the section is to be construed as confined to the narrower scope shown by the head note. (In re Wilson, 30 Cal. App. 567; People v. Richards, 86 Cal. App. 86; In re Wilson, 196 Cal. 515; Messick v. Superior Court, 57 Cal. App. 340.)

Note: Section 7 of the Vehicle Code makes this rule inapplicable to that code).

Where, however, the black letter headings or head notes to a section or chapter were placed there by the publishers of the statute, and not by the legislature as a part of the statute, they can not be considered in interpreting the statute. (In re Holcomb, 21 Cal. 2d 126.)

Where a statute, which originally had to be given a limited application by reason of its head note which was part of the statute when enacted, is amended by an act which includes no such limiting head note such amendment acts as the repeal of such head note and the amended statute is to be construed without regard to such former head note. (People v. Schlachter, 136 Cal. App. 184.)

English Language—Statutes must be in

Section 24 of Article IV of the Constitution provides that all official writings, and the executive, legislative and judicial proceedings shall be conducted, preserved and published in no other than the English Language.

Where the defendant was charged with a violation of section 11500 of the Health and Safety Code (the narcotic law) with possession of "Genus Lophorphora . . . also known as peyote" the court held that the use of "Genus Lophophora" was not a departure from the use of the English language and that if a Latin word as been in common use and carried in English dictionaries for many years it is proper to put it into a statute (People v. Johnson, 147 Cal. App. 2d. 417). Where the definition of a crime is not in the English language the statute is unconstitutional (In re Lockett, 179 Cal. 581). When a word, whether coming from a foreign language or coined to meet a particular need of expression, has been used as an English word in speech or writing to such an extent that its meaning has become commonly understood by people dealing with the subject to which it relates, it becomes a part of the English language with the meaning attached to it by such use even though it is not in the English dictionary (People v. Beesley, 119 Cal. App. 82, 88).

Vague and Uncertain Statute

A statute, so vague and uncertain that the subject matter, the persons subject thereto or the act made punishable thereby becomes a matter of opinion or conjecture instead of being determinable by the language used, is invalid. (Matter of Peppers, 189 Cal. 682; In re Harder, 9 Cal. App. 2d 153; see also cases collected in Pacific Coast Dairy v. Police Court, 214 Cal. 668; People v. McCaughan, 49 Cal. 2d.)

Statute Denouncing a Series of Acts

Where a statute, in defining a crime, enumerates and denounces a series of acts or methods in which such statute is violated, the commission of any one of such acts will constitute the offense, (People v. Lawlor, 21 Cal. App. 63, 65) and the doing of two or more of such acts on a single occasion will constitute but one offense. But where a statute, for example section 337a of the Penal Code, is written in the disjunctive throughout and the several offenses therein are separately defined and are apparently as separate and distinct from each other as if they had been enacted in separate sections of the code, each offense defined therein is a separate offense to be construed as if it stood alone in a separate section and were read in connection with the general words applicable to all. (Matter of Robers, 157 Cal. 472; see also People v. Lawlor, 21 Cal. App. 63; People v. Plath, 166 Cal. 227; People v. Cahan, 126 Cal. App. 2d. 785.)

Local Ordinance Conflicting With State Law

Where a state statute and a local ordinance both undertake to make the same act or omission punishable as a crime, the state law prevails and the ordinance is void, (Ex parte Sic, 73 Cal. 142; Ex parte Mansfield, 106 Cal. 400; Ex parte Stephen, 114 Cal. 282; People v. Huchstep, 114 Cal. App. 769; In re Mingo, 190 Cal. 769; People v. De Ferrari, 63 Cal. App. 671; Ex parte Daniels, 183 Cal. 636; In re Portnay, 21 Cal. 2d. 237; People v. Villarino, 134 Cal. App. 2d 893) and the same rule applies where the local law is a provision of a city charter. (In re Shaw, 32 Cal. App. 2d. 84.)

Where, however, while the local ordinance is upon the same general subject matter as that of a state statute, such ordinance does not conflict with or cover the same act or omission as that punishable by the state law, but makes punishable as a crime an act not covered by the statute the ordinance is valid. (In re Iverson, 199 Cal. 582; In re Simmons, 199 Cal. 590.)

The legislature may, however, by including in the state statute a provision that no local subdivision of government shall legislate upon a particular subject covered by such statute or by other language declaring the legislative intent to occupy exclusively a particular field of legislation, thereby take unto itself the exclusive right of passing legislation thereon and in such case a local ordinance in the same field is invalid. (Ex parte Daniels, 183 Cal. 636; In re Iverson, 199 Cal. 582.)

Conflict Between State Statutes

Where two legislative enactments punish exactly the same act or omission as crimes they are in conflict (Ex parte Stephen, 114 Cal. 278, 282; In re Murphy, 190 Cal. 286, 290; In re Mingo, 190 Cal. 769, 771) and the one latest in time will control (People v. Lewis, 4 Cal. App. 2d 775; People v. Carter, 131 Cal. App. 177; People v. Breyer, 139 Cal. App. 547; Spreckels v. Graham, 194 Cal. 516; Patchett v. Weber, 198 Cal. 440; In re Bryson, 131 Cal. App. 546) but provisions of the earlier act, not included and not in conflict with the law of later date, remain in effect. (People v. Breyer, 139 Cal. App. 547; People v. Carter, 131 Cal. App. 177.)

A later act, containing no repealing clause, does not repeal a prior act except so far as the two are clearly inconsistent or it is manifest that the later act is intended as a substitute for the former in all respects and to cover the entire subject to which both relate. The law does not favor repeal by implication and where two statutes treat of the same subject, one being special and the other general, unless they are irreconcilably inconsistent, the latter, though later in date will not be held to have repealed the former but the special act will prevail in its application to the subject matter so far as coming within its provisions. (People v. Edwards, 28 Cal. App. 716.) Sections 7028 and 7030 of the Business and Professions Code, making it a misdemeanor to conspire to engage in the business of contractor has been held to take such conspiracies out of the scope of section 182, the general conspiracy law (In re Williamson, 43 Cal. 2d. 651).

"Crime" Defined

"A crime or public offense is an act committed or omitted in violation of a law forbidding or commanding it, and to which is annexed, upon conviction, either of the following penalties: 1. Death; 2 Imprisonment; 3. Fine; 4. Removal from office; or 5. Disqualification to hold and enjoy any office of honor, trust or profit in this state." (Penal Code, sec. 15.) To constitute an act or omission a crime it must not only be in violation of a statute or ordinance but such violation must carry with it one or more of the penalties listed in section 15. (Matter of Ellsworth, 165 Cal. 677; see also People v. McNulty, 3 Cal. Unrep. 441, and People v. McNulty, 93 Cal. 427; People v. Vincent, 95 Cal. 425, 429.)

Felonies and Misdemeanors Distinguished

"Crimes are divided into: 1. Felonies; and 2. Misdemeanors." (Penal Code, sec. 16.)

"A felony is a crime which is punishable with death or by imprisonment in the state prison. Every other crime is a misdemeanor. When a crime, punishable by imprisonment in the state prison, is also punishable by fine or imprisonment in a county jail, in the discretion of the court, it shall be deemed a misdemeanor for all purposes after a judgment imposing a punishment other than imprisonment in the state prison.

Where a crime is declared to be a felony by the statute defining it but no specific penalty is provided for its violation such crime is a felony (In re Belotti, 12 Cal. App. 2d 103) and the penalty is provided for in the general statutes covering cases wherein no penalty is specially provided. (See **General Provisions as to Penalties** in following sub-title.) If the offense carries, by express statutory provision, either the sole penalty of death, or the sole penalty of imprisonment in the state prison, or carries the penalty of death or the alternative of imprisonment in the state prison and no other possible penalty the offense is at all times a felony.

Offenses Punishable by Imprisonment in State Prison or Jail or by Fine

Where an offense is punishable either as a felony by imprisonment in the state prison or as a misdemeanor by fine or by imprisonment in a jail the offense is a felony up to the time the sentence is imposed. (People v. Williams, 27 Cal. 2d 220; People v. War, 20 Cal. 117; Doble v. Superior Court, 197 Cal. 556, 799; People v. Lippner, 219 Cal. 395; People v. Pryor, 17 Cal. App. 2d 397; People v. Kennedy, 21 Cal. App. 2d 185; People v. Cowan, 38 Cal. App. 2d 231; People v. Boren, 139 Cal. 210; People v. Boggess, 75 Cal. App. 499.)

Probation without Sentence

If, upon conviction of an offense punishable either as a felony or as a misdemeanor, the defendant is placed on probation without any sentence having been pronounced he still stands convicted of a felony. (People v. Lippner, 219 Cal. 395.)

Effect of Sentence

Where in such a case the defendant is sentenced to imprisonment in the state prison the offense is at all times a felony but if he be sentenced to a term in jail or to pay a fine the offense is deemed a misdemeanor for all purposes after such judgment has been pronounced (People v. Cornell, 16 Cal. 187; People v. Perini, 94 Cal. 573; In re Sullivan, 3 Cal. App. 193; In re O'Shea, 11 Cal. App. 468; People v. Picetti, 124 Cal. 361; People v. Gray, 137 Cal. 267; People v. Sacramento Butchers, 112 Cal. App. 481, and interesting discussion therein; People v. Lippner, 219 Cal. 395; People v.

Rowland, 19 Cal. App. 2d 540; People v. Wilson, 59 Cal. App. 2d 610) even though the statute declares the offense to be a felony. (People v. Trimble, 18 Cal. App. 2d 350; People v. Rowland, 19 Cal. App. 2d 540.)

The question as to whether an offense is a felony or a misdemeanor can not, however, be determined solely by the sentence imposed. Where the offense is punishable only by imprisonment in the state prison it is always a felony and its character is not changed if the illegal sentence imposed provided for imprisonment in the county jail. And where a defendant is convicted of what in law can only be a misdemeanor but is sentenced to and serves under such sentence a term of imprisonment in the state prison the crime is only a misdemeanor and in such a case the defendant could truthfully say he had not been convicted of a felony even though he had never by appeal or otherwise attacked the illegality of his imprisonment. (Lesser v. Collins, 1 Cal. App. 2d 161.)

Lesser Offense

If a defendant is convicted of an offense less than that with which he was charged in the indictment, information or complaint the question as to whether he has been convicted of a felony or misdemeanor depends not upon the offense with which he was charged but upon the penalty of the offense of which he was convicted. (People v. Apgar, 35 Cal. 389; People v. Ambrey, 53 Cal. 427.)

State Prison or Death Not in Penalty

An offense the penalty for which does not include either the death penalty or imprisonment in the state prison and which is not expressly declared to be a felony is a misdemeanor only. (People v. Phair, 137 Cal. App. 612; In re Humphrey, 64 Cal. App. 572.)

Where Place of Imprisonment Not Stated

Where the law provides that a particular crime is punishable by a specified period of imprisonment but is silent as to the place of imprisonment and the offense is not declared to be either a misdemeanor or a felony the place of imprisonment is a jail and the offense is a misdemeanor (In re Humphrey, 64 Cal. App. 572; Union Ice Co. v. Rose, 11 Cal. App. 356) but there may be additional factors which would classify such an offense a felony. Thus where the legislature created the offense of burglary with explosives (Penal Code, sec. 464) with the penalty of imprisonment of not less than twenty-five nor more than forty years but the statute neither declared the place of imprisonment nor whether the offense was a felony or a misdemeanor, it was held that, considering the severity of the penalty and the fact that it was included in the same chapter as first and second degree burglary, felonies, the offense was a felony. (In re Wilson, 196 Cal. 515.)

Imprisonment as Condition of Probation Not a Sentence

The imposition of a period of detention in the county jail as a condition of probation is not the imposition of a sentence or a judgment (People v. Wallach, 8 Cal. App. 2d 129; People v. Gibbons, 39 Cal. App. 2d 671; People v. Johnston, 37 Cal. App. 2d 606) and has no bearing upon the question as to whether the offense is a felony or a misdemeanor. (See also In re Hays, 120 Cal. App. 2d. 308.)

CHAPTER II.

PENALTIES

General Provisions as to Penalties

Where there is no specific statute fixing both the maximum and minimum penalty for a particular crime, the punishment is fixed by general statutes.

("Punishment of felony when not otherwise prescribed). Except in cases where a different punishment is prescribed by any law of this State, every offense declared to be a felony is punishable by imprisonment in any of the state prisons, not exceeding five years; provided, however, every offense which is prescribed by any law of this state to be a felony punishable by imprisonment in any of the state prisons or by a fine, but without an alternate sentence to the county jail, may be punishable by imprisonment in the county jail not exceeding one year or by a fine, or both.

"This section shall not be construed to apply to an offense set forth in Division 10 of the Health and Safety Code, nor to any offense which is prescribed by any law of this State to be a felony punishable by imprisonment in any of the state prisons, but without alternative of a fine" (Penal Code, sec. 18).

Every offense which is prescribed by law to be a felony punishable by imprisonment in the state prison or by a fine, but without any alternate sentence to the county jail, may be punishable by imprisonment in the county jail not exceeding one year or by a fine, or both. (Penal Code, sec. 18).

Except where a different minimum punishment is prescribed by law for an offense punishable by imprisonment in the state prison, the minimum imprisonment in the state prison shall be for six months. (Penal Code, sec. 18a).

In all cases where the maximum term for an offense punishable by imprisonment in the state prison is 15 years or less, the minimum term shall be six months. (Penal Code, sec. 18b).

Except where a different punishment is prescribed for a misdemeanor it is punishable by imprisonment in the county jail not exceeding six months or by fine not exceeding five hundred dollars or both. (Penal Code, sec. 19).

Whenever any person is declared punishable for a crime by imprisonment in the state prison for a term not less than any specified number of years, and no limit to the duration of such imprisonment is declared, punishment for such offender shall be imprisonment during his natural life subject to the provisions of Part 3 of this code. (Penal Code, sec. 671).

9

Fine May Be Added

"Upon conviction of any crime punishable by imprisonment in any jail or prison, in relation to which no fine is herein prescribed, the court may impose a fine on the offender not exceeding five hundred dollars ($500) in cases of misdemeanor or five thousand dollars ($5,000) in cases of felonies, in addition to the imprisonment prescribed." (Penal Code, Sec. 672). The words "any crime" in this section include both felonies and misdemeanors and include all crimes whether included in the Penal Code or in any other statute. (People v. Shah, 91 Cal. App. 2d 843.)

Imprisonment Limited for Misdemeanors

"Maximum term of commitment to jail, etc). In no case shall any person sentenced to confinement in a county or city jail, or in a county or joint county penal farm, road camp, work camp, or other county adult detention facility, or committed to the custody of the sheriff for placement in any such county adult detention facility, on conviction of a misdemeanor, or as a condition of probation upon conviction of either a felony or a misdemeanor, or upon conviction for civil contempt, or upon default in the payment of a fine upon conviction of either a felony or a misdemeanor, or for any reason except upon conviction or more than one offense when consecutive sentences have been imposed, be comitted for a period in excess of one year; provided, however, that the time allowed on parole shall not be considered as a part of the period of confinement." (Penal Code, sec. 19a).

Does Not Apply in Felony Probation

Section 19a has no application to a case in which the defendant is placed on probation on a felony conviction and, as a condition of probation, is required to spend a period of detention in a county jail. Such order is not a sentence and furthermore section 19a applies only to cases of misdemeanor. (In re Marquez, 3 Cal. 2d 625; In re Brown, 5 Cal. App. 2d 218; In re Tantlinger, 8 Cal. App. 2d 157; In re Weber, 95 Cal. App. 2d 183.)

Where, upon conviction of manslaughter in driving a motor vehicle with gross negligence, the defendant was placed on probation on condition that he spend the first eight months in the county jail and, after serving such time less a good time allowance, probation was revoked and defendant was sentenced to serve a year in the county jail, the sentence was valid since the time spent as a condition of probation was not the service of a sentence (In re Hays, 120 Cal. App. 2d. 308).

Consecutive Sentences for Misdemeanor

Where a defendant is convicted of two or more misdemeanors, either in the same on in separate prosecutions, the court may commit the defendant to the county jail under each of such convictions and an order directing that such terms of imprisonment shall run consecutively is valid. (People v. Carr, 6 Cal. 2d 227; People v. Rozier, 4 Cal. App. 2d 250; People v. Flanagan, 7 Cal. App. 2d 214; In re Somerville, 32 Cal. App. 2d 671; People v. De Casaus, 150 Cal. App. 2d 274).

Second Violation of Same Law

There are some offenses which, when committed the first time, are punishable as misdemeanors but, upon a second commission of the same offense, the latter is made a felony and jurisdiction is in the Superior Court. There are also some felonies for which the penalty upon a second violation is greater than upon the first conviction.

Where the prior conviction was had under a particular numbered section of the Vehicle Code and the second prosecution was had under a section of that code bearing a different section number, but both sections defined and punished the same offense, it was held that upon, the conviction of the latter offense, the penalty for a second violation applied and that, while the first violation was a misdemeanor, the second violation was a felony of which the Superior Court had jurisdiction, the difference in numbering the sections being immaterial (People v. Atkinson, 115 Cal. App. 2d. 425).

Increased Penalties After Prior Conviction

Where a defendant has suffered one or more prior convictions of felony the penalty upon a subsequent conviction of a felony is subject to being increased by reason of such prior conviction upon the theory that, not having benefited by his prior experience but having displayed a continuing tendency to commit crime, he should, for his subsequent crime, receive a greater punishment or a longer period of segregation from society than if it had been his first offense.

Pleading Prior Conviction

"Whenever it shall be discovered that a pending indictment or information does not charge all prior felonies of which the defendant has been convicted either in this state or elsewhere,

12 CALIFORNIA CRIMINAL LAW

said indictment or information may be forthwith amended to charge such prior conviction'' (Penal Code, sec. 969a) and similar provision is made for the amendment of a complaint before a magistrate to which the defendant has entered a plea of guilty. (Sec. 969½, Penal Code.) Unless the defendant admits the allegation it is deemed denied and the issue must be tried and verdict rendered thereon. (Sec. 1158, Penal Code.)

Conviction—Appeal Pending

A conviction is the ascertainment of guilt by plea or at the conclusion of a trial and a person has been convicted even though the judment has been suspended during an appeal (People v. Clapp, 67 Cal. App. 2d. 197,200; People v. Morgan, 140 Cal. App. 2d 796).

A prior conviction may be pleaded and proved and given the effect of a prior conviction even though the former conviction case is on appeal (People v. Hurley, 155 Cal. App. 2d ......, cases cited).

Petty Theft After Prior Felony Conviction

Where a defendant is convicted under section 667 of the Penal Code on a charge of petty theft after a prior conviction of a felony ''no greater penalty can be imposed than imprisonment for five years notwithstanding the fact that the defendant has suffered other convictions and served time thereunder on more serious charges than the petit charge of which he was lastly convicted.'' (In re Boatwright, 210 Cal. 677, 683).

Minimum Where One Prior

Where the defendant admits, or it is found by verdict, that the defendant has suffered a prior conviction of a felony either in this state or elsewhere, and he is sentenced to the state prison, his minimum term of sentence and imprisonment is five years nothwithstanding any other provisions of law specifying a lesser sentence for his crime. (Sec. 3024, subd. c, Penal Code.) This section does not apply unless the prior conviction is alleged in the indictment or information and either admitted or found upon trial to have been suffered and the admission of such conviction by the defendant under cross examination does not constitute the admission which will make the section applicable (In re Harris, 80 Cal. App. 2d. 173 and cases cited).

A conviction of a felony under the laws of another state makes this provision of section 3024 applicable even though the act upon which such conviction was based would not, if committed in this state, have been a felony (People v. Gut-kowsky, 100 Cal. App. 2d. 635).

Where Accused was Armed

Section 969c in connection with section 3024 of the Penal Code similarly provides that whenever a defendant was, at the time of the commission of the crime or at the time of his arrest, armed with a firearm, blackjack, slungshot, billy, sandclub, sandbag, metal knuckles, and dirk, dagger or knife having a blade longer than five inches, any razor with an unguarded blade or any metal pipe or bar used or intended to be used as a club the fact that defendant was so armed shall be charged in the indictment, information or complaint and if the defendant plead not guilty the question whether he was so armed must be determined at the trial. If he plead guilty the court must determine, either upon his admission in court or by evidence, whether he was so armed.

Section 3024, subd. a, provides that, where the defendant was armed with one or more of the specified (in subd. f of section 3024) deadly weapons either at the time of his commission of the offense or a concealed deadly weapon at the time of his arrest, his minimum term of imprisonment if sentenced to state prison shall be five years notwithstanding any provision of law specifying a lesser sentence for his offense. Where the crime is one which can only be committed with a deadly weapon, this subdivision of section 3024 does not apply 'In re Shull, 23 Cal. 2d. 745; People v. Bryant, 154 Cal. App. 2d. ...... (assault with a deadly weapon; In re Rodgers, 121 Cal. App. 370, exconvict in possession of a gun).

The Dangerous Weapons Control Law, Penal Code, section 12022 provides that any person who commits or attempts to commit any felony within this state while armed with any of the weapons specified in section 12020 or a firearm capable of being concealed upon the person, without a permit to carry the same, shall, in addition to the punishment for the crime committed, serve a consecutive term as prescribed in section 12022 of the Penal Code (see Dangerous Weapons, infra). Where the crime of which the prisoner is convicted involves the element of the perpetrator being armed with or using such a weapon these additional penalties do not apply (In re Shull, 23 Cal. 2d. 745). Having used the weapon element to make up the crime charged it cannot again be used to impose the additional punishment.

Prior Conviction and Armed

Subdivision b of Section 3024 Penal Code provides that if the defendant was both previously convicted of a felony and armed with a deadly weapon at either the time of his commission of the offense or a concealed deadly weapon at the time of his arrest his minimum term, if sentenced to the state prison, shall be ten years notwithstanding any provision of law specifying a lesser sentence for his offense.

(Note: The requirement that the possession of a deadly weapon at the time of the arrest which will make applicable the special minimum sentence is the possession of a "concealed" deadly weapon quite obviously does not include a case in which the weapon was not "concealed." This gives rise to such an anomolous situation as that, where at the time of arrest the defendant was armed with a revolver, not "concealed" but displayed and used to resist arrest, this provision of law does not apply.)

Prior Felony Conviction in Another Jurisdiction

"Every person who has been convicted in any other state, government, country, or jurisdiction of an offense for which, if committed within this state, such person could have been punished under the laws of this state by imprisonment in a state prison, is punishable for any subsequent crime committed within this state in the manner prescribed in sections 644, 666 and 667, and to the same extent as if such prior conviction had taken place in a court of this state." (Penal Code, sec. 668).

Where the prior conviction was in another state for a crime which may or may not be a felony under the law of this state, depending on the facts of the case, an allegation of a prior felony conviction is not sustained unless it is shown that under such facts the said crime would at the time have been a felony under the law of this state (People v. Hayes, 3 Cal. App. 2d 59) and if it appears that the facts upon which such foreign conviction is based would not be a felony in California under our law as it existed at the time of such conviction then such prior conviction can not be considered a prior felony conviction which would make applicable the California law increasing the penalty. (People v. Pace, 2 Cal. App. 2d 464; People v. McChesney, 39 Cal. App. 2d 36; People v. Shaw, 137 Cal. App. 523; In re Williams, 76 Cal. App. 2d 161.) A conviction of felony in another state at a time when the act involved would have been a felony in California

is a prior felony conviction in this state for all purposes even
though at the time of sentence on a subsequent conviction in
California, due to amendment of the California law in the
interim, such act would only be a misdemeanor. (People v. Mc-
Connell, 20 Cal. App. 2d 196). Where the prior felony conviction was for an act which was punishable as a misdemeanor
under one section of our law but was also punishable under
another section of our law as a felony, such prior conviction
may be considered as a conviction of a felony (In re Digiuro,
100 Cal. App. 2d. 260).

Federal Convictions

Due to the nature of the federal offenses involved it has
been held that California will not, for the purpose of increasing the penalty, consider a conviction under the Jones Miller
Act (People v. Albritten, 110 Cal. App. 188) but will so consider a conviction under the Harrison Narcotic Act, (People v.
Bigelow, 94 Cal. App. 28; People v. Albritten, 110 Cal. App.
188) and the Dyer Act; (People v. Fitzwater, 5 Cal. App. 2d
187.) or other law where the offense of which the defendant
was convicted would be a felony under California law (In re
McVickers, 29 Cal. 2d. 264). A prior conviction of conspiracy
to use the mails to defraud is a prior felony conviction (People
v. Ashley, 42 Cal. 2d. 246).

Service of Term Not Necessary

Since section 3024 applies the increased penalty by reason
of a prior felony conviction without regard to whether the defendant served a term of imprisonment therefor, such prior conviction will have effect under this section even though the
defendant served no term of imprisonment for such former
conviction (People v. Velvin, 116 Cal. App. 650) and even
though he was placed on probation after such prior conviction
and probation was later terminated, the conviction set aside
and a plea of not guilty entered and the case was then dismissed. (People v. Acosta, 115 Cal. App. 103; People v. Hain-
line, 219 Cal. 532; People v. Barwick, 7 Cal. 2d 696; People v.
Majado, 22 Cal. App. 2d 323.)

What Is a Prior Felony Conviction

A prior felony conviction which was suffered by the defendant after the commission of the offense for which he is
presently being tried is not a prior felony conviction within
the meaning of the law relating to penalties. In this connec-

tion a prior felony conviction means such a conviction suffered prior to the commission of the offense in the prosecution of which such prior conviction is charged in the indictment, information or complaint. (People v. McGee, 1 Cal. 2d 611.)

Effect of Pardon

The fact that the defendant had been pardoned for his prior felony conviction does not alter its effect as increasing the penalty for a subsequent offense committed by him. (People v. Dutton, 9 Cal. 2d. 505; People v. Biggs, 9 Cal. 2d. 508) but any sentence based on a conviction of which the person was previously pardoned on the express ground that he was not guilty shall not be counted as a previous conviction (Penal Code, sec. 3045).

Habitual Criminals

"Every person convicted in this state of robbery, burglary of the first degree, burglary with explosives, rape with force and violence, arson as defined in section 447a of this code, murder, assault with intent to commit murder, train wrecking, felonious assault with a deadly weapon, extortion, kidnaping, escape from a state prison by use of force or dangerous or deadly weapon, rape or fornication or sodomy or carnal abuse of a child under the age of 14 years or any act punishable under section 288 of this code, conspiracy to commit any one or more of the aforementioned felonies who shall have been previously twice convicted upon charges separately brought and tried, and who shall have served separate terms therefor in any State prison and/or Federal penitentiary, either in this state or elsewhere, of the crime of robbery, burglary, burglary with explosives, rape with force or violence, arson, murder, assault with intent to commit murder, grand theft, bribery of a public official, perjury, subornation of perjury, train wrecking, feloniously receiving stolen goods, felonious assault with a deadly weapon, extortion, kidnaping, mayhem, escape from a State prison, rape or fornication or sodomy or carnal abuse of a child under the age of 14 years or any act punishable under section 288 of this code, conspiracy to commit any one or more of the aforementioned felonies, shall be adjudged an habitual criminal and shall be punished by imprisonment in the State prison for life." (Penal Code, Sec. 644, subd. a.)

Every person who in like manner shall have been three times convicted of felonies included in those so listed "shall be adjudged an habitual criminal and shall be punished by imprisonment in the State prison for life." (Penal Code, sec. 644, subd. b.)

This section does not subject a defendant to a second punishment or double jeopardy and is constitutional (In re Rosencrantz, 205 Cal. 534; People v. Millwood, 150 Cal. App. 2d. 154).

May Be Adjudged Not Habitual Criminal

"In exceptional cases, at any time not later than sixty days after the actual commencement of imprisonment, the court may, in its discretion, provide that the defendant is not an habitual criminal, and in such case the defendant shall not be subject to the provisions of this section or of Sections 3047 and 3048 of this code." (Penal Code, sec. 644, subd. c.)

Effect of Habitual Criminal Law

Section 644 does not affect or abrogate the death penalty in crimes so punishable. (Penal Code, sec. 644, subd. d.)

Section 3047 provides that an habitual criminal imprisoned under subdivision (a) of Section 644 should not be eligible for a release on parole until he shall have served a minimum term of at least fifteen years with benefit of good conduct credits and section 3048 provides that any habitual criminal imprisoned under subdivision (b) of Section 644 shall not be eligible for parole until he shall have served a minimum term of at least twenty years with benefit of good conduct credits.

Section 3047.5 provides that an habitual criminal under paragraph "a" of section 644, received after January 1, 1948, shall not be eligible for release on parole until he shall have served a minimum of at least nine years and section 3048.5 provides that in a case under paragraph "b" of section 644 the prisoner must serve a minimum of at least twelve years. The effect of these statutes of 1947 is the fixing of minimum periods of imprisonment even though good conduct credits would, under section 3047, permit a parole at an earlier time.

What Convictions Included

The habitual criminal law applies only where (1) the prior felony convictions were separate and successive, each sentence being served before the next conviction is had; (2) where each of the prior convictions was for one of the offenses named in the section and (3) only those prior convictions can be considered in which the terms of imprisonment were served in a

State prison and/or Federal penitentiary. (In re Miller, 133 Cal. App. 228; People v. Valdez, 3 Cal. App. 2d 700.) It has been held that serving in a state reformatory constitutes serving a term in a prison. (In re Brady, 5 Cal. 2d 224; In re Gilliam, 26 Cal. 2d 860; In re Loncarie, 71 Cal. App, 2d 144; People v. Stein, 31 Cal. 2d 630; People v. McConnell, 86 Cal. App. 2d 578.)

Under the language of section 644, the prior convictions must have been separately brought and tried and the defendant must have served separate terms therefor or the section does not apply (People v. Sukovitzen, 138 Cal. App. 2d. 159).

Where a defendant's prior convictions consisted of two robbery convictions which had been ordered to run consecutively but the first sentence had not yet been fully served and the second had not yet begun he does not come within the habitual criminal law since he has not served any term for the second conviction (In re Brees, 99 Cal. App. 2d. 328).

The service of a term, after conviction of a felony, in a facility of the Youth Authority is not the service of a prison term within the meaning of the habitual criminal law (People v. Lockwood, 146 Cal. App. 2d. 189).

Prior Convictions Outside of State

Where the conviction in another state or in a federal court was on a state of facts which under the law of California would amount only to a misdemeanor it can not be treated as a felony conviction under Sec. 644 of the Penal Code (People v. Shaw, 137 Cal. App. 533; People v. Hayes, 3 Cal. App. 2d 59; People v. Pace, 2 Cal. App. 2d 464; In re Howard, 69 Cal. App. 2d 164; In re Thompson, 72 Cal. App. 2d 747; In re Williams 76 Cal. App. 2d 161; In re Seeley 29 Cal. 2d 294) but the determination of whether the facts amounted to a felony conviction must be made according to the law of California as it existed at the time the prior conviction was suffered. (People v. McConnell, 20 Cal. App. 2d 196.) In re Williams 76 Cal. App. 2d 161; In re Seeley, 29 Cal. 2d 294.)

The pleading and proof, or admission, of a conviction of a felony in another state of an offense which may or may not be a felony if committed in the State of California, without more, merely establishes that the defendant was convicted of a felony under the law of that foreign state. Thus a conviction of grand theft in Utah (where a theft is grand theft if the value of the property is over $50) must be assumed, until proven otherwise, to be a theft of property barely over $50 in value which would only be a petty theft in California (In re McVickers, 29 Cal. 2d 264; People v. Bramble, 31 Cal. 2d 43) and, since the theft of property under the law of Texas is a felony if the property taken is of a value over $50, a Texas conviction can not be considered a felony conviction under the habitual criminal law unless there is proof that the property taken exceeded the $200 requirement for felony theft in California (In re Martin, 115 Cal. App. 2d 188).

Where, under the law of another State the elements of the offense pleaded as a prior conviction are different or less demanding than such offense under California law, it must be proved that the offense charged would have been a violation of the California statute had it been committed in this State or the prior conviction can not be used as a basis of a finding that the defendant was an habitual criminal (People v. Taylor, 155 Cal. App. 2d ....).

California Convictions

Where the prior conviction charged was suffered in this state its status is determined by the law in effect at the time of such conviction. If the prior conviction be for grand theft the question as to the value of the property involved was determined by the conviction itself and it need not be shown that the facts of the prior case were such as to constitute grand theft (People v. Vega, 136 Cal. App. 2d. 202).

Priors Must Be Pleaded and Proved

The prior convictions served must be both pleaded and proved and found by verdict or admitted by the defendant before the court can adjudicate him to be an habitual criminal (In re Fontino, 135 Cal. App. 466; In re Tartar, 1 Cal. App. 2d 400) but even though not pleaded, if the defendant admits on arraignment for judgment having suffered the required prior convictions, the court could adjudicate him an habitual criminal. (People v. Birdsell, 6 Cal. App. 2d 749.)

Where the defendant admits in open court the prior felony convictions charged, this is sufficient to establish the truth of such allegations and the court is not required to thereafter receive proof thereof and may adjudge the defendant an habitual criminal on the basis of such admissions (People v. Gilliam, 26 Cal. 2d 860; People v. Allen, 119 Cal. App. 2d 365).

The facts necessary to an adjudication that a defendant is an habitual criminal must be proved beyond a reasonable doubt (People v. Morton, 41 Cal. 2d. 536, 539).

Limited to Specified Felony Convictions

For the purpose of adjudicating a defendant an habitual criminal the court cannot consider any conviction for a felony not included in the list set forth in section 644, (People v. Hayes, 3 Cal. App. 2d 59; In re McVickers, 29 Cal. 2d 264) as for example a conviction under the Dyer Act (People v. Lohr, 28 Cal. App. 2d 397), a burglary conviction in Louisiana due to the fact that what is there burglary may not be burglary under our law (People v. McChesney, 39 Cal. App. 2d 36), a conviction under the National Motor Vehicle Theft Act (In re Galloway, 78 Cal. App. 2d 880), or a conviction under section 146 of the California Vehicle Act, now section 503 of the Vehicle Code (People v. McChesney, 39 Cal. App. 2d 36).

Effect of Pardon

The fact that the defendant has been pardoned for a prior conviction does not affect its being considered in adjudging him to be an habitual criminal. (People v. Biggs, 9 Cal. 2d 508; People v. Dutton, 9 Cal. 2d. 505) but any sentence based on a conviction of which the person was previously pardoned on the express ground that he was not guilty shall not be counted as a previous conviction (Penal Code, sec. 3045).

Foreign Prior Conviction

"Every person who has been convicted in any other state, government or country, of an offense which, if committed in this state, would be punishable by the laws of this state by imprisonment in the state prison, is punishable for any subsequent crime committed within this state in the manner prescribed in sections 644, 666 and 667, and to the same extent as if such prior conviction had taken place in a court of this state." (Penal Code, sec. 668.) Even though the offense is called a "high misdemeanor" under the law of the foreign jurisdiction it will be considered a felony conviction here if the offense is one which would be a felony under California law (People v. Stein, 31 Cal. 2d 630).

To constitute a felony conviction in another state the offense must have been one which, had it been committed at the same time in California, would have been a felony under the laws of this state (In re Harincar, 29 Cal. 2d 403; In re Wolfson, 30 Cal. 2d, 20).

Law in Force at Time of Offense Governs

Whether a prior felony conviction can be considered as a basis of adjudicating and punishing a defendant as an habitual criminal depends upon the language of section 644 as it existed at the time of the commission of the offense charged and not as it existed at the time of such prior conviction. (People v. McConnell, 20 Cal. App. 2d 196; Spivey v. McGilvray, 29 Cal. App. 2d 357; In re Kingsbury, 74 Cal. App. 2d 959; In re McVickers 29 Cal. 2d 264; In re Wolfson, 30 Cal. 2d, 20.)

Sexual Psychopaths

A convicted person found to be a sexual psychopath may be confined for a period no less than the maximum time provided for the offense committed plus the time spent in a hospital under sexual psychopath proceedings (People v. Gross, 115 Cal. App. 2d. 503; People v. Gross, 139 Cal. App. 2d. 607).

Death Penalty—Minor Under Eighteen

Section 190.1 of the Penal Code provides that the death penalty shall not be imposed upon any person who was under the age of eighteen years at the time of the commission of the crime and that the burden of proof as to age shall be upon the defendant.

CHAPTER III.

CORPUS DELICTI—ELEMENTS OF CRIME

Every crime consists of a group of elements laid down by the statute or law defining the offense and every one of these elements must exist or the statute is not violated. This group of essential elements is known as the "corpus delicti." (People v. Watters, 202 Cal. 154, 157.) This term is not limited to cases of homicide, and, People v. Simonsen, 107 Cal. 345, 347, notwithstanding, it does not mean the dead body. Generally the definition of a crime very clearly lists the elements of the corpus delicti of that crime but in some instances an important element of the corpus delicti is not disclosed by a mere reading of the definition because it is included within one of the terms used in the definition. Thus in larceny we have the element that the unlawful taking must be with the specific intent to permanently deprive the owner of his property, an element not evident in the definition of larceny but necessarily a part of that definition because of the use of the word "steal" in the definition.

Since every element of the crime must be established before there can be a conviction, the failure of the prosecution to prove the corpus delicti is the basic defense to a criminal charge, and, while the defense relied upon for an acquittal or a reversal on appeal may appear under some title such as justification, excuse, mistake of fact, unconsciousness of the accused, consent, lack of knowledge on the part of the accused, the time of forming the intent, authority for the act, or cause of death in a case of homicide, such defenses are merely specific instances of the basic defense that the corpus delicti has not been established.

The law of corpus delicti is also of great importance in the determination of a case in which, while the act of the accused was criminal, there still remains the question as to whether such act constitutes the crime charged, a lesser included offense, or some other crime not included within the allegations of the indictment or information, or, as in a prosecution for theft, it becomes important to determine which specific offense, if any, has been committed.

Identity of Perpetrator Not Part of Corpus Delicti

Proof of the corpus delicti of a crime is complete when there is evidence of the existence of every element of the offense even

22

though there is no evidence as to who committed it. Identity of the perpetrator is never a part of the corpus delicti. (People v. Tarbox, 115 Cal. 57; People v. Ward, 134 Cal. 301; People v. Moran, 144 Cal. 48; People v. Ford, 25 Cal. App. 388; People v. Eldridge, 72 Cal. App. 386; People v. Rodway, 77 Cal. App. 738, 783; People v. Garcia, 101 Cal. App. 213; People v. Samaniego, 118 Cal. App. 165; People v. Cowling, 6 Cal. App. 2d 466; People v. Stephens, 30 Cal. App. 2d 67; People v. Wilt, 40 Cal. App. 2d 124; People v. Cowan, 41 Cal. App. 2d 586; People v. Hubbell, 54 Cal. App. 2d 49; People v. Fierro, 58 Cal. App. 2d 215; People v. Ives, 17 Cal. 2d 493; People v. Wade, 71 A. C. A. 71 Cal.App. 2d 646, People v. Leary, 28 Cal. 2d 727; People v. Sparks, 82 Cal. App. 2d 145; People v. Mehaffey 32 Cal. 2d 535; People v. Cullen, 37 Cal. 2d 614; People v. Amaya, 40 Cal. 2d. 70; People v. Parker, 122 Cal. App. 2d. 867; People v. Cobb, 45 Cal. 2d. 158).

Provable by Circumstantial Evidence

While the law is otherwise in some other jurisdictions it is settled in California that the corpus delicti of any offense may be established solely by circumstantial evidence. (People v. Mar Gin Suie, 11 Cal. App. 42, 50; People v. Clark, 70 Cal. App. 531; People v. Cullen, 37 Cal. 2d 614; People v. Bedoy, 80 Cal. App. 783; People v. Hill, 2 Cal. App. 2d 141; People v. Hamilton, 49 Cal. App. 30; People v. Alviso, 55 Cal. 230, 235; People v. Wilkins, 158 Cal. 530; People v. Domenighini, 81 Cal. App. 484, 488; People v. Bermijo, 2 Cal. 2d 270; People v. D'Angelo, 60 Cal. App. 2d 73; People v. Sparks, 82 Cal. App. 2d 145; People v. Mehaffey, 32 Cal. 2d 535; People v. Corrales, 34 Cal. 2d 426; People v. Gulbrandsen, 35 Cal. 2d 512, forcible rape; People v. Kittrelle, 102 Cal. App. 2d 149, burglary; People v. Kennedy, 101 Cal. App. 2d 709, robbery and kidnaping; People v. Hubler, 102 Cal. App. 2d 689, robbery; People v. Reed, 38 Cal. 2d 423, murder in the perpetration of rape; People v. Amaya, 40 Cal. 2d. 70, murder in attempted robbery; People v. Moore, 48 Cal. 2d ...., Murder in attempt to commit rape).

The law recognizes no distinction, in the degree of proof required for conviction, between direct and circumstantial evidence. All that is required for a conviction is that guilt be established beyond a reasonable doubt (People v. Kennedy, 101 Cal. App. 2d 709; People v. Hubler, 102 Cal. App. 2d 689.)

Prima Facie Case

"The corpus delicti may be proved by circumstantial evidence and the reasonable inferences drawn therefrom. . . .

If a prima facie case is presented that the deceased met his death by means of the unlawful act of another, the evidence is sufficient.'' ''To prove a prima facie case of corpus delicti all that was required was to show a reasonable probability that a criminal act of another had been the direct cause of death.'' (People v. Ives, 17 Cal. 2d 459, murder by administration of chloral hydrate followed by drowning; People v. Du Bois, 16 Cal. App. 2d 81, death caused by wounds that could not have been self inflicted; People v. Black, 103 Cal. App. 2d 69, homicide by stab wounds; People v. Mercer, 103 Cal. App. 2d 462, burglary with explosives.)

Cannot Be Proved by Admission or Confession

Before there can be a legal conviction every element of the corpus delicti must be established by proof independent of and without any consideration of any admission, declaration or confession of the accused (People v. Mehaffey, 32 Cal. 2d 535; People v. Frank, 2 Cal. App. 283; People v. Jones, 31 Cal. 565, 567; People v. LaRue, 62 Cal. App. 276; People v. Black, 73 Cal. App. 13; People v. Jenkins, 77 Cal. App. 158; People v. Kay, 34 Cal. App. 2d 691; People v. Chan Chuan, 41 Cal. App. 2d 586; People v. Seymour, 54 Cal. App. 2d 266; People v. Quarez, 196 Cal. 404; People v. Gilbert, 86 Cal. App. 8; People v. De Martini, 50 Cal. App. 109; People v. Clark, 70 Cal. App. 530; People v. Murphy, 60 Cal. App. 2d 762; People v. Cornett, 61 Cal. App. 2d 98; People v. Cullen, 37 Cal. 2d 614; People v. Amaya, 40 Cal. 2d. 70; People v. Byrd, 42 Cal. 2d. 200) and no element of the corpus delicti can be established solely by an extrajudicial statement of the defendant. (People v. Simmonsen, 107 Cal. 345; People v. Tapia, 131 Cal. 647; People v. Ward, 145 Cal. 736; People v. De Martini, 50 Cal. App. 109; People v. Clark, 70 Cal. App. 531; People v. Quarez, 196 Cal. 404; People v. Bispham, 26 Cal. App. 2d. 216; People v. Davis, 47 Cal. App. 2d. 331; People v. Seymour, 54 Cal. App. 2d. 266; People v. Corrales, 34 Cal. 2d. 426.) Thus for example, if proof that a burglary was committed in the night-time is essential to a conviction of first degree burglary a conviction cannot be sustained if there is no proof of the time of the burglary other than an extrajudicial statement of the defendant. (People v. Vertrees, 169 Cal. 404; People v. Frey, 165 Cal. 140; People v. Parker, 122 Cal. App. 2d. 867). Where the charge has as an element of the corpus delicti the fact that the defendant was an agent, such fact cannot be established solely by the extrajudicial statement of the defendant (People v. Lambe, 125 Cal.

App. 2d. 877). Where the defendant was charged with burglary of a vehicle, an offense in which one of the elements is that the doors of the vehicle must have been locked, the latter element must be proved by evidence other than that of an extrajudicial statement of the defendant or his failure to deny an accusatory statement including that element of the offense (People v. Burns, 114 Cal. App. 2d. 566).

Where there was evidence establishing the corpus delicti of murder, the death of a human being and the existence of a criminal agency as a cause of the death, independently of any extrajudicial statements of the accused, the prosecution is not bound to establish by independent evidence the attendant circumstances of the killing (such as that it occurred in the attempt to perpetrate a robbery) before the extrajudicial declarations of the accused (such as the planning and execution of the attempted robbery) may be used to prove the degree of the murder and the corpus delicti of murder having been established by independent evidence, the circumstances surrounding the commission of the murder can be shown by such extrajudicial statements and such statements may be used to establish the degree of the crime (People v. Miller, 37 Cal. 2d. 801,806; People v. Williams, 151 Cal. App. 2d. .... A.C.A. ....; see also People v. Amaya, 40 Cal. 2d. 70). Note: These cases indicate that, in the case of other crimes divided into degrees, the corpus delicti of the crime having been shown by independent evidence, the degree of the crime may be proved by the extrajudicial declarations of the accused and that the cases (supra) in which it has been held that the degree of burglary must be established by evidence independent of such declarations are no longer the law).

Prima Facie Proof Sufficient

To render the voluntary confession or admission of a defendant admissible prima facie proof of the corpus delicti is all that is required. (People v. Selby, 198 Cal. 426; People v. Cullen, 37 Cal. 2d 614; People v. Amaya, 40 Cal. 2d 70; People v. Bausell, 18 Cal. App. 2d 15; People v. Davis, 47 Cal. App. 2d 351; People v. Kay, 43 Cal. App. 2d 802; People v. Roche, 49 Cal. App. 2d 590; People v. Fierro, 58 Cal. App. 2d 215; People v. Seymour, 54 Cal. App. 2d 266; People v. Ives, 17 Cal. 2d 493; People v. McMonigle, 29 Cal. 2d 730; People v. Sparks, 82 Cal. App. 2d 145; People v. Corrales, 34 Cal. 2d 426; People v. Amaya, 40 Cal. 2d 70.) The declarations of the accused, when received in evidence, may be considered along with the other evidence in determining whether the guilt of the defendant has been established beyond a reasonable doubt and may remove such doubt which, in the absence of such declarations, would otherwise exist. (People v. Powell, 34 Cal. 2d 196.)

Proof by Photograph

A photograph showing defendants in the commission of an act in violation of section 288a of the Penal Code, showing on its face to have been taken in the defendants' apartment and to be a genuine photograph and not a "composite" or "faked" was held admissible and sufficient to prove a violation of section 288a although no witness was produced who was present when the picture was taken (People v. Doggett, 83 Cal. App. 2d 405.)

INTENT

"In every crime or public offense there must exist a union or joint operation of act and intent or criminal negligence." (Penal Code, sec. 20.) This section merely puts in statutory form the rule that mere intent without action can not be punishable as a crime.

Defined

Criminal intent is the intent to perform an act of such a nature that the law declares its commission punishable as a criminal offense. It does not require a knowledge that such act is unlawful or a belief that the act is wrong and may even exist in the presence of a belief that the act is right and not unlawful. To constitute criminal intent it is never necessary that the defendant shall have intended to violate the law. (People v. Dillon, 199 Cal. 1; People v. Hartman, 130 Cal. 487.) Criminal intent exists whenever a person intentionally does that which the law declares to be a crime, even though he may not know that his act is a crime. (People v. McClenegan, 195 Cal. 445; People v. Gonzales, 74 Cal. App. 291; People v. Sheasby, 82 Cal. App. 459.)

Where the statute makes an act punishable as a crime and that act is voluntarily committed, the law implies that the act knowingly done was done with criminal intent even though the accused did not know that such act was punishable or was mistaken as to the meaning of the law. (People v. McCalla, 63 Cal. App. 783; People v. Maciel, 71 Cal. App. 213; People v. Medagli, 94 Cal. App. 543; People v. Settles, 29 Cal. App. 2d 78; People v. Harris, 29 Cal. 678, 681; People v. Hunt, 59 Cal.

430; People v. Ah Gee Yung, 68 Cal. 144; People v. McClenegan, 195 Cal. 445; People v. Gonzales, 74 Cal. App. 291; People v. Sheasby, 82 Cal. App. 459; People v. Dillon, 199 Cal. 1; People v. McLaughlin, 111 Cal. App. 2d 781.)

How Proved

Criminal intent need not be proved by direct and positive evidence and it is deemed sufficient to prove the unlawful act and from such proof infer the intent. (People v. Hunt, 59 Cal. 430, 433; People v. Cadd, 60 Cal. 640; People v. O'Brien, 96 Cal. 171; People v. Wolfrom, 15 Cal. App. 732; People v. Phillips, 27 Cal. App. 291; People v. Gonzales, 72 Cal. App. 626; People v. Smith, 84 Cal. App. 2d 509.)

Where it is necessary to establish the intent it may be proved by direct evidence, such as the expressed intent of the accused or by proof of the circumstances connected with the commission of the offense (People v. Welsh, 63 Cal. 167; People v. Bones, 35 Cal. App. 429; People v. Tellez, 32 Cal. App. 2d 217; People v. Deininger, 36 Cal. App. 2d 649; People v. Watson, 125 Cal. 342; People v. Crowl, 4 Cal. Unrep. 355; People v. Browning, 132 Cal. App. 136; People v. Collins, 5 Cal. App. 654; People v. Hadley, 175 Cal. 118) and for this purpose the conduct of the defendant before and after the principal fact in issue is provable. (People v. Welsh, 63 Cal. 167; People v. Collins, 60 Cal. App. 263.)

"The intent or intention is manifested by the circumstances connected with the offense and the sound mind and discretion of the accused." (Penal Code, sec. 21.) Upon the trial of the issue raised by the plea of not guilty the defendant "shall be conclusively presumed to have been sane at the time the offense is alleged to have been committed" (Penal Code, sec 1026) and this latter provision supplements the latter portion of section 21 by conclusively presuming that the accused was of sound mind.

Motive

"In every criminal case, proof of the moving cause is permissible and oftentimes it is valuable; but it is never essential. Where the perpetration of a crime has been brought home to a defendant, the motive for its commission becomes unimportant. Evidence of motive is sometimes of assistance in removing doubt, and completing proof which might otherwise be unsatisfactory, and that motive may either be shown by positive testimony, or gleaned from the facts and surroundings of the act. The motive then becomes a circumstance, but nothing more than a circumstance, to be considered by the jury, and its absence is equally a circumstance in favor of the accused, to be given such weight as it deems proper. But proof of motive is never indispensable to a conviction." (People v. Durrant, 116 Cal. 179, 208; People v. Owens, 132 Cal. 469; People v. Besold, 154 Cal. 363; People v. Muhly, 15 Cal. App. 416; People v. Hall, 27 Cal. App. 2d 440; People v. Soeder, 150 Cal. 12; People v. Weston, 169 Cal. 393; People v. Simons, 25 Cal. App. 723; People v. Oh Fung, 17 Cal. 377; People v. Bowers, 1 Cal App. 501; People v. Botkin, 9 Cal. App. 240; People v. Klempke, 19 Cal. App. 672; People v. Galloway, 104 Cal. App. 422; People v. Kawamoto, 216 Cal. 531; People v. Perez, 19 Cal. App. 2d 472; People v. O'Neill, 78 Cal. App. 2d 888.)

Motive is not part of the corpus delicti of any crime and need not be proved. (People v. Aranda, 12 Cal. 2d 307; People v. Greig, 14 Cal. 2d 548; People v. Rongo, 169 Cal. 1; People v. Kelley, 208 Cal. 387; People v. Northcott, 209 Cal. 639; People v. Larrios, 220 Cal. 236.)

Effect of Proof of

Absence of motive does not necessarily establish innocence or even raise a reasonable doubt of guilt (People v. Baueraerts, 164 Cal. 696) but evidence of motive is admissible to show the intent with which the act was committed (People v. Miller, 121 Cal. 343), as tending to rebut a claim of self defense (People v. Brown, 130 Cal. 591), to show that the act was rational and not that of an insane person (People v. Donlan, 135 Cal. 489; People v. Soeder, 150 Cal. 12), to remove doubt as to the identity of the perpetrator (People v. Wright, 144 Cal. 161; People v. Soeder, 150 Cal. 12), to solve a doubt as to the degree of the offense (People v. Soeder, 150 Cal. 12), or as to the justification or excusability of the act (People v. Soeder, 150 Cal. 12).

A good motive does not prevent an act from being a crime if all the elements of the corpus delicti are present and the same is true even though there be no apparent motive. On the other hand, no matter how much motive there be for committing a crime no crime has been committed unless there exists a complete corpus delicti.

Of Person Other Than Defendant

Evidence of a motive on the part of a person other than the defendant to commit the crime charged is inadmissible unless coupled with other evidence having an inherent tendency to connect such other person with the commission of the crime. (People v. Mendez, 193 Cal. 39; People v. Montezuma, 117 Cal. App. 125; People v. Gentekos, 118 Cal. App. 177; People v. Perkins, 8 Cal. 2d 502; People v. Wagner, 21 Cal. App. 2d 92.)

Specific Intent

Under the definition of some crimes it is an essential part of the corpus delicti that the act in question be done with a particular or specific intent. Thus in burglary the entry must have been with the specific intent to commit either grand or petty theft or some felony and an entry without such intent is not burglary. And there are various felonious assaults with intent to commit a specific crime such as rape, robbery, murder, etc., and in such cases to constitute the crime it is necessary that the perpetrator have in mind, in committing the assault, the specific intent to perform acts which, if accomplished, would constitute the crime the commission of which is charged as the intent with which the assault was committed. Thus in assault with intent to commit murder it is not sufficient to prove that the defendant intended to do an act which might cause the death of the victim, which death if so caused would be murder, but the proof must show that the assault was committed with the intent to take human life. (People v. Weston, 32 Cal. App. 571.) And there are crimes in which the corpus delicti includes the element that they must be done "maliciously," and, as the word maliciously "imports a wish to vex, annoy or injure another person, or an intent to do a wrongful act" (Penal Code, sec. 7, subd. 4) such specific state of mind must be present to constitute the crime.

Defendant May Disprove

Where a specific intent is an element of the corpus delicti the defendant must be allowed to prove any fact tending to show that he had no such intent (People v. Brierton, 132 Cal. App. 471; People v. Martel, 21 Cal. App. 573) and may himself testify to his intent, state of mind or belief (People v. Sheasby, 82 Cal. App. 459) and may offer proof that he acted under advice of legal counsel (People v. Wyatt, 101 Cal. App. 396).

Specific Intent Not Presumed

While the intent may properly be inferred from the circumstances attending the commission of an act and it is proper in a murder case for the court to instruct the jury that a person is presumed to intend the natural and probable consequences of his voluntary acts (People v. Mize, 80 Cal. 41; People v. Wilson, 36 Cal. App. 489; People v. Cook, 15 Cal. 2d 507; People v. Besold, 154 Cal. 363; People v. Botkin, 9 Cal. App. 240) such an instruction is erroneous in every case other than murder in which a specific intent is an element of the corpus delicti.   In such other cases the specific intent must be established by proof and cannot be presumed from the act and its probable consequences. (People v. Mize, 80 Cal. 41; People v. Landman, 103 Cal. 577; People v. Flores, 86 Cal. App. 235; People v. Jones, 160 Cal. 358; People v. Miller, 2 Cal. 2d 527; People v. Brown, 27 Cal. App. 2d 61; People v. Snyder, 15 Cal. 2d 706.)

Transferred Intent (No Such thing)

on Test

Where a person commits a crime with the intent of injuring one person, such as shooting with intent to kill, but the bullet misses the intended victim and kills another whose death was not intended, the intent to kill is transferred and the assailant is guilty of the felonious death of the person slain, and, if death did not result, would be guilty of an assault to kill such other person (People v. Wells, 145 Cal. 138; People v. Ramirez, 64 Cal. App. 358; People v. Suesser, 142 Cal. 367; People v. Buenaflore, 40 Cal. App. 2d 713; People v. Torres, 38 Cal. 141; People v. Halbert, 78 Cal. App. 598; People v. Brannon, 70 Cal. App. 225; People v. Trebilcox, 149 Cal. 307; People v. Larrios, 220 Cal. 236; People v. Pivaroff, 138 Cal. App. 625; People v. Rothrock, 21 Cal. App. 2d 116; People v. Walker, 76 Cal. App. 2d 10; People v. Henderson, 34 Cal. 2d 340; People v. Sutic, 41 Cal. 2d. 483) for under such circumstances all of the elements of the corpus delicti, including the necessary specific intent, are present: Where the defendant committed a murder by shooting his victim and one of his shots missed the victim and struck a third person a conviction of assult with a deadly weapon upon such third person was sustained (People v. Carr, 72 Cal. App. 2d 191).   Where the defendant attempted to murder R by setting fire to a building in which R was sleeping it was held also an attempt to murder the wife of R who was sleeping with him (People v. Neal, 97 Cal. App. 2d 668), but it must be noted that the wife in this case was actually injured and the decision would not apply to a similar case but in which the wife suffered no injury and there was no intent to injure the wife and no knowledge that she was in the building on the part of the defendant.

Criminal Negligence

Section 7, subd. 2, of the Penal Code provides "The following words have in this code the signification attached to them in this section unless otherwise apparent from the context. * * * 2. The words 'neglect', 'negligence', 'negligent' and 'negligently' import a want of such attention to the nature or probable consequences of the act or omission as a prudent man ordinarily bestows in acting in his own concerns."

(For rule in cases of Manslaughter see that subject.)

Knowledge—Knowingly.

"The word 'knowingly' imports only a knowledge that the facts exist which bring the act or omission within the provisions of this code. It does not require any knowledge of the unlawfulness of such act or omission." (Penal Code, sec. 7, subd. 5.)

There are certain crimes—receiving stolen property, obtaining property by false pretenses, failure to stop after an automobile collision, possession of narcotics, etc.,—in which knowledge is an element of the corpus delicti and without which the crime has not been committed; in others knowledge may be an evidence factor only. A person may lack knowledge and yet act intentionally or deliberately as where a person does an act through mistake or unawareness of fact as where a person makes a representation, such as would constitute a basis for a charge of obtaining property by false pretenses, without knowledge of its falsity and under an honest belief that it is true or might intentionally pull the trigger of a firearm believing that it was not loaded. On the other hand a person may have knowledge of a fact but, inadvertently, may perform an act intentionally but inadvertently, not intending or intending the act which he in fact performs as where a person, though knowing that one of the bills in his wallet is counterfeit, inadvertently pays it out while honestly intending to use a good bill.

The mere denial of knowledge by the accused is not conclusive and the jury is not bound thereby and may, upon evidence of circumstances, conclude that he had knowledge (People v. Henry, 23 Cal. App. 2d 155).

Wilfully.

"The word 'wilfully' when applied to the intent with which an act is done or omitted implies simply a purpose or willingness to commit the act or make the omission referred to. It does not require an intent to violate the law, or to injure another or to acquire an advantage." Penal Code, sec. 7, subd. 1.)

The word "wilfully" as used in criminal statutes implies a purpose or willingness to commit the act and, although it does not require an evil intent, it implies that the person knows what he is doing, intends to do what he is doing and is a free agent (In re Trombley, 31 Cal. 2d 801).

CHAPTER IV.

CONSENT—ENTRAPMENT

Since a crime is an offense against the state no individual can by consenting to the commission of a criminal act by another afford him any immunity or defense. However, in crimes such as rape by force and larceny it is an essential element of the crime that the act be without the consent of the ostensible victim and in such cases consent would be a defense.

Where consent is a defense it must be a free and voluntary consent, not induced by fraud, threats, force or duress; the person consenting must have been legally and mentally capable of consenting and must have had knowledge of the true nature of that to which he consented. Mere assent or lack of objection without an appreciation of the facts is not consent, but a failure to object to a transaction with full knowledge of all the facts, where it becomes the duty of one to dissent, would warrant the inference that there was consent. (People v. Bousquet, 116 Cal. 75.) As stated in People v. Dong Pok Yip, 164 Cal. 143, "Consent in law means a voluntary agreement by a person in the possession and exercise of sufficient mentality to make an intelligent choice, to do something proposed by another. 'Consent' differs materially from 'assent.' The former implies some positive action and always involves submission. The latter means mere passivity or submission which does not include consent." (See also People v. Kangieser, 44 Cal. App. 345; People v. Mack, 24 Cal. App. 438; People v. Hanselman, 76 Cal. App. 460, 462; People v. Carmelo, 94 Cal. App. 2d. 301, 307; People v. Claasen, 152 Cal. App. 2d. ....).

In addition to consent being a defense to some offenses it is also of importance in the determination of the question as to whether, under some circumstances, a witness is an accomplice. (See further discussion under **Accomplice.**)

ENTRAPMENT

See also: Feigned accomplice, pg. 99.

The question of consent is sometimes involved in those cases in which, having information that a crime is being contemplated, plans are formed and carried out to catch the perpetrator. If the crime is one in which consent is a defense, then the accused cannot be convicted if the means of entrapment amount to consent, but, if the crime is fully consummated, the fact that, it being known that the crime was about to be committed, nothing was done to prevent it and the officers lay in wait and captured the offender in the criminal act is no defense.

Also, if a person join in the commission of a crime solely for the purpose of apprehending and securing evidence against his guilty associate or associates, he will not be criminally responsible for his acts in associating with the criminals provided he does nothing of his own initiative to promote the criminal enterprise, but acts merely as the tool of the actual criminals who will be fully liable for any crime committed. (See People v. Caiazza, 61 Cal. App. 505; People v. Heusers, 58 Cal. App. 103; People v. Lanzit, 70 Cal. App. 498; In re Moore, 70 Cal. App. 483; People v. Ramirez, 95 Cal. App. 140.)

In such a case it is, however, necessary that the plan be carried out for, unless the corpus delicti is complete, no conviction for the crime planned can be had. Thus, where a man proposed to another that he join him in a burglary and the other fell into the plan for the purpose of entrapping the intending burglar but, in carrying out the enterprise the feigned—*not real* accomplice entered the building while the proposer remained outside, no burglary was committed because the man who entered the building did so solely with the intent of entrapment, and the burglarious intent, an essential element of the corpus delicti, was absent. (People v. Collins, 53 Cal. 185; see also People v. Lanzit, 70 Cal. App. 498.)

"Under the doctrine of entrapment the *(apparent)* overt acts essential to the commission of the offense charged are assumed to have been committed by the defendant. But the criminal intent, as here, also essential to the completion of the crime, is not assumed to have been established. It is assumed to be lacking when it did not originate in the mind of the defendant but was conceived in the minds of the enforcement officers for the unlawful purpose of inducing him to commit a crime" (People v. Jackson, 42 Cal. 2d. 540, in which the sole contention of the defendant was that he claimed that his acts, upon which the charge of bribery were based, were done by him solely to test the integrity of the officer whom he was charged with bribing, the court holding that the sole issue was the question of defendant's criminal intent).

Entrapment as a Defense — *public policy defense*

The law will not tolerate a person, particularly a law enforcement officer, generating in the mind of a person, who is innocent of any criminal purpose, the original intent to commit a crime thus entrapping him into the commission of a crime which he would not have committed or even contemplated but for such inducement and where a crime is committed as a consequence of such entrapment no conviction can be had of the person so entrapped. (In re Moore, 70 Cal. App. 483; People v. Malone, 117 Cal. App. 629; People v. Tomasovich, 56 Cal. App. 520; People v. Gallagher, 107 Cal. App. 425; People v. Barkdoll, 36 Cal. App. 25, 28; People v. Jackson, 42 Cal. 2d. 540, 548). "Where the criminal intent originates in the mind of the entrapping person and the accused is lured into the commission of the offense charged in order to prosecute him, no conviction can be had." (People v. Crawford, 105 Cal. App. 2d. 530).

"It is only when the criminal design is conceived in the mind of the officer and does not originate with the accused, and a decoy is used to insnare the innocent and law abiding by persuasion, inducement or allurement into the commission of a crime that there is entrapment." (People v. Lindsey, 91 Cal. App. 2d 914, 917; People v. Lagomarsino, 97 Cal. App. 2d 92 and cases cited: People v. Finkelstein, 98 Cal. App. 2d 545; People v. Crawford, 105 Cal. App. 2d 530).

There is a distinction, however, between inducing in the mind of a person the commission of an unlawful act and setting a plan to capture and secure evidence of guilt against a person who commits a crime of his own volition and conception. If the criminal intent is that of the perpetrator and the criminal offense is completed, the fact that an opportunity is furnished, or that the accused is aided in the commission of the crime in order to secure the evidence necessary to prosecute and convict him constitutes no defense. (People v. Caiazza, 61 Cal. App. 505; People v. Lanzit, 70 Cal. App. 498; People v. Norcross, 71 Cal. App. 2; People v. Makovsky, 3 Cal. 2d 366; People v. Bunkers, 2 Cal. App. 197; People v. Hall, 133 Cal. App. 40; People v. Fitzpatrick, 78 Cal. App. 37; People v. Settles, 29 Cal. App. 2d 781; People v. Ah Sam, 41 Cal. 645; People v. McDonnell, 80 Cal. 293; People v. Malone, 117 Cal. App. 629; People v. Billingsley, 59 Cal. App. 2d 845; People v. Lindsey, 91 Cal. App. 2d 914; People v. Finkelstein, 98 Cal. App. 2d 545.)

Entrapment is a positive defense imposing upon the defendant the burden of showing that he was induced to commit the act for which he is in trial (People v. Terry, 44 Cal. 2d. 371, and cases cited). Entrapment as a matter of law is not established where there is any substantial evidence in the record from which it may be inferred that the criminal intent to commit the particular offense originated in the mind of the accused (People v. Terry, supra).

Thus the jury can, as to an illegal prescription for narcotics, infer the defendant's criminal intent from the fact that he charged $150 for writing four prescriptions, did not examine the fictitious patient and prescribed an inordinate quantity of the narcotic (People v. Nunn, 133 Cal. App. 2d. 460).

There is no entrapment if the officers use no more persuasion than is necessary to an ordinary sale and the accused is willing to and does in fact make the sale (People v. Gonzales, 136 Cal. App. 2d. 437, selling narcotic).

Entrapment to Secure Evidence

"Officers, if they know or suspect that a crime is about to be committed, may, through a feigned accomplice, facilitate or even aid in its consummation." (People v. Lagomarsino, 97 Cal. App. 2d. 92).

The question of whether entrapment is a tenable defense is more difficult in those cases in which, in order to secure evidence against and secure the conviction of a person who has not as yet declared an intention to commit a criminal act but who is believed to be planning a crime or is engaged in a series of law violations, such person is approached by an officer or a person in the interest of law enforcement with a request that he join in such a crime or carry out a criminal transaction of the nature of that in which he is believed to be engaged, such as the unlawful sale of narcotics, the investigator merely intending to engage in such a transaction for the purpose of entrapment. In such case if the illegal act is committed the vital question is whether it was the voluntary and intentional act of the suspect carrying out a criminal purpose of his own in which case entrapment would not be a defense or whether the person suspected had in fact no intent to commit a criminal act and his participation in the act committed would not have occurred but for such inducement in which case entrapment would be a defense. (In re Moore, 70 Cal. App. 483; People v. Lanzit, 70 Cal. App. 498.) (see also Feigned Accomplice).

"It is not the entrapment of a criminal upon which the law frowns, but the seduction of innocent people into a criminal career by its officers is what is condemned and will not be tolerated. Where an accused has a preexisting criminal intent, the fact that, when solicited by a decoy he committed a crime raises no inference of an unlawful entrapment." (People v. Roberts, 40 Cal. 2d. 483.)

Illustrative Cases

The question as to which of such situations existed is to be determined from all the facts and circumstances. (In re Moore, 70 Cal. App. 483.) Thus if the person asked to make an illegal sale of liquor or narcotics proceeds to a place with which he is evidently familiar and there secures the contraband (In re Moore, 70 Cal. App. 483) or was apparently a willing vendor (People v. Ramirez, 95 Cal. App. 140; In re Wong Poy, 113 Cal. App. 677; People v. Harris, 80 Cal. App. 328; People v. Mesa, 121 Cal. App. 345; People v. Lee, 9 Cal App. 2d 99; People v. Heusers, 58 Cal. App. 103; People v. Amort, 60 Cal. App. 29; People v. Norcross, 71 Cal. App. 2; People v. Mahovsky, 3 Cal. 2d 366) or where an officer offered to the defendant whom he believed to be a bookmaker a bet on a horse race (People v. Cherry, 39 Cal. App. 2d 149; People v. Kennedy, 66 Cal. App. 2d 522; People v. Lindsey, 91 Cal. App. 2d 914) the defense of entrapment is not tenable.

The mere fact that a defendant committed a crime when solicited by a decoy raises no inference of unlawful entrapment (People v. Jalifi, 139 Cal. App. 2d. 368; People v. Nunn, 46 Cal. 2d. 460).

"Where an accused has a preexisting criminal intent, the fact that when solicited by a decoy he committed a crime raises no inference of unlawful entrapment" (People v. Alamillo, 113 Cal. App. 617, sale of narcotics). Merely allowing a willing seller an opportunity to make an illegal sale, such as a sale of narcotics, is insufficient to compel a finding of entrapment (People v. Candillo, 138 Cal. App. 2d. 183 and cases cited). Where an accused has a preexisting criminal intent, the fact that, when solicited by a decoy, he committed a crime raises no inference of unlawful entrapment (People v. Branch, 119 Cal. App. 2d. 490, quoting People v. Schwartz, 109 Cal. App. 2d. 450, 455 and citing cases). Where a doctor gave to an inspector of the Bureau of Narcotics Enforcement a prescription for narcotics on the latter's representation that his wife used and needed narcotics when in fact such was not the case and the name given by the inspector and that of the wife were fictitious and there was evidence that defendant stated that he had been selling prescriptions for narcotics because he needed the money and the evidence showed as a whole that the defendant had been a willing seller of narcotics and the evidence as to entrapment was in conflict, the conviction was sustained (People v. Braddock, 41, Cal. 2d. 794). It is not entrapment for an officer to misrepresent himself as a seaman and solicit the defendant to accept horse racing bets where the defendant had the preexisting intent to accept bets on horse races (People v. Ungaro, 122 Cal. App. 2d. 57).

Where operatives of the medical board visited the defendant saying that they were husband and wife and desired an abortion and paid defendant the fee he requested and then defendant placed the woman upon a table and attempted an abortion, there was no illegal entrapment. (People v. Raffington, 98 Cal. App. 2d. 455).

Where, however, a police officer induced a drug addict and peddler to approach the defendant and the peddler asked defendant whether he wanted to buy some morphine and the defendant replied in the negative and the peddler then made a good offer and defendant said he would accept and the peddler then agreed to leave the drug at a designated place and when defendant picked it up there he was placed under arrest and there was no evidence that defendant had any thought of securing any morphine until he was approached by the police agent it was held that entrapment was a good defense to the charge of illegal possession of narcotics. (People v. Gallagher, 107 Cal. App. 425.) *Failure to Instruct Jury (Conflict) on issue of entrapment (case to be retried)*

"Where a person is innocent of any intention to commit a crime and is inveigled into its commission by an officer of the law for the purpose of advancing his standing for efficiency or to obtain revenue by fine for the municipality it might be said that to uphold such practices would be repugnant to any just conception of good morals and violative of sound public policy." (People v. Barkdoll, 36 Cal. App. 25, 28.)

A witness who had been approached by the accused with the proposal that he cooperate in the commission of a crime may testify as to the proposal and also to his report to the law enforcement officials and their directions as to his future conduct in apparent cooperation with the criminal to show he was acting in good faith and for the purpose of apprehending the guilty person and not with criminal intent. (People v. Squires, 99 Cal. 327; People v. Lanzit, 70 Cal. App. 498; People v. Fitzpatrick, 78 Cal. App. 37.)

When Defense Not Available

The defense of entrapment is not available to a defendant who denies that he committed the act in question (People v. Johnson, 99 Cal. App. 2d. 559; People v. Lee, 9 Cal. App. 2d.

Calling for evidence from another case

99; People v. Tillman, 142 Cal. App. 2d. 404). The invocation
of the defense of entrapment assumes that the act charged as
a public offense was committed (People v. Gelardi, 77 Cal.
App. 2d. 467, 477; People v. Schwartz, 109 Cal. App. 2d. 450,
455; People v. Tillman, 142 Cal. App. 2d. 404). The defense
of entrapment may not be raised for the first time on appeal *— call upon*
(People v. Jalifi, 139 Cal. App. 2d. 368) *a'd support sympathy*
a person or authority for proof of decision in one's favor.

Burden of Proof

(fact is so)

Entrapment is an affirmative defense imposing upon the
accused the burden of proving that he was unlawfully induced
to commit the crime of which he is charged (People v. Guiterrez, 128 Cal. App. 2d. 35; People v. Terry, 44 Cal. 2d. 371).

CHAPTER V.

LESSER OFFENSE

"The jury, or the judge if a jury trial is waived, may find the defendant guilty of any offense the commission of which is necessarily included in that with which he is charged, or of an attempt to commit the offense." (Penal Code, sec. 1159.) An offense necessarily included in the crime charged is an offense the elements of which are included in the elements, or corpus delicti, of the crime charged. Unless the corpus delicti of the lesser offense is so included, there can be no conviction of a lesser offense solely on the basis that the evidence shows its commission, for it is a basic rule that no person can be convicted of an offense not covered by the complaint, indictment or information under which he is being tried. Whether a lesser offense is included in the crime charged is a question of law to be determined solely from the definition and corpus delicti of the offense charged and of the lesser offense, and the language used in the accusatory pleading and whether the elements of the lesser offense are shown by the evidence. If all of the elements of the corpus delicti of a lesser crime can be found in a list of all of the elements of the offense charged and are shown by the evidence then and then only is the lesser included in the greater. In applying the test it must be borne in mind that the elements of the corpus delicti of a crime are not always clearly apparent from the definition of the offense. Thus in larceny the essential element that the taking must be with the intent to permanently deprive the owner of his property is not expressly stated in the definition of that offense and the same is true of the element of assault in the crimes of rape and robbery.

A person cannot be convicted of an offense (other than a necessarily included offense) not charged against him by indictment or information, whether or not there was evidence at his trial to show that he had committed that offense (In re Hess, 45 Cal. 2d. 171 and cases cited).

The fact that the evidence shows a lesser or other offense than that charged does not necessarily or of itself make it an included offense. No person can be convicted of an offense the elements of the corpus delicti of which are not included within the allegations of the accusatory pleading and, where the lesser offense shown by the evidence includes an element of its corpus delicti which is not an element of the offense charged, such lesser offense is not an included offense and the defendant cannot be convicted thereof.

Where the trial court has jurisdiction of the offense charged it also has jurisdiction upon conviction of the defendant of a lesser offense even though such lesser offense is one of which trial jurisdiction, if it were directly charged, would be in an inferior court. (Ex parte Bell, 4 Cal. Unrep. 309; People v. Spreckels, 125 Cal. App. 2d. 507; Penal Code, sec. 1159.)

Included Offenses—What Are

It has been said that "The test in this state of a necessarily included offense is simply that where an offense cannot be committed without necessarily committing another offense, the latter is a necessarily included offense." (People v. Greer, 30 Cal. 2d. 589; In re Hess, 45 Cal. 2d. 171). "If, in the commission of acts made unlawful by one statute, the offender must always violate another, the one offense is necessarily included in the other" (People v. Whitlow, 113 Cal. 2d. 804; People v. Krupa, 64 Cal. App. 2d. 598). Before a lesser offense can be said to constitute a necessary part of the greater, all of the elements of the corpus delicti of the lesser offense must be included in the elements of the greater offense (People v. Whitlow, supra; Pople v. Greer, 30 Cal. 2d. 589).

As indicated by the cases where the crime charge is assault with a deadly weapon with intent to commit murder, infra, and People v. Marshall, 48 Cal. 2d. .... the test is not merely the elements of the lesser offense are included within the language of the statute defining the offense charged but also whether the elements of the lesser offense are included within the allegations in the accusatory pleading.

"The offense of robbery, as defined by section 211 of the Penal code does not include all of the elements of a violation of section 503 of the Vehicle Code. . . . A person charged simply with robbery in the words of the statute . . . could not properly be convicted of the offense described by section 503 because the accusatory pleading would not inform the defendant that he must be prepared, at the trial, to contravene evidence that he took a particular kind of personal property, a vehicle." Where, however, the pleading alleges that the property taken in the robbery was an automobile, the specific language of the pleading makes the offense of violating section 503 a necessarily included offense (People v. Marshall, 48 Cal. 2d. 394). Note: This rule will no doubt be limited to cases where the specific allegation is a proper part of the charge but will exclude cases in which the specific language is surplusage and not a proper element in pleading the offense charged. Thus if burglary be pleaded and there be an added allegation that, in the perpetration of the burglary, certain property was stolen the crime of theft would not be an included offense.

The crime of simple assault is included in a charge of battery (People v. McDaniels, 137 Cal. 192), assault with a deadly weapon (People v. Apgar, 35 Cal. 389; People v. Holland, 59 Cal. 364; People v. Lee, 23 Cal. App. 2d 168), wife beating under section 273d of the Penal Code (People v. Van Os, 96 Cal. App. 2d. 204; People v. Burns, 88 Cal. App. 2d. 867), assault with intent to commit a felony (People v. Jones, 112 Cal. App. 68; People v. De Masters, 105 Cal. 669; People v. Mallon, 103 Cal. 513; People v. Day, 199 Cal. 78), forcible rape (People v. Chevaz, 103 Cal. 407), robbery (People v. Foss, 85 Cal. App. 269), or sodomy without the consent of the victim. (People v. Hickey, 109 Cal. 275.)

The crime of assault with a deadly weapon is included in a charge of assault with a deadly weapon with intent to commit murder. (People v. Watson, 125 Cal. 342; People v. Davidson, 5 Cal. 133; People v. English, 30 Cal. 215; Ex parte Ah Cha, 40 Cal. 426; People v. Congleton, 44 Cal. 94; People v. Pope, 66 Cal. 367; People v. Lightner, 49 Cal. 226; People v. Bentley, 75 Cal. 410; People v. Mock Ming Fat, 82 Cal. App. 618.)

The crime of assault with intent to commit rape is included in a charge of forcible rape (People v. Chevaz, 103 Cal. 407; People v. Rupp, 41 Cal. 2d. 371; People v. Kimball, 122 Cal. App. 2d. 211) or statutory rape (People v. Babcock, 160 Cal. 537, but see contra People v. Spady, 64 Cal. App. 567).

The attempt to commit the crime of sodomy is included in a charge of assault with intent to commit that crime (People v. Jensen, 76 Cal. App. 558) which gives us the rule that an assault with intent to commit a particular felony includes the offense of an attempt to commit that crime. Vagrancy is necessarily included within the infamous crime against nature (People v. Babb, 103 Cal. App. 2d. 326).

The crime of compounding the offense of manslaughter is included in the crime of compounding the crime of murder (People v. Raymond, 87 Cal. App. 510), the crime of manslaughter being included in a charge of murder. (People v. Gilmore, 4 Cal. 380; People v. Backus, 5 Cal. 278.)

The crime of petty theft is included in a charge of robbery (People v. Covington, 1 Cal. 2d 316) or grand theft (People v. Stanhope, 37 Cal. App. 2d 631).

The crime of grand theft is included in a charge of robbery in which the taking is alleged to have been from the person (People v. Gannon, 61 Cal. 476; People v. Moreland, 150 Cal. App. 2d. 417) or the nature or value of the property of which the victim was robbed is such that its theft would be grand theft (People v. Marshall, 48 Cal. 2d. 394).

The offense of contributing to the delinquency of a minor is included in a charge of statutory rape. (People v. Lopez, 46 Cal. App. 2d 857; People v. Greer, 30 Cal. 2d 589) and in a charge of violating section 288 of the Penal Code (People v. Greer, 30 Cal. 2d 589.) Even though the trier of fact, court or jury, finds the defendant guilty of a lesser offense though, if guilty at all, he is guilty of the greater offense charged, the defendant cannnot complain of the error which is favorable to him (People v. Powell, 34 Cal. 2d. 196). Where the defendant is charged with a violation of section 288a of the Penal Code and there is no allegation that the victim was under the age of twenty-one years, the offense of contributing to the delinquency of a minor is not an included offense and a verdict convicting the defendant of the latter offense is void (People v. Kennedy, 133 Cal. App. 2d. 693).

The crime of driving while under the influence of intoxicating liquor, defined in section 501 of the Vehicle Code, includes the lesser offense of violating section 502 of that Code (People v. Gossman, 95 Cal. App. 2d 293, also holding that a violation of section 367d of the Penal Code is also included). (Since sections 501 and 502 of the Vehicle Code only require that the driver be "under the influence of intoxicating liquor" and do not require that the driver be "intoxicated" as does section 367d, and the quoted terms are not synonymous (see discussion in Chapter XXXI, infra) it would seem that a violation of section 367d is not included in either of these Vehicle Code sections as a pleading under those sections would not allege that the driver was intoxicated). (Note:—Since a violation of section 502 under the law as of 1954 requires the element that the vehicle be driven upon a "highway" while no such element exists in the corpus delicti of the offense defined in section 501, a violation of section 501 does not include a violation of section 502 as a necessarily and lesser included offense.)

The crime of abortion under Penal Code section 274 includes the lesser offense of an attempt to commit that offense (People v. Reed, 128 Cal. App. 2d. 497; People v. Berger, 131 Cal. App. 2d. 127).

Conviction of Attempt

The defendant may be convicted of an attempt to commit the crime charged (People v. Vanderbilt, 199 Cal. 461; People v. McConnell, 80 Cal. App. 789; People v. Clements, 111 Cal. App. 173) even though the attempt carries a greater penalty than the crime charged (People v. Lavine, 115 Cal. App. 289) and even though the evidence shows that he was guilty of the consummated crime. (Penal Code, sec. 663; People v. Vanderbilt, 199 Cal. 461.)

Offenses Not Included

The offense of accessory after the fact (Penal Code, sec. 32) is not included in a charge of committing the crime itself (People v. Brown, 131 Cal. App. 2d. 643).

A charge of assault with a deadly weapon does not include battery (People v. Helbing, 61 Cal. 620; People v. McCaffrey, 118, Cal. App. 2d. 611; People v. Mueller, 147 Cal. App. 2d. 233) or the offense (Penal Code, sec. 417) of exhibiting a deadly weapon in an angry and threatening manner (People v. Diamond, 33 Cal. App. 2d 518; People v. Piercy, 16 Cal. App. 13; People v. Torres, 151 Cal. App. 2d. ....).

A charge of assault with intent to commit murder does not include assault with a deadly weapon when the charge does not state that the assault was committed with a deadly weapon. (People v. Murat, 45 Cal. 281; People v. Arnett, 126 Cal. 680.)

The offense of assault by a public officer under color of authority is not an offense included in a charge of assault by means of force likely to produce great bodily injury (People v. Lantz, 120 Cal. App. 2d. 787).

A charge of burglary does not include larceny or theft (People v. Devlin, 143 Cal. 128; People v. Curtis, 76 Cal. 57; People v. Garnett, 29 Cal. 622; People v. Arnarez, 68 Cal. App. 645; In re Howe, 135 Cal. App. 2d. 604) or an attempt to commit larceny or theft (People v. Curtis, 76 Cal. 57) nor the offense of receiving stolen property (People v. Russell, 34 Cal. App. 2d. 665).

The offense of soliciting another to commit burglary (Penal Code sec. 653f) does not include, as a lesser offense, a violation of section 650½ of that code which punishes, among other acts, an act which endangers public peace and outrages public decency (People v. Proctor, 46 Cal. 2d. 481).

Where the accusatory pleading charges embezzlement by a public officer under section 504 of the Penal Code the offense of petty theft, a misdemeanor, is not an included offense even though a sum of less than $200 is involved (People v. Marquis, 153 Cal. App. 2d. ......).

Since forcible rape can be committed without contributing to the delinquency of a minor (e. g. where the female is over 21 years of age) it does not include, as a lesser included offense, the latter offense (In re Hess, 45 Cal. 2d. 171).

A charge of prescribing a narcotic in violation of section 11163 of the Health and Safety Code is not included in a charge of issuing a prescription for a narcotic in violation of section 11165 of that code (People v. Whitlow, 113 Cal. 2d 804).

When charged in the language of the statute (Penal Code, sec. 464) the crime of burglary with explosives does not include either degree of burglary.   (People v. Black, 73 Cal. App. 13.)

Neither the charge of theft of an automobile nor the charge of robbery in which the victim's automobile was taken include the offense of driving an automobile in the absence of the owner and without his consent under section 503 of the Vehicle Code (People v. O'Neal, 2 Cal. App. 2d 551; People v. Deininger, 36 Cal. App. 2d 649; People v. Tellez, 32 Cal. App. 2d 217) nor the charge (Penal Code, sec. 499b) of temporarily using such automobile (cases last cited). A defendant charged with grand theft in the taking of sheep can not be convicted of petty theft as that offense is not an included offense and in such a case the defendant is either guilty of grand theft (subd. 3, sec. 487a, Penal Code) or not guilty (People v. Piazza, 115 Cal. App. 2d 811; People v. Kuhl, 28 Cal. App. 2d 471, a calf).

Where the defendant is charged with a violation of section 480 of the Vehicle Code, involving injury to a person, that charge does not include as a lesser offense a violation of section 481 of that code since the latter section is applicable by its express terms only to a case "resulting only in damage to property".

The offense of reckless driving in violation of the Vehicle Act is not necessarily included in the charge of manslaughter even though both are based upon the same incident (People v. Herbert, 6 Cal. 2d. 541, 545).

The charge of grand theft does not include the crime of receiving stolen property (People v. Stanley, 90 Cal. App. 132); battery is not included in either robbery or attempted sodomy (People v. Romero, 62 Cal. App. 2d 116); driving an automobile under the influence of intoxicating liquor does not include reckless driving (People v. McGrath, 94 Cal. App. 520); and the manufacturing of intoxicating liquors does not include the possession of intoxicating liquor. (People v. Arnarez, 68 Cal. App. 645.)

The crime of robbery does not include the offense of receiving stolen property (People v. Mora, 139 Cal. App. 2d. 266) nor does it include a violation of section 503 of the Vehicle Code if pleaded in the language of the statute and there is no specification that the property taken in the robbery was a vehicle (People v. Marshall, 48 Cal. 2d. ....).

When Charge Is Conspiracy

While it has been held that a conspiracy to commit a crime does not include a lesser offense (Doble v. Superior Court, 197 Cal. 556, 799) that case must be limited in its application to the facts and the particular charge under consideration and it seems reasonable, in the light of the authorities on the question of lesser included offenses, that under a charge of conspiracy to commit a crime, which crime includes a lesser offense, that the offense of conspiracy to commit such lesser offense is included in the offense charged.

Conviction of Lesser-Evidence Showing Greater Offense

A defendant cannot complain, after conviction of a lesser offense, on the ground that the evidence and the charge would sustain a conviction of a greater offense (People v. North, 81 Cal. App. 113; People v. Post, 208 Cal. 433; People v. Clensey, 97 Cal. App. 71; People v. Gebiba, 138 Cal. App. 94; People v. Glab, 15 Cal. App. 2d 120; People v. Borrego, 7 Cal. App. 613; People v. Huntington, 8 Cal. App. 612) even though the defendant, if guilty at all, is guilty of the offense charged (People v. Tugwell, 32 Cal. App. 520; People v. Washburn, 54 Cal. App. 124; People v. Dong Pok Yip, 164 Cal. 143; People v. Lopez, 21 Cal. App. 188), and the same rule applies where the defendant is convicted of a lesser degree of the crime charged. (People v. North, 81 Cal. App. 113; People v. Clensey, 97 Cal. App. 71; People v. Jenkins, 118 Cal. App. 115; People v. Latourell, 118 Cal. App. 386.) The same principal applies where the defendant is tried by the court without a jury (People v. Powell, 34 Cal. 2d 196.)

Instructions to Jury as to Lesser Offense

Where the defendant is either guilty of the offense charged or of the higher degree of the crime charged the court may properly exclude from consideration by the jury any lesser offense or degree (People v. Franklin, 70 Cal. 641; People v.

Guidice, 73 Cal. 226; People v. Madden, 76 Cal. 520; People v.
Chun Hong, 86 Cal. 329; People v. O'Brien, 88 Cal. 483; People
v. Barry, 90 Cal. 41; People v. Scott, 93 Cal. 516; People v.
Wright, 93 Cal. 564; People v. Chevaz, 103 Cal. 407; People v.
Davis, 4 Cal. Unrep. 524; People v. Rasmussen, 25 Cal. App.
2d 399; People v. Melendrez, 25 Cal. App. 2d 490; People v.
Petters, 29 Cal. App. 2d 48; People v. Kuhl, 28 Cal. App. 2d
471; People v. Hickok, 28 Cal. App. 2d 574; People v. King,
30 Cal. App. 2d 185; People v. Louviere, 34 Cal. App. 2d 62;
People v. Mitchell, 14 Cal. 2d 237; People v. Griffin, 36 Cal.
App. 2d 59) and may properly refuse to instruct the jury on the
lesser degree. (People v. Green, 13 Cal. 2d 37; People v.
King, 13 Cal. 2d 521; People v. Mitchell, 14 Cal. 2d 237; People
v. Rogers, 163 Cal. 476; People v. Di Donato, 90 Cal. App. 366;
People v. Northcott, 209 Cal. 639; People v. Samaniego, 118 Cal.
App. 165; People v. Pianezzi, 48 Cal. App. 2d 270; People v.
Mandell, 48 Cal. App. 2d 806; People v. Madison, 3 Cal. 2d 668;
People v. McCoy, 25 Cal. 2d 177; People v. Dorman, 28 Cal.
2d 846 and cases last above cited). Thus where the defendant,
if guilty of felonious homicide at all is guilty of first degree
murder, "It is proper in such a case for the court to advise
the jury that the defendant is either guilty or innocent of
first degree murder." (People v. Sanford, 33 Cal. 2d 590). Also
where the evidence shows that the crime charged was consummated the court may properly refuse to submit to the jury
the possibility of a verdict of an attempt to commit the crime
charged. (People v. Stanton, 106 Cal. 139; People v. Dukes, 16
Cal. App. 2d 105; People v. Lionberger, 19 Cal. 2d 284.)
Where the defendant was either guilty of a violation of section 288 of the Penal Code or not guilty and denied the
conduct upon which the charge was based, instructions as
to the lesser included offense of contributing to the delinquency of a minor were properly refused (People v. Romersa,
111 Cal. App. 2d 173).

While it has been held error to instruct the jury on the law
of a lesser included offense where, under the evidence, the accused was either guilty of the offense charged or not guilty,
the later and best considered decisions hold that in such a case
the defendant cannot complain where the jury which found him
guilty returned a verdict of a crime of a lesser degree which was
more favorable to him than the facts warranted. (People v.
Tugwell, 32 Cal. App. 520; People v. Stevens, 5 Cal. 2d 92;
People v. Washburn, 54 Cal. App. 124; People v. Alderson, 105
Cal. App. 202; People v. Jenkins, 118 Cal. App. 115; People v.

Wolcott, 139 Cal. App. 355; People v. Rucker, 11 Cal. App. 2d 609; People v. Cota, 53 Cal. App. 2d 455.) In such cases the rational interpretation of the verdict must be that the jury found the defendant guilty under the charge upon which he was tried and convicted the defendant of the lesser offense either through a misunderstanding of the law which led them to the conclusion that it was the lesser offense of which the defendant was guilty or from a desire to extend a degree of leniency to the accused, but, regardless of the error in favor of the accused, the verdict is valid.

CHAPTER VI.

ATTEMPTS

Mere intention to commit an act constituting a particular crime is not punishable but there is a point between the formation of the evil intent and actual commission of the crime where the criminal has, by overt action toward the accomplishment of the intended crime, gone so far in the carrying out of his purpose as to be guilty of an attempt to commit such crime. An attempt to commit a crime is itself punishable as a public offense.

Penalties

In some instances, such as the attempt to commit arson (Penal Code, sec. 451a), attempts to escape (Penal Code, secs. 107, 4531, 4532), and attempted extortion (Penal Code, sec. 524), the attempt is directly declared to be a crime and specific provision made for its punishment. Since most crimes include as a lesser offense the attempt to commit such crimes the law also provides that:—

"Every person who attempts to commit any crime, but fails, or is prevented or intercepted in the perpetration thereof is punishable, where no provision is made by law for the punishment of such attempt, as follows:

"1. If the offense so attempted is punishable by imprisonment in the state prison for five years, or more, or by imprisonment in the county jail, the person guilty of such attempt is punishable by imprisonment in the state prison, or in a county jail, as the case may be, for a term not exceeding one-half the longest term of imprisonment prescribed upon a conviction of the offense so attempted; provided, however, that if the crime attempted is one in which there is no maximum sentence set by law or in which the maximum sentence is life imprisonment or death the person guilty of such attempt shall be punishable by imprisonment in the state prison for a term of not more than 20 years.

"2. If the offense so attempted is punishable by imprisonment in the state prison for any term less than five years, the person guilty of such attempt is punishable by imprisonment in the county jail for not more than one year.

"3. If the offense so attempted is punishable by a fine, the offender convicted of such attempt is punishable by a fine

49

not exceeding one-half the largest fine which may be imposed upon a conviction of the offense so attempted.

"4. If the offense so attempted is punishable by imprisonment and by a fine, the offender convicted of such attempt may be punished by both imprisonment and fine, not exceeding one-half the longest term of imprisonment and one-half the largest fine which may be imposed upon a conviction of the offense so attempted." (Penal Code, sec. 664.)

The word "punishable" in Section 664 means "liable to punishment by" (People v. Superior Court, 116 Cal. App. 412).

Application of the Statute

Subdivision one governs attempts to commit all felonies the maximum penalty for which felonies is five years or more in the state prison. If the felony attempted has a maximum penalty of less than five years in the state prison the attempt is punishable under subdivision 2. If the crime attempted is a misdemeanor the attempt is punishable under subdivision 1 if the only penalty provided for such misdemeanor is imprisonment in a county jail; if the misdemeanor is punishable by a fine only the attempt is punishable under subdivision 3; and an attempt to commit a misdemeanor is punishable under subdivision 4 if the penalty for such misdemeanor may be both a fine and imprisonment. Subdivision 4 also applies to cases where the felony attempted is punishable by both a fine and imprisonment.

In attempted burglary, since the maximum sentence of the two degrees of burglary is different, the degree of the burglary should be fixed by the verdict or, if a jury is waived or the defendant pleads guilty, by the court.

What Constitutes An Attempt

In order to constitute an attempt there must be, in addition to the wicked intent, some overt act done toward the ultimate commission of the proposed crime. (People v. Stites, 75 Cal. 570.) Acts amounting to mere preparation, before or unaccompanied by an overt act toward the actual commission of the intended crime, do not amount to an attempt to commit such crime. (People v. Lombard, 131 Cal. App. 525.) A mere agreement by the defendant to perform an abortion and the payment of the fee therefor does not constitute an attempt to commit the crime of abortion (People v. Holbrook, 45 Cal. 2d. 228). The preparation consists in devising or arranging the means or measures, making the plans, getting ready the necessary tools or implements, gathering together the persons necessary to be gotten together before the immediate steps are taken toward the commission of the crime. (People v. Murray, 14 Cal. 2d. 159.)

The attempt consists of an overt act toward the commission of the crime following the preparation and planning and amounting to the commencement of the actual perpetration which would end in the consummation of the crime if not interrupted or stayed (People v. Di Donato, 90 Cal. App. 366; People v. Fiegelman, 33 Cal. App. 2d 100; People v. Murray, 14 Cal. 159; People v. Lanzit, 70 Cal. App. 498; People v. Parrish, 87 Cal. App. 2d 853; People v. Poluma, 18 Cal. App. 131; People v. Mann, 113 Cal. 76; People v. Gilbert, 86 Cal. App. 8) and, when the design and intent to commit a crime is clearly evidenced by an act, even though slight, in furtherance of the design and constituting an actual step toward the perpetration of the crime, this will constitute an attempt to commit that crime. (People v. Fiegelman, 33 Cal. App. 2d 100, and cases last cited; People v. Hecht, 133 Cal. App. 2d. 25.)

"An attempt to commit a crime is an endeavor carried beyond mere preparation but falling short of execution of the ultimate design. It is an act immediately and directly tending to the execution of the principal crime, and committed by the prisoner under such circumstances that he had the power of carrying his intentions into execution and would have done so but for some intervening cause. The law recognizes a distinction between an intention to commit a crime and an attempt to commit such crime. An intention followed by no overt act cannot be punished. There is also a distinction between an attempt to commit a crime and merely soliciting one to commit it, as there is between an attempt and mere preparation." (Ex parte Floyd, 7 Cal. App. 588.) The making of arrangements for transporting a woman to Mexico for the purpose of there performing an abortion is merely preparatory and does not constitute an attempt (People v. Buffum, 40 Cal. 2d 709; see also People v. Gallardo, 41 Cal. App. 2d. 57,66).

"In order to establish an attempt it must appear that the defendant had a specific intent to commit a crime and did a direct, unequivocal act toward that end; preparation alone is not enough and some appreciable fragment of the crime must have been accomplished" (People v. Gallardo, 41 Cal. 2d. 57). (Note:—The last clause of this quotation is not clear. If it means that some element of the crime must be committed, it is contrary to prior decisions. In People v. Werner, 16 Cal. 2d 216, 221 and People v. Buffum, 40 Cal. 2d 709 and People v. Miller, 2 Cal. 2d 527, cited to support this clause the elements of an attempt are stated to be "an intent and a direct ineffectual act done toward its commission" and it must be assumed that, since these cases are followed and not overruled, that this is what is meant in the Gallardo case).

Overt Act

The overt act required to constitute an attempt differs from the overt act essential to the crime of conspiracy in that, while in conspiracy any act, even though it be an act of mere preparation and may be a lawful act, beyond mere planning and agreement, toward the accomplishment of the object of the conspiracy is an overt act, the overt act necessary to an attempt must be an actual step in the perpetration of the crime, a beginning in the action toward its commission. (People v. Parrish, 87 Cal. App. 2d 853).

The required overt act need not be the last proximate act prior to the commencement of the crime itself. Whenever the design of a person to commit a crime is clearly shown, a slight act done in furtherance of that design will constitute the overt act and at attempt to commit the crime has been committed (People v. Fiegelman, 33 Cal. App 2d 100; People v. Parrish, 87 Cal. App. 2d 853; People v. Lanzit, 70 Cal. App. 498; People v. Fratiano, 132 Cal. App. 2d. 610, attempted extortion).

Examples of Attempts

Appellant and his codefendant, each wearing a handkerchief around his neck with eyeholes cut therein and each being armed with a revolver, pushed open the swinging doors of a saloon shortly after midnight and, seeing a crowd inside, promptly departed. The court held that an attempt to commit robbery had been committed and that pushing open the doors was an overt act. (People v. Moran, 18 Cal. App. 209.)

Entering the automobile of another without his permission and operating the levers and starter in an apparent effort to start the motor is an attempt to commit theft. (People v. Carter, 73 Cal. App. 495; People v. Edwards, 79 Cal. 514.

Where two men, one armed with a pistol, approached a parked car and the one with the gun pointed it at the driver and the gun was discharged, killing the driver, this consti-

tuted an attempt to commit robbery, making the killing first
degree murder. (People v. Samaniego, 118 Cal. App. 165.)

The defendant intending to kill his wife had his associate
prepare a dynamite bomb equipped with a time device to
explode it and they then went to the place where the wife
had her bedroom to place it thereunder. As the associate
began to prepare the bomb for placement the officers, tipped
off by the associate, arrested the defendant. It was held
that this constituted an attempt to commit murder. (People
v. Lanzit, 70 Cal. App. 498; People v. Parrish, 87 Cal. App. 2d
853.)

Where the defendant walked into a theatre entrance,
pulled out a gun and advanced toward the ticket window and,
as he was about to raise the gun, it was discharged, a conviction of attempt to commit robbery was sustained. (People v.
Anderson, 1 Cal. 2d 687.)

Where the evidence showed preparations to kidnap a person for the purpose of extorting money, providing a cabin in
which to keep the victim and means of tying and gagging him,
and the defendants, as the overt act, drove to Redlands for
the purpose of delivering the extortion note and at the same
time to kidnap the victim, the crime attempted kidnapping was
committed (People v. Lombard, 131 Cal. App. 525).

Where a person approaches a dwelling and climbs over a
balcony on the second floor (People v. Gilbert, 86 Cal. App. 8)
or was arrested with his hands raised against the screen of a
window (People v. Machen, 3 Cal. App. 2d 499; People v.
Davis, 24 Cal. App. 2d 408) was seen a few feet from a window,
the screen of which had been cut, and there was physical evidence that the defendant had cut the screen (People v. Cagle,
141 Cal. App. 2d. 612) or broke the glass door of a clothing
store in early morning hour and ran when a patrol officer approached (People v. Guiterrez, 152 Cal. App. 2d. ......). or pried
at the door of a store with a tool (People v. Wilson, 25 Cal.
App. 2d 332; see also People v. Martone, 38 Cal. App. 2d 392,
and illustrative cases cited), severing a lock with a bolt cutters
(People v. Walker, 31, 33 Cal. 2d 290), approached the rear of
a store carrying a 14 foot ladder, set down a bag of tools including a 30 foot rope ladder, sledge hammer, brace and bit,
gloves and a flashlight, and walked along the edge of the
buiding looking up (People v. Bigson, 94 Cal. App. 2d 468)
such person having no business to be where he was found, he is
guilty of an attempt to commit burglary.

Where the defendant, charged with attempted extortion, told the victim that he would call for the money and would ring her doorbell the next night and did so call, his so calling constituted an overt act completing the attempt (People v. Franquelin, 109 Cal. App. 2d 774).

A conviction for attempt to commit robbery was sustained on evidence that two men seized a woman who was on her way home about midnight, tried to knock her down, and ran when she screamed. (People v. Sanchez, 35 Cal. App. 2d 316.)

While an attempt to commit a crime does not necessarily include an assault, an assault with intent to commit a crime necessarily includes an attempt to commit that crime. (People v. Akens, 25 Cal. App. 373; see also cases under FELONIOUS ASSAULTS.)

Where the defendant who asked to be shown a diamond ring was shown a tray of rings by the jeweler and fled when he was detected in attempting to substitute a bogus ring for a good one he was held guilty of an attempt to commit larceny. (People v. Gilmore, 25 Cal. App. 332; People v. Isenberg, 25 Cal. App. 334.)

A person who has done all the acts necessary to constitute a larceny by trick and device except the obtaining of the victim's money is guilty of an attempt to commit larceny (People v. Vaughn, 25 Cal. App. 736) even though the completion of the crime was frustrated by the defendant's arrest. (People v. Mayen, 188 Cal. 237.)

Where a man and a woman represented themselves as husband and wife to defendant, a doctor, at his office, stating that the woman was pregnant, discussed an abortion and paid the defendant the fee requested, the woman was placed upon a table and defendant sterilized his instruments and prepared materials which he said would produce an abortion, the crime of attempted abortion was committed (People v. Raffington, 98 Cal. App. 2d. 455). Where the defendant agreed to perform an abortion, told the woman to get upon the operating table and that he was going to dilate her uterus and scrape her and took a speculum from a sterilizer and ran cold water over it, a conviction of attempted abortion was sustained (People v. Reed, 128 Cal. App. 2d. 499; People v. Bowlby, 135 Cal. App. 2d 519). Where arrangements were made for the performance of an abortion at the house of the complainant and surgical instruments were delivered to this home and the codefendant came to the house and placed the instruments in pans in the stove and placed cotton and medicinal preparations on a side table, it was held that this constituted an attempt to commit the crime defined by section 274 of the Penal Code, commonly referred to as abortion (People v. Berger, 131 Cal. App. 2d. 127). Where a woman in the company of an investigator for the State Board of Medical Examiners told the defendant, a doctor, that she thought she was pregnant and the defendant examined her and told her that she was definitely pregnant and asked whether she desired an abortion and made an appointment for a later date at which time he received $300 and had the woman remove her lower clothing and get onto a surgical table, inserted a speculum and stated that he was going to scrape the uterus which would prevent her from having a baby and picked up a curette, an instrument used for such purpose, at which time he was arrested, the crime of attempt to commit abortion had been committed even though the woman was in fact not pregnant, the court holding that the crime of attempted abortion is committed if one, believing that a woman is pregnant and intending to produce a miscarriage does a direct unequivocal act toward the consummation of a miscarriage (People v. Cummings, 141 Cal. App. 2d 193).

Where the evidence showed a declared and premeditated intent to kill and the defendant fired one shot from a pistol over the head of the complainant, pointed the gun at complainant and the gun misfired and defendant ejected the shell and put another in the gun and again aimed at the complainant, the crime of attempted murder was commited (People v. Van Buskirk, 113 Cal. App. 2d 789).

Attempt—What Is Not

To constitute an attempt to commit a crime there must be a direct, unequivocal act and a specific intent to commit the crime and some appreciable fragment of the crime must have been accomplished (People v. Gallardo, 41 Cal. 2d 57,76). Acts merely preparatory and equivocal are not sufficient (People v. Goldstein, 146 Cal. App. 2d 268).

To sustain a charge of attempted grand theft the prosecution introduced evidence that two inspectors visited appellant at his workshop, representing that they were naturopaths and had heard that appellant had a device that was effective in the treatment of many diseases and that appellant showed them his machine and the inspectors offered to buy two of the machines and, when appellant agreed, paid him $250 on

(No attempt at all)

account and there was evidence that the machine had no value as a means of diagnosis or treatment of disease but that the inspectors did not rely on the statements of appellant as to what the machine would do and never intended that appellant should keep the money, the court, calling attenion to the rule (citing cases) that to constitute an attempt it must appear that the accused had a specific intent to commit the crime and did a direct unequivocal act toward that end, held that the crime charged had not been committed (People v. Schroeder, 131 Cal. App. 2d 1).

Abandonment of Attempt

(Stop commission of offense (will not constitute defense)) — End crime is not committed with attempt.

When a person has once committed acts which make the complete corpus delicti of a criminal offense he cannot avoid responsibility by not proceeding further or by making restitution. If the act of a person amounts to an attempt to commit a crime, the fact that he abandoned all further effort to commit the crime intended will not relieve him from responsibility for the attempt. (People v. Jones, 112 Cal. App. 68; People v. Johnson, 131 Cal. 511; People v. Stewart, 97 Cal. 238.) In the case last cited the court said, "It is no less a crime, though the aggressor should abandon his intentions before the consummation of the act, by reason of the pains of a stricken conscience alone." (See also People v. Lutes, 79 Cal. App. 2d 233.) A failure to complete a crime because of threatened arrest or the appearance of the police is not such a free and voluntary act as to constitute an abandonment (People v. Walker, 33 Cal. 2d 250). The fact that the attempt failed because of an intervening cause which prevented the consummation of the ultimate intent of the perpetrator is immaterial and is not a defense (People v. Grant, 105 Cal. App. 2d. 347). "Abandonment is a defense if the attempt to commit a crime is freely and voluntarily abandoned before the act is put in process of final execution and when there is no outside cause prompting such abandonment." (People v. Von Hecht, 133 Cal. App. 2d. 25).

Specific Intent

Since an attempt is an overt act in carrying out an intent to commit a particular crime, it is obvious that to constitute an attempt there must exist the specific intent to commit the crime which the accused is charged with having attempted. (People v. Lanzit, 70 Cal. App. 498; People v. Mize, 80 Cal. 41; People v. Fleming, 94 Cal. 308; People v. Keefer, 18 Cal. 636.)

Attempt to Commit Crime
Not Capable of Consummation *(State of mind not capable of going thru)*

There appears some confusion in the authorities as to the law of attempts applicable to those cases in which by reason of the circumstances the completion of the intended crime was not possible. Where the crime is to the mind of the perpetrator possible of perpetration and the elements of the corpus delicti of the attempt of that crime are present the circumstance that the absence of some physical fact makes the consummation of the crime impossible will not constitute a defense to a charge of an attempt to commit the crime. Thus where a man shot at a hole in the roof with the intention of killing a police officer who he believed was there stationed, he was guilty of an attempt to commit murder even though at the time the officer was out of range of the bullet. (People v. Lee Kong, 95 Cal. 666.) An attempt to steal money from the pocket of another is punishable even though the pocket was empty. (People v. Fiegelman, 33 Cal. App. 2d 100.) An attempt to obtain money by false pretenses is committed, the other elements of the offense being present, even though the intended victim did not rely on the false representations. (People v. Grossman, 28 Cal. App. 2d 193.) An attempt to receive stolen property is complete even though, when the intending receiver went to the place where the property had been concealed and was ready to receive it, the property was not there because it had been removed by the officers. (In re Magidson, 32 Cal. App. 566.) And the fact that the intended victim of an attempt to obtain money by false pretenses did not have the necessary money is no defense. (People v. Arberry, 13 Cal. App. 749.) Where a deputy sheriff proposed to a member of the sheriff's narcotic detail that the latter furnish him with narcotics for sale and the narcotic officer, acting under orders of his superiors, had further conversations on the subject with the defendant and finally met him at his home and delivered to him a white powder which in fact was not a narcotic but only talcum powder and arrested the defendant when he was about to put the package into his safe, a conviction of attempted possession of narcotics was sustained the court holding that the essential elements, a specific intent to commit the crime and a direct ineffectual act done towards its commission, were shown by the evidence (People v. Siu, 126 Cal. App. 2d. 41).

Where, after examining a woman and declaring that she was pregnant, defendant attempted to use an instrument, inserted in the uterus, to produce an abortion, the fact that she was not pregnant is not material and the crime of attempted abortion was committed (People v. Cummings, 141 Cal. App. 2d 193).

Legal impossibility — Known liable

Inability in Law to Commit the Crime *(is a defense)*

Where the crime attempted is one which as a matter of law could not be committed, where by reason of the law an essential element of the corpus delicti can not exist and the intended crime is a legal impossibility, there can be no attempt to commit such crime. Since a lottery ticket can not be the subject of larceny there can be no attempt to steal it. *not law anymore* Again certain crimes can be committed against only a particular class of persons. A violation of section 288 of the Penal Code can only be committed upon a minor under the age of fourteen years and there could not be an attempt to commit this crime upon a minor who was over that age. Rape can only be committed upon a woman and an attempt to rape committed upon a man dressed in woman's clothes, even though believed by the accused to be a woman, could not constitute an attempt to commit rape. "The defense of impossibility means a legal impossibility" (People v. Fratiano, 132 Cal. App. 2d. 610, attempted extortion).

It does not necessarily follow that where a person attempts to commit a crime which is impossible of commission as a matter of law that he can entirely escape punishment, for it may be that, while the charge of an attempt must fail, he has by his act committed some other crime for which he may be prosecuted.

CHAPTER VII.

REASONABLE DOUBT

"A defendant in a criminal action is presumed to be innocent until the contrary is proved, and in case of a reasonable doubt whether his guilt is satisfactorily shown, he is entitled to an acquittal, but the effect of this presumption is only to place upon the state the burden of proving him guilty beyond a reasonable doubt. Reasonable doubt is defined as follows: It is not a mere possible doubt because everything relating to human affairs, and depending on moral evidence, is open to some possible or imaginary doubt. It is that state of the case, which, after the entire comparison and consideration of all the evidence, leaves the minds of jurors in that condition that they can not say they feel an abiding conviction, to a moral certainty, of the truth of the charge." (Penal Code, sec. 1096.) The presumption of innocence ends with the conviction of the accused (People v. Shorts, 32 Cal. 2d 502).

"The law does not require demonstration, that is, such a degree of proof as, excluding possibility of error, produces absolute certainty; because such proof is rarely possible. Moral certainty only is required, or that degree of proof which produces conviction in an unprejudiced mind." (Code Civ. Proc. 1826). This section applies exclusively to criminal cases (People v. Miller, 171 Cal. 649, 657; see also People v. Derenzo, 46 Cal. App. 2d. 411, 416; People v. Castro, 68 Cal. App. 2d. 491).

Instruction in Language of Statute Sufficient

Where the court gives to the jury the instruction in the language of section 1096 of the Penal Code, "no further instruction on the subject of the presumption of innocence or defining reasonable doubt need be given." (Penal Code, sec. 1096a; People v. Cohen, 94 Cal. App. 4; People v. Knocke, 94 Cal. App. 55; People v. Lloyd, 97 Cal. App. 664; People v. Galloway, 104 Cal. App. 422; People v. Barnes, 111 Cal. App. 605; People v. Bettencourt, 115 Cal. App. 387; People v. Annunzio, 120 Cal. App. 89; People v. Emmett, 123 Cal. App. 678; People v. O'Shaughnessy, 135 Cal. App. 104; People v. Cancino, 137 Cal. App. 73; People v. Thompson, 3 Cal. App. 2d 359; People v. Madison, 3 Cal. 2d 668; People v. Kynette, 16 Cal. 2d 731; People v. McEvers, 53 Cal. App. 2d 548.)

Court May Give Further Instruction

The court may, however, in its discretion, give further proper instructions on the subject (People v. Carillo. 104 Cal. App. 586; People v. Sheffield, 108 Cal. App. 721; People v. Eggers, 30 Cal. 2d. 676) such as:—"But while the defendant cannot be convicted unless his guilt is established beyond a reasonable doubt, still the law does not require demonstration; that is, such a degree of proof as, excluding possibility of error, produces absolute certainty, because such proof is rarely possible. Moral certainty only is required, or that degree of proof which produces conviction in an unprejudiced mind." (People v. Arnold, 199 Cal. 471; People v. Derenzo, 46 Cal. App. 2d. 438.)

Judicial Interpretation of Rule

In the endeavor to clarify the meaning of the term "reasonable doubt" our courts have said that a reasonable doubt is a doubt for which a reason can be given, arising from the evidence but it is not a doubt arising from mere caprice or groundless conjecture (People v. Bo, 72 Cal. 623, 626; People v. Manasse, 153 Cal. 10, 14; People v. White, 116 Cal. 17, 19; People v. Botkin, 9 Cal. App. 240, 257; People v. Del Cerro, 9 Cal. App. 764, 769); that it is not the rule that guilt must be established to an "absolute moral certainty" (People v. Nelson, 85 Cal. 421; People v. Hecker, 109 Cal. 451), and that "most conclusive proof" is not required (People v. Hall, 94 Cal. 595); that it is not necessary that proof of guilt "must nearly approach absolute certainty" or "exclude the possibility of doubt" (People v. Smith, 105 Cal. 676); and that reasonable doubt does not mean "a mere possible doubt" or "a conjectural or speculative doubt." (People v. Arnold, 199 Cal. 471.)

The presumption of innocence and rule of reasonable doubt operate in favor of the defendant from the beginning of the trial until the jury has arrived at a verdict (People v. Mc-Namara, 94 Cal. 509, 514), and it is essential to a conviction that the jury be satisfied beyond a reasonable doubt that every essential element of the corpus delicti has been proved. (People v. Morino, 53 Cal. 67; People v. Cohn, 76 Cal. 386; People v. Sheffield, 108 Cal. App. 721.)

As to Degree of Guilt or Penalty

Where a jury is satisfied beyond a reasonable doubt that the defendant is guilty but entertains a reasonable doubt as to whether he is guilty of the offense charged or of a lesser included offense or as to the degree of the crime they must give him the benefit of the doubt and return a verdict of guilty as to the lesser offense (People v. Iams, 57 Cal. 115) and, where the case is one in which the jury has the duty of fixing the penalty the jury, if entertaining a reasonable doubt as to which penalty should be imposed, should fix the lesser penalty. (People v. Cancino, 10 Cal. 2d 223.)

When Rule Does Not Apply

The reasonable doubt rule, depending upon the presumption of innocence, does not apply to an issue not covered by that presumption. Thus, where the defense is that of insanity, idiocy or unconsciousness at the time of the commission of the crime and there being a presumption contrary to such abnormal mental conditions, it is the rule that the burden of proving such defense is upon the defendant. (See further discussion under the heading CAPACITY TO COMMIT CRIME.)

Issues of fact not relating to the question of the guilt of the defendant need not be proved beyond a reasonable doubt. Thus issues of fact as to the statute of limitations (People v. McGill, 10 Cal. App. 2d 155) or venue (People v. Harkness, 15 Cal. App. 2d 133; People v. Carter, 10 Cal. App. 2d 387; People v. West, 34 Cal. App. 2d. 55; People v. Cavanaugh, 44 Cal. 2d. 252) are decided by the jury according to the preponderance of evidence and if the defendant in a murder case contends that he is not subject to the imposition of the death penalty because he was under eighteen years of age the burden of proving that fact is upon the defendant and he must do more than raise a reasonable doubt on that point. (People v. Ellis, 206 Cal. 353.) The presumption of innocence does not apply upon the trial of the issues under the plea of not guilty by reason of insanity (People v. Harmon, 110 Cal. App. 2d 545). So also if the prosecution introduces evidence of the commission of a criminal offense other than that for which the defendant is on trial, such other crime need not be proved beyond a reasonable doubt. (People v. Lisenba, 14 Cal. 2d 403; People v. Gray, 52 Cal. App. 2d 620; People v. Albertson, 23 Cal. 2d 550.) A fact not necessary to a conviction need not be established beyond a reasonable doubt. (People v. Machado, 6 Cal. Unrep. 600; People v. Durrant, 116 Cal. 185; People v. Liera, 27 Cal. App. 346.) The venue of the prosecution need not be proven beyond a reasonable doubt (People v. Montgomery, 32 Cal. App. 2d 43; People v. De Soto, 33 Cal. App. 2d 478; In re Ryan, 61 Cal. App. 2d 310; People v. Guernsey, 80 Cal. App. 2d 463); People v. Harkness, 51 Cal. App. 2d 133). The reasonable doubt rule does not apply to proof of a violation of probation (People v. Sweeden, 116 Cal. App. 2d 891; People v. London, 28 Cal. App. 2d 395). Upon a motion to change a plea of guilty to one of not guilty the doctrine of presumption of innocence and reasonable doubt does not apply (People v. Burkett, 118 Cal. App. 2d 204). It is not necessary before considering testimony corroborating an accomplice that the jury be satisfied beyond a reasonable doubt of the truth of the corroborating testimony (People v. Baker, 89 Cal. App. 2d 503). To render admissible the declarations and acts of a conspirator the existence of the conspiracy need only be established by prima facie proof (People v. Kulwin, 102 Cal. App. 2d 104) and to render a declaration of a defendant admissible prima facie proof of the corpus delicti is sufficient (see Corpus Delicti—Prima Facie Proof). The reasonable doubt rule is not pertinent to the appraisal of the testimony of a witness (People v. Shannon, 147 Cal. App. 2d 300).

Habitual Criminal

"The people must prove the alleged prior convictions beyond a reasonable doubt" (People v. Morton, 41 Cal. 2d. 536).

Rule of Convenience

Positive Assertion

Where the subject matter of a negative averment in an accusatory pleading, or a fact relied upon by the defendant as a justification or excuse, relates to him personally or otherwise lies peculiarly within his knowledge, the general rule is that the burden of proof as to such fact or averment is on him (People v. Osaki, 209 Cal. 169, 191; People v. Agnew, 16 Cal. 2d 655, 663); People v. Hassen, 144 Cal. App. 2d 334). The recognition of the rule of convenience does not deprive the accused of the presumption of innocence (People v. Cline, 79 Cal. App. 2d 11, 15; People v. Osaki, 209 Cal. 169, 186; People v. Hassen, 144 Cal. App. d 334).

Burden of Proof of License, etc.

Where an act is made criminal by reason of its having been done without a license permit required by law it is not incumbent upon the prosecution to prove that the defendant did not have a license since it will be taken as proved that the defendant did not have a license unless the defendant proves that he did have such a license. Practicing medicine (People v. Boo Doo Hong, 122 Cal. 606; People v. Wah Hing, 47 Cal. App. 329; People v. Machado, 99 Cal. App. 702; People v. Saunders, 61 Cal. App. 341; People v. Ramsey, 83 Cal. App. 2d 707; People v. Kendall, 111 Cal. App. 2d 204); manufacturing liquor without a license (People v. Spagnoli, 58 Cal. App. 154); possession of an unlicensed still (People v. Dal Porto, 17 Cal. App. 2d 755); carrying concealed weapons (People v. Ross, 60 Cal. App. 163); selling corporate securities (People v. Dean, 131 Cal. App. 228); possession of narcotics without a lawful prescription (People v. Bill, 140 Cal. App. 389; People v. Moronati, 70 Cal. App. 17).

Other Presumptions

It is not the law that the presumption of innocence is the only presumption allowable in a criminal case nor is it the law that the presumption of innocence is not overcome by any other presumption or that it overcomes all other presumptions. "All presumptions are evidence. Conclusive presumptions (Code Civ. Proc., secs. 1961, 1962) are not overcome by the presumption of innocence nor are many disputable presumptions so overcome." (People v. Le Doux, 155 Cal. 535, 553; followed and quoted in People v. Agnew, 16 Cal. 2d 655, 662; People v. Theodore, 121 Cal. App. 2d. 17).

CHAPTER VIII.

CAPACITY TO COMMIT CRIME

"All persons are capable of committing crimes except those belonging to the following classes:

"**One.** Children under the age of fourteen, in the absence of clear proof that at the time of committing the act charged against them, they knew its wrongfulness.

"**Two.** Idiots.

"**Three.** Lunatics and insane persons.

"**Four.** Persons who committed the act or made the omission charged under an ignorance or mistake of fact, which disproves any criminal intent.

"**Five.** Persons who committed the act charged without being conscious thereof.

"**Six.** Persons who committed the act or made the omission charged through misfortune or by accident, when it appears that there was no evil design, intention, or culpable negligence.

"**Seven.** Married women (except for felonies) acting under the threats, command, or coercion of their husbands.

"**Eight.** Persons (unless the crime be punishable with death) who committed the act or made the omission charged under threats or menaces sufficient to show that they had reasonable cause to and did believe their lives would be endangered if they refused." (Penal Code, sec. 26.)

Minors

The common law rule that children under seven years of age are conclusively presumed to be mentally incapable of committing any crime does not exist in California. In this state it is assumed that a child who is under fourteen years of age is incapable of committing a crime but, if the proof clearly shows that the child, regardless of its age, knew the wrongfulness of its act at the time of its commission such child is fully responsible and, if the act is a crime, is legally as liable therefor as if over fourteen years of age. Minors fourteen years of age and over are as capable of committing crime as an adult. The term "age of fourteen" means an actual attained age, that the individual has lived fourteen years since birth, and has no reference whatever to the mentality

64

or "mental age", (People v. Day, 199 Cal. 78), impaired mentality and subnormality, if of such a degree as to render a person incapable of committing crime, being provided for under the second and third subdivisions of the statute.

(Note: for a case of a thirteen year old girl with a mental age of eleven years convicted of murder see People v. Nichols, 22, 88 Cal. App. 2d 22).

Idiots

The term "idiot" in its commonly accepted sense applies to a person who is virtually without mentality. The test of criminal capacity of the mentally subnormal is that one who has sufficient capacity mentally to appreciate the character of his act knew that it violated the rights of another and was in itself wrong and thus could appreciate the character and comprehend the consequences of his act, is to be judged accordingly and is liable for his crimes regardless of how deficient mentally he may have been otherwise. (People v. Oxnam, 170 Cal. 211; People v. Keyes, 178 Cal. 794.)

Where the defense of idiocy is interposed the rules as to the insanity defense requiring a special plea and separate trial of the issue raised thereby (see **Insanity**, infra) do not apply and the defense of idiocy is provable under the issues raised by the plea of not guilty.

Insanity

Insanity which will render a person incapable of committing a crime is such a diseased and deranged condition of his mental faculties as to render him incapable of appreciating the character and quality of the act or incapable of distinguishing between right and wrong as to the act.

Insanity is not a defense unless it exists to such a degree that at the time of the commission of the offense the defendant was so disordered or deranged mentally that he was incapable of appreciating the true nature and quality of his act, that is, that due to his disease the incident did not appear to him in its true but in a distorted, illusionary or delusionary form, or, if he was mentally capable of appreciating the nature of the act, that mental disease had so confused and deranged his faculties that he was incapable of distinguishing between right and wrong as to his act or was under the deluded belief that what he was doing was right. (People v. Harris, 169 Cal. 53; People v. Williams, 184 Cal. 590; People v. Zari, 54 Cal. App. 133; People v. Griffith, 146 Cal. 339; People v.

Gilberg, 197 Cal. 306; People v. Sloper, 198 Cal. 238; People v. Kimball, 5 Cal. 2d 608; People v. Troche, 206 Cal. 35; People v. French, 12 Cal. 2d 720.)

(Note: For a discussion of the so called Durham test, whether the act was the product of mental disease or mental defect see State v. Collins, 314 Pac. 2d 660).

When Not a Defense

Unless it meets this test, insanity is not a defense to a criminal charge. It is interesting to note that as to one charge a defense of insanity may be good but as to another offense, committed at the same time and by the same defendant, he may be criminally responsible. (People v. Perry, 99 Cal. App. 90.) An adjudication, in another proceeding, by a competent court, that a person is insane is not conclusive proof of his insanity nor does it establish the defense of insanity upon his trial on a criminal charge. (People v. Jackson, 105 Cal. App. 2d 811; People v. Willard, 150 Cal. 543; People v. Puter, 85 Cal. App. 2d 348). Proof of such adjudication is merely evidence which the jury may weigh in its consideration of the question whether the defendant was at the time of the offense incapable of committing the crime by reason of insanity. (People v. Dale, 7 Cal. 2d 156; People v. Rothrock, 21 Cal. App. 2d 116; In re Gibson, 78 Cal. App. 794; People v. McConnell, 80 Cal. App. 789; People v. Lee, 108 Cal. App. 609; People v. Little, 68 Cal. App. 674; In re Stevenson, 187 Cal. 773; People v. Prosser, 56 Cal. App. 454; People v. Grace, 88 Cal. App. 222; People v. Keyes, 178 Cal. 794; People v. Hickman, 204 Cal. 470; People v. Willard, 150 Cal. 543; People v. Coleman, 50 Cal. App. 2d 592; People v. Williams, 20 Cal. 2d 273; People v. Shuman, 64 Cal. App. 2d. 382; People v. Gilberg, 197 Cal. 306). Soundness of mind and legal sanity are not synonymous (People v. Baker, 42 Cal. 2d. 550).

It is immaterial as to the cause which brings about the insanity urged as a defense. Thus, though voluntary intoxication is not a defense, nor is mere temporary mental derangement produced by the recent use of intoxicants, still if the continued use of intoxicants produces settled insanity the measure of responsibility and capacity to commit crime is the same as insanity resulting from any other cause. (People v. Travers, 88 Cal. 239; People v. Findley, 132 Cal. 307; People v. Griffith, 146 Cal. 344; People v. Crimmin, 57 Cal. App. 202.)

Partial Insanity—Insane Delusion

Whenever partial insanity or insane delusion or hallucination is relied upon as a defense, it must appear that the crime charged was the product or offspring of such insanity, insane delusion or hallucination and not the result of some sane reasoning and natural motive and was not committed with an appreciation of its wrongfulness. Although the defendant may have been partially insane—as, for example, suffering from insanity producing an insane delusion or hallucination—there must be the relation of cause and effect between the insanity and the act and, if he understands the nature and character of his act and that it is wrong, such insanity is not a defense. (People v. Hubert, 119 Cal. 223; People v. Griffith, 146 Cal. 346; People v. Willard, 150 Cal. 554; People v. Lizarraga, 108 Cal. App. 153.)

Moral Insanity

Moral insanity, as an independent state, if such a state exists, is not recognized by the law as a defense to crime, and does not constitute such insanity as makes it a legal defense and, in itself, is not a bar to responsibility for criminal acts; hence, however perverted the feelings, conscience, affections and sentiments of a defendant may be, he is responsible to the law for his criminal acts unless the intellectual faculties and reasoning powers are so affected by mental disease that he does not know the nature and quality of his act or is incapable of distinguishing between right and wrong in relation to the act with which he is charged. (People v. McCarthy, 115 Cal. 262; People v. Gilberg, 197 Cal. 306; see also People v. French, 12 Cal. 2d 720; People v. Troche, 206 Cal. 35; People v. Johnson, 115 Cal. App. 704; People v. Lizarraga, 108 Cal. App. 153.)

Irresistible Impulse

A diseased condition of the mind wherein, though the patient knows the nature and quality as well as the wrongfulness of his act, still, by reason of an irresistible impulse, he cannot prevent himself from committing a criminal act, is not recognized in California as a form of insanity which is a defense to a criminal charge. (People v. Morisawa, 180 Cal. 148; People v. Methever, 132 Cal. 332; People v. Hubert, 119 Cal. 216; People v. Ward, 105 Cal. App. 343; People v. McCarthy, 115 Cal. 255; People v. Hoin, 62 Cal. 120; People v. Harris, 169 Cal. 53; People v. Estes, 188 Cal. 511; People v.

Elder, 55 Cal. App. 644; People v. Buck, 151 Cal. 667; People
v. Spraic, 87 Cal. App. 724; See State v. Maish, 185 Pac. 2d
486 for discussion; also see Sollars v. State, 316 Pac. 2d 917,
Nevada, for reasons against irresistable impulse as a defense).

Lucid Intervals

There are forms of insanity in which the person afflicted
at times is controlled by his disease and is irresponsible but
has, at times, lucid intervals when he is able to distinguish
between right and wrong and knows the nature and quality
of his acts. The law presumes that a crime committed by a
person so afflicted was committed by him during one of his
lucid intervals and that he is responsible for his crime, and to
secure his acquittal upon the ground of insanity the defendant
must prove by a preponderance of evidence that he was actually legally insane, as measured by the right and wrong test,
at the time the crime was committed. (People v. Keyes, 178
Cal. 794.)

Temporary Insanity

Insanity of short duration, referred to in the law as temporary insanity, as a defense to a criminal charge is as fully
recognized as insanity of a longer duration or of a chronic
character if, by reason of his disease, he is either incapable of
appreciating the nature and quality of his acts or to know
the difference between right and wrong with reference to his
act and the fact he was sane shortly before his commission of
the criminal act or recovered his sanity shortly after the act
does not in any degree impair his defense of insanity. (People
v. Ford, 138 Cal. 140.)

Burden of Proof—Presumption of Sanity

Since the law presumes every person to be sane and free
from such mental disease as would constitute a defense to a
criminal charge the prosecution is not required to prove, as a
part of its case in chief, that the defendant was sane at the
time of the commission of the crime charged. If the defendant interposes the plea of "not guilty by reason of insanity"
the burden of proving that defense is upon the defendant
to prove his insanity by a preponderance of the evidence. If
the preponderance of the evidence is in favor of sanity or if
the evidence on the issue of insanity is evenly balanced the
jury should find that the defendant was sane. (People v.
Loomis, 170 Cal. 347; People v. Harris, 169 Cal. 53; People v.

Keyes, 178 Cal. 794; People v. Estes, 188 Cal. 511; People v. Nikell, 144 Cal. 202; People v. Troche, 206 Cal. 35; People v Busby, 40 Cal. App. 2d 193; People v. Daugherty, 40 Cal. 2d 876).

The presumption of sanity may, of itself, be sufficient to overcome the proof offered by the defendant (People v. Chamberlain, 7 Cal. 2d 257, where the finding of sanity by the jury was sustained on appeal in a case wherein the prosecution offered no evidence, relying on the presumption of sanity alone to rebut the case of the defendant who introduced the testimony of ten lay witnesses and three medical experts, two of them appointed by the court, all of whom testified that the defendant was insane; see also People v. Darling, 107 Cal. App. 2d 635; People v. Harmon, 110 Cal. App. 2d 545).

What Is Not Legal Insanity

The standards of legal capacity applied in testing the testator's competency to make a will, to have a guardian appointed because of his incompetence to care for his own affairs, or to warrant his commitment by a lunacy commission to a hospital for the insane (People v. Field, 108 Cal. App. 2d 496) are not applicable in determining whether a person has legal capacity to commit crime. While a person may be found insane when measured by these tests such insanity will not impair his capacity to commit crime unless it measures up to the right and wrong test set forth in the beginning of this discussion. (See People v. Willard, 150 Cal. 543, where the defendant, immediately after being committed by a court to a hospital for the insane as "homicidal and dangerous," shot and killed the sheriff and his conviction was affirmed on appeal.)

A person falling within the definition of the term "sexual psychopath" (sec. 5500, Welfare and Institutions Code) or adjudicated to be a "sexual psychopath" is not an insane person (People v. Tipton, 90 Cal. App. 2d. 603; People v. Cooper, 123 Cal. App. 2d. 353).

Insanity Produced by Intoxication

"Insanity produced by intoxication does not destroy responsibility when the party when sane and responsible made himself voluntarily intoxicated." (People v. DeMoss, 4 Cal. 2d 409.)

A sane man who voluntarily becomes intoxicated is not excused because the result is to cloud his judgment, unbalance his reason, impair his perceptions, derange his mental faculties, and lead him to the commission of an act which in his sober senses he would have avoided. (People v. Fellows, 122 Cal. 233, 239; People v. Lim Dung Dong, 28 Cal. App. 2d 135; People v. Reid, 193 Cal. 491; the last two cases laying down the rule that the rule is the same where the condition is produced by the effect of the use of narcotics.)

Other Examples

Even though a defendant was irrational, mentally abnormal or defective, or suffered from a nervous disorder he is liable for his crimes unless he measures up to the right and wrong test. (People v. Dugger, 5 Cal. 2d 337; People v. Kimball, 5 Cal. 2d 608; People v. Zari, 54 Cal. App. 372.)

An inability to distinguish between right and wrong, not due to any disease of the brain or mind, is not insanity and savors of either the doctrine of irresistible impulse or the effect of jealousy and passion. (People v. Reynolds, 108 Cal. App. 69.)

Melancholia which impaired the defendant's will and rendered him likely to commit a homicide (People v. Barthleman, 120 Cal. 7, 12), or an unbalanced mind (People v. Goldsworthy, 130 Cal. 600, 606), or a mental condition due to epilepsy and the use of alcohol (People v. Kloss, 115 Cal. 567) which do not measure up to the right and wrong test are not such insanity which is a defense. A person may be unable to reason correctly upon the plan which he is formulating to execute a crime, and, notwithstanding his defective reasoning, be responsible to the law if he comes within the legal test. (People v. Koehn, 207 Cal. 605.) The fact that the accused had, some years before, received a violent head injury which greatly impaired his physical condition, standing by itself, may not be proved as it does not tend to prove that he did not have the capacity to commit crime. (People v. Davis, 4 Cal. Unrep. 524.)

Evidence that defendant's will power was weak and his physical condition bad and that he was without sufficient force to resist the impulse of his codefendant to accompany him in the perpetration of robberies does not tend to show incapacity to commit crime and is inadmissible. (People v. Villegas, 29 Cal. App. 2d 658.)

Insanity Not Provable on Trial to Determine Guilt

A defendant who does not enter a plea of not guilty by reason of insanity is conclusively presumed to have been sane at the time of the commission of the offense charged. If the defendant enters such a plea without also pleading not guilty he thereby admits the commission of the offense charged. (Penal Code, sec. 1016.)

When a defendant pleads both not guilty and not guilty by reason of insanity he must first be tried as if he had entered the plea of not guilty only "and in such trial he shall be conclusively presumed to have been sane at the time the offense is alleged to have been committed." (Penal Code, sec. 1026.) It has been decided that the plea of not guilty does not raise any issue under which evidence of insanity is admissible (People v. Leong Fook, 206 Cal. 64; People v. Phillips, 102 Cal. App. 705) and that "The insanity of a defendant cannot be used for the purpose of reducing his crime from murder in the first degree to murder in the second degree. If responsible at all in this respect he is responsible in the same degree as a sane man, and if he is not responsible at all he is entitled to an acquittal in both degrees." (People v. Troche, 206 Cal. 35; People v. French, 12 Cal. 2d 720.)

Where, however, upon the trial under the plea of not guilty an issue arises as to an event occurring at a time other than the time when the offense is alleged to have been committed the statute does not have the effect of excluding evidence of insanity of the accused at that time. Thus it has been held that evidence of insanity is admissible to determine whether an alleged confession of the defendant was the product of a diseased mind (People v. Dias, 210 Cal. 495), and the court also added that since the evidence of insanity in such a case was before the jury the defendant's mental status could be considered by the jury in fixing the penalty in a murder case but could not be considered by them as to the degree of the crime. This latter remark of the court suggests that the court might, if the point were directly presented in a future case, hold that such evidence would be admissible if offered for the sole purpose of being considered by the jury in fixing the penalty in a first degree murder case.

(Note: Since mental condition, whether the result of intoxication or disease not amounting to insanity may be proved and considered in fixing the degree of the crime it would seem that mental condition amounting to insanity, if shown by the evidence, may be considered for the same purpose. As to the language in section 1026 of the Penal Code that, in a trial of the issue raised by the plea of not guilty, the defendant "shall be conclusivey presumed to have been sane at the time the offense is alleged to have been committed" in the author's opinion the word "sane" should be construed as "sufficiently sane to have the capacity to commit the crime charged" and that insanity of any lesser or other degree should be provable as relevant to the issues of intent and degree of the crime).

Mistake of Fact

An act or omission committed under an ignorance or mistake of fact under circumstances which disprove any criminal intent is not criminal. Where a person in good faith believes in the existence of certain facts and acts or omits to act with reference to such believed facts in a manner which would be lawful if such facts were as he believes them to be, he is not guilty of a crime even though his act or omission is such that, if committed by one who knew the true facts, it would constitute a criminal offense. In such a case there would be no criminal intent since an act is not knowingly committed where there is an honest ignorance or mistake of fact with reference to which the act is committed. As it is not larceny for a customer at a restaurant to take his overcoat with him upon his departure it would not be larceny if, intending to take his own coat, he, under an honest mistake, took the coat of another which closely resembled and was hung near his own. Here the circumstances disprove the larcenous intent and mistake of fact is a defense. (People v. Mullaley, 16 Cal. 44.) Where a person joins what actually is a conspiracy in ignorance of its true character and under an honest belief that it is a lawful association with a lawful purpose only, he is not guilty of conspiracy (People v. Flanagan, 65 Cal. App. 268 and cases cited.)

When Not a Defense

Mistake of fact is not, however, a defense where a person intends to do an act the commission of which is a criminal offense and the result of which act produces a result different from that intended but which also constitutes a crime, nor can he escape the legal consequences of his negligence because he did not know what the results of his carelessness would be. Thus a person who sets fire to a barn which he believes to be empty under circumstances which constitute arson will be guilty of first degree murder if in fact there be in the barn a person whose death is caused by the fire; nor could a person escape responsibility, if he were driving his automobile on the left side of the highway at night without lights and thereby caused the death of a pedestrian, merely because he assumed it to be a fact that no one else was upon the highway. Also a person cannot escape responsibility under the claim that he did not intend the criminal results of his voluntary act since he is under the law responsible for the natural and probable consequences of an act he intended to perform even though he did it with the object of attaining a different result. There is a difference between assuming a state of facts to exist when investigation would disclose that no such state of facts exist and mistaking or misinterpreting the facts which are known to the person who acts with reference thereto.

In considering mistake of fact as a possible defense it must always be borne in mind that, when a person voluntarily does that which the law declares punishable as a crime, the element of criminal intent exists and the defense is not tenable and that it is only where the ignorance or mistake of fact operates as proof of a lack of criminal intent that this defense can succeed.

Knowledge of the Material Fact

There are some statutes, prominently those enacted to protect health, safety and morals, under which a person may be criminally responsible whether he has knowledge of the material fact or not. Among these laws are those punishing the sale of adulterated foods or alcoholic intoxicating liquor (People v. Bickerstaff, 46 Cal. App. 764; People v. Schwarz, 28 Cal. App. 2d 775; People v. Beggs, 69 Cal. App. 2d 819) where the seller is liable for the prohibited sale even though he did not know that the article was of the character the sale of which was prohibited or the sale of an adulterated drug (sec. 26280 Health and Safety Code) which is a crime even though the seller was ignorant of the fact of adulteration and his ignorance was not due to his negligence (People v. Stuart, 47 Cal. 2d 167, see also Sandstrom v. Racing Board, 31 Cal. 2d 401 and cases cited). So also it is not a defense to a charge of statutory rape that the defendant did not know that the girl was under the age of consent nor can a charge of bigamy be defended on the ground that the defendant believed his former marriage had been terminated by death or divorce or had not been consumed. (People v. Hartman, 130 Cal. 487).

Mistake of Law

It is the general rule that if, in ignorance of the existence of a law or a mistake as to what the law is or as to its interpretation, a person voluntarily does an act which the law has declared to be a crime this fact that he did not know that his act was unlawful, or honestly believed it to be lawful, is no defense. And this is true even though the accused had previously received legal advice in good faith upon which he based his knowledge or belief. (People v. McCalla, 63 Cal. App. 783; People v. Simonsen, 64 Cal. App. 97; People v. Doble, 203 Cal. 510; People v. Stewart, 115 Cal. App. 681; People v. Rubens, 11 Cal. App. 2d 536; People v. Aresen, 91 Cal. App. 2d 26.) (In the Doble and Simonsen cases wherein the defendants were charged with selling securities without a permit from the corporation commissioner, it was held that the advice of the commissioner that no permit was required was not provable as a defense but in People v. Ferguson, 134 Cal. App. 41, it was held that such statement of the commissioner was admissible and that, a license permit having been refused, the defendant was thereby placed in a position where he would either have to sell his securities without a permit or not sell them at all. Under such circumstances it does not seem that sound public policy should permit the prosecution or conviction of a defendant who thereafter in good faith sold his securities without a permit.) Where, however the offense charged involves the doing of an act "knowingly", such as knowingly selling a security without a permit, it would be a defense that the accused had been informed by his attorney that the necessary permit had been secured (People v. Flumerfelt, 33 Cal. App. 2d 495). While it has been said that that every person is presumed to know the law and ignorance thereof is no defense to a charge of crime (People v. Flanagan, 65 Cal. App. 268, 274) there is really no such presumption, the true rule being rather that where a person intentionally and knowingly does that which the law declares to be a crime, he is acting with criminal intent even though he may not know that his act is in violation of law (see Intent).

As a Defense

Where the charge was maliciously injuring a public highway, evidence of ample ground to believe that the highway had been legally abandoned at the time he fenced it was held admissible as tending to prove that the act was not done by the defendant maliciously. (People v. Goodwin, 136 Cal. 455.)

Where the offense charged involves, as a necessary part of the corpus delicti, a specific intent or knowledge the defendant may, to prove that he acted without such intent or knowledge, prove that he acted after receiving legal advice where such advice tends to disprove the existence of such intent or knowledge. (People v. Wyatt, 101 Cal. App. 396.)

And where one in good faith takes the property actually that of another but believing it legally to be his own or that he has a legal right to its possession he is not guilty of larceny although his belief is based on a misconception of the law, for in such a case the specific intent to deprive the owner of his property, an essential element of the crime of larceny, is missing. (People v. Photo, 45 Cal. App. 2d 345.)

Unconscious Acts

Since it is the voluntary act of an individual which makes him subject to punishment for a criminal offense the law does not punish a person "who committed the act charged without being conscious thereof." (Penal Code, sec. 26, subd. 5.) This provision does not cover or apply to cases of insanity, mental defect, or voluntary intoxication, "but on the contrary contemplates only cases of sound mind as, for example, somnambulists or persons suffering with the delirium of fever or drugs," those cases in which there is no functioning of the conscious mind and the person's acts are controlled solely by the subconscious mind. (People v. Denningham, 82 Cal. App. 2d 119; People v. Methever, 132 Cal. 326, 329; People v. Lim Dum Dong, 26 Cal. App. 2d 135; People v. Freeman, 61 Cal. App. 2d 110; People v. Anderson, 87 Cal. App. 2d 857). As further illustration there are the cases of unconsciousness produced by epilepsy (People v. Freeman, 61 Cal. App. 2d 110) or by a blow on the head (People v. Cox, 67 Cal. App. 2d 166).

While there has been no decision by our courts on the point it seems clear that where a person is in a condition of involuntary intoxication, where his condition is not the result of having knowingly or voluntarily partaken of an intoxicating liquor or drug, and such intoxication is of such a degree as to amount to unconsciousness, such person may avail himself of the defense of unconsciousness. If, however, such intoxication does not go to the extent of unconsciousness or if the condition of intoxication results from the voluntary use of intoxicating liquor or drugs the case is governed by the law relating to voluntary intoxication. (People v. Samaniego, 118 Cal. App. 165; People v. Lim Dum Dong, 26 Cal. App. 2d 135; People v. Taylor, 31 Cal. App. 2d 723; see also People v. Freeman, 61 Cal. App. 2d 110.) "Subdivision 5, section 26, Penal Code, is inapplicable in cases where temporary interference of the mental faculties results from voluntary intoxication. Such a situation is governed by section 22, Penal Code." (People v. Anderson, 87 Cal. App. 2d. 857.)

In a case of manslaughter in the driving of an automobile while under the influence of intoxicating liquor it would not be a defense that the defendant was rendered unconscious by his voluntary act in becoming intoxicated (People v. Mead, 126 Cal. App. 2d. 164).

The mere statements of the defendant, introduced by the prosecution, that he did not or could not remember "are not sufficient to establish unconsciousness at the time of the commission of the particular act" (People v. Martina, 140 Cal. App. 2d 17).

Unconscious Acts—Burden of Proof *Complete defense*

The burden of proving the defense of unconsciousness, like that of insanity, is upon the defendant for, in the absence of proof to the contrary, a person who conducts himself as one in the full possession of his faculties is presumed to be conscious. (People v. Nihell, 144 Cal. 200, 202.) (Note:—The case of People v. Smith, 39 Cal. App. 2d 277, which declares that this is not the rule wholly failed to consider the rule laid down in the Nihell case and relied for its authority upon People v. Flanelly, 128 Cal. 83, 92, a case not only prior to the Nihell case but also one in which the defense was not unconsciousness but that of self defense and what is said in the Flanelly case is therefore dicta so far as its application to the defense of unconsciousness is concerned. The difference between the conscious and intentional act of a person in possession of his mental faculties acting in self defense, a normal mental condition, and a person performing an unintentional act in a condition of unconsciousness, an abnormal mental state, is obvious.) In the last decision on the point the court recognizes that there is a presumption of consciousness which is rebuttable but rules that it is sufficient to entitle a defendant to an acquittal if there is a reasonable doubt as to the issue raised by the defense of unconsciousness and that, as to this defense, the defendant need not prove it by a preponderance of evidence as is the case where insanity is a defense (People v. Hardy, 33 Cal. 2d 52; People v. Butler, 118 Cal. App. 2d 16).

Misfortune or Accident

Where the defendant contended that, if he committed the acts charged, he lacked the specific intent or was incapable of committing crime because he was unconscious, the rule of subd. 6 of Penal Code section 26 does not apply (People v. Gorgol, 122 Cal. App. 2d. 281).

(In connection with Homicide cases see:—Excusable and Justifiable Homicide, infra.)

"Misfortune" when applied to a criminal act is analagous with the word "misadventure" and has the connotation of accident while doing a lawful act (People v. Gorgol, supra).

Where the defendant was riding in the back seat of a taxicab and the driver, believing that the defendant was going to rob him, left the vehicle while it was in motion and there was a question as to whether the subsequent acts of the defendant were merely an attempt to control the car or to violate section 503 of the Vehicle Code, the defendant was entitled to have the jury instructed as to the law of accident and misfortune (People v. Acosta, 45 Cal. 2d 538).

Married Women

Married women are as fully liable for felonies committed by them as any other female, subject to a few exceptions due to the particular nature of the crime, as for example the rule that a husband and wife cannot commit the crime of conspiracy. (See CONSPIRACY.) Thus a married woman may be guilty of the larceny of her husband's separate property or of forgery by forging his name (People v. Graff, 59 Cal. App. 706) or of a crime committed against the person or property of her husband and in such a case he is a competent witness against her. (Penal Code, sec. 1322). A husband may be guilty of setting fire to and burning the community property (People v. Schlette, 139. App. 2d 165).

Where, however, the crime committed is a misdemeanor only, a married woman is not liable if the act was committed under the threats, command or coercion of her husband, and was not her voluntary act or in pursuance of her own criminal intent. The old presumption that a married woman who commits a crime in the presence of her husband was acting under his coercion no longer exists in this state (People v. Statley, 91 Cal. App. 2d 943).

Duress and Coercion

Where the crime, except it be a crime punishable with the death penalty, is committed under the threats or menaces of another, sufficient to show that the person so coerced had not only the belief that his life would be immediately endangered if he refused but also that he had reasonable cause for such belief, the law declares him incapable of committing such crime. (Penal Code, sec. 26, subd. 8.) To establish this defense it must be shown that the act of the defendant was done under such threats or menaces as show that his life was at the very time of his criminal act in present, active and immediate peril or that there was reasonable cause to believe, and actual belief on the part of the defendant, that his life was in imminent danger. (People v. Sanders, 82 Cal. App. 778.) The danger of death at some future time in the absence of danger of death at the time of the commission of the offense will not relieve a defendant of guilt. (People v. Sanders, 82 Cal. App. 778.) Thus, even though his codefendant, who induced him to participate in the crime, displayed a gun and ordered the defendant about and defendant participated because of the orders, this is not sufficient to constitute a defense unless it also appears that by reason of the threats or menaces of his codefendant he acted and cooperated because he was in fear of imminent death. (People v. Lindstrom, 128 Cal. App. 111; People v. Hart, 98 Cal. App. 2d 514, defendant displayed a knife.) The fact that a defendant, who seeks to evade liability for his cooperation in the commission of a crime on the ground of coercion, is a minor does not change the rule as stated. (People v. Martin, 13 Cal. App. 96.) The fear which will relieve a person from liability must not only be a fear of death if he does not comply with the demand made upon him but it must be a fear of immediate death if he refuse to comply and a fear of future danger to his life does not in any degree relieve him from responsibility. (People v. Martin, 13 Cal. App. 96.)

Where it appeared that the defendant and his co-defendant planned the robbery and divided the money and the co-defendant did not threaten to harm the defendant in any way, the mere fact that the co-defendant had a knife which he held to the victim's neck and that he ordered the defendant to continue driving the car wholly fails to support the defendant's claim that he cooperated in the robbery under duress (People v. Sierra, 115 Cal. App. 2d 498).

Where the crime committed is one punishable by the death penalty, no amount of threats, coercion or duress will relieve a person who cooperates in the commission of the offense. Threats or menaces which in any other case would be a complete defense will not help in the slightest the person who by reason thereof joins in a crime carrying the death penalty. (People v. Petro, 13 Cal. App. 2d 245; defendant claimed he was forced to participate in the robbery in which his codefendant killed the victim, indicating that the penalty test is applied to the crime committed and not to the crime in which the defendant claims he was forced to participate.)

CHAPTER IX.

INTOXICATION

In considering the effect upon the guilt of a defendant the law makes a distinction between intoxication at the time of the commission of the offense which is voluntary and intoxication which is involuntary. (defense)

Intoxication is voluntary when it is the result of the individual knowingly and willingly partaking of any intoxicant and where intoxication thus results it is immaterial whether he intended to become intoxicated or not or whether the intoxicant consumed had a greater effect than he anticipated.

Intoxication is involuntary when a person becomes intoxicated not as a result of his knowingly and voluntarily partaking of an intoxicant, but where it is brought about by the stratagem or fraud of another or without his knowledge as, for example, where it results from partaking of a medicine prescribed by his physician.

Involuntary Intoxication

Where a person is in a state of involuntary intoxication to such a degree that he does not know what he is doing he is not criminally responsible for his acts since the law declares that a person is incapable of committing crimes if he commits the act charged without being conscious thereof. (Penal Code, sec. 26, subd. 5.) Where involuntary intoxication does not produce unconsciousness, the person having a greater or lesser ability to appreciate what he is doing, his intoxication may be considered in the same manner and to the same extent as if his intoxication were voluntary since, being conscious, he is as responsible for his acts as if his intoxication were voluntary.

Voluntary Intoxication

"No act committed by a person while in a state of voluntary intoxication is less criminal by reason of his having been in such condition. But whenever the actual existence of any particular purpose, motive or intent is a necessary element to constitute any particular species or degree of crime, the jury may take into consideration the fact that the accused was intoxicated at the time in determining the purpose, motive or intent with which he committed the act." (Penal Code, sec. 22.) DRUNKENNES no excuse for crime,

80

This simply means that when a particular motive, purpose or intent constitutes a necessary element going to make up the corpus delicti of the crime charged, or the degree of such crime, then evidence of intoxication may be introduced and considered by the jury or judge trying the case as casting light upon the operation of the defendant's mind, in ascertaining the purpose, motive or intent with which he did the act. (People v. Smith, 14 Cal. 2d 541; People v. Blake, 65 Cal. 275; People v. Ferris, 55 Cal. 588; People v. Phelan, 93 Cal. 111; People v. Gordon, 103 Cal. 568).

Where the defendant, charged as being a passive participant in a violation of section 288a of the Penal Code, contended that, by reason of voluntary intoxication, he was not aware that the act was being performed upon him, the appellate court approved the instruction that drunkenness was not of itself a defense but that where a person committed an act without being conscious thereof, however that condition may have been caused, he does not thereby commit a crime though such an act would constitute a crime if committed by a person while conscious (People v. Guthrie, 113 Cal. App. 2d 720).

Where No Motive or Specific Intent Is Involved

Where the offense charged involves no particular purpose, motive or intent it is immaterial whether the defendant was in a condition of voluntary intoxication at the time of the crime. (People v. Avanzi, 25 Cal. App. 2d 301.) Thus it has been held in trials for manslaughter (People v. Nichol, 34 Cal. 211; People v. Laughton, 67 Cal. 428), assault with a deadly weapon (People v. Franklin, 70 Cal. 641; People v. Marseiler, 70 Cal. 98; People v. Gordon, 103 Cal. 568; People v. Lim Dum Dong, 26 Cal. App. 2d 135; People v. Sanchez, 35 Cal. 2d 522), and in cases of murder committed in the perpetration of rape, robbery, arson, burglary or mayhem or by poison, torture or lying in wait (People v. King, 27 Cal. 507, 514; People v. Nichol, 34 Cal. 211, 215, 217), but the rule applicable to such cases of murder is subject to the modification that evidence of intoxication should be considered in determining whether the accused was capable of forming the specific intent necessary to constitute the crime of rape, robbery, arson, burglary or mayhem, as the case might be, in the perpetration or attempt to perpetrate which the killing occurred.

Intoxication will not aid in the defense of a person who while sober planned the crime and formed the necessary specific intent and went to the scene of the intended crime with his co-conspirator and there committed the crime even though by reason of intoxication he lost consciousness while the offense was being committed. (People v. Norwood, 39 Cal. App. 2d 503.)

Evidence of intoxication may also be considered and received as tending to show that by reason thereof the accused was incapable of performing the act in question or of conducting himself in the manner alleged by other witnesses.

In Murder Cases

In cases of murder intoxication may be considered for the purpose of establishing the degree of the crime (People v. Methever, 132 Cal. 332; People v. Lewis, 36 Cal. 531; People v. Williams, 43 Cal. 344; People v. Vincent, 95 Cal. 425; People v. Smith, 14 Cal. 2d 541) and whether there was deliberation and premeditation. (People v. Belencia, 21 Cal. 544; People v. Harris, 29 Cal. 658; People v. King, 27 Cal. 507; People v. Williams, 43 Cal. 352.)

Mental Impairment Not the Test

"A sane man who voluntarily drinks and becomes intoxicated is not excused because the result is to cloud his judgment, unbalance his reason, impair his perceptions, derange his mental faculties, and lead him to the commission of an act which in his sober senses he would have avoided. . . . Obviously mere temporary derangement resulting from the use of intoxicants, whether it manifests itself in the form of delirium tremens or in some milder form, cannot operate to absolve a person from liability for a criminal act." (People v. Goodrum, 31 Cal. App. 430; People v. Fellows, 122 Cal. 233; People v. Hower, 151 Cal. 643; People v. Brewer, 24 Cal. App. 317; People v. Clifton, 185 Cal. 143; People v. Lim Dum Dong, 26 Cal. App. 2d 135; People v. Taylor, 31 Cal. App. 2d 735; People v. Ferris, 55 Cal. 588.)

"To relieve one of responsibility for the commission of an offense on the ground of voluntary intoxication from the effect of liquor or narcotics it is necessary to prove that the brain has become permanently affected thereby" (People v. Lim Dum Dong, 26 Cal. App. 2d 135) and then only if the condition amounts to Insanity. (q. v.)

Intoxication by Drugs

The language of section 22 of the Penal Code does not limit the rule to intoxication which is caused by alcoholic beverages but includes intoxication produced by narcotic drugs. (People v. Samaniego, 118 Cal. App. 165, 173; People v. Lim Dum Dong, 26 Cal. App. 2d 135.) Also the rule applies equally to all defendants and is not affected by the fact that due to disease a defendant was more subject to the effects of an intoxicant. (People v. Foster, 3 Cal. App. 2d 35.)

To Show Absence of Specific Intent

While intoxication, voluntarily acquired, is not a defense to crime, still, where the offense charged is one requiring the existence of a specific intent or state of mind, if the proof is such as to show that such intent or state of mind did not exist the accused is entitled to an acquittal and the absence of such intent or state of mind may be proved by evidence that at the time of the alleged offense the accused was so intoxicated as to be incapable of forming or entertaining such intent or state of mind. This rule is not so much one relating to intoxication as it is a concrete application of the rule that, where a specific intent is an element of the corpus delicti, the accused is entitled to an acquittal if the jury has a reasonable doubt of the existence of such intent. (People v. Demartini, 63 Cal. App. 747; People v. Fellows, 122 Cal. 233; People v. Hower, 151 Cal. 643; People v. Keyes, 178 Cal. 794.)

CHAPTER X.

PRINCIPAL AND AGENT

A principal is not liable for the criminal acts of his agent which he did not authorize or direct even though such acts were in the course of the agent's employment. (People v. Doble, 203 Cal. 510; see also People v. Blackman, 127 Cal. 248; People v. Green, 22 Cal. App. 45; People v. Moore, 82 Cal. App. 739.) If, however, the principal is an actual participant in the offense or aids and abets the agent in his criminal act or has advised its commission he is equally guilty with the agent because by such action he becomes an actual party to the crime and not because of the relation of principal and agent. (People v. Doble, 203 Cal. 510; People v. Waxman. 114 Cal. App. 2d 399.) An agent is as fully liable for his criminal acts committed in the service of his principal as though the acts were solely in his own interests. (People v. Woods, 190 Cal. 513.)

Where the criminal intent exists solely in the mind of the principal and the agent though performing the act constituting the offense, acts innocently and without criminal intent and without knowledge of the true character of the act, the principal alone is guilty. (People v. Keller. 79 Cal. App. 612; People v. Leach, 106 Cal. App. 442.)

An employer is legally liable for an illegal sale of liquor by a clerk made with the employer's knowledge (People v. Deibert, 117 Cal. App. 2d 410).

However, where the penal statute positively forbids certain acts and imposes liability upon the principal if the act done by the agent knowingly is within the scope of the latter's authority, such as the sale of intoxicating liquor, pure food and drug statutes, short weighting of commodities, etc., the principal may be convicted for the violation of the law by his agent even though he himself had no knowledge of such violation (In re Marley, 29 Cal. 2d 525).

Partnerships

A partnership is not such a legal entity that the partnership itself may commit a crime but, while the partnership cannot be prosecuted for a criminal offense committed as an act of the copartnership, the member or members of the firm who committed the offense may be individually prosecuted and

84

punished therefor. (People v. Schomig, 74 Cal. App. 109; People v. Maljan, 34 Cal. App. 384.)

But in a prosecution for the sale of inedible eggs in violation of section 1103 of the Agricultural Code it was held that such a sale by one partner made his copartner criminally liable even though he had no knowledge of the sale. (In re Casperson, 69 Cal. App. 2d 441.)

Corporations

A corporation is capable of committing a crime where the penalty may be a fine but it can not be prosecuted for an offense which is not so punishable. (People v. Jevne Co., 179 Cal. 621.) But, though in many instances the corporation cannot be prosecuted for criminal acts and conduct, the officer or agent of a corporation who, in carrying out the interests of the corporation, commits a crime is individually liable to prosecution. (People v. Schomig, 74 Cal. App. 109.)

CHAPTER XI.

PRINCIPALS AND ACCESSORIES

At common law the one who personally did the criminal act or committed the offense through a wholly innocent agent was known as a principal in the first degree, one who was actually or constructively present at the commission of the offense, knowingly and wilfully assisting the actual perpetrator, was known as a principal in the second degree and one who, though absent when the crime was committed, had procured, counselled, ordered or abetted the actual perpetrator was known as an accessory before the fact. These distinctions and the barriers to prosecution which accompanied them do not exist in California but the terms are sometimes used to indicate the particular relationship which an individual may bear to a crime which has been committed. (Penal Code, sec. 971.)

Principals Defined

"All persons concerned in the commission of a crime, whether it be a felony or misdemeanor, and whether they directly commit the act constituting the offense, or aid and abet in its commission, or, not being present, have advised and encouraged its commission and all persons counseling, advising, or encouraging children under the age of fourteen years, lunatics or idiots, to commit any crime, or who, by fraud, contrivance, or force, occasion the drunkenness of another for the purpose of causing him to commit any crime, or who, by threats, menaces, command, or coercion, compel another to commit any crime, are principals in any crime so committed." (Penal Code, sec. 31.)

Co-Principals Equally Guilty

All persons who are principals under the law are equally guilty. Thus, where one of the perpetrators of a robbery is armed with a deadly weapon and, hence, guilty of first degree robbery, each of his co-principals is also guilty of first degree robbery (People v. Perkins, 37 Cal. 2d 62; People v. Silva, 143 Cal. App. 2d 162; People v. Machado, 150 Cal. App. 2d 190), first degree murder).

Aiding and Abetting

For one person to aid and abet another in the commission of a criminal offense means to knowingly and with criminal intent aid, promote, encourage or instigate by act or counsel, or by both act and counsel, the commission of such offense. (People v. Elliott, 103 Cal. App. 329; People v. Best, 43 Cal. App. 2d 100.) Mere aiding without criminal intent is not sufficient, for a person may innocently aid another in the commission of a crime, and to be held liable as a principal one must both aid and abet in its commission. One who merely stands by watching an offense being committed and even approving of it is not aiding and abetting (People v. Hill, 77 Cal. App. 2d 287; People v. Luna, 140 Cal. App. 2d 662).

The effect of section 31 is that all persons who would at common law have been classed as principals of the first or second degrees or as accessories before the fact are all considered as principals under the law of California and equally guilty of the offense committed, and this rule applies to cases of misdemeanors as well as felonies. (People v. Witt, 170 Cal. 104; People v. Wood, 56 Cal. App. 431; People v. Frankovitch, 64 Cal. App. 184.)

It is not necessary to constitute a person an aider and abettor that the actual perpetrator of the offense communicate to him the purpose of such perpetrator, if it appears from the circumstances that the person accused as an aider and abettor knew that the crime in question was to be committed and knowingly assisted in accomplishing it; nor is it necessary to prove that the parties conspired to commit the crime (People v. Gischott, 107 Cal. App. 2d 631).

The aider and abetter is not only guilty of the crime the contemplated commission of which was known to him but also of the natural and reasonable or probable consequences of the acts which he knowingly aided and encouraged (People v. Godstein, 146 Cal. App. 2d 268).

Evidence in a robbery case, in which defendant's car was used by the robbers, that defendant knew, at the time he loaned them the car, that the car was going to be used for some illegal purpose but did not know what that purpose was, held sufficient to show that he aided and abetted in the robbery (People v. Hailey, 149 Cal. App. 2d 560 A.C.A. 518; Query: Can a person be an aider and abetter in an offense without knowing, before the crime is committed, what specific crime the principals intend to commit?)

Examples

Where the defendant sent two men to a house to get certain property and the property was taken under circumstances constituting larceny he was held guilty as a principal in the crime of burglary. (People v. Peterson, 96 Cal. App. 373.) While the mere act of driving a criminal to the place where he commits a crime does not necessarily make the driver a party to the offense (People v. Griggs, 114 Cal. App. 133), further circumstances tending to show guilty participation in the plan or knowledge of the purpose of the trip will sustain the conviction of the driver as a principal by reason of his aiding and abetting the commission of the offense (People v. Cowling, 6 Cal. App. 2d 456, People v. Martin, 12 Cal. 2d 466; People v. Moe, 116 Cal. App. 740; People v. Jaggers, 120 Cal. App. 733; People v. Ratten, 39 Cal. App. 2d 267; People v. Silva, 143 Cal. App. 2d 162), and this would also be the case of one who drove the perpetrators of the crime from the place where it had just been committed, the driver waiting outside while the criminal act was in progress. (People v. Spahn, 28 Cal. App. 2d 149; People v. Anderson, 37 Cal. App. 2d 615; People v. Gianello, 68 Cal. App. 214; People v. Wilson, 93 Cal. App. 632; People v. Davis, 106 Cal. App. 179; Peope v. Miller, 126 Cal. App. 162; People v. Silva, 143 Cal. App. 2d 162).

One who procured a room for another knowing that the room was to be used in the perpetration of a crime is a principal if such crime is thereafter committed in the room. (People v. Wood, 56 Cal. App. 431.) Where the driver of an automobile involved in an accident fails to stop as required by law an occupant who urged him to drive on is as guilty of the offense as the driver. (People v. Graves, 74 Cal. App. 415; People v. Steele, 100 Cal. App. 639.) Where each of four men raped the prosecutrix while the others stood by, each of the three is as guilty as the actual perpetrator. (People v. Mummert, 57 Cal. App. 2d 849.) Where a taxi-cab driver heard one of his passengers suggest to the other passenger that they rob a gas station they were passing and stopped the cab around the corner and the passengers got out and committed the proposed robbery, the driver was held guilty as a principal in the commission of the robbery (People v. Lincoln, 89 Cal. App. 2d 795). Where the two appellants, one of them the driver of the car, drove to the place where the other two occupants got out and robbed a storekeeper and, when shots were exchanged between an officer and one of the bendits, appellants drove away in a hurry, the conviction of robbery was sustained on the theory that appellants were aiders and abetters (People v. Armindarez, 141 Cal. App. 2d 608). Defendant assisted one Caro to take a hypodermic injection by holding a tourniquet around the arm of the latter from which injection Caro died, and was held a principal in the crime of manslaughter in the commission of an unawful act, that of Caro in using the narcotic (People v. Hopkins, 101 Cal. App. 2d. 704). One who holds the victim while the latter is assaulted by a companion of the former is equally guilty of the assault (People v. Whalen, 124 Cal. App. 2d. 713). Evidence that several of the defendants took an injection of heroin in the presence of a female minor who then received an injection of heroin from another defendant, their conduct being designed to and did demonstrate that the injection would be free from pain and produce an agreeable reaction, made them liable as principals (People v. Rios, 127 Cal. App. 2d. 620). Where one person is committing an assault upon a third person and the defendant keeps back and prevents other people from stopping the attack the defendant is an aider and abetter in the assault and the homicide resulting therefrom (People v. Le Grant, 76 Cal. App. 2d. 148; People v. Cayer, 102 Cal. App. 2d. 643). Where two persons were racing on a city street in a residence district and, in coming to an intersection, one of the cars caused the death of the driver of a car then in the intersection under circumstances constituting manslaughter with gross negligence, conviction of both defendants was sustained (People v. Kemp, 150 Cal. App. 2d. 654).

It is not necessary to constitute a person a principal because of his aiding and abetting or encouraging that he take any actual part in the commission of the crime; it is sufficient if his relation to the crime is such that he knowingly helped or encouraged its commission. Thus, if a person joined with one or more others in kidnaping a female for the purpose of raping her and he stood idly by while the rape was being committed, he would be a principal as to the rape perpetrated (People v. Griffin, 106 Cal. App. 2d 531; People v. Mummert, 57 Cal. App. 2d 849). Where the defendant and one Soto were charged with statutory rape and the evidence showed that one C engaged in an act of sexual intercourse with a girl under the age of 18 after the defendant had showed them two motion pictures depicting the sexual act after which the defendant took pictures of C and the prosecutrix while engaged in sexual intercourse at a place to which Soto had driven them, it was held that while the mere presence and the taking of the pictures might not make the defendant an aider and abettor, the further evidence that he had previously showed the active participants the motion pictures could be the basis of the inference that this was done for the purpose of persuading the prosecutrix to engage in the act and the conviction was sustained (People v. Lewis, 113 Cal. App. 2d 468). Where one of the three co-defendants charged with robbery took no active part in the robbery but merely stood by and, when the three were shortly thereafter apprehended, the money stolen from the victim and the knife used by the perpetrators was found in his possession, his conviction as a principal was sustained (People v. Moore, 120 Cal. App. 2d. 303). Where the defendant knowingly drove his confederate to a place for the purpose of the latter obtaining heroin, he was an aider and abettor in the offense of possession of narcotics secured by his companion at that place (People v. Henderson, 121 Cal. App. 2d. 816). Where the defendant suggested the commission of a robbery and provided a pistol to be used in its commission and later took his share of the loot, he was guilty as a principal (People v. Eddy, 123 Cal. App. 2d. 826). Where the defendant, a physician, knowing that certain persons were engaged in a conspiracy to commit abortions, agreed to and did furnish preoperative and postoperative care to the women aborted and sent women desiring abortions to the place where arrangements for such operations were made, he was held to have aided and abetted in the crimes of conspiracy and abortion (People v. Sherman, 127 Cal. App. 2d. 230). The driver of the car which was used in the burglary is as responsible as his companion who directly committed the burglary (People v. Martin, 128 Cal. App. 2d. 361).

Unusual Cases

A person may be guilty of a crime by reason of his aiding and abetting or advising and encouraging another in the commission of a crime which, as a matter of law, he could not directly and personally commit. Thus a female may be convicted as a principal under a charge of rape where she aided and abetted the man who committed the offense (People v. Bartol, 24 Cal. App. 659; People v. Haywood, 131 Cal. App. 2d. 259) and a man may be convicted, under the same reasoning, for a rape committed upon his wife (In re Kantrowitz, 24 Cal. App. 203) or of pimping in which the perpetrator must be a male (People v. Young, 132 Cal. App. 770). Where the crime is one which can only be committed by a public officer, such as certain forms of bribery or the embezzlement of public funds, a person not a public officer may be convicted as a principal if he aided and abetted another who was a public official in the commission of such an offense. (People v. Little, 41 Cal. App. 2d 797; People v. West, 3 Cal. App. 2d 568; People v. Anderson,

75 Cal. App. 365) and one who aids and abets an officer who destroys public records in violation of section 6200 of the Government Code may be convicted as a principal (People v. Thompson, 122 Cal. App. 2d. 567). And a person not standing in a fiduciary capacity may be guilty of embezzlement by aiding and abetting one who holds funds in such capacity. (People v. Zimmer, 23 Cal. App. 2d 581; People v. Colton, 92 Cal. App. 2d 704; People v. Frank, 82 Cal. App. 465; People v. Little, 41 Cal. App 2d 797; People v. Hess, 104 Cal. App. 2d 642).

Even though the actual perpetrator of the crime is entitled to an acquittal because of his intoxicated condition those who aided and abetted him are guilty as principals (People v. Ojeda, 132 Cal. App. 593) and the acquittal of the actual perpetrator has no effect upon the conviction of his aider and abettor. (People v. Terman, 4 Cal. App. 2d 345.)

Withdrawal of Adviser

"The responsibility of one who has counselled and advised the commission of a crime or engaged in a criminal undertaking does not cease unless, within time to prevent the commission of the contemplated act, he has done everything to prevent its consummation. It is not enough that he may have changed his mind and tried when too late to avoid responsibility. He will be liable if he fails within time to let the other party know of his withdrawal and does everything in his power to prevent the commission of a crime." (People v. King, 30 Cal. App. 2d 185; People v. Ortiz, 63 Cal. App. 662). (see also Withdrawal from Conspiracy.)

Prosecution of Co-Principals

"The distinction between an accessory before the fact and a principal, and between principals in the first and second degree is abrogated; and all persons concerned in the commission of a crime, who by operation of other provisions of this code are principals therein, shall hereafter be prosecuted, tried and punished as principals and no other facts need be alleged in any accusatory pleading against any such person than are required in an accusatory pleading against a principal." (Penal Code, sec. 971.) *Distinction between accessory before the fact & principal abrogated.*

"An accessory to the commission of a felony may be prosecuted, tried and punished, though the principal may be neither prosecuted nor tried, and though the principal may have been acquitted." (Penal Code, sec. 972.)

These sections entirely do away with the old common law rules which made it difficult to prosecute aiders and abettors and especially accessories after the fact. Under our law all persons coming within the definition of section 31 as principals are prosecuted as if they were the ones who actually did the unlawful act and may be convicted upon proof either that they did the act or aided and abetted or advised and encouraged its commission (People v. Wood, 56 Cal. App. 431; People v. Desmond, 24 Cal. App. 408; People v. Ah Gee, 37 Cal. App. 1; People v. Groenig, 57 Cal. App. 495; People v. Fronk, 82 Cal. App. 465; People v. Latona, 2 Cal. 2d 714; People v. Burdg, 95 Cal. App. 257) and the actual perpetrator need not be tried in order to prosecute a co-principal (People v. Arnold, 199 Cal. 471) and it is not necessary that all of the co-principals be prosecuted. (People v. Patterson, 102 Cal. 239.)

Accessories After the Fact

"Every person who after a felony has been committed, harbors, conceals or aids a principal in such felony, with the intent that said principal may avoid or escape from arrest, trial, conviction or punishment, having knowledge that said principal has committed such felony or has been charged with such felony or convicted thereof, is an accessory to such felony." (Penal Code, sec. 32.) To distinguish such a case from one of accessory before the fact (a principal under California Law) the perpetrator of this offense is properly referred to as an accessory after the fact.

Penalty

"(Punishment of Accessories) Except in cases where a different punishment is prescribed, an accessory is punishable by a fine not exceeding five thousand dollars, or by imprisonment in the state prison not exceeding five years or in a county jail not exceeding one year, or by both such fine and imprisonment." (Penal Code, sec. 33).

Elements of Offense

To be guilty of the offense of being an accessory after the fact it is necessary that the accused knew either that the principal whom he is charged with helping has committed a felony, or that he has been charged with or convicted of a felony. (Ex parte Goldman, 7 Cal. Unrep. 254). The word "felony" in section 32 includes all crimes punishable by death or imprisonment in the state prison and, where the offense is also punishable by a fine or a jail sentence, it is a felony until a sentence imposing a penalty less than confinement in a state prison has been imposed (see Felonies and Misdemeanors Distinguished; People v. McLaughlin, 111 Cal. App. 2d 781). This offense has also as an element that in helping the principal the accused had the intent to assist the principal to avoid arrest, trial, conviction or punishment.

The word "charged" as used in section 32 means more than that the person has merely been accused. As here used "charged" means that an indictment or information or a complaint has been filed against the principal or at least that he has been placed under arrest on a felony charge. (People v. Garnett, 129 Cal. 364.) The word "conceal" means more than merely withholding knowledge or remaining silent. To amount to concealment there must be an act of concealing or hiding. (People v. Garnett, 129 Cal. 364, 366.)

Unless the act comes within the language of section 32 describing what acts are necessary to constitute the offense or if there is no intent to enable the principal to avoid or escape arrest, prosecution or punishment, the offense of accessory after the fact is not committed. Thus a person who, with guilty knowledge that certain property is stolen, aids the thief in selling and disposing of such property is not guilty of being an accessory after the fact, though he may be guilty of receiving stolen property (People v. Staken, 4 Cal. 599), nor does knowingly aiding a thief in concealing stolen property come within the scope of section 32. (Ex parte Goldman, 7 Cal. Unrep. 254.) Also there can be no crime of accessory after the fact except where the crime committed by the principal is a felony. One who, after a murder has been committed, aids the murderer in disposing of the body and burying it is an accessory after the fact and, in such case, the murderer, having aided and abetted the accessory, is also guilty of being an accessory after the fact (People v. Wallin, 32 Cal. 2d. 803). Where the evidence showed that the defendant knew that one L was serving a term of imprisonment in the county jail with 120 days to serve and that, about three hours after seeing L in jail, the defendant met him several blocks from the jail and took him by automobile to another place, a conviction of harboring, concealing and aiding an escaped prisoner was sustained (People v. Parker, 122 Cal. App. 2d. 867).

CHAPTER XII.

COMPOUNDING CRIMES

"Every person who, having knowledge of the actual commission of a crime, takes money or property of another, or any gratuity or reward, or any engagement, or promise thereof, upon any agreement or understanding to compound or conceal such crime, or to abstain from any prosecution thereof, or to withhold any evidence thereof, except in the cases provided for by law, in which crimes may be compromised by leave of court, is punishable as follows:

1. By imprisonment in the state prison not exceeding five years, or in the county jail not exceeding one year, where the crime was punishable by death or imprisonment in the state prison for life;

2. By imprisonment in the state prison not exceeding three years, or in the county jail not exceeding six months, where the crime was punishable in the state prison for any other term than for life;

3. By imprisonment in the county jail not exceeding six months, or by fine not exceeding five hundred dollars, where the crime was a misdemeanor." (Penal Code, sec. 153.)

Gist of Offense

The gist of the offense of compounding a felony is the unlawful agreement or understanding to settle or conceal a crime or refrain from the criminal prosecution of another or to withhold evidence as to a crime, felony or misdemeanor, which has been committed, in consideration of anything of value, either actually received or promised. This offense differs from that of accessory after the fact in that in the crime of compounding it is the agreement or understanding which makes the act criminal and it is not necessary that anything be done towards carrying out the agreement while to be an accessory after the fact there must be an affirmative act of assistance. Also while an accessory after the fact may be guilty if he knows that his principal has been charged with or convicted of a felony, a person can not be guilty of compounding a crime unless he has knowledge of the actual commission of a crime which he agrees to compound or conceal or as to which he agrees not to prosecute or to withhold evidence. As the law makes no exceptions as to who may violate its provisions it applies as much to the injured victim of the crime as to some third party. Thus if the owner of stolen goods agrees with the thief that he will not prosecute him if the thief returns the stolen property and it is returned he is guilty of compounding the theft. Also

94

it is not necessary that the money or other consideration shall have been received from the person who committed the crime.

Mere Reimbursement Not Compounding

There is, however, nothing in the law which makes it unlawful for a person who has been injured by the commission of a crime from receiving reimbursement or compensation for the damage he has suffered. Where injury results from the commission of a crime the injured party has a civil cause of action, a claim which he can enforce in a civil lawsuit, and he is acting wholly within the law if he agrees to accept or actually does accept an agreed reimbursement or compensation for the damage he has suffered provided he refrains from promising to compound or conceal the crime or to abstain from prosecution or to withhold evidence thereof. (Morris v. Moore, 61 Cal. App. 314.)

Compromising Misdemeanors

The exception provided at the end of the first paragraph of section 153 is provided in sections 1377, 1378 and 1379 of the Penal Code.

"When the person injured by an act constituting a misdemeanor has a remedy by civil action, the offense may be compromised as provided in the next section except when it is committed:

1. By or upon an officer of justice, while in the execution of the duties of his office;

2. Riotously;

3. With an intent to commit a felony." (Penal Code, sec. 1377.)

"If the person injured appears before the court in which the action is pending at any time before trial, and acknowledges that he has received satisfaction for the injury, the court may, in its discretion, on payment of the costs incurred, order all proceedings to be stayed upon the prosecution, and the defendant to be discharged therefrom; but in such case the reasons for the order must be set forth therein, and entered on the minutes. The order in a bar to another prosecution for the same offense. (Penal Code, sec. 1378).

"No public offense can be compromised, nor can any proceeding or prosecution for the punishment thereof upon a compromise be stayed, except as provided in this chapter." (i. e., except as provided in the two preceding sections.) (Penal Code, sec. 1379.)

CHAPTER XIII.

ACCOMPLICES

[handwritten: Judge Instructs Jury]
[handwritten: must test against person on trial (trial rule only)]

While the word "accomplice" generally means a guilty associate in crime it has a special significance in our California law, because by statute, "A conviction cannot be had upon the testimony of an accomplice unless it be corroborated by such other evidence as shall tend to connect the defendant with the commission of the offense; and the corroboration is not sufficient if it merely shows the commission of the offense or the circumstances thereof. An accomplice is hereby defined as one who is liable to prosecution for the identical offense charged against the defendant on trial in the cause in which the testimony of the accomplice is given." (Penal Code, sec. 1111.) Historically speaking, the uncorroborated testimony of an accomplice was sufficient to sustain a conviction under the common law (People v. Clough, 73 Cal. 348; People v. Hooker, 126 Cal. App. 2d. 394).

Further defining the term it has been said that, "An accomplice is one who, knowing that a crime is being committed, wilfully and with criminal intent, aids, abets and assists another in the commission of such crime or criminal act." (People v. Howell, 69 Cal. App. 239.) As used in section 1111 the word "accomplice" refers to a principal in the crime who gives testimony essential to the conviction of a co-principal on trial. (People v. King, 30 Cal. App. 2d 185.)

Rule Applies Only to Conviction Upon Trial

Section 1111 applies only to trials. Thus the uncorroborated testimony of an accomplice may be a sufficient basis for the order of a committing magistrate holding a defendant to answer after a preliminary examination. (Ex parte Schwitalla, 36 Cal. App. 511; People v. McRae, 31 Cal. 2d. 184) or to sustain an indictment (Stern v. Sup. Ct., 78 Cal. App. 2d. 9, 17).

When Uncorroborated Testimony Is Sufficient

Even at a trial the rule merely provides that a defendant cannot be convicted upon the uncorroborated testimony of an accomplice. The uncorroborated testimony of an accomplice is sufficient to identify an exhibit and admit it in evidence (People v. Santos, 134 Cal. App. 736) and is sufficient to prove the corpus delicti (People v. Siderius, 29 Cal. App. 2d 361; People v. Briley, 9 Cal. App. 2d 84; People v. Snyder, 74 Cal. App. 730; People v. Fraser, 80 Cal. App. 464; People v. Meyers, 7 Cal. App. 2d 351; People v. Earl, 10 Cal. App. 2d 163:

People v. White, 48 Cal. App. 2d 90; People v. Parker, 80 Cal. App. 2d 128; People v. Pearson, 111 Cal. App. 2d 9; People v. Barclay, 40 Cal. 2d. 146; People v. Simpson, 43 Cal. 2d. 553) or to fix the degree of the crime (People v. Barclay, 40 Cal. 2d. 146, robbery; People v. Clark, 116 Cal. App. 2d. 219, burglary), but in a prosecution of a public officer for bribery where the testimony of the accomplice was uncorroborated not only as to defendant's connection with the offense charged but wholly uncorroborated as to any crime having been committed the court intimated that in such case the corpus delicti could not be established through the testimony of the accomplice alone (People v. Davis, 210 Cal. 540), but since the court also held that there was no corroborating evidence tending to connect the defendant with the offense charged, a complete reason by itself for a reversal of the conviction, and since the only corroboration required by section 1111 is evidence which "tends to connect the defendant with the commission of the offense" the case is of doubtful value as a precedent, especially since all the other authorities hold that the corpus delicti may be established by the uncorroborated testimony of an accomplice.

When Question for Jury or One of Law

If the facts are in dispute the question as to whether a witness is an accomplice is one of fact for the jury (People v. Allison, 200 Cal. 404; People v. Gibbs, 87 Cal. App. 177; People v. Payton, 36 Cal. App. 2d 41; People v. King, 30 Cal. App. 2d 185; People v. Roderick, 118 Cal. App. 457), but, if there is no conflict as to this issue, the question is one of law for the trial judge, and, if the witness is an accomplice as a matter of law it is the duty of the judge to so instruct the jury and it would be error in such a case to leave the determination of the question to the jury (People v. Allison, 200 Cal. 401; People v. Schumann-Heinck, 98 Cal. App. 225; People v. Brown, 25 Cal. App. 2d 513; People v. Ferlin, 203 Cal. 587) but not necessarily sufficient to call for a reversal (People v. Clark, 116 Cal. App. 2d 219).

While it has often been held that such error is not ground for a reversal, either because the record shows ample corroboration of the accomplice or upon the theory that, where the jury is correctly instructed on the law of accomplice, it is presumed that the jury followed the instructions (People v. Wahnish, 20 Cal. App. 2d 58; People v. Ferlin, 203 Cal. 587; People v. McDermott, 75 Cal. App. 718; People v. Calvert, 93 Cal. App. 568; People v. Knoth, 111 Cal. App. 250; People v. Bonner, 5 Cal. App. 2d 314), there have been cases in which such error has been held ground for a reversal on appeal (People v. Heddens, 12 Cal. App. 2d 245; People v. Schumann-Heinck, 99 Cal. App. 225; People v. Warren, 16 Cal. 2d 103), and this is the rule where it appears from the record that, had such instruction been given, the jury might or should have returned a verdict of not guilty instead of a verdict of guilty.

Where there is a conflict in the evidence as to whether a witness was an actual accomplice or a feigned accomplice the question is one for the jury to decide (People v. Griffin, 98 Cal. App. 2d 1).

Who Is An Accomplice

In considering the question of who is an accomplice it must be remembered that our present definition of the term was inserted in section 1111 by the legislature in 1915 and that many of the decisions prior to the amendment are no longer the law (see People v. Williams, 7 Cal. App. 2d 600, 602, for discussion).

In spite of the clear and simple test for determining whether a witness is an accomplice which is given to us by section 1111 our appellate courts are constantly called upon to review this question. The test may be thus stated: that to be an accomplice a person must have testified against the defendant and must himself be liable to prosecution for the identical offense charged against the defendant on the trial in which such testimony is given.

The term "liable to prosecution" must not be construed in its broadest sense for even a wholly innocent person may be liable to prosecution if there is probable cause to suspect him. As here used the phrase means that the evidence produced at the trial in which he testifies will warrant the conclusion that he was a principal in the commission of the crime for which the defendant is then on trial. (People v. Allison, 200 Cal. 404; People v. Howell, 69 Cal. App. 239; People v. Stanley, 92 Cal. App. 778; People v. Frahm, 107 Cal. App. 253; People v. Layman, 117 Cal. App. 476; People v. Schumann-Heinck, 98 Cal. App. 225.)

While it is the general rule that the thief is not the accomplice of the person prosecuted as the receiver of the stolen property, an exception to the rule exists where the thief and the receiver conspired for one to steal and deliver the property to the other and this plan was carried out, in which case the receiver is an accomplice of the thief and the thief is an accomplice of the receiver since they may both be convicted of each of such offenses. (People v. Lima, 25 Cal. 2d 573). Where three men entered into a conspiracy that two of them would commit a robbery of a jeweler and the third would receive the stolen goods and these objectives were accomplished, the third conspirator was an accomplice of the other two in the robbery and they of the third man in receiving the stolen property (People v. Brumback, 15 Ca. App. 2d. ...... A.C.A. 427). Mere submission to an act of sodomy is not sufficient to render the passive party to that offense an accomplice (People v. Westek, 31 Cal. 2d 469).

Examples

Subject to the exceptions where the crime is committed against the consent of the other party to the act or his legal incapacity to commit the crime such party is an accomplice in a prosecution for violating section 288a of the Penal Code (People v. McCollum, 116 Cal. App. 103; People v. McCollum, 214 Cal. 601; People v. Williams, 12 Cal. App. 2d 207; People v. Brown, 25 Cal. App. 2d 513), incest (People v. Adinolfi, 106 Cal. App. 26; People v. Stoll, 84 Cal. App. 99), or the crime against nature (People v. Robbins, 171 Cal. 466; People v. Casey, 79 Cal. App. 295) but if such act were committed upon a victim against his will and consent the latter would not be an accomplice (People v. Willis, 129 Cal. App. 2d. 330). The mere fact that the defendant exhibited and passed a knife from hand to hand when he proposed to the other party a violation of section 288a of the Penal Code would still leave such other person liable to prosecution for the violation of section 288a which followed and hence an accomplice unless it appears that he did believe that his life would be in danger if he refused (Penal Code, sec. 26, subd. 8; People v. Hart, 98 Cal. App. 2d. 514).

A conspirator is an accomplice in the prosecution of a co-conspirator where the latter is charged either with the crime of conspiracy or with a crime committed in pursuance of the object of the conspiracy (People v. Doble, 203 Cal. 510; People v. Lafrenz, 134 Cal. App. 687; see also People v. Bailey, 82 Cal. App. 700), and persons who contributed to a fund to be used to bribe a public official are accomplices in a prosecution for giving or offering the bribe. (People v. Southwell, 28 Cal. App. 431). In a prosecution for conspiracy to commit abortion the mother, of one of the girls who underwent an abortion, who was with her daughter at the time some of the preliminaries to the abortion were discussed with one of the conspirators was an accomplice (People v. Buffum, 40 Cal. 2d 709).

Where an offense is committed through an agent or intermediary who has knowledge of the nature of the transaction and is aiding and abetting therein by so acting, such agent or intermediary may be the accomplice not only of the principal who enlisted his aid but, where the crime is one requiring the act of two persons, such as the giver and receiver of a bribe, he may be the agent and accomplice of each of the parties. (People v. Davis, 210 Cal. 540). Where, in a prosecution for soliciting one M to offer and join in an offer to bribe the police, M, a bookmaker, requested one R to find someone who could secure police protection for his bookmaking operations and R secured the services of the defendant W and it was agreed that defendant was to get 20% of the net take of the book for a payoff to be divided between R, the defendant and the police, the court held that since M had joined the conspiracy of R and defendant and was an active participant, he could be held liable for his own solicitation and hence was an accomplice (People v. Wayne, 117 Cal. 2d. 268). Where, under a charge of preparing a writing to be used in presenting a false claim for insurance under a fire insurance policy, the witness, though he did not prepare the fraudulent claim, had burned the property at the request of the defendant, knowing that such destruction was to be used as a basis of the insurance claim, it was held that he was an aider and abettor to the filing of the claim and an accomplice (People v. Zelver, 135 Cal. App. 2d. 226).

Minors As Accomplices (exception)

Since an accomplice must be a principal in the commission of the crime charged and since a minor under the age of fourteen is presumed to be incapable of committing crime in the absence of clear proof that he knew the wrongfulness of the act (Penal Code, sec. 26), such a minor will not be considered an accomplice unless, in addition to proof that he cooperated by acts which would make a person over the age of fourteen a principal, there also be clear proof that he knew that the transaction constituting the crime was wrong. (People v. Singh, 62 Cal. App. 450; see also People v. Kangiesser, 44 Cal. App. 345; People v. Dong Pok Yip, 164 Cal. 143; People v. Wyett, 49 Cal. App. 289; People v. Camp, 26 Cal. App. 385; People v. Delgado, 37 Cal. App. 807; People v. Singh, 121 Cal. App. 107; People v. Mack, 24 Cal. App. 2d 438; People v. Becker, 140 Cal. App. 162; People v. Slobodion, 31 Cal. 2d 555.) Even though the minor knows the wrongfulness of the act involved, he is not an accomplice unless the evidence as a whole will sustain the conclusion that he was a principal in the commission of the crime (People v. Westek, 31 Cal. 2d 469; People v. Claasen, 152 Cal. App. 2d. A.C.A. 700).

Where the prosecutrix in a case of incest is under the age of consent, 18 years, she is not an accomplice and need not be corroborated (People v. Hamilton, 88 Cal. App. 2d 398.)

When Minor Has Capacity to Commit Crime

Where, however, though under the age of fourteen, his knowledge of the wrongfulness of the act is clearly established, the presumption of incapacity to commit crime no longer continues to operate and the ordinary test as to a witness being an accomplice is applicable. (People v. Robbins, 171 Cal. 466; People v. Singh, 121 Cal. App. 107; People v. McCullum, 214 Cal. 601; People v. Williams, 12 Cal. App. 2d 207.)

While, under the provisions of the Juvenile Court Act, a minor under the age of eighteen cannot, if the age be called to the attention of the court, be tried for a criminal offense until his case has been passed upon by the Juvenile Court and that court has declined to handle his case as that of a juvenile delinquent and has certified him for trial on the criminal charge, it is not the rule (People v. Johnson, 115 Cal. App. 704, notwithstanding) that a minor under the age of eighteen cannot be considered an accomplice unless the Juvenile Court has so acted. The phrase "liable to prosecution" does not involve the question whether an attempt to prosecute will be successful but merely contemplates that the facts be such as to warrant the conclusion that the witness is guilty of the offense in question. While the ultimate decision in the Johnson case was correct it is justified, not upon the failure of the Juvenile Court to declare the minor prosecutrix unfit, but upon the ground that being under the age of consent she could not legally consent to an act of sexual intercourse. In the later case of People v. McCullum, 214 Cal. 601, the offense there being a violation of section 288a of the Penal Code, a minor under the age of eighteen was held to be an accomplice regardless of the fact that no action had been taken by the Juvenile Court. (See also People v. Stoll, 84 Cal. App. 99; People v. McRae, 31 Cal. 2d 184; People v. Cox, 102 Cal. App. 2d 285.)

Who Is Not An Accomplice
(See also Feigned Accomplice, infra)

Merely aiding in the commission of a criminal offense without guilty knowledge or intent is not criminal and will not make one an accomplice. (People v. Dole, 122 Cal. 492; People v. Warren, 130 Cal. 686.)

The mere fact that the witness was held to answer as a codefendant (People v. Acosta, 115 Cal. App. 103) or that he had been charged with the same offense (People v. Kosta, 14 Cal. App. 696; People v. Frahm, 107 Cal. App. 253; People v. Stan-

ley, 92 Cal. App. 773; People v. Acosta, 115 Cal. App. 103;
People v. Johns, 69 Cal. App. 2d 737; People v. Morgan, 87
Cal. App. 2d 674; People v. Lawson, 114 Cal. App. 2d 217;
People v. Clark, 116 Cal. App. 2d 219) does not of itself
make him an accomplice.

The fact that the witness is guilty of an offense similar to
that charged does not make him an accomplice since it is only
his guilt of the identical offense charged which could have that
effect. (People v. Galli, 68 Cal. App. 682; People v. Allison, 200
Cal. 404.)

Thus where, upon the trial, evidence of an offense other
than that charged is introduced against the defendant, the
fact that the witness was a principal in the commission of such
other offense does not make him an accomplice. (People v.
Troutman, 187 Cal. 313.) And a witness, who took no part in
the commission of a burglary but, after its commission, assisted
the burglars in conveying the loot from the scene of the crime,
would not be an accomplice since such action would not make
him a principal in the burglary. (People v. Piscitella, 90 Cal.
App. 528; see also People v. King, 30 Cal. App. 2d. 185.) Where
the defendant was charged with using a minor for the purpose
of transporting narcotics (Sec. 11714, Health and Safety Code)
the minor is regarded as a victim and is not an accomplice
(People v. De Paula, 43 Cal. 2d. 643).

In a prosecution for a lewd and lascivious act committed
upon a child under the age of fourteen (Penal Code, sec. 288)
the minor is not an accomplice, unless the defendant on trial
were also under the age of fourteen, since a person can only be
guilty of this offense where the other party to the act is under
the age of fourteen. (People v. Hulbart, 55 Cal. App. 112;
People v. Troutman, 187 Cal. 313; People v. Nichols, 2 Cal.
App. 2d 99; People v. Agullana, 4 Cal. App. 2d 34; People v.
Maine, 93 Cal. App. 141; People v. Geonzalis, 106 Cal. App.
434; People v. Kocalis, 140 Cal. App. 566; People v. Von Benson, 38 Cal. App. 2d 43; People v. Slaughter, 45 Cal. App. 2d
724; People v. Slobodian, 31 Cal. 2d 555; People v. Becker, 80
Cal. App. 2d 691; People v. Westek, 31 Cal. 2d 469; People v.
Terry, 99 Cal. App. 2d. 579.) While in a prosecution for
sodomy or violation of section 288a of the Penal Code a voluntary participant, having the capacity to commit crime, is an
accomplice, the victim of such an act committed against his
will and without his consent is not an accomplice (People v.
Willis, 129 Cal. App. 2d. 330). The woman upon whom an
abortion is performed is not an accomplice of the person
charged with performing or attempting to perform the abortion. (People v. Clapp, 24 Cal. 2d 835; People v. Wilson,

25 Cal. 2d 341; People v. Ramsey, 83 Cal. App. 2d 707; People v. Buffum, 40 Cal. 2d 709; People v. Gallardo, 41 Cal. 2d. 57.) Upon a prosecution for conspiracy to commit abortion in which the evidence showed that, in pursuance thereof, the women were aborted, the women are not accomplices (People v. Buffum, 40 Cal. 2d. 709). The person solicited to commit a crime is not an accomplice of the person charged with soliciting him to do so. (People v. Baskins, 72 Cal. App. 2d 728; People v. Haley, 102 Cal. App. 2d 159). In a prosecution of a husband for placing his wife in a house of prostitution, two persons who conducted such house, with whom defendant discussed such placement but who did not know of the relation of husband and wife, could not be convicted of that offense and are not accomplices (People v. Stein, 55 Cal. App. 2d 417). A person whose knowledge is acquired after the crime has been committed is not an accomplice (People v. Watson, 113 Cal. App. 2d 799). Even though a witness was guilty as a matter of law of the crime of concealing the felony charged, this of itself will not make him an accomplice (People v. Barclay, 40 Cal. 2d 146). Where a defendant is tried for two separate violations of the same statute, committed upon two separate individuals, while each of the victims may be an accomplice as to the crime in which he is involved, this does not make him an accomplice in the offense committed against the other (People v. Mahon, 116 Cal. App. 2d 883; People v. Wertz, 145 Cal. App. 2d. 395). Where the defendant and others entered a building with intent to steal a safe and its contents but, due to its weight, were unable to remove it and left and returned with other persons and then succeeded in removing the safe, the burglary was complete upon the first entry and the persons who participated in the second but not in the first entry were accessories after the fact but not accomplices in the burglary based on the first entry (People v. Piscitella, 90 Cal. App. 528).

A verdict of not guilty as to one of several defendants is a finding of fact that he was not an accomplice of another defendant convicted of the same crime with which both were charged (People v. Lawson, 114 Cal. App. 2d 217).

Illustrative Cases

Further illustrating that a witness is not an accomplice unless there is proof that he was a principal in the commission of the identical crime charged it has been decided in this state that the following are not accomplices: the thief who stole the property in the trial of the person charged with receiving the

stolen property (People v. Gordon, 41 Cal. App. 2d 226; In re
Morton, 179 Cal. 51; People v. Williams, 7 Cal. App. 2d 600;
People v. Sischo, 79 Cal. App. 576; People v. Haack, 93 Cal.
App. 590; People v. Burness, 53 Cal. App. 2d 214; People v.
Lima, 25 Cal. 2d 573; People v. McKinney, 71 Cal. App. 2d 5)
or the vendor in the prosecution of the vendee for receiving
stolen property (People v. Burness, 53 Cal. App. 2d 214);
the person who knowingly received stolen property in the
trial of the thief (People v. Haack, 93 Cal. App. 590; People
v. Evans, 34 Cal. App. 2d 284; People v. Sischo, 79 Cal. App.
576; see also People v. Williams, 7 Cal. App. 2d 600) or
in the trial for the burglary in which the property was
stolen (People v. Gibson, 33 Cal. App. 459; People v. Monteverde, 111 Cal. App. 2d. 156; People v. Conrad, 125 Cal. App.
2d. 184) except where the thief and the receiver had agreed
before the theft that the thief was to steal and the receiver
would receive the property when it was stolen in which case
each would be the accomplice of the other (People v. Lima,
25 Cal. 2d. 573); "The thief and the one knowingly receiving
stolen property from him are guilty of distinct and separate
offenses and are not accomplices of each other" (People v.
Raven, 44 Cal. 2d. 523). "An exception to the rule is recognized
when the thief and the receiver conspire together in a pre-
arranged plan whereby one is to steal and the other is to buy"
(People v. Raven, supra) in which case they are each an
accomplice of the other; where an officer testifies to the
declarations of a coconspirator made in pursuance of the object
of the conspiracy the accomplice rule has no application
(People v. Robinson, 43 Cal. 2d. 132); the woman prosecutrix
in a case of pandering (People v. Montgomery, 47 Cal. App.
2d. 1; People v. Brown, 62 Cal. App. 96) or pimping (People
v. Simpson, 79 Cal. App. 555; People v. Wilkins, 135 Cal. App.
2d. 371; People v. Prayer, 140 Cal. App. 2d.......), but if a procured woman aids and abets in the procurement of another
woman, the former could be an accomplice (id); the minor in a
prosecution for contributing to his delinquency (People v.
Barbera, 78 Cal. App. 277; People v. Doetschman, 69 Cal. App.
2d. 486; People v. Stanley, 78 Cal. App. 2d. 358; People v.
Deibert, 117 Cal. App. 2d. 410); the female victim of incest
committed against her will and consent (People v. Stoll, 84
Cal. App. 99; People v. Kemp, 139 Cal. App. 48; People
v. Gama, 2 Cal. 2d. 274; People v. Lachuk, 5 Cal. App. 2d.
729; People v. Hobday, 131 Cal. App. 626; People v. Lee,

55 Cal. App. 2d. 163; People v. Hamilton, 88 Cal. App. 2d.
398; People v. Pettis, 95 Cal. App. 2d. 790; People v. Herman,
97 Cal. App. 2d. 272; People v. Jahn, 99 Cal. App. 2d.
236); the female victim of rape who is under the age of
consent (People v. Bernon, 29 Cal. App. 424) or any victim
of rape since this crime is one which can only be perpetrated
by a male; the person who places a bet on a horse race in
a prosecution of the bookmaker for receiving the bet (People
v. Mirapol, 33 Cal. App. 2d. 297; People v. Grayson, 83 Cal.
App. 2d. 516); a conspirator who withdrew from the conspiracy before the commission of the crime charged and which
was the product of the conspiracy (People v. Cowan, 38 Cal.
App. 2d 23); the victim of sodomy committed against his will
and consent (People v. Miller, 68 Cal. App. 758, People v.
Battalina, 52 Cal. App. 2d 685); the purchaser in the prosecution of the seller upon the charge of the unlawful possession
of intoxicating liquor (People v. Lein, 204 Cal. 84) or narcotics
(People v. Galli, 68 Cal. App. 682); the buyer or receiver in
a prosecution for the illegal sale or furnishing of intoxicating
liquor or narcotics (People v. Kinsley, 118 Cal. App. 593; People
v. Galli, 68 Cal. App. 682; People v. Lein, 204 Cal. 84; People
v. Heusers, 58 Cal. App. 103; People v. Grijalva, 48 Cal. App.
2d. 882); upon the trial of a charge of possession of narcotics
the person to whom the defendant sold and delivered the
narcotics is not an accomplice (People v. Candelaria, 126 Cal.
App. 2d. 408) and the rule is the same where the defendant
is on trial for the sale of narcotics and the witness was the
buyer (People v. Lamb, 134 Cal. App. 2d. 582); but it was
held that where the officers met one Leiva who stated that
he would take them to a party who would sell narcotics and,
arriving at the defendant's home, the officers gave Leiva three
five dollar bills and a ten dollar bill to purchase heroin from
the defendant and Leiva went into the house and returned with
the heroin and, upon the defendant returning from a store
where she had gone in the meantime, she was placed under
arrest and had in her possession one of the five dollar bills,
the court held that Leiva was an accomplice (People v. Ramirez,
113 Cal. App. 2d. 842). (Note: Since under section 11710 of
the Health and Safety Code a person working under the
direction, supervision or instruction is immune from prosecution under the narcotic law, a provision not considered in the
Remirez case, the witness Leiva was not "liable to prosecution"
and hence was not an accomplice. See next subtitle, infra); the
witness who gave the perjured testimony in a prosecution for
the suborning of such perjury (People v. Layman, 117 Cal.

App. 476; People v. Nickell, 22 Cal. App. 2d 117; People v. De Vaughn, 2 Cal. App. 2d 572). The giver and receiver of a bribe are nor accomplices (People v. Bompensiero, 142 Cal. App 2d. 693). The person of whom the defendant is charged with asking a bribe (People v. Skaggs, 80 Cal. App. 2d. 83); where a bribe is solicited the victim is not an offender and cannot be considered an accomplice of the person seeking the bribe (People v. Lyon, 135 Cal. App. d. 558 and cases cited); one of the defendants on trial testifies in his own behalf but who does not give any testimony against his codefendant (People v. Burnette, 39 Cal. App. 2d 215); and the victim of a murder wherein death was caused by an illegal abortion is not an accomplice and her dying decalaration does not require corroboration. (People v. Wilson, 54 Cal. App. 2d 555). The person who has committed a murder who thereafter aids and abets another in disposing of the body is an accomplice of such other person who is being prosecuted as an accessory after the fact (People v. Wallin, 32 Cal. 2d 803). In a prosecution under section 653f of the Penal Code, soliciting the commission of a crime, the person solicited could be found to be an accomplice where he actively encouraged another person to solicit him (People v. Wayne, 41 Cal. 2d 814, decisions, holding that a woman who solicits and encourages an abortion upon herself is not an accomplice of an abortionist, distinguished).

While the husband of the woman aborted who plays an active part in arranging for the abortion is an accomplice of the abortionist (People v. Wilson, 25 Cal. 2d. 341) he is not an accomplice as a matter of law where he had no conversation or transaction with the abortionist and was merely present in his home where the abortion was performed and paid the abortionist at the request of his wife after the abortion had been performed (People v. Brenon, 138 Cal. App. d. 795 and cases cited and discussed).

Where one of the defendants who testified is acquitted, he cannot be classified as an accomplice (People v. Goldstein, 136 Cal. App. 2d 778, 789).

Where a person is immune from prosecution he is not an accomplice (People v. Nunn, 46 Cal. 2d. 460).

Immunity From Prosecution

"All duly authorized peace officers, while investigating violations of this division in performance of their official duties, and any person working under their immediate direction, supervision or instruction, are immune from prosecution under this division." (Health and Safety Code, sec. 11710; the "division" referred to is that part of said code relating to narcotics.)

Feigned Accomplice

When there is reason to believe that a person is about to commit a crime, or is committing or intending to commit a series of similar violations of the law a peace or law enforcement officer, or at times a private person, who, seemingly becoming a party to the criminal project but actually acting for the sole purpose of apprehending or securing evidence against the guilty party, joins with him or affords him an opportunity of committing his intended criminal act while under such surveillance, even though he cooperate with the suspect in the commission of the crime, is not guilty of the offense committed (see ENTRAPMENT) and is not an accomplice as to the crime committed. (People v. Bolanger, 71 Cal. 17; People v. Keseling, 35 Cal. App. 501, and cases cited; People v. Rodriguez, 1 Cal. App. 69; People v. Caiazza, 61 Cal. App. 505; People v. Spaulding, 81 Cal. App. 615; People v. Calvert, 93 Cal. App. 568; People v. Fitzgerald, 14 Cal. App. 2d 180; People v. Norcross, 71 Cal. App. 2; People v. Barric, 49 Cal. 342; People v. Fong Ching, 78 Cal. 169; People v. Lanzit, 70 Cal. App. 498; People v. Heusers, 58 Cal. App. 103; In re Moore, 70 Cal. App. 483; People v. Lombard, 131 Cal. App. 325; People v. Hicks, 62 Cal. App. 2d 859; People v. Griffin, 98 Cal. App. 2d 1; see also cases under ENTRAPMENT.)

It is not essential to the status of a person as a feigned accomplice that, before the offense was committed, he consulted or informed officers of the law (People v. Pigg, 149 Cal. App. 2d. 737).

However, where a person becomes an actual party to a crime as by formulating the plan for a robbery, or by other acts which make him a principal in its commission, he cannot justify his conduct or escape being an accomplice under the contention that his associates were criminals and that he merely induced them to commit the crime to bring about their conviction and punishment. (People v. Scott, 1 Cal. Unrep. 68; People v. McCormick, 76 Cal. App. 688; also cases under ENTRAPMENT.)

Corroboration of Accomplice

The basic rule of the law of accomplice is that "A conviction cannot be had upon the testimony of an accomplice unless it be corroborated by such other evidence as shall tend to connect the defendant with the commission of the offense." (Penal Code, sec. 1111.) The corroboration required is merely such as will show that the defendant was connected with the commission of the crime. The test as to whether the necessary corroboration exists is stated by our Supreme Court, "We suggest this as a proper test: eliminate from the case the evidence of the accomplice and then examine the testimony of the other witnesses with a view to determine if there be inculpatory evidence—evidence tending to connect the defendant with the offense—if there is, the accomplice is corroborated; if there is no inculpatory evidence then there is no corroboration, though the accomplice may be corroborated in regard to any number of the facts sworn to by him." (People v. Morton, 139 Cal. 719, 724; see also People v. Kempley, 205 Cal. 441; People v. White, 35 Cal. App. 2d 61; People v. Janssen, 74 Cal. App. 402; People v. Davis, 210 Cal. App. 540; People v. Kazatzky, 18 Cal. App. 2d 105; People v. Hoyt, 20 Cal. 2d 306). "In view of the more recent decisions of the Supreme Court we conclude that the test suggested in People v. Morton, supra . . . is not an exclusive method of analyzing the sufficiency of evidence corroborative of the testimony of an accomplice . . . such evidence may be held sufficient if it connect the defendant with the crime in such a way as reasonably to satisfy the fact finding body that the accomplice is telling the truth" (People v. Griffin, 98 Cal. App. 2d. 1). The substitution of the words "that portion of the testimony of the accomplice which tends to connect the defendant with the commission of the offense" for the words "the evidence of the accomplice" in the above quotation from People v. Morton is a correct statement of the law (People v. Keene, 128 Cal. App. 2d. 520). (Note:—Since the accomplice need be corroborated only as to that portion of his testimony which tends to connect the defendant with the offense charged, the suggestion in the Morton case is too broad since, if the entire testimony of the accomplice were eliminated from consideration, we would exclude testimony of the accomplice as to matters as to which he need not be corroborated such as the sole proof of the corpus delicti. The true rule is whether there is any evidence, other than the testimony of the accomplice which tends to connect the defendant with the commission of the offense and, if there is, the accomplice is corroborated and, if there is no such evidence, then there is no such corroboration as is required by law).

The corroborative evidence must be in itself of an inculpatory character without the aid of the testimony which is to be corroborated but the corroborating evidence need not establish the actual commission of the offense, the corpus delicti (People v. Goldstein, 146 Cal. App. 2d. 268 and cases cited).

What Is Not Sufficient

The corroboration is not sufficient if it merely shows the commission of the offense or some or all of the circumstances thereof (People v. Robbins, 171 Cal. 466) or merely tends to raise a suspicion of the guilt of the defendant. (People v. Robbins, 171 Cal. 466; People v. Taylor, 70 Cal. App. 239; People v. Kelly, 69 Cal. App. 570; People v. Davis, 210 Cal. 540.) Corroboration is not adequate if it requires aid from the testimony of the person to be corroborated in order to connect the defendant with the commission of the offense charged (People v. McEwing, 45 Cal. 2d. 218. An accomplice cannot be corroborated by the testimony of one or more other accomplices; the corroboration required by law must come from the evidence of circumstances or direct testimony from a witness or witnesses against whom the charge of accomplice will not lie. (People v. Shaw, 17 Cal. 2d. 820, 842; People v. Clapp, 24 Cal. 2d. 835.)

The testimony of an accomplice is not corroborated by the testimony of a witness to the effect that the defendant committed a separate offense of the same character since such evidence does not tend to connect the defendant with the crime charged (People v. Cox, 102 Cal. App. 2d 285). The failure of the defendant to testify does not tend to connect him with the offense charged and does not constitute evidence such as is required to corroborate an accomplice (People v. Cox, 102 Cal. App. 2d 285). (Note: The circumstances might however result in a different holding in another case since the evidence of the other offense might be such as would tend to prove that the defendant was the perpetrator of the offense charged and the undenied evidence might also have that effect).

On the other hand it is not necessary that the corroboration extend to every fact and detail covered by the testimony of the accomplice (People v. Nichols, 83 Cal. App. 172; People v. Adinolfi, 106 Cal. App. 261; People v. Whittaker, 18 Cal. App. 2d 396; People v. Smitherman, 58 Cal. App. 2d 121) nor need it necessarily show the commission of the crime (People v. Knowles, 75 Cal. App. 229; People v. Barr, 134 Cal. App. 383; People v. Whittaker, 18 Cal. App. 2d 396; People v. Parker, 80 Cal. App. 2d 128) unless the crime is of such character that the fact of the commission of the crime and the defendant's connection therewith are inseparable. (People v. Davis. 210 Cal. 540.)

What Is Sufficient Corroboration

The corroboration is sufficient if it, of itself, tends to connect the defendant with the commission of the offense although it is slight and entitled when standing by itself to but little consideration (People v. McLean, 84 Cal. 480; People v. Humphrey, 27 Cal. App. 2d 631; People v. Hickok, 28 Cal. App. 2d 574; People v. Yeager, 194 Cal. 452; People v. Watson, 21 Cal. App. 692; People v. Barker, 144 Cal. 617; People v. Klopfer, 61 Cal. App. 291; People v. Compton, 123 Cal. 411; People v. Fay, 82 Cal. App. 62; People v. Dahl, 107 Cal. App. 302; People v. Breitenstein, 111 Cal. App. 746; People v. Negra, 208 Cal. 64; People v. Tinnin, 136 Cal. App. 301; People v. Andrew, 43 Cal. App. 2d 126; People v. Trujillo, 32 Cal. 2d 105) and it is not necessary that the corroborative evidence shall connect the defendant with the commission of the offense beyond a reasonable doubt. (People v. Collier, 111 Cal. App. 215; People v. Looney, 9 Cal. App. 2d 335.) The corroborative evidence is sufficient if it connect the defendant with the commission of the crime in such a way as to reasonably satisfy the fact finding body that the accomplice is telling the truth (People v. Henderson, 34 Cal. 2d 340, 342; People v. Duarte, 96 Cal. App. 2d. 661; People v. Griffin, 98 Cal. App. 2d. 1; People v. Trujillo, 32 Cal. 2d. 105, 111; People v. McEwing, 45 Cal. 2d. 218); it is "sufficient if it tends in some slight degree, at least, to implicate the defendant (People v. Griffin, 98 Cal. App. d. 1) and the corroboration may be by circumstantial evidence alone and is sufficient" if the connection of the defendant with the alleged crime may be reasonably inferred from the corroborating evidence (People v. Griffin, 98 Cal. App. d 1 and cases cited). "It is not necessary that the corroborative evidence prove independently either that the defendant is guilty of the offense or that he is guilty beyond a reasonable doubt" (People v. Griffin, 98 Cal. App. 2d 1; People v. Williams, 101 Cal. App. 2d 624). "It is not necessary that the independent evidence be sufficient to establish the defendant's guilt. The prosecution is not required to single out an isolated fact which in itself, unrelated to other proven facts, is considered to be sufficient corroboration. It is the combined and cumulative weight of the evidence furnished by the non-accomplice witnesses which supplies the test" (People v. Trujillo, 32 Cal. 2d. 105, 111). An accomplice in a prosecution for abortion may be corroborated by the testimony of the woman who submitted to the abortion(People v. Gallardo, 41 Cal. 2d 57 and cases cited). The corroboration may be gathered from the defendant's own conduct and attitude while testifying (People v. Todd, 9 Cal. App.

2d 237; People v. Monteverde, 111 Cal. App. 2d. 156). False and contradictory statements of the defendant in relation to the charge, an attempt to rig a false alibi and flight are sufficient corroboration (People v. Santo, 43 Cal. 2d. 319). Possession of the probable means or instrument used in the commission of a crime may be sufficient corroboration (People v. Keene, 128 Cal. App. 2d. 520, printing press and type used to print blanks for forged checks). Possession of the property stolen is corroborative of the testimony of an accomplice (People v. Morrow, 127 Cal. App. 2d. 293, receiving stolen property).

Corroboration by Admission or Confession

An accomplice is sufficiently corroborated by proof of the defendant's confession or admission tending to connect him with the crime, (People v. Baker, 25 Cal. App. 2d 1; People v. Hickok, 28 Cal. App. 2d 574; People v. Wiley, 33 Cal. App 2d 424; People v. Desmond, 24 Cal. App. 408; People v. Richardson, 161 Cal. 552; People v. Groenig, 57 Cal. App. 495; People v. Tobin, 39 Cal. App. 76; People v. Kelly, 69 Cal. App. 558; People v. Fraser, 81 Cal. App. 281; People v. Graves, 74 Cal. App. 415; People v. Adinolfi, 106 Cal. App. 261; People v. Bonilla, 124 Cal. App. 212; People v. Briley, 9 Cal. App. 2d 84; People v. Earl, 10 Cal. App. 2d 163; People v. Rokes, 18 Cal. App. 2d 689; People v. Derenzo, 46 Cal. App. 2d 411; People v. White, 48 Cal. App. 2d 90; People v. Pritchard, 58 Cal. App. 2d 791; People v. Holt, 88 Cal. App. 2d 42; People v. Walker, 88 Cal. App. 2d 265; People v. Bennett, 93 Cal. App. 2d 549; People v. Griffin, 98 Cal. App. 2d 1; People v. Brickman, 119 Cal. App. 2d 253) or by testimony given by the defendant upon the trial having the same effect. (People v. Watson, 21 Cal. App. 692; People v. Sullivan, 144 Cal. 471; People v. Groenig, 57 Cal. App. 495.) Equivocal statements of the defendant when first arrested and when first accused of the crime and evidence of his conduct at other times may also be corroborative of the accomplice's testimony (People v. Carmelo, 94 Cal. App. 2d 301). Silence of the accused in the face of a confession of an accomplice implicating both of them in the crime is sufficient corroboration (People v. Hambright, 113 Cal. App. 2d 140).

False Statements of Defendant

"False and contradictory statements of a defendant in relation to the charge are themselves corroborative evidence" (People v. Simpson, 43 Cal. 2d. 553; see also cases under next subtitle).

By Circumstantial Evidence

It is not necessary that the corroboration be by direct evidence; the required proof connecting the defendant with the commission of the offense may be by proof of circumstances. (People v. Santo, 43 Cal. 2d. 319, 327; People v. Yeager, 194 Cal. 452; People v. Nikolich, 93 Cal. App. 356; People v. Freer, 104 Cal. App. 39; People v. Robinson, 107 Cal. App. 11; People v. Blunkall, 31 Cal. App. 778; People v. Bennett, 93 Cal. App. 2d 549). Thus it has been held that the accomplice was sufficiently corroborated where the corroborative evidence showed flight of the defendant from the scene of the crime or at the time of arrest (People v. Rice, 29 Cal. App. 2d 614; People v. Knoth, 111 Cal. App. 250; see also People v. Holt, 20 Cal. 2d 306), possession by the defendant of the stolen property (People v. Rice, 9 Cal. App. 2d 614; People v. Bettencourt, 64 Cal. App. 263; People v. Haughey, 79 Cal. App. 541; People v. Haney, 126 Cal. App. 473; People v. Richmond, 127 Cal. App. 538; People v. Sandow, 133 Cal. App. 559; People v. Miller, 54 Cal. App. 2d 384; People v. Shofstall, 56 Cal. App. 2d 121; People v. Bennett, 93 Cal. App. 2d 549; People v .Morrow, 127 Cal. App. 2d 293; People v. Antone, 141 Cal. App .2d 681). But merely finding the stolen property on the defendant's premises in a place where it could as well have been placed by some other person would not be proof of possession by the defendant. (People v. Curran, 3 Cal. Unrep. 643; People v. Hurley, 60 Cal. 74; People v. Ciani, 104 Cal. App. 596.) Falsehoods, contradictions or silence of the defendant in the face of accusation may also furnish the necessary corroboration. (People v. Hendricks, 71 Cal. App. 730; People v. Nikolich, 93 Cal. App. 536; People v. Holmes, 130 Cal. App. 507; People v. Collins, 4 Cal. App. 2d 86; People v. Bonner, 5 Cal. App. 2d 314.) Possession by the defendant of a weapon similar to that used in the robbery was held "substantial evidence" connecting the defendant with the crime. (People v. Henderson, 34 Cal. 2d 340). In the same case the District Court of Appeals said that corroboration of the testimony of the accomplice that the defendant's wife made the masks used in the robbery and that the barrel of the shotgun used was sawed off in the home of the defendant's father and that defendant's uncle took the accomplice for medical aid after the robbery for injuries received therein "is found in the failure of defendant to call his wife and father as witnesses." The Supreme Court, while affirming the conviction, does not express an opinion as to the language last above quoted, but does state that the relationship of the men and all of their acts may be considered in determining whether there is corroboration. (People v. Henderson, 34, Cal. 2d 340.)

Physical evidence connected with the commission of the crime and also connected with the defendant (possession of a gun similar to that fired, a scarf of defendant found at the scene of the crime, fibres of defendant's clothing shown to be the same as fibres found on objects directly connected with the crime) have been held sufficient corroboration (People v. Trujillo, 32 Cal. 2d 105). The testimony of a handwriting expert connecting the defendant through his handwriting with the forgery charged sufficiently corroborates the testimony of an accomplice (People v. Morris, 115 Cal. App. 2d 312).

Failure of Defendant to Testify

It has been indicated that the failure of the defendant to take the witness and his failure to introduce any evidence tending to show that he had no connection with the commission of the crime may be considered by the jury as tending to corroborate the testimony of an accomplice (People v. Arbaugh, 82 Cal. App. 2d. 971, 975; People v. Watkins, 126 Cal. App. 2d. 199) but in these cases there was other corroboration. In People v. Ashley, 42 Cal. 2d. 246, 268, the court points out that the failure of a defendant to testify will not supply any lack of proof in the case of the prosecution (see also People v. Hooker, 126 Cal. App. 2d. 394) from which it would follow that the failure of a defendant to testify or a failure to introduce evidence, or both, will not alone be sufficient to corroborate the testimony of an accomplice.

Accomplice—When Granted Immunity

While there is no objection to extending to the accomplice immunity from prosecution, in whole or in part, upon condition that he testify fairly and fully as to his knowledge of the facts, it is a miscarriage of justice where a conviction is obtained through the use of testimony of an accomplice who was granted immunity upon the condition that the testimony he is about to give shall be such as will result in the conviction of one who is or could be jointly charged with him (People v. Green, 102 Cal. App. 2d 831).

SOLICITING COMMISSION OF CRIME

"Every person who solicits another to offer or accept or join in the offer or acceptance of a bribe, or to commit or join in the commission of murder, robbery, burglary, grand theft, receiving stolen property, extortion, rape by force, perjury, subornation of perjury, forgery or kidnaping, is punishable by imprisonment in the county jail not longer than one year, or in the state prison not longer than five years, or by a fine of not more than five thousand dollars. Such offense must be proved by the testimony of two witnesses or of one witness and corroborating circumstances." (Penal Code, sec. 653f.)

"When any person solicits another to offer or join in the offer of a bribe, the solicitor has committed the offense described in section 653f." People v. Rissman, 154 Cal. App. 2d. ......). The gist of the offense is the solicitation to offer or join in the offer of a bribe and not the commission of the bribery." "A contemplated overt act is not an essential element of the offense." (People v. Rissman, supra). The offense "is complete when the solicitation is made and it is immaterial that the object of the solicitation is never consummated or that no steps were taken toward its consummation." (People v. Burt, 45 Cal. 2d. 311; People v. Rissman, supra).

The gist of the offense is the solicitation of the commission of one or more of the offenses listed in the statute (People v. Humphrey, 27 Cal. App. 2d 631) and the law is violated whether the person solicited responds favorably or unfavorably or not at all, whether or not the crime the commission of which was solicited was committed or attempted (People v. Gray, 52 Cal. App. 2d 620; People v. Haley, 102 Cal. App. 2d 159) and whether the idea was one which the person solicited had previously entertained or not or whether the solicitation was in response to some act or statement of the person solicited. It is essential to this crime that two or more persons must be involved and at least one person must be the solicitor and another person be the person solicited, but it does not follow that where both parties approach the crime as solicitors that the section is not violated for in such case each party may, by his act, be guilty of soliciting (People v. Wayne, 41 Cal. 2d. 814).

While there has been as yet no declaration by our appellate courts as to just what "corroborating circumstances" must be shown where there is but one witness to the commission of the offense it would seem that, since the requirement for corroboration in the crimes of obtaining property by false pretenses (Penal Code, sec. 1110) and perjury (Penal Code, sec. 1103a) is expressed in the same language as that used in section 653f, the law of corroboration as laid down with reference to those offenses would also apply to a prosecution for soliciting a person to commit a felony. (See People v. Wayne, 41 Cal. 2d. 814.)

An accomplice is a "witness" within the meaning of the last sentence of the section (People v. Rissman, 154 Cal. App. 2d. ......).

The corroborating evidence is sufficient if it tends to connect the defendant with the commission of the crime in such a way as may reasonably satisfy the trier of fact that the witness who must be corroborated is telling the truth (People v. Rissman, 154 Cal. App. 2d. ......).

The requirements as to corroboration apply only to the trial and do not apply to a preliminary examination and a defendant may be held to answer upon the testimony of one witness alone. (Kind v. Sup. Ct., 143 Cal. App. 2d. 100.)

The solicitation prohibited by the statute includes cases where the solicitation is to crime without as well as within the state (People v. Burt, 45 Cal. 2d. 311).

It is immaterial where the acts solicited are to be performed and where such act is to be performed without this state, proof that such act would constitute a crime in the foreign jurisdiction is unnecessary (People v. Burt, 45 Cal. 2d. 311).

The testimony of other persons who had been solicited to commit the same crime has been held sufficient corroboration. "The corroborative evidence need not be strong nor even sufficient in itself, without the aid of other evidence, to establish the fact." (People v. Baskins, 72 Cal. App. 2d 728.)

CHAPTER XIV

civil connotations
crim. "
2 Fold

CONSPIRACY ✓

"If two or more persons conspire:

1. To commit any crime; (Note: Under this subdivision the conspiracy must be one to commit a crime in California, People v. Buffum, 40 Cal. 2d 709). *charge with an offense*

conspiritorium

2. Falsely and maliciously to indict another for any crime, or to procure another to be charged or arrested for any crime;

obtained by mal. intent

3. Falsely to move or maintain any suit, action, or proceeding; *(ex) → stock sales*

4. To cheat and defraud any person of any property, by any means which are in themselves criminal, or to obtain money or property by false pretenses or by false promises with fraudulent intent not to perform such promises;

changing all the time

5. To commit any act injurious to the public health, to public morals, or to pervert or obstruct justice, or the due administration of the laws, (Note: Subdivision 5 evidently was not intended to cover cases of conspiracy in which the object thereof was a crime since such cases would be covered by subdivision 1. Subdivision 5 is constitutional (Calhoun v. Sup. Ct., 46 Cal. 2d. 18).

"When they conspire to do any of the other acts described in this section they shall be punishable by imprisonment in the county jail for not more than one year or in the state prison for not more than three years or by a fine not exceeding five thousand dollars ($5000) or both." (Penal Code, sec. 182.)

"No agreement amounts to a conspiracy, unless some act, besides such agreement, be done within this state to effect the object thereof, by one or more of the parties to such agreement and the trial of cases of conspiracy may be had in any county in which any such act be done." (Penal Code, sec. 184.)

"Upon a trial for conspiracy, in a case where an overt act is necessary to constitute the offense, the defendant cannot be convicted unless one or more overt acts are expressly alleged in the indictment or information, nor unless one of the acts alleged is proved; but other overt acts not alleged may be given in evidence." (Penal Code, sec. 1104; People v. Nunn, 65 Cal. App. 2d. 188.)

No Other Conspiracies Punishable

"No conspiracies other than those enumerated in the preceding section are punishable criminally" (Penal Code, sec. 183).

116

People — v — Roberts —

This section does not exclude conspiracies made punishable criminally by other statutes (see In re Williams, 43 Cal. 2d. 651).

Conspiracy Defined

A conspiracy is an agreement or understanding between two or more persons that they will commit one or more of the unlawful acts enumerated in section 182 of the Penal Code or to accomplish a lawful or unlawful ultimate purpose by the commission of one or more of the unlawful acts enumerated in section 182. In other words a conspiracy is a criminal partnership, differing from the partnership recognized by law as a legal method of legally transacting a business or profession in that the conspiracy has as its object the doing of one or more of the unlawful acts listed in section 182. It follows that a legal association of individuals engaged in a lawful enterprise may become a criminal conspiracy by including in its objects an unlawful act within section 182 or by an agreement to accomplish one of its lawful objects or purposes by such an unlawful act.

Conspiracy is not synonymous with aiding or abetting or participating. It implies an agreement to commit a crime; to aid and abet requires actual participation in the act constituting the offense (People v. Malotte, 46 Cal. 2d. 59).

A conspiracy may have as its object one unlawful act, or any number of the unlawful acts, listed in section 182, and it is proper in charging a conspiracy to set forth in one count of the indictment or information any number of the objects of the conspiracy. (People v. Gilbert, 26 Cal. App. 2d 1; People v. Yant, 26 Cal. App. 2d 725; People v. Head, 9 Cal. App. 2d 647; People v. Busick, 32 Cal. App. 2d 315.)

As in a lawful partnership, the members thereof are individually liable for the obligations arising out of and in the course of the business in which they are engaged even though they arise out of a transaction which was not contemplated at the time the partnership agreement was entered into, so in the case of a conspiracy each of its members is personally criminally liable for every unlawful act done by any one or more of his co-conspirators in an attempt to carry out and accomplish an object of the conspiracy.

The words "any crime" in section 182 include all crimes, felonies and misdemeanors, whether punishable by the provisions of the Penal Code or by any other statute of the state or by local ordinance (Doble v. Superior Court, 197 Cal. 556) and to constitute a conspiracy to commit a crime it is not necessary that the crime shall have been committed. (People v. Van, 30 Cal. App. 2d 663.)

To constitute a conspiracy within subd. 1 of section 182 the crime which is the object of the conspiracy must be a crime to be committed within this state (People v. Buffum, 40 Cal. 2d 709). Under this ruling it would seem that in such a prosecution the prosecution must prove not only that the conspiracy was to commit a crime but also that the crime was one agreed to be committed within this state (but in People v. Burt, 45 Cal. 2d. 311, it was held that the offense of soliciting the commission of crime, Penal Code, sec. 653f, includes cases where the crime is to be committed without as well as within the state).

A conspiracy to violate the Corporate Securities Law is punishable as a conspiracy under subdivision of section 182 of the Penal Code (Doble v. Sup. Ct., 197 Cal. 550; People v. Eiseman, 78 Cal. App. 223; People v. Sears, 138 Cal. App. 2d. 773).

A conspiracy to commit an act in violation of a penal statute which is unconstitutional cannot stand (People v. Drake, 151 Cal. App. 2d. ....).

Penalties

All conspiracies are felonies since, whether the object of the conspiracy includes the commission of a felony or whether its object be only the doing of any one or more of the unlawful acts listed in section 182, every conspiracy is punishable by imprisonment in the state prison and, where the object of a conspiracy is a felony which is punishable by the death penalty, it may be punishable by the supreme penalty. Thus a conspiracy to commit murder can only be a conspiracy to commit murder in the first degree and is punishable by either life imprisonment or the death penalty in the discretion of the jury (People v. Kynette, 15 Cal. 2d 731.)

A conspiracy to commit a misdemeanor is a felony (People v. Cossey, 97 Cal. App. 2d 101).

Proof of Conspiracy

It is not necessary to prove a conspiracy to show an actual meeting or actual agreement of the parties to the conspiracy and the existence of a conspiracy may be established either by direct testimony of the fact or by circumstantial evidence or by a combination of both direct and circumstantial evidence. (People v. Zimmerman, 3 Cal. App. 84; People v. Leavins, 12 Cal. App. 178; People v. Donnolly, 142 Cal. 398; People v. Eldridge, 147 Cal. 782; People v. Kaufman, 152 Cal. 148; People v. Yeager, 194 Cal. 452; People v. Lee, 23 Cal. App. 2d 168; People v. Jordan, 24 Cal. App. 2d 39; People v. Little, 41 Cal. App. 2d 797; People v. Malone, 20 Cal. App. 2d 1; People v. Schmidt, 33 Cal. App. 426; People v. Bucchierre, 57 Cal. App.

2d 153; People v. Burton, 91 Cal. App. 2d 695; People v. Griffin, 98 Cal. App. 2d 1; People v. Hess, 107 Cal. App. 2d 407.)

Common design can rarely be shown by direct evidence and a finding of the formation and existence of a conspiracy may stand on circumstantial evidence alone and, in the determination of this question, the relation of the parties to one another, their personal and business associations with one another, evidence of what transpired between them at or before the time of the alleged combination or agreement and the acts performed and the declarations or statements made by the various parties subsequent to the alleged confederation in respect to and in pursuance and furtherance of the object or objects of the conspiracy shed light on the question. (Cases last cited.) Evidence that two or more persons, pursued by their acts the same object, so as to complete it with a view of attaining the same object, will justify the conclusion that such persons were engaged in a conspiracy to effect that object. (People v. Bentley, 75 Cal. 409; People v. Wagner, 65 Cal. App. 704; People v. Torres, 84 Cal. App. 2d. 787; People v. McManis, 122 Cal. App. 2d. 891.) Existence of a conspiracy may be established by acts or declarations of one or more of the conspirators where the acts or declarations were made in pursuance of the object of the conspiracy. (People v. Rodley, 131 Cal. 240; People v. Daener, 96 Cal. App. 2d 827) by the testimony at the trial of one of the conspirators (People v. Zimmerman, 3 Cal. App. 84) or by the testimony of one who has been a conspirator but had withdrawn from the conspiracy (People v. Cowan, 38 Cal. App. 2d 23) or by the dying declaration of the victim of a homicide committed in pursuance of the conspiracy. (People v. Amaya, 134 Cal. 531.)

It is not necessary that each conspirator see the others or know who all of the members of the conspiracy are (People v. Buffum, 40 Cal. 2d. 700, 725 and cases cited).

Not Provable by Admission or Confession

A conspiracy can not be proved by the ex parte declarations of a conspirator not made as a verbal act evidencing the agreement (People v. Doble, 203 Cal. 510) nor can the existence of the conspiracy be proved by the extra-judicial admission or confession of one or more of the conspirators as the law is settled that no part of the corpus delicti of the crime may be so established.

The Overt Act

Mere agreement or understanding between two or more persons to do an unlawful act included within section 182 is not

sufficient to make the crime of conspiracy complete and before
the agreement amounts to a conspiracy there must be the
performance of some act by at least one of the conspirators
as the first step toward accomplishment of the purpose and
object of the conspiracy, an overt act evidencing that the parties have gone beyond the mere agreement and that the conspiracy has begun an active existence. It is not ncessary, however, that the overt act amount to an attempt to perform the
object of the conspiracy (People v. George, 74 Cal. App. 440;
People v. Ragone, 84 Cal. App. 2d 476), although such an
attempt would clearly be an overt act, but to constitute an
overt act within the requirement of the law (Penal Code, sec.
184) there must be an act or step, lawful or unlawful, beyond mere planning and agreement, toward the accomplishment of the object of the conspiracy. An overt act
need amount to no more than an act showing that the conspiracy has gone beyond the stage of a mere meeting of the minds
upon the attainment of an unlawful object and that action by
the conspirators, as such, has begun (People v. George, 74 Cal.
App. 440; People v. Stevens, 78 Cal. App. 395; People v. Yant,
26 Cal. App. 2d 725; People v. Beck, 60 Cal. App. 417, citing
illustrations) and it is not necessary that the overt act be of a
criminal or unlawful nature. (People v. Gilbert, 26 Cal. App.
2d 1; People v. Daniels, 105 Cal. 262; People v. Stevens, 78 Cal.
App. 395; People v. Yant, 26 Cal. App. 2d 395; People v. Beck,
60 Cal. App. 417; People v. Corica, 55 Cal. App. 2d 130;
People v. Ragone, 84 Cal. App. 2d 476; People v. Sica, 112
Cal. App. 2d 574; People v. Frankfort, 114 Cal. App. 2d 680;
People v. Shaw, 115 Cal. App. 2d. 597; People v. Robinson,
43 Cal. 2d. 132), nor is it necessary that each conspirator
commit an overt act or that more than one conspirator commit
an overt act (People v. Robinson, 43 Cal. 2d. 132).

Proof of But One Objective

Where it is charged that the defendants conspired to
commit two or more crimes the offense of conspiracy is established and a conviction is warranted if the proof shows that
there was a conspiracy to commit any one of such crimes even
though it fails to show any other crime as the object of that
conspiracy (People v. Marvin, 48 Cal. App. 2d 180; People
v. Griffin, 98 Cal. App. 2d 1).

Examples

Where, following the agreement to kidnap a motion picture
actress and hold her for ransom, two of the conspirators stationed themselves in an automobile outside of the studio where

she was employed for the purpose of making observations to assist them in planning the details of the kidnaping it was held that an overt act had been committed. (People v. Stevens, 78 Cal. App. 395.) Raising funds to be used in carrying out a conspiracy to bribe a public officer is an overt act (People v. Beck, 60 Cal. App. 417), as is an attempt to open the door in a conspiracy to commit burglary (People v. Rodriguez, 61 Cal. App. 69), as are acts not of a criminal nature in preparation for carrying out the object of the conspiracy (People v. Gilbert, 26 Cal. App. 2d 1) such as purchasing postage stamps in order to mail poison in pursuance of a conspiracy to commit murder. (People v. Corica, 55 Cal. App. 2d 130). Where there was an agreement to perform abortions in this state and arrangements were made to contact the women by telephone to make the necessary arrangements and the women were transported over California highways headed for the place where the abortions were to be performed, the conspiracy would be complete and the subsequent transportation of the women to Mexico for the abortions would not nullify the acts which had already been done in this state (People v. Buffum, 40 Cal. 2d 709).

Crimes Committed in Pursuance of Conspiracy — Rule of Evidence & procedure probable

Where two or more persons join together in a criminal venture and the crime is one likely to result in the death of a human being or the parties to the conspiracy are prepared to kill any person who may interfere in their criminal undertaking all of the conspirators are equally guilty of any crime, including murder, committed as the natural and probable consequence of such enterprise by any one of the co-conspirators. (People v. La Vers, 27 Cal. App. 2d 336; People v. King, 30 Cal. App. 2d 185; People v. Waller, 14 Cal. 2d 693; People v. Cowan, 38 Cal. App. 2d 231; People v. Rowell, 64 Cal. App. 58; People v. Bringhurst, 192 Cal. 748; People v. Pickens, 61 Cal. App. 405; People v. Thomas, 135 Cal. App. 654; People v. Brown, 59 Cal. 345; People v. Pedde, 25 Cal. App. 34; People v. Yeager, 194 Cal. 452; People v. Pool, 27 Cal. App. 572; People v. Welch, 89 Cal. App. 18; People v. Perry, 195 Cal. 623; People v. Sutton, 17 Cal. App. 2d 561; People v. Ferdinand, 194 Cal. 555; People v. Jones, 136 Cal. App. 722; People v. La Frenz, 134 Cal. App. 687; People v. Harper, 25 Cal. 2d 862; People v. Miller, 37 Cal. 2d 801.)

"A conspirator does not have to participate in the crime conspired" (People v. Malotte, 46 Cal. 2d. 59).

The rule stated and the cases cited are based upon the proposition that where a conspiracy exists every act done by any one of the conspirators in pursuance of the object of the con-

spiracy is the act of all even though it is not an act planned
or even contemplated by the members of the conspiracy (People
v. Coffelt, 140 Cal. App. 444; People v. MacPhee, 26 Cal.
App. 218; People v. Schmidt, 33 Cal. App. 426; People v. Mazzurco, 49 Cal. App. 275; People v. Rooley, 131 Cal. 240; People
v. Zimmerman, 3 Cal. App. 84; and cases last above cited) and
even though the act so committed is a greater crime than that
which was the object of the conspiracy as, for example, the
commission of a murder in pursuance of the object of the conspiracy which was robbery. (People v. Ferdinand, 194 Cal.
555; People v. Perry, 195 Cal. 623; People v. Jones, 136 Cal.
App. 722; People v. Lafrenz, 134 Cal. App. 687; People v. Sutton, 17 Cal. App. 2d 561.)

Acts Not Originally Intended

The fact that an act so committed was not planned or intended as a part of the design (People v. Creeks, 170 Cal. 368;
People v. Palmer, 92 Cal. App. 323; People v. Sberno, 22 Cal.
App. 2d 392; and cases above cited under this heading), even
though the act was done by one of the conspirators in the absence of his co-conspirators (People v. Correa, 44 Cal. App.
634; People v. Mazzurco, 49 Cal. App. 275; People v. Ferlin, 203
Cal. 587; People v. Cook, 10 Cal. App. 2d 54), is not a defense
to the other members of the conspiracy. Nor is it a defense
to any member of the conspiracy which resulted, for example,
in a murder, that he did not intend to take human life or that
he expressly forbade his associates to do so (People v. Law-
rence, 143 Cal. 148; People v. Vasquez, 49 Cal. 560) or that
when the victim to the planned robbery made resistance he
made no effort to shoot but was about to drop his gun at the
time his co-conspirator shot the intended victim. (People v.
Sberno, 22 Cal. App. 2d. 392.) Where there was a common
design to beat up the deceased, both persons who took an
active part in the beatings are responsible for the death of
the victim resulting from such assault and battery (People
v. McMannis, 122 Cal. App. 2d. 891).

Where, in order to carry out and accomplish the object of
a conspiracy, one or more of the conspirators commits a crime
not specifically agreed upon or contemplated, all of the conspirators are equally guilty thereof if such crime was one
which would naturally occur in the perpetration of the ultimate
purpose of the conspiracy. Thus a kidnaping, in the perpetration of a robbery, which was the ultimate object of the conspirators, would be a crime of which all are guilty. (People v.
Salter, 59 Cal. App. 2d 59.)

Acts and Declarations of Co-Conspirators

Where persons have entered into a conspiracy each is as
responsible, as though he himself had performed the act, for

every act done by any one of his confederates in furtherance of the object of the conspiracy, even though he was not present and whether the act by itself constituted a crime or was only an act in furtherance of the criminal design (People v. Coffelt, 140 Cal. App. 444; People v. McPhee, 26 Cal. App. 218; People v. Prather, 23 Cal. App. 721; People v. Correa, 44 Cal. App. 634; People v. Kempley, 205 Cal. 441; People v. Williams, 30 Cal. App. 2d 234; People v. Schmidt, 33 Cal. App. 426; People v. Temple, 15 Cal. App. 2d 336), and the same rule applies to declarations or statements made by one of the conspirators in pursuance of the course of action planned by the conspirators. (People v. Prather, 23 Cal. App. 721; People v. Trim, 39 Cal. 75; People v. Cook, 10 Cal. App. 2d 54; People v. Cory, 26 Cal App. 735; People v. Lichtenstein, 22 Cal. App. 592; People v. Ford, 81 Cal. App. 449; People v. Ferlin, 203 Cal. 587; People v. Eppstein, 108 Cal. App. 72; People v. Whittaker, 18 Cal. App. 2d 396; People v. Shaffer, 38 Cal. App. 2d 421). The acts and declarations of a co-conspirator in the course of the conspiracy are not rendered inadmissible because he is not joined with the defendants on trial (People v. Arnold, 199 Cal. 471).

Act or Declaration Not in Scope of Conspiracy

Where, however, a conspirator makes a statement after the conspiracy is at an end, such statement is not that of his former co-conspirators and is, and can be used, only as the statement of the one who made it (People v. Oldham, 111 Cal. 648; People v. Collum, 122 Cal. 186; People v. Opie, 123 Cal. 294; People v. Smith, 151 Cal. 619; People v. Sidelinger, 9 Cal. App. 298; People v. Ayhens, 16 Cal. App. 618; People v. Mazzurco, 49 Cal. App. 275; People v. Doble, 203 Cal. 510), and declarations by a conspirator showing merely past acts and not in furtherance of the conspiracy are not binding upon his co-conspirators (People v. Irvin, 67 Cal. 494; People v. Erickson, 66 Cal. App. 307; People v. Doble, 203 Cal. 510; People v. Rober, 168 Cal. 316), for as to them the statements are inadmissible hearsay.

Where a conspirator commits an act which is not in furtherance of the object of the conspiracy nor the natural and probable consequence of an attempt to attain that object he alone is responsible for and bound by that act and no responsibility therefor attaches to any of his confederates. (People v. Little, 41 Cal. App. 2d 797; People v. Gilliland, 39 Cal. App 2d 250.)

Scope of the Conspiracy

It does not follow that, when the declared object of a conspiracy has been accomplished, the conspiracy is at an end and that there is no further liability to any of the conspirators because of an act of one of its members. In a conspiracy to commit a crime the conspiracy continues not only until that crime has been committed but until the ultimate object of the crime has been accomplished and the liability of the conspirators, as such, extends beyond the mere consummation of the crime. (People v. Tinnin, 136 Cal. App. 301; People v. Kavanaugh, 107 Cal. App. 571; People v. Wagner, 133 Cal. App. 775; People v. Lorraine, 90 Cal. App. 317.) Thus a conspiracy to commit the crime of robbery is not ended until the spoils of the robbery have been divided (People v. Dean, 66 Cal. App. 602) or, if the crime be kidnaping for ransom, until the ransom has been paid. (People v. Wagner, 133 Cal. App. 775.)

While it may not be expressly so agreed, it is obviously tacitly understood by the persons who conspire to commit a criminal offense, and the law is justified in assuming, that the conspiracy includes the evading and resisting of arrest and acts done to that end (People v. Welch, 89 Cal. App. 18; People v. Corkery, 134 Cal. App. 294; People v. Thomas, 135 Cal. App. 645; People v. La Vere, 130 Cal. App. 708; People v. Kauffman, 152 Cal. 334) and, as indicated in the cases cited, a murder in such an effort to escape arrest makes each conspirator guilty thereof. (See also cases cited under this title.)

The common design of the conspiracy "may extend in point of time beyond the actual commission of the act constituting the crime for which the accused is being tried, such as for the purpose of concealing the crime, securing the proceeds thereof, or bribing or influencing witnesses. . . . Of course it must reasonably appear that such acts were committed in furtherance of the common design of the conspiracy. . . ." (People v. Suter, 43 Cal. App. 2d 444; see also People v. Ross, 46 Cal. App. 2d 385; People v. Derenzo, 46 Cal. App. 2d 411.)

Where the charge is that of conspiracy to commit grand theft the mere fact that, while thefts were committed in pursuance of the conspiracy, no theft amounted to grand theft, does not show that the conspiracy was merely one to commit grand theft where under the facts it could be found that the conspiracy contemplated taking any sum big or little (People v. Berger, 44 Cal. 2d. 459).

Joining a Conspiracy Already Formed — (RULE OF EVIDENCE)

Any person, who, after a conspiracy has been formed, joins therein thereby becomes a party thereto from that time on, as if he had originally conspired and, upon his trial for an offense resulting from the acts of the conspirators, the acts and declarations of the co-conspirators done and made before he became a member of the conspiracy may be introduced in evidence against him subject only to the condition that such acts and declarations were in pursuance of the object or objects of the conspiracy. (People v. Jones, 25 Cal. App. 2d 517; People v.

Kiser, 22 Cal. App. 11; People v. Fitzgerald, 14 Cal. App. 2d 246; People v. Griffin, 98 Cal. App. 2d. 1.) Where a person joined a conspiracy after it was formed and actively participated therein he "thereby adopted the previous acts and declarations of his fellow conspirators" (People v. Jones, 25 Cal. App. 2d. 517, 520; People v. Sherman, 127 Cal. App. 2d. 230). Whether a conspirator was one of the originators of the conspiracy or later joined and participated in the common design is immaterial (People v. Drake, 151 Cal. App. 2d..........). Where three men conspired that two of them were to commit a robbery and the third was to receive the stolen property and these objectives were accomplished and the defendant then joined them, received a substantial part of the stolen property and placed it in a safe deposit box which he rented, the conviction of defendant of conspiracy to receive stolen property was sustained the court holding that defendant's contention, that he could not be guilty of conspiracy unless he was a member of the conspiracy before the robbery, was not the law and applying the rule that one who joins a conspiracy after it is formed and actively participates therein thereby adopts the previous acts and declarations of his fellow conspirators (People v. Brumback, 152 Cal. App. 2d........ A.C.A. 427).

Where a person joins an existing criminal conspiracy in ignorance of its criminal character and under an honest belief that it is a lawful enterprise with a lawful purpose, he does not become a co-conspirator and incurs no liability as such since we have here an honest ignorance or mistake of fact which disproves criminal intent (Penal Code, sec. 26, subd. 4; People v. Flanagan, 65 Cal. App. 268 and cases cited; see also People v. McLaughlin, 111 Cal. App. 2d 781) but ignorance of the law, knowing the object of the conspiracy but not knowing that it is unlawful, is not a defense (People v. McLaughlin, supra).

Withdrawal from Conspiracy — *way of terminating consp.*

A person who, by conspiring with others, advises and encourages the commission of an unlawful act cannot escape responsibility by quietly withdrawing from further activity or by remaining away from the scene of the crime at the time it is perpetrated or by fleeing from the scene and personally abandoning the criminal design before the unlawful planned act has been committed. (People v. Madsen, 93 Cal. App. 711.) Once a person is a member of a criminal conspiracy he continues to be a member and is liable as a co-conspirator until he withdraws by informing and bringing home to the knowledge of his confederates that he desires to entirely sever his relationship with his co-conspirators and will no longer be a member of the unlawful partnership. Until his withdrawal becomes actual and is communicated to his confederates he remains fully liable as a conspirator for all of the acts of the members of the conspiracy committed toward the accomplishment of the purpose of the conspiracy. (People v. Wilson, 76 Cal. App. 688; People v. Albritton, 110 Cal. App. 188; People v. Jones, 136 Cal. App. 722; People v. Corkery, 134 Cal. App. 294; People v. Madsen, 93 Cal. App. 711; People v. Graft, 61 Cal. App. 7; People v. Chait, 69 Cal. App. 2d 503; Loser v. Superior Court, 78 Cal. App. 2d 30.)

While there is no authority in point in this state our courts would no doubt follow the rule in other jurisdictions that notice of withdrawal by one conspirator to his confederates is not limited to verbal or written notice but may be by such act and conduct as clearly have the same effect.

Since there will be cases in which a conspirator, desiring to withdraw from the conspiracy, does not know all of its members and may even be wholly ignorant of the fact that certain persons are members thereof and it would be illogical and unreasonable to require him to give notice of his desire to withdraw from the conspiracy to persons whose participation in the conspiracy was wholly unknown to him, the requirements for withdrawal from the conspiracy would be satisfied if notice of withdrawal were given to all of the conspirators known to him.

Prosecution of Conspirators

Where the indictment charges the commission of the crime of conspiracy and all of the conspirators are jointly charged and tried and all but one of the defendants are found not guilty, the remaining conspirator cannot be found guilty of conspiracy and a verdict of guilty as to him would be invalid. (People v. Gilbert, 26 Cal. App. 2d 1; People v. MacMullen, 134 Cal. App. 81.) The reason for this rule is that when the jury by its verdict found that all the other defendants were not guilty such verdicts have the effect of a finding that there was no conspiracy and the one remaining defendant could not be guilty of conspiracy if he had no co-conspirator. If, however, in such a case so prosecuted, the action were dismissed during the trial as to all but one of the conspirators a conviction of the remaining defendant would be good since, while as to the defendants who were thus eliminated from the case the dismissal would operate as a bar to another prosecution to the same effect as if they had been acquitted by verdict, the dismissal would not have the effect of a finding that there was no conspiracy. (People v. Gilbert, 26 Cal. App. 2d 1.)

The rule just discussed has, however, no application to a case in which all of the conspirators are not jointly tried, nor does it apply to a trial on a charge of a criminal offense other than the crime of conspiracy. A conviction of two or more defendants is not dependent upon a conviction of all the conspirators (People v. Schwarz, 79 Cal. App. 98, 752) and, as all of the conspirators are principals in the crime of conspiracy, any one of them may be convicted even though, in a separate prosecution against the others, such others were acquitted. It is not essential to the conviction of a coconspirator that another or all other conspirators shall be tried and convicted (People v. Calhoun, 150 Cal. App. 2d. A.C.A. 527, indictment severed and defendant tried alone).

Husband and Wife as Conspirators

While it has been decided that a conspiracy cannot be formed where the sole parties to the agreement are husband and wife (People v. Miller, 82 Cal. 107; People v. Richards, 67 Cal. 412; People v. MacMullen, 134 Cal. App. 81; People v. Little, 41 Cal. App. 2d 797) on the common law theory that husband and wife are but one person and hence cannot make the agreement which is the very essence of the crime of conspiracy, this rule has no application where some third person joins with them (People v. Gilbert, 26 Cal. App. 2d 1; People v. Ingles, 117 Cal. App. 22) nor does it prevent the prosecution and conviction of either husband or wife or both, where a crime is committed by one as a result of an agreement between them that the crime be committed, if the prosecution is for the crime committed in pursuance of the agreement, for in such a case both the actual perpetrator and the other spouse would be guilty as principals. (People v. Eppstein, 108 Cal. App. 72.) In this connection it should be noted that while all conspirators are principals in the commission of a crime in pursuance of the object of a conspiracy, mere aiding and abetting or advising and encouraging another in the commission of a public offense is not of itself sufficient to constitute a conspiracy.

Prosecution of the Crime Committed in Pursuance of the Conspiracy

While the crime of conspiracy was originally intended to punish the agreement to commit a crime and at common law if a conspiracy to commit a felony, pursued by the conspirators, resulted in the commission of the felony the conspiracy was merged in the felony and there could only be prosecution for a felony, our law in such case permits a prosecution for either the conspiracy or the crime committed in pursuance thereof

(People v. McPhee, 26 Cal. App. 218; People v. Keyes, 103 Cal. App. 264; People v. Head, 9 Cal. App. 2d 647) and a conviction can be had of both the conspiracy to commit a crime and the consummated crime committed in pursuance of its purpose. (People v. Hoyt, 20 Cal. 2d 306; People v. Martin, 114 Cal. App. 392; People v. Eiseman, 78 Cal. App. 223; People v. Head, 9 Cal. App. 2d 647; People v. Chait, 69 Cal. App. 2d 503; People v. Gordon, 71 Cal. App. 2d 606.)

Where one or more conspirators are prosecuted for the commission of a crime committed in pursuance of the object of the conspiracy it is permissible for the prosecution to prove the conspiracy and the acts and declarations of the conspirators in pursuance of its object and it is not necessary that the indictment or information shall set forth that the crime was committed as a product of a conspiracy. (People v. La Vers, 27 Cal. App. 2d 336; People v. Siderius, 29 Cal. App. 2d 361; People v. Anderson, 34 Cal. App. 2d 48; People v. Kelly, 69 Cal. App. 558; People v. Tanner, 3 Cal. 2d 279; People v. Gregory, 12 Cal. App. 2d 7; People v. Ford, 25 Cal. App. 388; People v. Kelly, 69 Cal. App. 588; People v. Bryant, 101 Cal. App. 84; People v. Sampsell, 104 Cal. App. 431; People v. Duran, 57 Cal. App. 2d 369.)

Conspiracy to Commit Crime Outside of This State

A conspiracy to commit abortions upon women in Mexico, carried out by transporting the women to that country where they were operated upon, is not punishable in this state (People v. Buffum, 40 Cal. 2d 709).

Corroboration

Where the charge is that of conspiracy to commit abortion the woman upon whom the offense was committed must be corroborated as if the crime charged were abortion (People v. Buffum, 40 Cal. 2d. 709; People v. MacEwing, 45 Cal. 2d. 218).

CHAPTER XV.

HOMICIDE—MURDER—MANSLAUGHTER

Homicide, the killing of a human being, may be either justifiable or excusable, in which event it is not unlawful, or it may be felonious and therefore punishable. A felonious homicide is either murder or manslaughter unless, by special statute, provision is made for punishing a homicide committed under some specific state of facts such as the now repealed statute punishing negligent homicide caused by the unlawful operation of an automobile.

Corpus Delicti

The corpus delicti of a felonious homicide consists of two elements: (1) death of a human being and (2) an unlawful act or criminal agency causing such death. (People v. Frank, 2 Cal. App. 283; People v. Vicunia, 105 Cal. App. 145; People v. Bonilla, 114 Cal. App. 219; People v. Samaniego, 118 Cal. App. 165; People v. Durborrow, 130 Cal. App. 615; People v. Du Bois, 16 Cal. App. 2d 81; People v. Wray, 56 Cal. App. 2d 347; People v. Duenas, 74 Cal. App. 2d 846; People v. Williams, 151 Cal. App. 2d.........; People v. Miller, 37 Cal. 2d 801; People v. Amaya, 40 Cal. 2d 70, 75).

Mere proof of death by producing the dead body does not establish the corpus delicti (People v. Simonsen, 107 Cal. 345) even though it also be shown that death was the result of a bullet wound (People v. Frank, 2 Cal. App. 283) or violence (People v. Eldridge, 3 Cal. App. 648) and where there is no proof that the violent injury causing death was caused by some other person and was not accidental or suicidal (People v. Lewis, 36 Cal. 53) the evidence is insufficient to prove the corpus delicti. Where, however, the death is the result of bodily injury, and the circumstances surrounding the death show prima facie that it was not the result of accident or the act of the deceased, the corpus delicti of a felonious homicide is established. (People v. Searle, 33 Cal. App. 228; People v. Spencer, 58 Cal. App. 197; People v. Wilson, 61 Cal. App. 611; People v. Valenti, 61 Cal. App. 242; People v. Ybarra, 68 Cal. App. 259; Ex parte Heacock, 8 Cal. App. 420; People v. Clark, 70 Cal. App. 531; People v. Coker, 78 Cal. App. 151; People v. Valenti, 103 Cal. App. 249; People v. Vicunia, 105 Cal. App. 145; People v. Westlake, 106 Cal. App. 247; People v. Bonilla, 114 Cal. App. 219; People v. Durborow, 130 Cal. App. 615; People v. Wolcott, 137 Cal. App. 355; People v. Meyers, 7 Cal. App. 2d 351; People v. Du Bois, 16 Cal. App. 2d 81; People v. Crawford, 41 Cal. App. 2d 198; People

129

Prima facie—Literally on first Appearance.
" " Evidence—
" " "sufficient to est. the FACT in ques.

v. Bollinger, 196 Cal. 191; People v. Selby, 198 Cal. 426; People
v. Spinelli, 14 Cal. 2d. 137; People v. Cook, 15 Cal. 2d. 507;
People v. King, 132 Cal. App. 2d 642; People v. Misquez, 152
Cal. App. 2d........ A.C.A. 509). It is not necessary to proof of the
corpus delicti that there be evidence as to the means used to
accomplish the killing (People v. Bonila, 114 Cal. App. 219)
nor is it necessary that there have been an autopsy performed.
(People v. Wood, 145 Cal. 659; People v. Ong Git, 23 Cal. App.
148). Proof of the corpus delicti as to the identiy of the body is
sufficient if it shows "a reasonable probability" that the deceased was the man alleged to have been killed. (People v.
Mehaffey, 32 Cal. 2d 535). It is not necessary to support a con-
vition that the body be found (People v. Cullen, 37 Cal. 2d 614).

While not a part of the corpus delicti the law provides that:
"To make the killing either murder or manslaughter, it is
requisite that the party die within a year and a day after the
stroke received or the cause of death administered; in the com-
putation of which the whole of the day on which the act was
done shall be reckoned the first". (Penal Code, sec. 194.)
This provision is on the assumption that, unless death occurred
within the specified period, it was not the result of the unlawful act. The statute, however, merely prevents a prosecution
for murder or manslaughter and would not affect a prosecution
for the act preceding the death, such as a prosecution for felonious assault, administering poison with intent to kill, or attempt
or conspiracy to commit murder.

Proof by Circumstantial Evidence

While in some jurisdictions a contrary rule exists, in California both elements of the corpus delicti—death and the criminal agency causing the death—may be proved wholly by circumstantial evidence. People v. Mehaffy, 32 Cal. 2d 535; People v. Alviso, 55 Cal. 230; People v. Clark, 70 Cal. App. 531;
People v. Hamilton, 49 Cal. App. 30; People v. Watters, 202
Cal. 154; People v. Corales, 34 Cal. 2d 426; see also discussion under CORPUS DELICTI for the general rules governing
that subject.)

Cause of Death

To constitute a felonious homicide the unlawful act or
criminal agency causing death may be either an affirmative
act, a failure to act, or criminal negligence and such act, failure or negligence must be a proximate cause of the death but
not necessarily the sole cause of death. Thus, where the death
of the deceased was attributed to two causes, the wound inflicted by the accused and the shock of the operation for the removal of the bullet, the accused was held responsible for the

death because it was the shot fired by him which was the proximate cause which made the operation necessary and the fact that the victim of the shooting might have lived had there been no operation or that the operation was performed so negligently that death resulted and could have been avoided had it been carefully and skilfully performed would not change the rule and the court properly excluded evidence to show whether or not the deceased would have survived in the absence of resulting complications. (People v. Williams, 27 Cal. App. 297; People v. McGee, 31 Cal. 2d 229; People v. Freudenberg, 121 Cal. App. 2d. 564). Where deceased suffered a broken neck which proximately resulted in his death, the defense claimed that, but for his removal from the hospital a month later, he might have lived more than a year and a day and that the defendant could not be convicted if the death was accelerated to bring it within the year and a day period. The court rejected this contention and said, "The fact that death may have been accelerated becomes unimportant unless it can be shown that the accelerating cause was also the supervening cause in which case the defendant is relieved of responsibility for the death in that the unlawful act of the accused was manifestly not the proximate cause of the death." (People v. Clark, 106 Cal. App. 2d 271.) The element that death was caused by an unlawful act or acts may be established by circumstantial evidence (People v. Martina, 140 Cal. App. 2d 17).

Proximate Cause

The fact that the person killed was enfeebled by disease or physical injury, but for which the injury inflicted by the accused would not have caused death, is no defense where his act did cause the death and, even though the victim was on the verge of death, if the unlawful act accelerated his death, the defendant is guilty of an unlawful homicide. (People v. Moan, 65 Cal. 532.) Thus where the deceased had been struck a fatal blow on the head by a third party and the defendant thereafter fired fatal shots into the body of the deceased, the conviction of the defendant was sustained. (People v. Liera, 27 Cal. App. 346.) Where the bullet wound inflicted on the deceased injured the aorta but did not cause death for some time, the fact that death resulted from the wound reopening by reason of exertion on the part of the deceased would not relieve the accused from liability for the death as the original wound was the proximate cause of the death. (People v. Cord, 157 Cal. 562.) In another case the defendant struck the deceased with intent to kill him and left him lying in the road, believing him to be dead. The court held that the claim that death may have been caused by an automobile running over the unconscious but still living victim of the assault would not avail the defendant, since, even if the evidence would sustain this theory, the accused would still be liable for the death as his act of striking down his victim and leaving him helpless where he might be run over by a passing vehicle would be the proximate cause of the death. (People v. Fowler, 178 Cal. 657; People v. Johnson, 93 Cal. App. 484.) If, however, in such a case the injury inflicted upon the victim was not a fatal injury and the death was caused by the driver of the automobile intentionally running over the victim as he lay in the road it would be the act of the driver of the vehicle which would be the cause of death and it would be the driver who would be liable and guilty of the homicide. Where the evidence warranted the conclusion that after he was mortally shot in the abdomen and in intense pain the deceased, in his pain, thereafter cut his throat, inflicting a mortal wound which accelerated his death, the defendant who inflicted the bullet wound was held responsible for the death. (People v. Lewis, 124 Cal. 551, 555; People v. Dallen, 21 Cal. App. 770.) Even though the immediate cause of death is the surgical shock following the operation to save the life of the deceased, the stab wound inflicted by the defendant and which necessitated the operation is the proximate cause of the death. (People v. Nerida, 29 Cal. App. 2d 11.) Where the evidence showed that defendant placed a fatal dose of strychnine in a glass of milk and induced her husband to drink it and shortly after, attempting to arise, he fell, striking his head against the mantel and against an iron smoking stand and died thirty-five minutes later, it was held that if it be assumed that death was caused by a brain injury due to the fall, such injury was proximately caused by the administration of the poison and that the conviction was justified either on that theory or the theory that death was caused by the poison. (People v. Cobler, 2 Cal. App. 2d 375.) A conviction of murder was sustained where death was caused by coronary thrombosis contributed to by multiple bruises and abrasions and fractures of several ribs and the transverse process of two lumbar vertebrae (People v. Osborn, 37 Cal. 2d 380).

Unlawful Act as Cause of Death

The mere fact, however, that a person is killed while the law is being violated by the accused does not establish the unlawful act as the cause of death and, where a group of persons gathered together under circumstances constituting an unlawful assembly and one member of the party killed another, the unlawful assembly could not be considered a proximate cause of the death. (People v. Kerrick, 86 Cal. App. 542.) In People v. Studer, 59 Cal. App. 547, the defendant had pushed his mother and she fell to the steps, became unconscious in half an hour and died that night. The deceased was 86 years old and suffered from an enlarged heart and high blood pressure and death was caused by a hemorrhage of the brain and there was medical testimony that the acts of the defendant, together with the attendant excitement and commotion, superinduced the hemorrhage causing death. The case was reversed because of error in the admission of evidence as to a prior occurence. The Supreme Court, on hearing, withheld its approval of the statement in the opinion of the District Court of Appeal to the effect that, if a person creates a breach of the peace and through the excitement thus induced the death of a bystander by a brain hemorrhage, the death is the natural and probable consequence of such disturbance of the peace and such person may be convicted of manslaughter, but no comment is made by the Supreme Court as to the law if, as in the case at bar, there was also actual violence upon the person of the deceased.

A licensed cosmetologist who applies to a human being a solution of phenol greater than 10% is guilty of a misdemeanor and, where such application is the proximate cause of death, the crime of manslaughter, the killing of a human being in the commission of an unlawful act not amounting to a felony, would be committed (see People v. Penny, 44 Cal. 2d. 861).

One who makes an unlawful attack upon another, but through interference or other cause, the injury attempted is not inflicted, but the intended victim, justified in believing he is in danger of great bodily injury and in his attempt to escape or avoid the injury threatened, does an act which causes his death, such as jumping off a moving railroad train or running into the street where he is struck by a passing vehicle, the assailant is guilty of a felonious homicide since the death is the natural and probable result of, and caused by, the assault. Where a person, knowing that another is afflicted with a heart disease or suffering from some other ailment and that fear or excitement may and probably will cause his death, intentionally does that which produces in his victim terror, excitement or nervous shock and thereby causes his death, he is as guilty of a felonious homicide as if he had caused death by direct application of physical force.

Where death was caused by phenol poisoning as the result of applying a solution of phenol to the face of deceased as a means of facial rejuvenation, the lack of a license to practice cosmetology can not be said to be the proximate cause of death (People v. Penny, 44 Cal. 2d. 861).

Human Being—Newborn Child

The only question which has caused any difficulty in determining who is a "human" being with reference to the law of homicide relates to the question as to when the existence of a human being begins. It is now well settled that a child is considered a human being when it has been born and has established a circulation independent of its mother whether the umbilical cord has been severed or not. The killing of a child while in its mother's womb is not homicide, but if an injury is inflicted upon a child before its birth and it dies after it has been born and has established a circulation of its own the killing is a homicide. The question of whether after birth the child had breathed or not has no significance other than as being corroborative of the answer to the test question as to whether an independent circulation has been established.

The only California case on the question declares that when a child has reached a stage of development where it is capable of living an independent life as a separate being and where in the natural course of events it will live if given normal care and is in the process of being born, such child is a human being within the homicide statutes (People v. Chavez, 77 Cal. App. 2d. 621).

MURDER

"Murder is the unlawful killing of a human being with malice aforethought." (Penal Code, sec. 187.)

Malice

"Such malice may be express or implied. It is express when there is manifested a deliberate intention unlawfully to take away the life of a fellow-creature. It is implied, when no considerable provocation appears, or when the circumstances attending the killing show an abandoned or malignant heart." (Penal Code, sec. 188.)

The definition of "malice" in Section 7, Sub. 4 of the Penal Code is not applicable in a case of murder, as here Section 188 applies. (People v. Harris, 169 Cal. 53; People v. Chavez, 37 Cal. 2d 656.666).

Malice aforethought, either express or implied, is manifested by the doing of an unlawful and felonious act intentionally and without legal cause or excuse. It does not imply a preexisting hatred, enmity or ill will toward the person killed. (People v. Balkwell, 143 Cal. 259; People v. Fallon, 149 Cal. 287; People v. Fleming, 218 Cal. 300; People v. Coleman, 50 Cal. App. 2d 592; People v. Cornett, 61 Cal. App. 2d 98.)

Where a person, without provocation, fired shots into a group of people causing the death of one of them, an implication of malice is warranted and the circumstances show an abandoned and malignant heart although the perpetrator had no actual malice against any of the persons in the group (People v. Stein, 23 Cal. App. 108, conviction of first degree murder sustained). The ruthless disposition of the body of the deceased is evidence as to an abandoned and malignant heart on the part of the slayer (People v. Johnson, 203 Cal. 153).

Volitional Performance of Felony

When an unlawful act which results in the death of a human being is deliberately performed by a person who knows, or under the circumstances should know, that his conduct endangers the life of another, and it is executed without extenuating circumstances, provocation or sudden passion such as would reduce the killing to manslaughter, malice is presumed (People v. Hamblin, 68 Cal. 101; People v. Goslaw, 73 Cal. 323; People v. Semone, 140 Cal. App. 318; People v. Hoover, 107 Cal. App. 635) and this is true even if there was no intent to kill. (People v. Doyell, 48 Cal. 95; People v. Hubbard, 64 Cal. App. 27.)

Corpus Delicti

simple crime

In a murder charge the corpus delicti consists of two elements: the death of the alleged victim and the existence of some criminal agency as the cause either or both of which may be proved circumstantially or inferentially (People v. Amaya, 40 Cal. 2d 70, 75; People v. Miller, 37 Cal 2d 801, 806; People v. Williams, 151 Cal App. 2d........; People v. Misquez, 152 Cal. App. 2d........ A.C.A. 509; Penal Code sec. 1105) and, that corpus delicti having been established by independent evidence, and the degree of the crime not being a part of the corpus delicti, the circumstances of the murder and the degree of the murder may be shown by the extra judicial statements of the accused (People v. Williams; People v. Miller, supra).

Intent to Kill *does not automatically make it 1° murder*

While an intent to kill is an element which, if formed as the result of deliberation and premeditation, will make the subsequent killing murder of the first degree, it is not necessary that an intent to kill shall exist to raise a killing to the crime of murder. If there be malice aforethought, express or implied, the unlawful killing will be murder even though there is no intent to kill. The killing of a human being is also murder if it occurs in the perpetration or attempt to perpetrate a felony since the law attaches the felonious intent accompanying the contemplated crime to the act of killing and constitutes it murder even though the killing was unintended and accidental.

(People v. Doyell, 48 Cal. 94; People v. Oleson, 80 Cal. 122; People v. Hubbard, 64 Cal. App. 27; People v. Reid, 193 Cal. 491; People v. Milton, 145 Cal. 169; People v. Hoover, 107 Cal. App. 635; People v. Wallace, 2 Cal. App. 2d 238; People v. Robertson, 67 Cal. 646.)   The crime could also be murder, even though the killing was unintentional, if it occurs in the commission of an unlawful act not amounting to a felony but which in its consequences naturally tends to destroy human life. (People v. Hubbard, 64 Cal. App. 27; People v. Doyell, 48 Cal. 95.)   Even though no intent to kill existed, where a man strangled a woman intending to render her insensible and then committed a felonious sexual act upon her and she died from the strangulation, the crime was first degree murder (People v. Renoso, 109 Cal. App. 2d 793).

But even though the intent to kill is present the homicide may amount only to voluntary manslaughter or murder of the second degree where the killing is in the heat of passion (see People v. Valentine, 28 Cal. 2d. 121, 131). It is only where the killing is also wilful, deliberate and premeditated that the killing will amount to first degree murder (in addition, of course, to those murders which are expressly designated as of the first degree by statute by reason of the elements of poison, torture or lying in wait or which are committed in the perpetration or attempt to perpetrate one of the specified felonies, and which are generally referred to as statutory first degree murder.)   Those cases, such as People v. Burkhart, 211 Cal. 726, which declare that an intent to kill is a necessary element of the corpus delicti of first degree murder or murder of either degree, do not correctly state the law.   (People v. Thomas, 25 Cal. 2d 880; People v. Holt, 25 Cal. 59; People v. Bender, 27 Cal. 2d 164.)

Killing One Person in Attempt to Kill Another — Just as liable

Where a person wilfully, deliberately and premeditatedly attempts to kill one person but by mistake or inadvertence kills another the law transfers the intent to the killing to the same effect as if the person killed was the person intended. (People v. Suesser, 142 Cal. 367; People v. Brannon, 70 Cal. App. 225; People v. Piraroff, 138 Cal. App. 625; People v. Bender, 27 Cal. 2d 164; see also Transferred Intent.)

DEGREES OF MURDER

"All murder which is perpetrated by means of poison, or lying in wait, torture, or by any other kind of willful, deliberate and premeditated killing, or which is committed in the perpetration or attempt to perpetrate arson, rape, robbery, burglary, mayhem or any act punishable under section 288 is murder of the first degree, and all other kinds of murder are of the second degree.'' (Penal Code, sec. 189.)

The division of murder into degrees is to classify as murders of the first degree all murders which are willful, deliberate and premeditated and every other unlawful killing of a human being with malice aforethought is murder of the second degree.

First Degree—Statutory

The section specifies certain kinds of murder as murders of the first degree. These cases are of two classes:

First: Where the killing is perpetrated by means of poison, lying in wait or torture. Here the means used is held to be conclusive evidence of premeditation and such killings are, as a matter of law, always murder of the first degree.

Second: Where the killing is done in the perpetration or attempt to perpetrate arson, rape, robbery, burglary or mayhem or act punishable under section 288 of the Penal Code. Here the occasion is made conclusive evidence of premeditation.

Where a case falls within either of these two classes the test question: Is the killing willful, deliberate and premeditated is answered by the statute itself and if the accused is guilty of the killing he is guilty of murder in the first degree and the jury have no option but to find him guilty of murder in the first degree and, if the jury is properly instructed, the court will submit to the jury only two possible verdicts—not guilty or guilty of murder in the first degree.

A person who kills by torture or poison may intend only to inflict suffering not death . . . but where the jury has found that the killing was by poison, lying in wait or torture, it is not their function to go farther and draw inferences as to the manner of the formation and carrying out of an intent to kill. In such a case the question which the statute (Pen. Code sec. 189) affirmatively answers is not ''Is the killing willful, deliberate and premeditated?'', it is ''Is the killing murder of the first degree?'' Killings by the means or on the occasions under discussion are murders of the first degree because of the substantive statutory definition of the crime (People v. Valentine, 28 Cal. 2d 121, 136).

In spite of the clarity and unambiguity of the statute expressly declaring all murders of these two classes to be of the first degree our courts have had not infrequent occasion to pass upon the questions involved.

Court Decisions on Statutory First Degree Murder.

By Poison

A murder perpetrated by the use of poison can only be first degree murder. (People v. Cobler, 2 Cal. App. 2d 375, defendant administered strychnine to her husband who, in falling to the floor, fractured his skull and the court held that, if the strychnine taken by the deceased was sufficient to cause his death, the fact that the brain injury may have been fatal in itself did not affect defendant's responsibility.) The word "poison" includes any substance which, when applied to the human body externally or in any way introduced into the human system (without acting mechanically,) is capable of destroying life. It does not include a substance which may mechanically produce death such as powdered glass (People v. Van Deleer, 53 Cal. 147).

By Torture (popular form of kill.)

Where the murder is committed by torture it is murder of the first degree. (People v. Fountain, 170 Cal. 460, People v. Duggan, 61 Cal. App. 2d, 379 deceased strangled to death; (People v. Chandler, 208 Cal. 243, deceased beaten to death with a chair and a stick; People v. Murphy, 1 Cal. 2d 37, deceased beaten to death with a belt buckle and fists; People v. Cardoza, 57 Cal. App. 2d 489, deceased fatally beaten with an axe handle.) The language, "A defendant who, after inflicting injuries which later prove fatal, abandons his victim and leaves him to die without medical or other assistance, is guilty of murder by torture", in People v. Cardoza, 37 Cal. App. 2d 489, 498, is not the law (People v. Kerr, 37 Cal. 2d 11). Where defendant threw gasoline over his wife and set it on fire causing about three-fourths of her body to be covered by second and third degree burns which caused her death it was held that the verdict of first degree murder was sustainable as of a killing by torture (People v. Martinez, 38 Cal. 2d 556).

A murder is not, however, a killing by torture merely because the means used caused severe pain to the victim (People v. Bender, 27 Cal. 2d 164, killing with two blows of a blunt instrument held not a killing by torture). The language of the statute indicates that it is not sufficient that the victim suffered torture but that it must also appear, to constitute murder of the first degree, that the torture must have caused the death. "Physical suffering, a concommitant of all violent deaths, is not enough by itself to show murder by torture.

There must also be the intent that the victim shall suffer
(People v. Caldwell, 43 Cal. 2d. 864, woman struck on head
and choked to death not a killing by torture). To constitute a
killing by torture there must exist an intent to cause pain
and suffering, evidenced by the declared intent of the accused
or manifested by the nature of the acts and the attendant
circumstances. (People v. Heslen, 27 Cal. 2d 520; People v.
 Tubby, 34 Cal. 2d 72, aged man severely beaten and skull
fractured in an assault continuing about fifteen minutes.)
Where the defendant, without provocation, beat up a fellow
prisoner who occupied the same cell in jail, knocking his
head against the wall and, while the victim was helpless on
the floor and apparently unconscious, continued kicking him,
picked him up and dropped him on the floor on his head and
again kicked him in the face with his heel, tearing the flesh
and displacing an eye, and kicked him in the groin, death
being caused by shock and hemorrhage caused by multiple
fractures of the skull, it was held that the verdict of first
degree murder carrying the death penalty was sustainable
on either of three theories, killing by torture, in the perpetration of mayhem or as a wilful, deliberate and premeditated
killing (People v. Gilliam, 39 Cal. 2d 235). Where the de-
defendant, after making threats against his wife from whom
he was separated, indicating an intent to kill and a wish to
seek vengeance, went to her abode, armed with a hunting
knife, and, when she fled, followed her and inflicted numerous stab wounds on her upper arm, shoulder, hips, abdomen
and forearm and a fatal wound in the breast which pene-
trated the heart, struck her in the face and kicked her while
she was lying on the ground still alive, the evidence was held
sufficient to show a killing by torture (People v. Daugherty,
40 Cal. 2d. 876). Murder is perpetrated by torture when the
assailant's intent was to cause cruel suffering on the part
of the person who was the object of the attack either for
the purpose of revenge, extortion or persuasion to satisfy
some other untoward propensity (People v. Tubby, 34 Cal.
2d. 72; People v. Daugherty, 40 Cal. 2d. 876, 886). Where
the brutal and revolting manner in which defendant fatally
beat and mistreated a two and a half year old girl led inevitably
to the conclusion that he intended to cause pain and suffering,
the crime was first degree murder by torture (People v. Misquez, 152 Cal. App. 2d. A.C.A. 409).

Lying in Wait, By

The killing of a human being with malice aforethought by lying in wait is murder of the first degree. The words "lying in wait" do not refer to the position of the body of the perpetrator. There may be a "lying in wait" within the meaning of the law where the perpetrator is sitting down, standing or moving about. The gist of lying in wait is that the perpetrator places himself in a position where he is waiting and watching with the intention of inflicting bodily injury likely to cause the death of another or the intention of killing him. There is nothing in the law that requires that the "lying in wait" exist for or consume any particular period of time before the firing of the shot or other act which causes the death. It is only necessary that the act causing death be preceded by and the outgrowth of lying in wait.

Section 189, defining the degrees of murder, does not state that a "killing" perpetrated by poison, torture or lying in wait is murder of the first degree but speaks only of "murder" so perpetrated and, to bring a case within section 189 it must appear that the killing amounted to murder nor is that section amenable to the construction that a killing by any one of these means is murder if the act causing death was committed accidentally (People v. Thomas, 41 Cal. 2d 470). By the phrase "or any other kind of wilful, deliberate and premeditated killing" in section 189 the Legislature identified murder commited "by means of poison, or lying in wait, torture" as kinds of wilful, deliberate and premeditated killings. It is not necessary to constitute a murder perpetrated by means of lying in wait as murder of the first degree that there be an intent to kill but the act causing death must be an intentional act (People v. Thomas. supra). Lying in wait is not limited to instances of concealment in ambush (People v. Sutic, 41 Cal. 2d. 483; People v. Thomas, supra; People v. Tuthill, 31 Cal. 2d 92, 100).

Where the defendant concealed himself for the purpose of shooting the deceased unawares and the fatal shot was fired without any words from either of them it was held a case of lying in wait (People v. Miles, 55 Cal. 207), and where a defendant, actuated by a desire for revenge, hid himself in a bathhouse near the residence of the deceased, cutting holes in the side to see out, and, when deceased went by, shot and killed him it was held a killing by lying in wait and murder of the first degree. (People v. Vukich, 201 Cal. 290.) To constitute lying in wait it is not necessary that there be a con-

cealment in ambush and, where a person arms himself with
a deadly weapon and awaits at a place for the appearance of
his intended victim, who is killed when he puts in an appearance, the facts sustain the conclusion that the killing was by
lying in wait (People v. Tuthill, 31 Cal. 2d. 92). Where the
defendant waited for four hours near his wife's house, armed
with a pistol, and upon the departure of her visitor immediately
entered the house and shot his wife, "The elements of waiting,
watching and concealment were all present as a basis for the
instruction on lying in wait." (People v. Byrd, 42 Cal. 2d. 200.)
Where the defendant had the store of the victims, in which
they were shot to death, under observation for a period of
twelve days excluding Sundays and there was evidence that
the defendant was seen in the building and had been around
the rear of the building at about the time of the homicide, it
was held error to instruct the jury on the subject of murder
by lying in wait (People v. Merkouris, 46 Cal. 2d. 540), this
apparently overrules the Byrd case supra).

"In the Perpetration" of a Felony

Where the killing is done in the perpetration or attempt to
perpetrate arson, rape, robbery, burglary or mayhem or any
act punishable under section 288 the murder is, as a matter
of law, murder in the first degree and this is the law whether
the killing was intentional or unintentional or even accidental.
(Rape or Attempted Rape:—People v. Leins, 220 Cal. 510;
People v. Lindley, 26 Cal. 2d. 780); (Attempted Burglary —
People v. Di Donato, 90 Cal. App. 366); (Burglary:—People
v. Witt, 170 Cal. 104; People v. Hadley, 175 Cal. 118; People v.
Morlock, 46 Cal. 2d. 141); (Robbery:—People v. Waller, 14 Cal.
2d 693; People v. King, 13 Cal. 2d 521; People v. Goodwin, 9
Cal. 2d 711; People v. Anderson, 1 Cal. 2d 687; People v. Green,
217 Cal. 176; People v. Boss, 210 Cal. 245; People v. Perry, 195
Cal. 687; People v. Reid, 193 Cal. 491; People v. Denman, 179 Cal.
497; People v. Cabaltero, 31 Cal. App. 2d 52; People v. Petro,
13 Cal. App. 2d 245; People v. Meyers, 7 Cal. App. 2d 351; People v. Hendricks, 129 Cal. App. 156; People v. Samaniego, 118
Cal. App. 165; People v. Peterson, 29 Cal. 2d 69; People v.
Rye, 33 Cal. 2d 688; People v. Osborne, 37 Cal. 2d 380; People
v. Coefield, 37 Cal. 2d 865; (Mayhem:—People v. Nolan, 126
Cal. App. 623; People v. Vaiz, 55 Cal. App. 2d 714); (See
also:—People v. Kaye, 43 Cal. App. 2d 802; People v. Sutton,
17 Cal. App. 2d 561); (attempted burglary, People v. Walker,
33 Cal. 2d 250). Where the killing is not wilful, deliberate and
premeditated and it is the theory of the prosecution that the

killing was in the perpetration of one of the felonies named in
section 189 of the Penal Code the accused is not guilty of first
degree murder unless had the specific intent to commit such
crime (People v. Cheary, 48 cal. 2d. 301).

In such cases it is immaterial whether the killer used his
hands or fists or something more inherently dangerous (People
v. Cheary, 48 Cal. 2d. 301).

Where there is no eyewitness, the killing, as having been
done in the perpetration of one of the enumerated felonies,
may be established by circumstantial evidence. Thus where
a woman was found beaten to death and the physical evidence tended to show sexual intercourse shortly before death,
a conviction of murder in the perpetration of rape was sustained (People v. Reed, 38 Cal. 2d 423).

Where the defendant entered a house with intent to commit
an assault with a deadly weapon and therein killed one of
the occupants, the killing was murder in the first degree, in
the perpetration of a burglary (People v. Laya, 123 Cal. App.
2d. 7; People v. Morlock, 46 Cal. 2d. 141, entry with intent to
commit assault with a deadly weapon upon one person and
after entry defendant killed another).

A murder is committed "in the perpetration" or attempt to
perpetrate a felony not only when it is committed during or at
the time the corpus delicti of such felony is completed but also
when the killing occurs thereafter while the criminal act is in
continued operation, and until the object of the crime has been
accomplished, including the departure of the perpetrators from
the scene of the crime (see People v. Chavez, 37 Cal. 2d 656).
Where the defendants left the store where they had committed a robbery and an employee of the store followed them
and was shot and killed by one of the robbers it was held
that this was a murder of the first degree because it was
committed "in the perpetration of" the robbery (People
v. Boss, 210 Cal. 245) and in a similar case where, as they
were running down the street, one of the robbers shot and
killed a uniformed police officer who ordered them to stop, it
was held a first degree murder in the perpetration of a robbery (People v. Doyell, 204 Cal. 109) and where, as the perpetrators of a robbery were about to leave the scene of the
crime one of their number shot at some persons who were approaching and was himself fatally shot by one of his associates,
apparently because the deceased had fired at the approaching
strangers, it was held a first degree murder in the perpetration
of the robbery irrespective of the fact that it was one of the
conspirators who was killed. (People v. Cabaltero, 31 Cal.

App. 2d 52; People v. Henderson, 34 Cal. 2d 340). Where two
defendants, armed with revolvers, entered a liquor store and
robbed three persons therein and, when a retired police officer
entered the store to make a purchase, he was told by defendant
A to go to the back of the store with the others but, after taking a few steps he fired at A wounding him and they then
exchanged shots and one of the shots fired by A killed one of
the original robbery victims, the conviction of first degree
murder was sustained under the proximate cause theory (People v. Wilburn, 153 Cal. App. 2d. .... A.C.A. 199, cases discussed). When, after the property had been taken into the
custody of the robbers, the victim was fatally injured by them
to prevent the discovery of their criminal acts and to facilitate
their successful flight from the scene of the robbery, the crime
was first degree murder though there was no intent to kill
(People v. Rye, 33 Cal. 2d 688). Where the defendant struck
the deceased on the head with a cleaver, inflicting the fatal
injury, and then stole the money box of the victim, a conviction
of first degree murder was sustained even though the defend-
and contended that the thought of taking the money did not
occur to him until after he had struck the victim (People v.
Kerr, 37 Cal. 2d 11). If, in fact the intent to take the property
of the victim did not exist until after the fatal injury was inflicted, the killing would not be one in the perpetration or
attempt to perpetrate a robbery (People v. Carnine, 41 Cal.
2d. 384; People v. Hudson, 45 Cal. 2d. 121). Where the defendant contended that the killing did not occur in an attempt
to commit rape but arose out of an assault with intent to commit rape, the court held that the latter offense was merely an
aggravated form of attempt to commit rape (People v. Rupp,
41 Cal. 2d. 371).

First Degree Murder Other Than Statutory

In addition to those murders which, by reason of the means
used or the occasion, are expressly declared by the statute to
be murders of the first degree there is a much larger class of
cases of equal aggravation included in the definition of first
degree murder and which includes all wilful, deliberate and
premeditated killings. To constitute first degree murder under this definition the unlawful killing must be accompanied
by a deliberate and premeditated intent to take human life.
The intent to kill must be the result of deliberate premeditation and formed upon a pre-existing reflection and not upon
a sudden heat of passion sufficient to preclude the idea of
deliberation. There need be, however, no appreciable space
of time between the intention to kill and the act of killing—

they may be as instantaneous as successive thoughts of the mind. It is only necessary that the act of killing be preceded by, and the result of, a concurrence of will, deliberation and premeditation on the part of the slayer, and if such is the case, the killing is murder of the first degree, no matter how rapidly these acts of the mind may succeed each other, or how quickly they may be followed by the act of killing. (People v. Nichol, 34 Cal. 213; People v. Morine, 61 Cal. 369; People v. Suesser, 142 Cal. 354; People v. Maughs, 149 Cal. 253; People v. Fleming, 218 Cal. 300; People v. Larrios, 220 Cal. 236; People v. Garcia, 2 Cal. 2d 673; People v. Dale, 7 Cal. 2d 156; People v. Patubo, 9 Cal. 2d 537; People v. Mar Gin Suie, 11 Cal. App. 42; People v. Russo, 133 Cal. App. 468; People v. Carmen, 36 Cal. 2d 768.)

"Direct evidence of a deliberate and premeditated purpose to kill is not required. Deliberation and premeditation may be inferred from proof of such facts and circumstances as will furnish a reasonable foundation for such an inference." (People v. Gulbrandsen, 35 Cal. 2d 514. The defendant, who was staying at a cabin with two other men, secured a stone pestle and killed both men while they lay asleep in bed, there being no evidence of motive or mitigating circumstances, and a conviction of first degree murder carrying the death penalty was sustained; see also People v. Caratitativo, 46 Cal. 2d. 68). Where defendant attempted to commit a violation of section 288 upon a female child and, when she objected and started to scream, choked her with his hands and then tied a necktie tightly around her neck and then with intent to kill struck the victim two hammer blows on the temple, inflicted three stab wounds, two in her chest and one in her back, with an ice pick and inflicted six skull fractures with an axe and finally severed the spinal cord with a knife, this was held to show a prima facie case of a deliberate and premeditated murder (People v. Stroble, 36 Cal. 2d 615. Note that the statute has been since amended to make the killing in the perpetration or attempt to perpetrate a violation of section 288 of the Penal Code a first degree murder as a matter of law). No rule can be laid down as to the character or amount of proof necessary to show deliberation and premeditation and each case must depend on its own facts and the required deliberation and premeditation need not be directly shown by the evidence but may be inferred from the facts and circumstances (People v. Eggers, 30 Cal. 2d 676; People v. Werner, 111 Cal. App. 2d 264). Where, after an altercation in a bar in which the deceased

struck defendant a violent blow in the mouth, defendant stated
to a third person that he would get even with the deceased even
if he had to go to jail for it, went to his room and secured a
knife and returned to the bar where he walked over to where
the deceased was seated and, with the first stab, stabbed deceased through the heart and then stabbed him twice more
and, upon the arrival of the police, told them that he had done
it and hoped that the deceased died but, at the trial, claimed
to have no recollection of the occasion other than that he had
a few drinks at the bar and, three hours after the homicide,
defendant had a blood alcohol content of .299 per cent, held
that, in spite of the alcohol in his system, defendant's acts and
conduct showed almost conclusively that he reasoned and premeditated and that the evidence sustained the conviction of
first degree murder (People v. Keeling, 152 Cal. App. 2d ....
A.C.A. 9).

It must, however, be born in mind that a murder is not of
the first degree merely because the killer formed the intent to
kill before the act of killing for such a homicide may be either
voluntary manslaughter or murder of the second degree only,
for, to constitute first degree murder the killing must be the
outgrowth of deliberation and premeditation, the killer must
have considered the situation and have formed the decision to
kill as a course he desired and selected to pursue in preference
to some other course of conduct. (People v. Bender, 27 Cal.
2d 164; People v. Honeycutt, 29 Cal. 2d 52.)

Murder By Transferred Intent

"Where a person purposely and of his deliberate and
premeditated malice attempts to kill one person but by mistake or inadvertence kills another instead, the law transfers
the felonious intent from the object of his assault and the
homicide so committed is murder in the first degree" (People
v. Suesser, 142 Cal. 354, 367; People v. Sutic, 41 Cal. 2d 483).

First Degree Murder—Penalty

"Every person guilty of murder in the first degree shall
suffer death, or confinement in the state prison for life, at the
discretion of the court or jury trying the same, and the matter
of punishment shall be determined as provides in section 190.1"
(Penal Code, sec. 190; for proceedings under section 190.1 see
California Criminal procedure Chapter XXVI).

"The death penalty shall not be imposed, however, upon
any person who was under the age of 18 years at the time of
the commission of the crime. The burden of proof as to the age

of said person shall be upon the defendant." (Penal Code, sec. 190.1).

The earlier cases (People v. Welsh, 49 Cal. 174; People v. French, 69 Cal. 169, 180) which held that the death penalty must follow unless the jury by unanimous verdict fixed the penalty at life imprisonment and that if the jury could not agree as to the penalty, the death penalty should be imposed, remain only as legal curios for it is now settled that there can not be a valid verdict of guilty of murder in the first degree unless the jury by unanimous verdict fixes one of the two penalties (People v. Hall, 199 Cal. 451) except where the jury finds the defendant was under the age of eighteen years at the time the murder was committed, in which case, while the jury must, by unanimous vote, fix the penalty, it can only fix the penalty at life imprisonment. Where a defendant contends that he was so under the age of eighteen the burden of proof is upon him to establish that fact by a preponderance of evidence. (People v. Ellis, 206 Cal. 353.)

Second Degree Murder

Murder of the second degree is distinguishable from murder in the first degree in that, while the element of malice aforethought is present in both degrees of murder, in murder of the second degree the killing is not wilful, deliberate and premeditated. All unlawful killings with malice aforethought are murder and if a particular murder does not measure up to the requirements of murder of the first degree it must be murder of the second degree. "Murder of the second degree may be defined as the unlawful killing of a human being with malice aforethought but which killing is not perpetrated by means of poison, lying in wait or torture, is not wilful, deliberate and premeditated and is not committed in the perpetration or attempt to perpetrate arson, rape, robbery, burglary or mayhem." (People v. Thomas, 25 Cal. 2d 880; People v. Holt, 25 Cal. 2d. 59. To the offenses named in these decisions should also be added "or any act punishable under section 288 of the Penal Code" which was added by amendment to section 189 since these decisions).

An unlawful killing in the perpetration or attempt to perpetrate a felony, other than the six felonies listed in the statutory definition of first degree murder, is murder of the second degree unless there also exists a specific wilful, deliberate and premeditated intent to kill in which event the murder would be of the first degree. Thus, where the death resulted from a severe beating (People v. Tubby, 34 Cal. 2d. 72; People v. Cayer, 102 Cal. App. 2d. 643; People v. Burns, 109 Cal.

App. 2d. 425) or where, as the result of an unlawful attempt to commit an abortion, the death of the woman is caused, the crime is murder of the second degree (People v. Powell, 34 Cal. 2d 196; People v. Huntington, 138 Cal. 261; Huntington v. Superior Court, 5 Cal. App. 288; Ex parte Wolff, 57 Cal. 94; People v. Wright, 167 Cal. 1; People v. Northcott, 45 Cal. App. 706; People v. Schafer, 198 Cal. 717; People v. De Vaughn, 2 Cal. App. 2d 447; People v. Knowles, 7 Cal. App. 2d 398; People v. Hickok, 28 Cal. App. 2d 574), and where the death of a pedestrian was the result of the defendant having feloniously driven an automobile while under the influence of intoxicating liquor the crime was held murder of the second degree. (People v. Wallace, 2 Cal. App. 2d 238; see also People v. McIntyre, 213 Cal. 50.) It has also been held that an unlawful killing resulting from and growing out of a conspiracy to commit a felony is murder of the second degree unless committed under circumstances making the crime murder of the first degree (People v. Cowan, 36 Cal. App. 2d 231) and an unlawful killing in the perpetration of larceny from the person, a felony, is murder of the second degree. (People v. Bauman, 39 Cal. App. 2d. 587.) The killing of a human being in the perpetration of felony false imprisonment is murder and not manslaughter (People v. Zillbauer, 44 Cal. 2d. 43).

Killing in Unlawful Act Dangerous to Life

If the killing is done in the commission of an unlawful act intentionally performed, the natural consequences of which are dangerous to human life the crime is murder of the second degree even though the unlawful act amounts only to a misdemeanor (People v. Hubbard, 64 Cal. App. 27; People v. Avila, 41 Cal. App. 279; People v. Copley, 32 Cal. App. 2d 74) unless there be, in addition, a further element raising the crime to first degree murder.

Where there is no specific intent to kill and the killing does not fall within either of the two classes of statutory first degree murder and the circumstances show an abandoned and malignant heart the killing is murder of the second degree. (People v. Hubbard, 64 Cal. App. 27.) One who commits an act with disregard of the fact that he is thereby endangering and likely to cause the loss of human life, there being no adequate provocation, justification or excuse, evidences an abandoned and malignant heart and the malice necessary to constitute murder is implied if the death of a human being results. The deliberate and unnecessary discharge of a gun into a crowd of people, with utter disregard for the consequences, whereby a person is killed shows, in the absence of adequate provocation, such an abandoned and malignant heart as will make the killing second degree murder. Where a woman by beating and bruising of her child, allowing the injuries to become infected, and the child was not properly nourished, thereby caused the death of the child she was held guilty of second degree murder. (People v. Murillo, 119 Cal. App. 59.) Where an unlawful killing is without malice and in the heat of passion engendered by adequate provocation the crime is manslaughter, but if there be no adequate provocation the crime is murder, for here the lack of provocation injects into the crime the element of malice. Where the defendant on successive occasions knocked the deceased down and kicked him in the upper part of his body and about the head and death was caused by shock and asphyxia, respiration having been stopped by blood fluid in the lungs, the fact that there was no considerable provocation and that the circumstances of the unprovoked assault showed an abandoned and malignant heart sustained a conviction of second degree murder (People v. Mears, 142 Cal. App. 2d. 198).

Second Degree Murder—Penalty

"Every person guilty of murder in the second degree is punishable by imprisonment in the state prison from five years to life." (Penal Code, sec. 190.)

Burden of Proof in Murder

"Upon a trial for murder, the commission of the homicide by the defendant being proved, the burden of proving circumstances of mitigation, or that justify or excuse it, devolves upon him, unless the proof on the part of the prosecution tends to show that the crime committed only amounts to manslaughter, or that the defendant was justifiable or excusable." (Penal Code, sec. 1105.)

Where the record warrants the conclusion that the defendant killed the deceased and there is nothing to show provocation or justification, malice aforethought will be implied (People v. Cole, 47 Cal. 2d. 99).

The effect of this statute is that when the proof of the prosecution shows that the defendant killed the deceased and there is no evidence as to the circumstances of the killing from which it can be determined whether the killing was murder or manslaughter or justifiable or excusable, the burden of proving that the killing was less than murder, that it was either manslaughter or excusable or justifiable, passes to the defendant and, if he fails to produce evidence to either of such effects sufficient to raise a reasonable doubt, the killing amounts to murder. This section does not apply unless the trial is had upon an indictment or information

which charges murder (People v. Turner, 93 Cal. App. 133;
People v. Lopez, 81 Cal. App. 199) nor does the section apply
when the evidence of the prosecution shows that the offense only amounts to manslaughter or that the defendant
was justifiable or excusable. (People v. Turner, 93 Cal. App.
133; People v. Lloyd, 97 Cal. App. 664.) The section, however,
merely declares a rule of procedure and does not relieve the
prosecution of the burden of proving guilt beyond a reasonable doubt (People v. Cornett, 33 Cal. 2d 33) and merely imposes upon the defendant a duty of going forward with
evidence of mitigating circumstances (People v. Deloney, 4
Cal. 2d. 832). Section 1105 has no application whatever in
determining the degree of a murder but is pertinent only in
the determination of whether the homicide constitutes murder
or manslaughter or is justifiable or excusable (People v.
Valentine, 28 Cal. 2d. 121, 133 and cases cited).

Where the proof of the prosecution, though establishing the fact that the defendant killed the deceased, furnishes no basis for a finding that the killing was manslaughter
or was justifiable or excusable, the evidence has established
a case of murder. The earlier cases held that in such a
case it should be found that the murder was of the second
degree (People v. Knapp, 71 Cal. 1; People v. Ford, 85 Cal.
App. 258; People v. Howard, 211 Cal. 328; People v. Ross, 34
Cal. App. 2d 574; People v. De La Roi, 36 Cal. App. 2d 287;
People v. Wells, 10 Cal. 2d 610) and this would seem the correct construction in such a state of the record, but later
cases (People v. Spinelli, 14 Cal. 2d 137, 142; People v.
Cook, 15 Cal. 2d 507; People v. Cornett, 61 Cal. App. 2d 98)
have quoted and followed the language of People v. Johnson, 203 Cal. 153, 164. "The defendant offered no proof
to meet the burden which the law casts upon him and as there
was no claim of justification or excuse offered for the killing
of decedent or pretense that the proof tended to show that the
crime committed only amounted to manslaughter, the crime
was murder of the first degree." The quoting of this language
was not precisely in point in the Spinelli case for there the
defendant tried, though rather ineffectually, to prove that he
had acted in self defense. Since section 1105, when applicable,
merely declares the killing to be murder but says nothing as
to the degree, the degree of the murder should be fixed as of
the second degree unless there be evidence of circumstances
from which it could legitimately be inferred (as was easily
possible in the Spinelli case) that the crime amounts to first
degree murder. (So held in People v. Thomas, 25 Cal. 2d 880;

had to be more than bruise on breast

People v. Bender, 7 Cal. 2d 164; People v. McGee, 31 Cal. 2d 229; People v. Craig, 49 Cal. 2d. ......). *1° reduced to 2nd °*

Burden of Proof Sustained by Creating Reasonable Doubt

The burden of proving mitigation, justification or excuse, when cast upon the defendant under the provisions of section 1105, is sustained when the proof on his part, when taken into consideration with the other evidence in the case, is sufficient to raise a reasonable doubt on the issue thereby joined (People v. Roe, 189 Cal. 548; People v. Post, 208 Cal. 433; People v. Semone, 140 Cal. App. 318; People v. Scott, 123 Cal. 434; People v. Wells, 10 Cal. 2d 610, 622; People v. Carson, 43 Cal. App. 2d 40), and a preponderance of evidence is not required. (People v. Marshall, 112 Cal. 422; People v. Bushton, 80 Cal. 160.)

Effect of Admission Justifying the Killing

Where the evidence of the prosecution, exclusive of the extrajudicial statement of the defendant merely shows the death of a human being, and there is nothing to show whether it was felonious or not, and the statement of the accused, while admitting the killing, gives a version thereof showing that the defendant had acted in self defense and there was nothing in the evidence to contradict that version of the affair, the prosecution is not aided by section 1105 of the Penal Code for the effect of such admission in evidence is to show that, while the defendant killed the deceased, the killing was justifiable and the defendant is entitled to an acquittal. (People v. Estrada, 60 Cal. App. 477; People v. Salaz, 66 Cal. App. 173; People v. Toledo, 85 Cal. App. 2d. 577; People v. Coppla, 100 Cal. App. 2d. 766). This rule does not apply where there is evidence contradictory of the defensory matter in the defendant's admission (People v. Salaz, 66 Cal. App. 173; People v. Jacobs, 111 Cal. App. 2d. 281; People v. Rutland, 120 Cal. App. 2d. 798; People v. Freudenberg, 121 Cal. App. 2d. 564).

Contradictory does not apply

MANSLAUGHTER

"Manslaughter is the unlawful killing of a human being without malice. It is of two kinds:

1. Voluntary—Upon a sudden quarrel or heat of passion.

prosecutable

2. Involuntary—In the commission of an unlawful act, not amounting to a felony; or in the commission of a lawful act which might produce death, in an unlawful manner, or without due caution and circumspection; provided that this subdivision shall not apply to acts committed in the driving of a vehicle.

3. In the driving of a vehicle—

(a) In the commission of an unlawful act, not amounting to felony, with gross negligence; or in the commission of a lawful act which might produce death, in an unlawful manner, and with gross negligence.

(b) In the commission of an unlawful act, not amounting to felony, without gross negligence; or in the commission of a lawful act which might produce death, in an unlawful manner, but without gross negligence.

This section shall not be construed as making any homicide in the driving of a vehicle punishable which is not a proximate result of the commission of an unlawful act, not amounting to felony, or of the commission of a lawful act which might produce death in an unlawful manner. (Penal Code, sec. 192, as amended in 1945.)

The effect of the 1945 amendment of section 192, when considered in connection with the 1945 amendment of section 193 prescribing the penalty for manslaughter is to create two degrees of manslaughter where the death results from the unlawful driving of a vehicle. This form of manslaughter is a felony when the act causing death is with gross negligence but is a misdemeanor only when such act is without gross negligence.

Penalty

"Manslaughter is punishable by imprisonment in the State Prison for not exceeding 10 years, except that a violation of subsection 3 of section 192 of this code is punishable as follows: In the case of a violation of subdivision (a) of said subsection 3 the punishment shall be either by imprisonment in the county jail for not more than one year or in the State prison for not more than five years, and in such case the jury may recommend by their verdict that the punishment shall be by imprisonment in the county jail; in the case of a violation of subdivision (b) of said subsection 3, the punishment shall be by imprisonment in the county jail for not more than one year. In cases where, as authorized in this section, the jury recommends by their verdict that the punishment shall be by imprisonment in the county jail, the court shall not have authority to sentence the defendant to imprisonment in the State prison, but may nevertheless place the defendant on probation as provided in this code." (Penal Code, sec. 193, as amended in 1945.)

Murder and Manslaughter Distinguished

The distinction between murder and manslaughter is that in murder the killing must have been with malice aforethought while in manslaughter the malice, express or implied, which is the very essence of murder is absent. (People v. Samsels, 66 Cal. 99.) The presence or absence in a homicide of an intent to kill is not a determining factor in drawing the distinction, for murder may be committed where no intent to kill exists in the mind of the slayer, while in spite of an intent to kill a homicide may amount only to manslaughter. (People v. Crowey, 56 Cal. 42; People v. Freel, 48 Cal. 436; People v. Elmore, 167 Cal. 205; People v. Avila, 62 Cal. App. 306; People v. McGee, 99 Cal. App. 178; People v. Mears, 142 Cal. App. 2d 198 and cases cited). Neither does the distinction depend upon whether or not a deadly weapon was used in the killing. (People v. Crowley, 56 Cal. 36; People v. Cayer, 102 Cal. App. 2d 643).

The former rule that no words of abuse are sufficient to reduce a killing from murder to manslaughter (see People v. French, 12 Cal. 2d 120, 144) is no longer the law; the heat of passion which will reduce a killing to manslaughter may be generated by words of abuse or reproach (People v. Valentine 28 Cal. 2d. 121, 137, lengthy discussion).

One who has instigated a quarrel and has failed to desist from a fistic encounter may not resort to the use of a deadly weapon and, if he so arms himself and kills his adversary, the crime is murder and not manslaughter upon a sudden quarrel and heat of passion (People v. Hoover, 107 Cal. App. 635).

Where the death is the proximate result of the doing of an unlawful act the question of whether the killing is murder or manslaughter depends upon the nature of the unlawful act. If the act is a felony the crime is murder but if the unlawful act does not amount to a felony the crime is only manslaughter unless it is committed with malice aforethought. Thus while the crime is murder where death is caused by the performance of an illegal abortion because the latter offense is a felony, the crime would only amount to manslaughter if the abortion were lawful, as where it is performed to save life, but death were caused by the operation, an act which might produce death being performed negligently, without due caution and circumspection. (People v. Long, 15 Cal. 2d 590.)

Voluntary Manslaughter

When the fatal injury, though unlawful, is inflicted in the heat of passion, excited by a sudden quarrel and adequate provocation, the law, even though at the time of the killing there existed in the mind of the slayer the intent to kill his adversary, will disregard the intent and reduce the offense to manslaughter. In such case, although an intent to kill exists, it is not that wilful, deliberate and premeditated intent which would make the offense murder, but rather an intent formed under the influence of passion induced by adequate provocation and the product of a mind *Emotion* so disturbed as to be incapable of deliberation and premeditation. (People v. Freel, 48 Cal. 437.) But, if the intent to kill be the result of deliberation and premeditation, an unlawful killing in the carrying out of that intent will be murder, even though done upon a sudden quarrel or heat of passion. And if there exist the intent to kill, though not that deliberate intent characteristic of murder, and even though the unlawful killing was done in the heat of passion or upon a sudden quarrel it will be murder unless "there be adequate provocation." (People v. Turley, 50 Cal. 471; People v. Tamkin, 62 Cal. 468; People v. Jackson, 78 Cal. App. 442; People v. Chutuk, 18 Cal. 768, 771.) *Specific*

"Voluntary manslaughter is a wilful act, characterized by the presence of an intent to kill, engendered by sufficient provocation and the absence of premeditation, deliberation and (by presumption of law) malice aforethought." "To be sufficient to reduce a homicide to manslaughter the heat of passion must be such as would naturally be aroused in the mind of an ordinary, reasonable person, under the given facts and circumstances or in the mind of a person of ordinary self control" (People v. Bridgehouse, 47 Cal. 2d. 406).

Provocation

It is for the jury to say whether or not there was such provocation as would be adequate to reduce a homicide to manslaughter. The heat of passion which will reduce a voluntary homicide to manslaughter must be such a passion as would naturally be aroused in the mind of an ordinarily reasonable person under the same facts and circumstances and no defendant may set up his own standards of conduct and justify or excuse himself because in fact his passions were aroused unless the facts and circumstances were such as would also have been sufficient to arouse the passion of the ordinarily reasonable person. A man of violent passion or a man of mildness or a man of courage or one who is cowardly are judged according to the manner in which the facts and circumstances would react upon the ordinarily reasonable man if placed in the position of the defendant.

The basic inquiry is whether or not the reason of the accused was, at the time of the killing, so obscured or disturbed by passion—not necessarily fear and never the passion for revenge or the passion induced by following the intent to commit a felony—to such an extent as would render the ordinary reasonable person of average disposition to act rashly and without due deliberation and reflection and from this passion rather than from judgment. (People v. Logan, 175 Cal. 45; People v. Valentine, 28 Cal. 2d 121.)

It is for the jury to say whether the facts and circumstances are sufficient to believe that the defendant did, or create a reasonable doubt whether or not he did, commit the offense under a heat of passion. The rule of some of the earlier cases that neither provocation by words only or gestures without an assault nor trespass against the lands or goods are of themselves sufficient to reduce an intentional homicide from murder to manslaughter is no longer the law (People v. Valentine, 28 Ca. 2d. 121, 137 et seq., lengthy discussion).

Whether provocation is adequate to reduce the killing to manslaughter must be determined by considering whether the provocation would have created the passion offered in mitigation in the ordinary man under the same circumstances. If so, then it is adequate and will reduce the offense to manslaughter. If not, it is inadequate even though the degree of passion was great. A defendant may not set up as a basis of the test his own disposition, his readiness to anger and fly into a passion or his voluntary intoxication. Neither is a defendant of unusually calm even disposition to be judged by his personal tendencies. Every defendant's conduct must be measured by the reactions of the ordinary person of average disposition under like conditions. (see People v. Valentine, 28 Cal. 2d. 121, 137).

Heat of Passion

The law recognizes that where a felonious homicide springs from a sudden quarrel or heat of passion the circumstances, taken in connection with the state of mind of the slayer, may be such that the crime is less than murder. But it is not every flash or outburst of passion which will reduce the grade of the killing, for the passion must be such as would be aroused in the mind of the ordinarily reasonable person similarly placed. No defendant may set up his own standard of conduct and claim mitigation because in fact his passion was aroused unless the facts and circumstances were such as would have aroused such passion in the ordinarily reasonable man. And the exciting cause of such passion must be such as would naturally tend to cause men of average and ordinary disposition to act rashly or without deliberation. The fundamental question of the inquiry is whether or not the defendant's reason was obscured by passion, not necessarily fear, and never of course the passion of desire or for revenge. (People v. Valentine, 28 Cal. 2d 121; People v. Danielly, 33 Cal. 2d 336; People v. Golsh, 63 Cal. App. 609; People v. French, 12 Cal. 2d 720; People v. Manzo, 9 Cal. 2d 594; People v. Turley, 50 Cal. 469; People v. Jackson, 18 Cal. App. 442; People v. Logan, 175 Cal. 45; People v. Hurtado, 63 Cal. 288; People v. Mendenhall, 135 Cal. 344; People v. Webb, 143 Cal. App. 2d. 402). "One may not instigate a quarrel, become the aggressor in any affray, and without first seeking to withdraw from the conflict, kill his adversary and expect to reduce the crime to manslaughter by merely asserting that it was accomplished upon a sudden quarrel or in the heat of passion." (People v. Montezuma, 117 Cal. App. 125; People v. Hoover, 107 Cal. App. 635).

Cooling Period *(artificial concept)*

To reduce a killing from murder to manslaughter not only must there have been a sudden quarrel or heat of passion but the killing must have occurred while the killer was acting under the direct and immediate influence of such quarrel or heat of passion. It follows that where the influence of the sudden quarrel or heat of passion has ceased to obscure the mind of the accused and sufficient time has elapsed for angry passion to cool and reason to control his conduct it will no longer mitigate a killing to manslaughter. The question as to whether the "cooling period" has elapsed is not measured by the standard of the accused but the duration of the cooling period is the time which it would take the average man or ordinarily reasonable person to have cooled and for his reason to have returned. (People v. Golsh, 63 Cal. App. 609; People v. Ashland, 20 Cal. App. 168, 170; People v. Gingell, 211 Cal. 532; People v. Fossetti, 7 Cal. App. 629.)

Involuntary Manslaughter *Negligent Act*

Involuntary manslaughter may occur:

1. In the commission of an unlawful act not amounting to a felony;

2. In the commission of a lawful act which might produce death in an unlawful manner; or

3. In the commission of a lawful act which might produce death without due caution and circumspection. (Penal Code, sec. 192.)

Killing in Commission of Unlawful Act

Manslaughter in the commission of an unlawful act not amounting to a felony bears a strong resemblance to murder where the killing is in the perpetration of a felony, but to be manslaughter the unlawful act which causes the death must not be a felony. One who violates laws designated to prevent injury to others is guilty of involuntary manslaughter if death is caused thereby (People v. Mitchell, 27 Cal. 2d. 678, 683, operating an automobile at excessive speed; People v. Penny, 44 Cal. 2d. 861, unlicensed cosmetologist using solution of phenol on face of customer). Where a person in committing an assault and battery without aggravating circumstances, without malice and without intent to kill unintentionally causes the death of his victim, as by his falling and fracturing his skull, the crime is manslaughter. (People v. Lee, 44 Cal. App. 2d 64; People v. Pierce, 46 Cal. 2d 731; People v. Munn, 65 Cal. 211; People v. Miller, 114 Cal. App. 293; People v. Anderson, 120 Cal. App. 5; People v. Kruse, 30 Cal. App. 2d 559; People v. Mullen, 7 Cal. App. 547; People v. McManis, 122 Cal. App. 2d. 891). Where defendant assisted deceased in the latter injecting a narcotic into his arm from which the latter died, defendant was held guilty of manslaughter since he aided and abetted such unlawful act of the deceased (People v. Hopkins, 101 Cal. App. 2d. 704). Where defendant kept other persons away while his associate committed an assault and battery resulting in the death of a third person a conviction of manslaughter was sustained on the theory that defendant had aided and abetted in the unlawful act causing death (People v. Le Grant, 76 Cal. App. 2d. 148; People v. Cayer, 102 Cal. App. 2d. 643). Where a person unlawfully exhibits a loaded gun in an angry manner (a misdemeanor under Penal Code, sec. 417) or is negligent in holding a loaded gun, and the gun is discharged and kills another, the offense is involuntary manslaughter (People v. Southack, 39 Cal. 2d. 578). And where the defendant drove an automobile at an unlawful rate of speed on the wrong side of the road, thereby killing a human being, "the case involved the doing of unlawful acts and not lawful acts" and the crime was held manslaughter on this theory. (People v. Seiler, 57 Cal. App. 195; People v. Cunningham, 64 Cal. App. 195; People v. Kelly, 70 Cal. App. 519. See, however, similar cases under **Killing in Commission of Lawful Acts, infra,** where convictions were sustained on that theory.)

Where a person applied a phenol solution to the face of a customer, an unlawful act because the accused was thereby practicing cosmetology without a license, and death resulted therefrom, a conviction of manslaughter could be sustained on the theory of death resulting from an unlawful act and also as resulting from a want of due caution and circumspection (People v. Penny, 44 Cal. 2d. 861).

Where the defendant, a pharmacist, without criminal intent or negligence, compounded a prescription which caused the death of a child by reason of an adulterant, not known to the defendant, included in one of the ingredients of the prescription the court held that to be an "unlawful act" within the meaning of section 192 of the Penal Code "the act in question must be dangerous to human life or safety and meet the conditions of section 20 of the Penal Code which requires that to constitute a crime there must be a union of act and intent or criminal negligence and, because of this and the element that the act of compounding the prescription with the adulterated ingredient was committed through ignorance and mistake of fact which disproved criminal intent, the conviction of manslaughter could not be sustained (People v. Stuart, 47 Cal. 2d. 167).

Causal Connection between unlawful act & the ensuing death.

It must be noted, however, that the fact that a person was committing an unlawful act and that he caused the death of another is not sufficient to make him guilty of manslaughter for, to justify a conviction there must be a causal connection between the unlawful act and the ensuing death. Where the unlawful act is not the cause or at least one of the causes proximately resulting in the death there is no felonious homicide. (People v. Kelly, 70 Cal. App. 519; People v. Kerrick, 86 Cal. App. 542; see also opinion of Supreme Court in People v. Studer, 59 Cal. App. 547, and discussion under Homicide—Unlawful Cause of Death).

Killing in Commission of a Lawful Act

The doing of an act ordinarily lawful which results in the death of a human being may be manslaughter where the act, being one which might cause death, is performed in an unlawful manner or without due caution and circumspection. It is difficult in cases of manslaughter committed in the operation of a motor vehicle to state positively that a particular case falls exclusively within a particular class of involuntary manslaughter. Where the cause of death is the driving of an automobile in violation of a provision of the California Vehicle Act such driving usually amounts to the driving of an automobile, an act lawful in itself but one which might produce death, without due caution and circumspection (People v. Thomas, 58 Cal. App. 308; People v. Seiler, 57 Cal. App. 195) but a conviction could also be sustained on the theory that death was caused by the doing of an unlawful act not amounting to a felony or on either or both theories. (People v. Cunningham, 64 Cal. App. 12.)

Convictions of manslaughter have been sustained where the death of a human being was the proximate result of:— driving beyond the speed limit while under the influence of intoxicating liquor (People v. Cunningham, 64 Cal. App. 12; People v. Kelly, 70 Cal. App. 519; People v. Haskins, 29 Cal. App. 2d 715); striking a pedestrian standing close to a street car track waiting for an approaching car (People v. Wilson, 193 Cal. 512); speeding at a poorly lighted intersection (People v. Black, 116 Cal. App. 90); unlawful speed driving on the left side of the road (People v. Seiler, 57 Cal. App. 195); speeding (People v. Emmons, 114 Cal. App. 26; People v. Wilson, 78 Cal. App. 2d 108); on the left side of street (People v. Eckartsberg, 133 Cal. App. 1); on left side of the road (People v. Collins, 195 Cal. 325; People v. Marconi, 118 Cal. App. 683); on left side of street with dim lights (People v. Thomas, 58 Cal. App. 308); under the influence of intoxicating liquor (People v. Collins, 195 Cal. 325; People v. Freeman, 16 Cal. App. 2d 101; People v. Crowe, 48 Cal. App. 2d 666); and driving in a manner expressly forbidden by law (People v. Seiler, 57 Cal. App. 195); driving into an intersection against a stop signal (People v. Barnett, 77 Cal. App. 2d 299; driving on the left side of the road without justification or excuse (People v. Abbott, 101 Cal. App. 2d. 200). (See also cases under Manslaughter in Driving a Vehicle, infra.)

Where death was caused by phenol poisoning, resulting from the application by defendant to the face of the deceased, as a face rejuvenating procedure, of a liquid containing phenol as an ingredient, the court, in applying that portion of section 192, subdivision 2, of the Penal Code (the killing of a human being in the commission of a lawful act which might produce death, in an unlawful manner or without due caution and circumspection) says that since the defendant knew that the substance used was poisonous and dangerous the jury could have concluded that the treatment was one which might produce death (People v. Penny, 44 Cal. 2d. 861).

Death Resulting From Negligence

In order to impose criminal liability for a homicide caused by negligence under subdivision 2, section 192, of the Penal Code there must be a higher degree of negligence than is required to establish negligent default on a mere civil issue.

The negligence must be aggravated, culpable, gross or reckless, that is, the conduct of the accused must be such a departure from what would be the conduct of an ordinarily prudent or careful man under the same circumstances as to be incompatible with a proper regard for human life or, in other words, a disregard of human life or an indifference to consequences. The facts must be such that the fatal consequences of the negligent act could reasonably have been foreseen. It must appear that the death was not the result of misadventure but the natural and probable result of a reckless or culpably negligent act (People v. Penny, 44 Cal. 2d. 861).

Where the death of a human being results from playing with or careless handling of a loaded firearm, there being no intent to injure any one, and the firearm is discharged, the offense is involuntary manslaughter, the killing being caused by the doing of a lawful act without due caution and circumspection. (People v. Sica, 76 Cal. App. 648; People v. Southack, 39 Cal. 2d 578; People v. Carmen, 36 Cal. 2d 768; People v. Freudenberg, 121 Cal. App. 2d. 564, and cases cited and discussed) defendant accidentally discharged a gun he had jokingly pointed at deceased; see also People v. Searle, 33 Cal. App. 228, in which the court says, "An unintentional homicide committed through the negligent handling of a firearm in a way indicating a reckless disregard of life is manslaughter. It is negligence to point a firearm at another without examining it to see whether or not it is loaded, or to handle or use it in a place where a discharge is likely to injure another"; see also People v. Freudenberg, 121 Cal. App. 2d. 564).

Imminent Peril

A person who, without negligence on his part, is suddenly and unexpectedly confronted with peril arising from either the actual presence or the appearance of imminent danger to himself or to others, is not expected or required to use the same judgment and prudence that is required of him, in calmer and more deliberate moments. His duty is only to exercise the care and caution that an ordinarily prudent person would be required to exercise in the same situation. If, at the moment of such peril he does what to him appears to be the best thing to do, and if his choice and manner of action are the same as might have been followed by any ordinarily prudent person under the same conditions and circumstances, he does all that the law requires of him, even though, in the light of after events, it should appear that a different course would have been better and safer. (See People v. Boulware, 41 Cal. App. 2d. 268).

Manslaughter in the Driving of a Vehicle — *Felony where the Act was committed with gross negligence.*

By the amendment in 1945 of section 192 of the Penal Code manslaughter, where death results from the driving of a vehicle, in the commission of an unlawful act not amounting to a felony or in the commission of a lawful act which might produce death in an unlawful manner, it is made a felony where the act was committed with gross negligence but, where the act was without gross negligence, it is only a misdemeanor. (Note: See also Killing in Commission of a Lawful Act, Supra).

Gross Negligence — *Not necessary that there exist & be present either wilfulness or wantonness*

Since the amended section does not define term "gross negligence" it must be assumed that the legislature intended that these words should be construed as having the same meaning as had been applied to them in the decisions of our appellate courts. In these cases gross negligence is defined as being such a degree of negligence or carelessness as to amount to the want of slight diligence, an entire failure to exercise care or the exercise of so slight a degree of care as to justify the belief that there was an entire indifference to the safety of the property and persons of others and a conscious indifference to consequences (People v. Costa, 40 Cal. 2d 160; and cases cited). To constitute gross negligence, it is not, however, necessary that there exist and be present either wilfulness or wantonness. (See Kastel v. Stieber, 215 Cal. 37, 46; Krause v. Rarity, 210 Cal. 644, 654; Cooper v. Kellogg, 2 Cal. 2d 504, 510.)

Where a driver did not see his victim until the instant of impact or not at all he is guilty of gross negligence (People v. Flores, 83 Cal. App. 2d. 11, victim struck while standing two feet from cars parked at the curb of a city street). Where the defendant, on a two lane highway the left side of which was occupied by a truck, driving at least 80 miles an hour, ran into the rear of a car ahead of him which was proceeding at about 50 miles an hour and caused the death of two of the occupants, conviction of manslaughter with gross negligence was sustained (People v. Markham, 153 Cal. App. d. A.C.A. 273).

The killing of a pedestrian standing in a marked safety zone, the visibility being good, when defendant swerved his car and crossed the safety zone was held manslaughter with gross negligence (People v. Leitgeb, 77 Cal. App. 2d. 764).

Where the defendant on a clear night, driving upon a fairly well lighted dry street at a high rate of speed, ran into the rear of a slow moving vehicle, having made no attempt to slow down, and a person riding in the defendant's car was killed by the collision, a verdict of manslaughter with gross negligence was sustained (People v. Clark, 106 Cal. App. 2d 271). Where the evidence showed that appellant and one Coffin were racing on a city street and, in crossing an intersection, Coffin's car struck another car causing the death of its driver but appellant succeeded in missing the car, a conviction of manslaughter with gross negligence was sustained the court holding that both appellant and Coffin were acting jointly in a series of acts which proximately caused the death (People v. Kemp, 150 Cal. App. 2d. 654).

Without Gross Negligence

Where the act causing death was "without gross negligence" a conviction may be had of misdemeanor manslaughter and the negligence need amount only to ordinary negligence (People v. Wilson, 78 Cal. App. 2d. 108). Where the driver was blinded by approaching lights but, instead of stopping, proceeded and killed a pedestrian in a cross-walk a conviction was sustained (People v. Lett, 77 Cal. App. 2d. 917).

The driving of a vehicle in a 25 mile an hour district at a rate in excess of 55 miles per hour is such an unlawful act that, if it proximately causes the death of a human being, the crime is involuntary manslaughter (People v. Mitchell, 27 Cal. 2d. 678, 683, and cases cited).

Death Resulting from Failure to Perform a Legal Duty

Where a duty is by law imposed upon a person and, through his failure to perform such duty the death of a human being is caused the crime is manslaughter, provided that such failure was not malicious, in which latter event the crime would be murder.

Thus the failure of a parent to furnish necessary food or medical aid to his child, thus causing the death of the child; the failure of an employer to furnish the protection to the life of his employe which the law requires, resulting in the killing of the employe; or a physician who failed in his duty to his patient to such an extent that the case did not receive that care and attention and skill which is exercised by the average physician in the same location and the patient died through such neglect—these are examples of manslaughter through failure to perform a legal duty. The test is:—was the duty a legal duty and was it one which, if left unperformed, would naturally result in causing or accelerating death? (See People v. Morales, 60 Cal. App. 2d 196, death of child caused by neglect, depriving of food and beatings resulting in death from pneumonia; People v. Montecino, 66 Cal. App. 2d 85, death caused by the failure of a person under contract as a practical nurse to properly care for a patient; see also People v. Murillo, 119 Cal. App. 59.) The mere failure on the part of a pregnant woman to make proper preparation for her expected confinement, the child being born without medical or other service, being born alive but dying shortly thereafter, is not sufficient to warrant her conviction of manslaughter predicated solely upon such failure and would be warranted only if death were proven to be due not to natural causes but some affirmative act of the accused (see discussion in State v. Osmus, 275 Pac. 2d. series, 469).

Contributory Negligence

The fact that the deceased or some other person was guilty of negligence which was a contributory cause of the death is no defense to a criminal charge since a criminal prosecution is not an action on behalf of the injured party but for an offense against the state. (People v. Collins, 195 Cal. 325; People v. Leutholtz, 102 Cal. App. 493; People v. Wilson, 193 Cal. 512; People v. Black, 111 Cal. App. 90; People v. Marconi, 118 Cal. App. 683; People v. Eckartsberg, 133 Cal. App. 1; People v. Barnett, 77 Cal. App. 2d 299; People v. Rodgers, 94 Cal. App. 2d 166). Negligence of the deceased would be a defense only if such negligence was the sole cause of the death (People v. Lett, 77 Cal. App. 2d 917).

CHAPTER XVI.

EXCUSABLE AND JUSTIFIABLE HOMICIDE *(Killing)*

Homicides which do not constitute crimes and which are not punishable are either excusable or justifiable. (Penal Code, sec. 199.)

Felonious is either murder or manslaughter)

Excusable Homicide *(Killing)*

"Homicide is excusable in the following cases:

1. When committed by accident and misfortune, in lawfully correcting a child or servant, or in doing any other lawful act by lawful means, with usual and ordinary caution, and without any unlawful intent. *Concur*

2. When committed by accident and misfortune, in the heat of passion, upon any sudden and sufficient provocation, or upon a sudden combat, when no undue advantage is taken, nor any dangerous weapon used, and when the killing is not done in a cruel or unusual manner." (Penal Code, sec. 195.)

Excusable homicide is distinguished from felonious homicide in that to be excusable the killing of the human being must have been by concurrence of both accident and misfortune. Where all the elements of the corpus delicti of a felonious homicide are present the fact that the death was accidental or unexpected is no defense. (People v. Kerrick, 86 Cal. App. 542; People v. Attema, 75 Cal. App. 642; People v. Hubbard, 64 Cal. App. 27; see also, under Murder, cases holding that a killing in the perpetration of a felony is murder even though the killing is accidental.)

Subdivision 1 of section 195 excuses those killings in which a person, doing a lawful act by lawful means and in a lawful manner, having no intention of doing any act which would constitute a crime and conducting himself with usual and ordinary care and caution, by accident and misfortune causes the death of another. The distinguishing characteristics of this form of excusable homicide are that the person whose act caused the death must have been doing a lawful act in an entirely lawful manner and the death must have been by accident and misfortune.

Subdivision 2 of section 195 refers to a type of excusable homicides which at first blush appears to bear a similarity to voluntary manslaughter but is readily distinguishable since to be excusable the intent to kill must be absent and the homi-

163

cide must be by accident and misfortune upon provocation both sudden and sufficient or upon a sudden combat. Also to be excusable there must have been no undue advantage taken nor any dangerous weapon used and the killing must have been in a manner neither cruel or unusual.

Even though the death was by misfortune and accidental, and was not intended or anticipated, the homicide will not be excused if it was caused by an unlawful act, or by the doing of a lawful act in an unlawful manner, or without due caution and circumspection. (People v. Attema, 75 Cal. App. 642; People v. Hubbard, 64 Cal. App. 27; and cases under MURDER and MANSLAUGHTER.)

Justifiable Homicide by Public Officers

"Homicide is justifiable when committed by public officers and those acting by their command in their aid and assistance, either:

1. In obedience to any judgment of a competent court; or,

2. When necessarily committed in overcoming actual resistance to the execution of some legal process, or in the discharge of any other legal duty; or,

3. When necessarily committed in retaking felons who have been rescued or have escaped, or when necessarily committed in arresting persons charged with felony, and who are fleeing from justice or resisting such arrest." (Penal Code, sec. 196.)

The characteristic of a justifiable homicide is that while it is the result of an intentional act likely to cause death, or even an intent to kill, the occasion is such that the law justifies the killing as a means of protecting and enforcing the rights of the individual, the community or the state.

Subdivision 1 justifies a public officer where a death sentence is carried out under a valid warrant and in a lawful manner and will also justify a homicide resulting from the lawful carrying out of a valid judgment.

Subdivision 2 justifies homicides committed by public officers in the lawful enforcement of their legal duties where the attempt to carry out such duties is met with such actual resistance that the homicide is necessarily committed. But to justify a homicide under such circumstances the killing must be actually necessary or must reasonably appear so and if the duty could reasonably be performed without such killing it would not be justified.

Homicide in Making an Arrest

Subdivision 3 relates particularly to the case of a peace officer making a lawful arrest in a lawful manner or in lawfully retaking a person charged with or convicted of a felony who has been rescued or who has escaped. An officer is justified when making an arrest for a felony in using as much force to compel the submission to arrest as appears reasonably necessary to accomplish the arrest with safety to himself, (People v. Brite, 9 Cal. 2d 666) provided the arrest is lawful and is attempted in a lawful manner and a homicide in the use of such force will be justified; but if, under the circumstances, viewed from the standpoint of the ordinarily reasonable and prudent person, such extreme force was not reasonably necessary and the arrest could have been accomplished without it, the homicide is not justifiable. (People v. Newsome, 51 Cal. App. 42.)

Where the arrest is only for a misdemeanor, the law does not justify the use of force to the extent of a homicide (People v. Wilson, 36 Cal. App. 589; People v. Lathrop, 49 Cal. App. 63, 67; People v. Bost, 107 Cal. App. 550), it being the policy of the law that it is better to allow a misdemeanant to escape than to kill him. If the person sought to be arrested makes an assault upon the person attempting the arrest the justification of the latter in resisting with force is governed not by subdivision 3 but by the law of self defense.

Justifiable Homicide Generally

"Homicide is also justifiable when committed by any person in either of the following cases:

1. When resisting any attempt to murder any person, or to commit a felony, or to do some great bodily injury upon any person; or,

2. When committed in defense of habitation, property, or person, against one who manifestly intends or endeavors, by violence or surprise, to commit a felony, or against one who manifestly intends and endeavors, in a violent, riotous or tumultuous manner, to enter the habitation of another for the purpose of offering violence to any person therein; or,

3. When committed in the lawful defense of such person, or of a wife or husband, parent, child, master, mistress, or servant of such person, when there is reasonable ground to apprehend a design to commit a felony or to do some great bodily injury, and imminent danger of such design being ac-

complished; but such person, or the person in whose behalf
the defense was made, if he was the assailant or engaged in
mutual combat, must really and in good faith have endeavored
to decline any further struggle before the homicide was committed; or,

4. When necessarily committed in attempting, by lawful
ways and means, to apprehend any person for any felony committed, or in lawfully suppressing any riot, or in lawfully
keeping and preserving the peace.'' (Penal Code, sec. 197.)

Bare Fear Not Sufficient

''A bare fear of the commission of any of the offenses
mentioned in subdivision two and three of the preceding section, to prevent which homicide may be lawfully committed,
is not sufficient to justify it. But the circumstances must be
sufficient to excite the fears of a reasonable person, and the
party killing must have acted under the influence of such
fears alone.'' (Penal Code, sec. 198.)

To Prevent a Felony

Subdivision 1 of section 197 must be applied and construed
with the qualification that a homicide to prevent the commission of a felony is justified only when it is reasonably
necessary, when the felony is such that force must be used to
prevent it, and when other means of preventing the commission of the felony would apparently fail.

Obviously an attempt to commit a felony involving no immediate injury to life or property would not justify a homicide to prevent its accomplishment. To render a killing reasonably necessary it is not required that the necessity be actual;
it is sufficient if it be apparently necessary even though in the
light of after acquired information it be learned that the danger
did not in fact exist. (See People v. Roe, 189 Cal. 548.) Thus
where the owner, believing a felony would be committed, conceals himself in his store and, upon the forcible entry of two
persons, fires a shot and kills one of them, the homicide is
justified and he has the right to assume that the intruders are
armed and he is not called upon to give the intruders any
warning before shooting. (Nakashima v. Takara, 8 Cal. App.
2d 35; see also Brooks v. Sessagesenio, 139 Cal. App. 679,
wherein the owner was held justified in killing a person who
was endeavoring to enter his chicken house in the night time,
an act constituting the felony of an attempt to commit a
burglary.)

Abandonment of Attempt by Felon

The law will not, however, justify the killing of a felon who has desisted from his attempt and fled, for there the occasion which would justify a homicide has ceased. (People v. Conkling, 111 Cal. 616.)

Defense of Habitation

Subdivision 2 of section 197 justifies the killing of one who manifestly intends or endeavors by violence or surprise to commit a felony against the habitation, property or person of another where such killing is necessary or appears to the slayer as a reasonable man to be necessary to prevent the commission of such felony. It also justifies the killing of a person who is obviously engaged in the endeavor to violently and tumultuously force his way into the house or habitation of another for the purpose of doing some violence to one of the inmates; here too, however, the killing must be either actually or apparently necessary. (See People v. Walsh, 43 Cal. 447, 449; People v. Flanagan, 60 Cal. 2, 3, 4.)

Killing of Trespasser

In cases involving the killing of a trespasser the distinction must be drawn between those cases in which the trespasser evidences an intention of committing a felony and those in which no such intent is apparent. "While one may use force, if necessary, to remove an intruder who refuses to leave after being requested to depart, it must not be assumed that he may intentionally kill another solely in defense of habitation. No person may intentionally kill merely because he cannot otherwise effect his object although the object sought to be effected is right. He can kill only in defense of life or person or to prevent a felony." (People v. Hubbard, 64 Cal. App. 27.) If a trespass is unaccompanied by any felonious attempt the law does not admit the force of the provocation sufficient to warrant the owner to make use, in repelling the trespass, of a deadly weapon (People v. Corlett, 67 Cal. App. 2d 33); and if, under such circumstances, the owner slays the trespasser with a deadly weapon, he is guilty of a felonious homicide. (People v. Doyell, 48 Cal. 85, 93.) But where the trespasser goes with the intent and means to commit a felony if necessary to accomplish his purpose the owner may, if it be apparently necessary, slay the trespasser to prevent the commission of a felony. (People v. Payne, 8 Cal. 341.) And "a person assailed in his own house is not bound to retreat from the house to avoid violence, even though a retreat may safely be made. If the intruder resists his ejection and assaults the lawful occupant, the latter need not retreat, but, in protecting his person, he may, if necessary, intentionally take the intruder's life if he has reason to believe and does believe that his own life is in danger or that he is in danger of receiving great bodily harm." (People v. Hubbard, 64 Cal. App. 27; see also People v. Will, 79 Cal. App. 101.)

Defense of Persons

Subdivision 3 of this section is particularly directed to homicides committed in defense of the person of the slayer or those related to him in the manner therein set forth. The circumstances under which such a homicide is justifiable are alike in either instance—there must be a reasonable ground to apprehend a design to commit a felony or to do some great bodily injury and real or apparent imminent danger of such design being accomplished. This rule is more fully covered under the subject of self defense next following and the principles there stated are equally applicable to homicides in defense of a person other than the slayer. (See People v. Roe, 189 Cal. 548; People v. Ortiz, 63 Cal. App. 662.)

Any person who sees a violent felony attempted is justified in using violence to prevent it. Thus, if, when assaulted with a fist, the person assailed draws a gun and the circumstances are not such as to warrant a belief on his part that he is in danger of death or great bodily injury and he nevertheless evidences the intent to kill his opponent, a third person is justified in killing him if it is apparently necessary to do so to prevent the threatened homicide. (People v. Travis, 56 Cal. 251.) Where a situation exists in which a person would be justified in killing another in self defense, a third person who handed him a gun with which he killed his assailant is also justified. (People v. Ortiz, 63 Cal. App. 662.)

Self Defense

The law justifying a homicide by a person acting in his own defense is founded upon necessity and in order to justify the taking of human life upon this ground it must appear to the slayer, as a reasonable man, not only that he has reason to believe and does believe that he is in danger of receiving great bodily harm but it must also appear that the facts and circumstances are such that an ordinarily reasonable man, placed in the position of the slayer, knowing what he knew and seeing what he saw, would believe that it was necessary for him to use in his own defense such force and means as might cause the death of his adversary in order to avoid the threatened great bodily injury. (People v. Morine, 61 Cal. 367; People v. Scroggins, 37 Cal. 675; People v. Howard, 112 Cal. 141; People v. Bruggy, 93 Cal. 482; People v. DeWitt, 68 Cal. 586; People v. Bradfield, 30 Cal. App. 721; People v. Head, 105 Cal. App. 331.) The acts which a person may do and justify under the law of self defense depend upon his own conduct, the conduct of his adversary and the circumstances attending the encounter. (People v. Hecker, 109 Cal. 462; People v. Brown, 15 Cal. App. 393.)

Bare Fear Not Sufficient

A bare fear on the part of the slayer that he in danger of great bodily injury is not sufficient to justify a homicide but the circumstances must be such that a reasonable and prudent person, situated as was the slayer, would believe that the danger of great bodily injury was present and imminent and the killing must have occurred under a well founded belief that it was necessary to save himself from great bodily harm. The accused cannot justify a killing by setting up his own standards and his own fear and belief of the danger threatened and of the necessity of killing. He who acts in self defense does so at his own peril; his act must be that of the ordinary careful and prudent individual and the jury are the judges of the reasonableness of his conduct. (People v. Glover, 141 Cal. 239; People v. Lynch, 101 Cal. 229; People v. Head, 105 Cal. App. 531; People v. Albori, 97 Cal. App. 537.) The fact that the defendant was in a peculiar mental state at the time of the homicide does not afford him any other or different right of self defense than if such mental state did not exist. (People v. Spraic, 87 Cal. App. 724; People v. Wells, 33 Cal. 2d 330.)

Danger Created by Act of Slayer

The doctrine of self defense presupposes that he who would avail himself of its benefits has, without fault on his part, found himself threatened by the danger of great bodily injury to avert which the law gives him the right to use all force necessary to his own protection. But the plea is not available to a person where he wilfully and without necessity for his own protection creates the danger with which he is threatened. (People v. Finali, 31 Cal. App. 479.) The right of self defense

is not available to a defendant who has sought a quarrel with
the design to force a deadly issue and thus, through his fraud,
contrivance or fault, to create a real or apparent necessity
for making a felonious assault. (People v. Hinshaw, 194 Cal.
1; People v. Burns, 27 Cal. App. 227; People v. Finali, 31 Cal.
App. 479.)

"Whenever an assault is brought upon a person by his own
procurement, or under an appearance of hostility which he
himself creates, with a view of having his adversary act upon
it, and he so acts, the plea of self defense under such circumstances is not available." (People v. Albori, 97 Cal. App.
537; People v. Westlake, 62 Cal. 303.) Where the accused,
while attempting to commit a burglary, was lawfully fired
upon by a watchman such action by the watchman did not
justify the accused in then firing back at the watchman.
(People v. Di Donato, 90 Cal. App. 366.)

Effect of Previous Threats

Previous threats by the deceased, unaccompanied by some
hostile act, do not justify a homicide. (People v. Gonzales, 33
Cal. App. 340; People v. Lynch, 101 Cal. 229.)

What Force May Be Used

Since the law will justify a homicide only when it appeared to the slayer, as a reasonable man, to have been necessary, it must also appear that the degree of resistance on the
part of the slayer was not clearly disproportionate to the injury
threatened. Thus, ordinarily, there would be no justification
for killing if the threatened injury was an assault and battery, though if it were under circumstances justifying a belief
that such assault and battery would cause grievous bodily
injury and the killing appeared necessary to prevent imminent danger thereof it would be justified. (People v. Campbell, 30 Cal. 312; People v. Williams, 32 Cal. 287; People v.
Hurley, 8 Cal. 390; People v. Morine, 61 Cal. 371; People v.
Anderson, 57 Cal. App. 721.)

"The person assaulted is justified in using so much force
as is necessary to his defense. To repel a slight assault the
person is not authorized to resort to measures of great violence.
He will not be justified in doing those acts that are calculated
to destroy the life of the assailant unless the assault is of such
character as to endanger his life or inflict on him great bodily
injury or to excite his fears as a reasonable man that such
would be the result. . . . The law does measure the degree of

the force that may be used to repel the assault; and although
it will not make the measurement with a nice hand and hold
the person assaulted to accountability for force slightly disproportionate to the assault yet it will hold him responsible
for a clearly marked excess." (People v. Shimonaka, 16 Cal.
App. 117, 123; People v. Campbell, 30 Cal. 312.)

Fear Based on Appearances (one may act on such)

Where the appearances are such as would justify, in the
mind of an ordinary prudent individual, placed in the same
position, the belief that one is in imminent danger of death
or great bodily injury, he may safely act on appearances and
kill his assailant if that course appears reasonably necessary,
and the killing will be justified although it may afterwards
be learned that the appearances were not representative of
the true facts and there was in fact no such danger. (People
v. Herbert, 61 Cal. 544; Nakashima v. Takara, 8 Cal. App. 2d
35; Brooks v. Sessagesimo, 139 Cal. App. 679; People v.
Hatchett, 63 Cal. App. 2d 144.) Thus, if an assailant were to
reach for the region of his hip pocket under circumstances
warranting the belief that he was about to draw a deadly
weapon and use it upon the person with whom he was quarrel-
ing, the latter would be justified in acting on these appearances and his right of self defense would not be impaired if
in fact the assailant was unarmed and had merely been reaching for his handkerchief.

Infliction of Injuries After Danger Has Passed

The right of self defense exists only as long as the danger
threatened continues to exist. Thus where the circumstances
justify a person in shooting his adversary in self defense and
the assailant has fallen to the ground or is rendered incapable
of inflicting injury, and the danger of great bodily injury with
which he was threatened has been removed, if the accused
thereafter fires a fatal shot into the body of his disabled adversary, such latter shot is not justified and the defendant is
guilty of felonious homicide regardless of the fact that the first
shot was justified under the law of self defense. (People v.
Barrett, 22 Cal. App. 780, 786; People v. Brown, 62 Cal. App.
96; People v. Smith, 61 Cal. App. 259; People v. McCurdy, 140
Cal. App. 499; People v. Spinelli, 14 Cal. 2d 137; People v
Keys, 62 Cal. App. 2d 903.)

No Duty to Retreat

The rule of some jurisdictions that, except when the encounter occurs in his own home, a person can not lawfully kill in self defense until he has retreated "to the wall" unless the danger threatened would be increased by retreat has no standing in California. It is well settled in this state that, in the exercise of his right of lawful self defense, a person may not only stand his ground and defend himself against the attack but he may pursue his assailant until he has secured himself from danger if that course is reasonably necessary. (People v. Kinowacki, 39 Cal. App. 2d 376; People v. Campanella, 39 Cal. App. 2d 384; People v. Weber, 26 Cal. App. 413; People v. Orosco, 73 Cal. App. 580; People v. Turner, 93 Cal. App. 133; People v. Cyty, 11 Cal. App. 702; People v. Flanelly, 128 Cal. 83; People v. Maughs, 149 Cal. 253; People v. Robertson, 67 Cal. 646; People v. Newcomer, 118 Cal. 263; People v. Lewis, 117 Cal. 186; People v. Hardwick, 204 Cal. 582; People v. Hatchett, 56 Cal. App. 2d 20; People v. Zuckerman, 56 Cal. App. 2d 366; People v. Holt, 25 Cal. 2d 59), and this is the rule even though he might more easily have gained safety by flight or by withdrawing from the scene. (Cases last cited.)

"When a defendant seeks or induces the quarrel which leads to the necessity for killing his adversary, the right to stand his ground is not immediately available to him, but, instead, he must first decline to carry on the affray and must honestly endeavor to escape from it. Only when he has done so will the law justify him in thereafter standing his ground and killing his antagonist." (People v. Holt, 25 Cal. 2d 59; People v. Soules, 41 Cal. App. 2d 298, 314.)

Where a person has reason to believe and expect that he will be attacked by another with a deadly weapon if he goes to a certain place, yet he has the right to go to such place and is not expected to go out of his way to avoid the attack. If he be attacked upon going to such place his right to self defense is measured by the same standards as if the attack were unexpected. (People v. Gonzales, 71 Cal. 569.)

Self Defense In Making an Arrest

Where a peace officer is making a lawful arrest in a lawful manner for either a felony or a misdemeanor and is attacked either by his intended prisoner or by some third party he has the same right of self defense as any other person who is attacked while he is acting lawfully (People v. Wilson, 36 Cal. App. 589), and he is under no obligation to retire to avoid a conflict. (People v. Hardwick, 204 Cal. 582.) Where a person believes that he is about to be arrested he cannot justify his act in drawing a gun and shooting the officer upon the ground that he believed the arrest was unwarranted if there was no reason to believe that the officer intended any unlawful injury. (People v. Giacobbi, 83 Cal. App. 12.)

Self Defense—Counter Attack

Where a person has made a felonious assault upon another or has created appearances justifying such other person in making a deadly counter attack the original assailant cannot kill his adversary and avail himself of the plea of self defense until he has first and in good faith declined further combat and has notified his assailant that he has abandoned the contest. Such notice must be brought home to his adversary so that he may be advised that he may safely cease his counter attack; in other words, he must have actual notice of the desire to terminate the contest. If the circumstances are such that by reason of injuries inflicted by the aggressor or the suddenness of the counter attack or other cause the aggressor cannot so notify him, the situation created is through the first assailant's fault and he is not justified in killing even though his life is in danger. (People v. Hecker, 109 Cal. 463; People v. Britton, 106 Cal. 628; People v. Scott, 123 Cal. 628; People v. Hoover, 107 Cal. App. 635; Penal Code, sec. 197, subd. 3.)

Killing in Mutual Combat

A killing is not justified if it is committed in a duel or deadly contest entered into by the consent of the parties. (People v. Hecker, 109 Cal. 451, 462.) Subdivision 3 of section 197 of the Penal Code provides that if a person is "engaged in mutual combat" he "must really and in good faith have endeavored to decline any further struggle" before he can justify a felonious homicide on the ground of self defense. The duty to decline further struggle before a killing in a mutual combat is the same as in the case of a person who was the original assailant. (See preceding topic, **Self Defense—Counter Attack.**) If two persons are engaged in a mutual combat, each of the parties to the agreement to fight is in effect an assailant and he cannot justify the killing of his adversary, no matter how great his danger of death or bodily injury may be, until he has in good faith endeavored to decline any further struggle and has brought home to the knowledge of his opponent his desire to cease fighting and has given his opponent an opportunity to cease the conflict. If, after the opponent has been so notified and afforded an opportunity to desist, such opponent continues the contest, the law regards such continuance of the conflict as a new assault against which his adversary may exercise his right of self defense.

When parties by mutual understanding engage in a conflict with deadly weapons and death ensues to either, the slayer is guilty of Murder. (People v. Bush, 65 Cal. 129.)

CHAPTER XVII.

ASSAULTS

"An assault is an unlawful attempt, coupled with a present ability, to commit a violent injury on the person of another." (Penal Code, sec. 240.)

By repeated usage the term "simple assault" has become a term recognized in the criminal law and is used synonymously with the word "assault" as defined in section 240 of the Penal Code. (People v. Egan, 91 Cal. App. 44.) Simple assault is a misdemeanor. (Penal Code, sec. 241.)

Since an assault is an attempt, the rules generally applicable to the law of attempts apply to cases of simple assault and also to felonious assaults. To constitute an assault there must be more than intention or preparation or words of threats; there must be an overt act from which the inference can be drawn that violent injury to the person of another was intended. It is not necessary that the injury intended or any injury at all shall have been inflicted; the attempt coupled with the present ability to inflict an unlawful injury are the essential elements of the offense (People v. Roder, 24 Cal. App. 477) and, where the unlawful attempt to injure another has been made, the fact that the assailant failed in his attempt, or was prevented or desisted from actually inflicting the injury he was attempting, does not affect his guilt. (People v. Bird, 60 Cal. 7; People v. Johnson, 131 Cal. 511; People v. Bowman, 6 Cal. App. 749.)

The words "violent injury" as used in defining the crime of assault do not import that the injury attempted must be a severe one or cause great physical pain but merely mean the unlawful application of physical force upon the person of another. "The kind of physical force is immaterial; it may consist in the taking of indecent liberties with a woman or laying hold of her and kissing her against her will." (People v. Bradbury, 151 Cal. 675; People v. Bumbaugh, 48 Cal. App. 2d. 791; People v. Whalen, 124 Cal. App. 2d. 713; People v. McCoy, 25 Cal. 2d. 177; People v. Flummerfelt, 153 Cal. App. 2d. ......). An unlawful attempt by one person to slap another, to spit on him, or to stop him from proceeding on his way or to push him aside would constitute a simple assault.

Attempt to Inflict Injury

The attempt to injure in many cases of assault is usually very evident, especially when actual injury results, and in

desist–to stop

175

other cases may be inferred from the circumstances. Where the defendant theatened to kill the prosecutrix and seized an axe and started toward her and she fled and escaped, his act was held to be an assault. (People v. Yslas, 27 Cal. 630; see also People v. Hunter, 71 Cal. App. 315 and cases under **Assault With a Deadly Weapon—Elements of Offense.** In a case in which defendant drove his automobile at night without lights on a public highway and struck a pedestrian it was held that the jury was warranted in finding that the defendant, by such conduct on his part, intended the natural and probable consequences of his acts. (People v. Vasquez, 85 Cal. App. 575). Where the defendant intentionally accelerated his automobile and steered directly at the victim striking the latter on the legs, a conviction of assault was sustained (People v. Flummerfelt, 153 Cal. App. 2d. ...... A.C.A. 112).

In order to constitute an assault there must be something more than a mere menace or threat. Thus the firing of a gun without aiming or pointing it at, and without intent to injure anyone, would not be an assault (People v. Carmen, 36 Cal. 2d 768). There must be violence begun to be executed. But where there is a clear intent to commit violence accompanied by acts which, if not interrupted, will be followed by personal injury, the violence is commenced and the assault is complete. A defendant need not have been in striking distance to inflict the blow he threatened; it is enough if he comes sufficiently near to the person threatened to warrant the belief that the blow will be instantly struck unless the intended victim defends or flees. (People v. Yslas, 27 Cal. 630.)

Present Ability

It is an essential element of the corpus delicti of an assault that in attempting the unlawful injury the defendant must have the "present ability" to inflict the injury threatened, that, so far as he personally is concerned, the means he intends to use in the manner in which he threatens and intends to use them will inflict the injury intended. Pointing an empty revolver at another at a distance of fifteen feet would not be an assault if the gun were not loaded because there is no present ability to carry the injury threatened into execution (People v. Bennett, 37 Cal. App. 324; People v. Sylva, 143 Cal. 62; People v. Montgomery, 15 Cal. App. 315), but the mere fact that the defendant testified that the gun was not loaded would not insure his acquittal, for the jury might be justified in finding from the circumstances, particularly the acts, declarations and conduct of the accused, that it was in fact loaded, as for example where the defendant evidenced a desire to shoot another by threatening to kill him and pointed the gun at his intended victim. (People v. Montgomery, 15 Cal. App. 315.) It is not, however, essential that the gun be pointed at the victim if the facts show an attempt to shoot. (See cases under **Assault With a Deadly Weapon.**) The fact that the gun with which the injury is threatened was not immediately capable of being fired, as, for instance, where it was first necessary to cock the gun or to operate its mechanism to transfer a cartridge from the magazine into the empty barrel, does not prevent the conclusion as a matter of law that the defendant had the present ability to commit an assault by an attempt to shoot. (People v. Simpson, 134 Cal. App. 646.)

The "present ability" referred to in the definition of assault relates solely to the ability of the person attempting the unlawful injury and does not refer to the fact that, by reason of some fact or condition not controlled by the defendant, the intended injury cannot be inflicted. If one person rush at another in an attempt to strike him but is prevented from carrying out his intention by being seized by a third person or by the intended victim; or if the person fired at were protected by a bullet proof vest or if the cartridge misfired or if the defendant slipped and fell and the gun were discharged into the ground, there would still be the present ability even though the attempt was unsuccessful. (People v. Yslas, 27 Cal. App. 630.)

Battery (Completed Attempt)

"A battery is any willful and unlawful use of force or violence upon the person of another." (Penal Code, sec. 242.) Battery is a misdemeanor. (Penal Code, sec. 243.) Battery includes and implies an assault for there can be no battery without an assault, but there can be an assault without a battery (People v. Daniels, 137 Cal. 192; People v. Helbing, 61 Cal. 620.) Battery is a consummated assault and the offense of simple assault is a necessarily included offense where battery is charged. (People v. Heise, 217 Cal. 671.) The force or violence necessary to constitute a battery need not be great nor need it necessarily cause pain. Detaining a person by grasping his coat sleeve, pushing a person out of the way or pouring water or spitting upon him would constitute sufficient force to furnish that element of a battery. It is not necessary that the assailant directly apply the force. Thus it would be a battery to apply a whip to a horse, causing it to run away with the rider, or to drive a team of horses or an automobile against a person or for one automobile driver to force another off the road or to set a dog on another which actually bites or touches him, if the act is willful and unlawful.

Felonious Assaults

Where an assault is committed with the specific intent to commit a felony this compound assault is a felony punishable by specific statute; viz., an assault with intent to commit murder is punishable by from one to fourteen years in the state prison (Penal Code, sec. 217), assaults with intent to commit rape, the infamous crime against nature, robbery or grand theft are punishable by from one to twenty years in the state prison (Penal Code, sec. 220) and an assault with intent to commit any felony other than those just enumerated is punishable by imprisonment in the state prison for not less than one nor more than five years in state prison or not exceeding one year in the county jail or by a fine of five hundred dollars or by both such fine and imprisonment. (Penal Code, sec. 221.)

Assault by Life Convict

If a person serving a life sentence in a state prison with malice aforethought commits an assault with a deadly weapon or by means of force likely to produce great bodily injury the penalty is death (Penal Code, sec. 4500) and if a convict in the state prison serving a term less than life commits such an assault the penalty is imprisonment in the state prison for not less than one year (Penal Code, sec. 4501) or any term of years up to life imprisonment. (Penal Code, sec. 671.)

Section 4500 is constitutional (People v. Jefferson, 47 Cal. 2d. 438).

It is not required that the assault be made with intent to kill (People v. McNabb, 3 Cal. 2d. 441.) The words "malice aforethought" denote the purpose and design of the assaulting party in contradistinction to accident and mischance (People v. McNabb, 3 Cal. 2d. 441, 456; People v. Wells, 33 Cal. 2d. 330, 338; People v. Silva, 41 Cal. 2d. 778, 782; People v. Berry, 44 Cal. 2d. 426). Section 4500 is constitutional (People v. Berry, 44 Cal. 2d. 426).

Section 4500 of the Penal Code is applicable not only to a prisoner whose term has been fixed at life imprisonment but also to a prisoner sentenced for an offense for which the penalty may be life imprisonment and as to whom no lesser penalty has been fixed (People v. Wells, 33 Cal. 2d 330; People v. Jefferson, 47 Cal. 2d. 438). An essential element of the offense is that the assault be committed with malice aforethought, by purposes and design (People v. Silva, 41 Cal. 2d. 778).

If death results from the assault, the findings of the autopsy surgeon and his opinion as to the cause of death are relevant to the amount of force used and admissible (People v. Berry, 44 Cal. 2d. 426).

Felonious Assaults by Reason of Means Used

Other assaults are made felonious by reason of the means used:— assault with a deadly weapon or by means of force likely to produce great bodily injury is punishable by imprisonment in the state prison by from one to ten years, or in a county jail not exceeding one year, or by fine of five thousand dollars, or by both such fine and imprisonment; administering any narcotic, anaesthetic or intoxicating agent with intent to facilitate the commission of a felony (Penal Code, sec. 222) is punishable by imprisonment in the state prison by a term of not less than six months or more than five years (Penal Code, secs. 18, 18a) and an assault with caustic chemicals carries a penalty of one to fourteen years in state prison (Penal Code, sec. 244). An attempt to wreck a railroad train, car or engine is punishable by imprisonment in the state prison for life without possibility of parole (Penal Code, sec. 218) and if the attempt is successful the penalty is either death or life imprisonment without possibility of parole and where any person suffers bodily harm the penalty is death (Penal Code, sec. 219). Any person who does an unlawful act with intent to wreck a vehicle operated by a common carrier and doing bodily harm and thereby wrecks the same and causes bodily harm is punishable by from one to fourteen years in the state prison. (Penal Code, sec. 219.1.) An assault with intent to commit a crime necessarily embraces an attempt to commit said crime but an attempt to commit such crime does not necessarily include an assault (People v. Akens, 25 Cal. App. 373, 374; People v. Rupp, 41 Cal. 2d. 371).

Assaults With Intent to Commit Felonies

In every charge of assault with intent to commit a particular felony the specific intent to commit that felony is an essential part of the corpus delicti and to sustain a conviction it must be established not only that an assault was committed but that it was committed with the specific intent to commit the crime alleged as being the object and purpose of the assault. Thus, while murder may be committed without an intent to kill, in the crime of assault with intent to commit murder the guilty person must specifically intend to take human life and must commit the assault with that intent (People v. Mize, 80 Cal. 41; People v. Weston, 32 Cal. App. 571; People v. Pineda, 41 Cal. App. 2d 100; People v. Mendenhall, 135 Cal. 344; People v. Kafoury, 16 Cal. App. 718) and the facts must be such that if death had resulted the crime would have been murder and not manslaughter (People v. Landman, 103 Cal. 577; People v. Maciel, 71 Cal. App. 213) but, since premeditation is not necessary in murder of the second degree, it is not a necessary element in the crime of assault with intent to commit murder (People v. Mendenhall, 135 Cal. 344). Where the defendant and his wife had separated and defendant telephoned his wife that if she did not let him have his daughter he would kill his wife and later appeared at the wife's residence and, after some conversation, threatened her whereupon she ran and the defendant fired a shot which passed very close to her, a conviction of assault with a deadly weapon with intent to commit murder was sustained (People v. Alexander, 41 Cal. App. 2d 275). Where the perpetrators of a robbery in their efforts to escape with the loot engaged in a gun battle with police officers a conviction of assault with intent to murder was sustained (People v. Anthony, 90 Cal. App. 2d 122).

Abandonment of Intent

If an assault with a specific intent is made, it is no less a crime though the aggressor should abandon his intentions before the accomplishment of the intent with which the assault was made (People v. Bradley, 71 Cal. App. 2d 114; People v. Harshaw, 71 Cal. App. 2d 146; People v. Stewart, 97 Cal. 238 240; People v. Bowman, 6 Cal. App. 749; People v. Lutes, 79 Cal. App. 2d 233).

Assault with Intent to Rape

To constitute the crime of assault with intent to commit rape, there must exist in the mind of the assailant the intent to so act that, if he carried his intent to consummation he would have commited the crime of rape. The old rule that, unless the defendant indicated a resolution to use all of his force to commit rape, then there is no satsifactory proof of such intent, has been considerably modified (People v. Nelson, 131 Cal. App. 2d. 57). The crime is complete if at any moment during the assault the accused intends to have carnal knowledge of the victim against her will and to use for that purpose whatever force may be required (People v. Meichtry, 37 Cal. 2d. 385, 388; People v. Furrh, 146 Cal. App. 2d. 740). The fact that he desisted prior to the accomplishment of his intended purpose is immaterial. (People v. Meichtry, 37 Cal 2d. 385; People v. Nye, 38 Cal. 2d. 34; People v. Stewart, 109 Cal. App. 2d. 334). The fact that his purpose was merely that of sexual intercourse would not be sufficient basis for a charge of assault with intent to commit rape against the will of the female. (People v. Fleming, 94 Cal. 308; People v. Norrington, 55 Cal. App. 103; People v. Mullen, 45 Cal. App. 297; People v. Parker, 74 Cal. App. 540.) If upon a trial of such a charge the circumstances negative the intent to commit rape the offense is merely simple assault. (People v. Manchego, 80 Cal. 306.) The intent need not be proved by direct evidence but may be inferred from the circumstances. (People v. Meichtry, 37 Cal. 2d 385.) Where the evidence showed that the defendant had attacked the prosecutrix on a street at a place where there were no lights, threw her down and put his hands under her clothes and tore her underclothing and struck her when she screamed and left when people approached a conviction of assault with intent to rape was sustained. (People v. Moore, 155 Cal. 237; see also People v. Singh, 59 Cal. App. 64; People v. Jones, 112 Cal. App. 68; People v. Cicerelli, 123 Cal. App. 48.) There need be, to sustain a conviction, no proof that the defendant was exposed so as to complete the act nor proof of sexual capacity and the absence of an immediate outcry on the part of the prosecutrix does not conclusively refute the hypothesis of guilt (People v. Meichtry, 37 Cal. 2d 385). Where the defendant grabbed a woman who had gone up a hill to look at a view and threatened to cut her throat if she screamed and struck her several blows across the face and head when she did scream and did not ask for any money and, when the woman fell to the ground, ran away, desisting when in the struggle he cut his thumb, a conviction of assault with intent to rape was sustained (People v. Collier, 113 Cal. App. 2d 861).

Incapable of Consenting

Since a girl under the age of eighteen years is incapable of consenting to an act of sexual intercourse with a man not

refute Prove to be false

her husband she is incapable of consenting to an assault with intent to commit rape (People v. Gordon, 70 Cal. 467; People v. Verdegren, 106 Cal. 211) and the crime of assault with intent to commit rape is included in a charge of statutory rape (People v. Babcock, 160 Cal. 537; see also People v. Verdegren, 106 Cal. 211; People v. Vann, 129 Cal. 118; People v. Johnson, 131 Cal. 511). There may be an assault with intent to commit rape where an assault is committed upon a female under the age of eighteen years with the intent to accomplish an act of sexual intercourse with her even though there be no intent to accomplish that act by force and against her will. (People v. Parker, 74 Cal. App. 540; People v. De Martini, 63 Cal. App. 647; People v. Laurintz, 114 Cal. 628; People v. Roach, 129 Cal. 33; People v. Vann, 129 Cal. 118; People v. Johnson, 131 Cal. 511.)

Assault With a Deadly Weapon

"Every person who commits an assault upon the person of another with a deadly weapon or instrument . . . is punishable by imprisonment in the state prison not exceeding ten years, or in a county jail not exceeding one year, or by fine not exceeding five thousand dollars, or by both such fine and imprisonment." (Penal Code, sec. 245.)

"Deadly Weapon" Defined

A deadly weapon is any object, instrument or weapon which, from the manner in which it is used, is capable and likely to produce death or great bodily injury. (People v. Franklin, 70 Cal. 641; People v. Valliere, 123 Cal. 576; People v. Lopez, 135 Cal. 3; People v. Rodrigo, 69 cal. 601; People v. Morlock, 46 Cal. 2d 141). Whether or not a particular object or instrument is a deadly weapon depends not upon the use for which it was originally suited or intended but upon whether it was used in a manner likely to produce death or great bodily injury. (People v. Robertson, 217 Cal. 671; see also People v. Lee, 23 Cal. App. 2d 168; People v. Russell, 59 Cal. App. 2d 660.) A comparatively innocent object in common use, a cane, a hatpin or a farming implement or (as in People v. Valliere, 123 Cal. 576) a sock filled with salt or a knife (People v. McCoy, 25 2d 177; People v. Arguilda, 85 Cal. App. 2d 623, a small knife); a bottle (People v. Cordero, 92 A.C.A. 270); a rifle with a loaded magazine but no cartridge in the chamber (People v. Simpson, 134 Cal. App. 646); an automatic pistol with shells in the clip but no cartridge in the chamber (People v. Pearson, 150 Cal. App. 2d 811), an unloaded pistol used as a bludgeon. (Peo-

ple v. White, 115 Cal. App. 2d 828) ; an iron pipe or bar (People
v. Car, 131 Cal. App. 644; People v. Lee, 23 Cal. App. 2d 168) ; a
blackjack (People v. Wilson, 33 Cal. App. 2d 194) ; a broken
bottle (People v. Sampson, 75 Cal. App. 2d 521) ; a club (People
v. Macias, 77 Cal. App. 2d 71) ; a hammer (People v. Porter, 82
Cal. App. 2d 585) or a nail file (People v. Russell, 59 Cal. App.
2d 660) may be a deadly weapon and is such if used in a manner likely to cause great bodily injury.

Other definitions of the term "deadly weapon" as used
in connection with other penal statutes have no application to
the crime of assault with a deadly weapon. Thus the definition of the term in section 3024, subd. f of the Penal Code,
has no application in a case of assault with a deadly weapon.
(People v. Petters, 29 Cal. App. 2d 48; People v. Cabrera,
104 Cal. App. 414.)

Weapon Used May Be Proved by Circumstantial Evidence

(Victim doesn't know what he was hit with)

Where there is no direct evidence as to the nature of the
weapon used this factor may be establishd by circumstantial
evidence. Thus where the victim suffered a severe wound
such as might have been caused by a sharp instrument the jury
is warranted in concluding that a deadly weapon was used
(People v. Stevens, 15 Cal. App. 294; People v. Henry, 25
Cal. App. 2d 49; People v. Urrutia, 58 Cal. App. 2d 468;
People v. Long, 70 Cal. App. 2d 470) and, where the defendant
pointed a gun at another with a threat to use it, the conclusion that the gun was loaded is warranted. (People v. Montgomery, 15 Cal. App. 315.)

Elements of Offense   must inflict bodily Injury

The crime of assault with a deadly weapon does not re- Hogwash
quire a specific intent (People v. Lopez, 81 Cal. App. 199;
People v. Lim Dum Dong, 26 Cal. App. 2d 135; People v. Gordon, 103 Cal. 575; People v. McCoy, 25 Cal. 2d 177; People v.
Corlett, 67 Cal. App. 2d 33; People v. Griffin, 90 Cal. App.
2d. 116; People v. Walker, 99 Cal. App. 2d. 238; People v.
Laya, 123 Cal. App. 2d. 7) or Malice (People v. Peak, 66 Cal.
App. 2d. 894) and intoxication is not a defense in such cases
and it is wholly immaterial whether the defendant was drunk
or sober at the time of the assault. (People v. Gordon, 103 Cal.
575, 576.)

To constitute an assault with a deadly weapon it is not
necessary that any injury be caused (People v. Macias, 77 Cal.
App. 2d 71; People v. Ingram, 91 Cal. App. 2d 912.) The gist
of the offense is the unlawful attempt to commit a violent

injury with a deadly weapon upon the person of another. If an injury be caused, that fact may be considered in determining the means used and the manner in which the injury was inflicted. (People v. Rader, 24 Cal. App. 477, 484.) Presenting a loaded gun in a threatening manner, pointed at the back of another and lowering it when the latter's wife screamed is, regardless of the defendant's reason for not firing, an assault with a deadly weapon. (People v. Dodini, 51 Cal. App. 179; see also People v. Bennett, 37 Cal. App. 324.)

It is not necessary, where the deadly weapon involved is a firearm that it shall actually be pointed at the intended victim to constitute the assault. A conviction was sustained where the defendant had entered the office of the complainant in an angry and intoxicated condition and without provocation abused the complainant and pulled a loaded revolver out of his pocket at which point he was disarmed by a bystander. (People v. Piercy, 16 Cal. App. 13.) Where a husband clearly evidenced an intent to shoot his wife and reached for his loaded revolver, but, before he could aim or fire, she escaped, it was held that the crime of assault with a deadly weapon was complete and that it was immaterial whether the defendant actually pointed the gun or not. (People v. Hunter, 71 Cal. App. 315; People v. Thompson, 93 Cal. App. 2d 780.) Where the defendant called upon the prosecuting witness in the latter's home and declared that she had come to kill her, took a loaded gun out of her purse and the two then struggled for the possession of the gun and, while so struggling, a third person took the gun from the defendant, a conviction was sustained (People v. Fite, 141 Cal. Ap. 2d 768). In one of our early decisions it appeared that the defendant drew a revolver and told the complainant that he would shoot him if he did not leave the land but did not point the gun at complainant and the court said. "Where a party puts in a condition which must at once be performed and which condition he has no right to impose and his intent is to immediately enforce performance by violence and places himself in a position to do so and proceeds as far as is then necessary for him to go in order to carry out his intention, then it is as much of an assault as if he had actually struck or shot at the other party and missed." (People v. Makin, 8 Cal. 547; People v. Thompson, 93 Cal. App. 2d 780; People v. McCoy, 25 Cal. 2d 177, assault with a knife.) By comparison, where during an argument the defendant pulled out a gun and stated, "Don't come any closer; your life is in danger," there being no attempt to use the gun, but merely the statement indicating that it might or would be used in the future no assault was committed. (People v. Diamond, 33 Cal. App. 2d 518.)

Where the defendant threw the complainant to the ground and held a knife close to her face and told her not to make a noise or he would use the knife a conviction of assault with a deadly weapon was sustained the court saying that it was not necessary that the defendant actually made an attempt to strike or use the knife upon the person of the prosecutrix and the fact that the defendant was thwarted in the act and did not inflict serious injury upon the prosecutrix did not render his conduct any the less criminal. (People v. McCoy, 25 Cal. 2d 177.)

Attempt Essential

doing of act with Specific Intent

To constitute an assault with a deadly weapon there must, as in all assaults, be an attempt and if there be no attempt to use the deadly weapon the crime of assault with a deadly weapon is incomplete even though the weapon be displayed. If the accused, for example, does no more than draw a knife from his pocket but at no time comes within striking distance of the complainant and moves away from rather than toward him and makes no attempt to use the knife there is no assault with a deadly weapon. (People v. Dodel, 77 Cal. 293.) Where a person discharges a firearm to frighten another person but without any intent of killing or injuring anyone, no assault has been committed since there is no attempt to inflict an injury upon another (People v. McGee, 31 Cal. 2d 229, 238; People v. Carmen, 36 Cal. 2d 768, 774).

Assault By Means of Force Likely To Produce Great Bodily Injury

"Every person who commits an assault upon the person of another . . . by any means of force likely to produce great bodily injury is punishable by imprisonment in the state prison not exceeding ten years, or in a county jail not exceeding one year, or by fine not exceeding five thousand dollars, or by both such fine and imprisonment." (Penal Code, sec. 245.)

To commit this form of felonious assault it is not necessary that the defendant shall have used a weapon or other instrument as the means of the assault as it is the violence and likelihood of the assault to produce great bodily injury that is the gist of this offense. (People v. Tallman, 27 Cal. 2d 209.) Convictions of this offense have been sustained where the means used were the hands and knees (People v. Kimmerle, 90 Cal. App. 186); throwing a person out of a window (People

v. Emmons, 61 Cal. 487); knocking a person down and kicking him (People v. Blake, 129 Cal. App. 196), choking the victim (People v. Bumbaugh, 48 Cal. App. 2d 791; People v. Schmidt, 66 Cal. App. 2d 253), and vicious assaults with the fists alone (People v. Hinshaw, 194 Cal. 1; People v. Nudo, 38 Cal. App. 2d 381;People v. Kinman, 134 Cal. App. 2d.). 419). Convictions have also been sustained under a charge of this form of assault where the means used was evidently a deadly weapon, viz., a brickbat (People v. Fahey, 64 Cal. 342), a beer bottle (People v. Mitchell, 40 Cal. App. 2d 204), an iron bar (People v. Hernandez, 70 Cal. App. 2d 190), and a rawhide whip brutally applied to the naked back of defendant's son (People v. Brown, 42 Cal. App. 462) and where the injuries were inflicted by forcibly pushing the victim so his head came in contact with a parking meter (People v. Conley, 110 Cal. App. 2d 731) or other vicious assault though no weapon is used (People v. Carnavacci, 119 Cal. App. 2d 14) or where the means used would normally not be considered a deadly weapon (People v. Hahn, 147 Cal. App. 2d 308, empty beer can). In this offense it is not necessary that actual injury be inflicted upon the intended victim (People v. Day 199 Cal. 78) but where there is actual injury it may be considered as evidence of the means and force used to produce it.

It is not essential in this crime that an intent to inflict serious injury be proved (People v. Schmidt, 66 Cal. App. 2d 253) and this offense may be perpetrated by the use of hands alone (People v. Tallman, 27 Cal. 2d 209).

The question as to what force is likely to produce great bodily injury is basically a question for the trial court (People v. Carnavacci, 119 Cal. App. 2d 14).

Where, after being stopped for questioning by officers, defendant fled in his car and, in departing from the scene, his left front fender struck one of the officers standing in the street, throwing him against another car and inflicting minor injuries, the conviction was sustained (People v. Dewson, 150 Cal. App. 2d 119), the court holding that the gist of the offense is the likelihood of great bodily injury and that the degree of force used is not as significant as the manner of its use. One who drives at a high rate of speed and then applies his brakes to skid his car to dislodge an officer may be convicted of this offense (People v. Fox, 82 Cal. App. 2d 913).

Assault With Caustic Chemicals

"Every person who willfully and maliciously places or throws, or causes to be placed or thrown, upon the person of another, any vitriol, corrosive acid, or caustic chemical of any nature, with the intent to injure the flesh or disfigure the body of such person, is punishable by imprisonment in the state prison not less than one nor more than fourteen years." (Penal Code, sec. 244.)

In a prosecution under this section there must be more than a mere assault and it must be shown that the corrosive or caustic chemical actually touched the person of another; a defendant could not be found guilty of this offense if his attempt to place or throw acid or caustic upon the person of another failed. "While it may often happen that the throwing of acids described by Section 244 of the Penal Code would have the result of producing great bodily injury, the fact that it does so, or even that it will have the properties of doing so, is not required by said section. The crime is complete if any quantity of acid so described, however small in quantity or however weak in strength and however incapable of producing great bodily harm, is thrown or placed upon the person of another, if done willfully and maliciously with intent to injure the flesh or to disfigure to the slightest extent the body of another." (People v. Day, 199 Cal. 78.)

It should be noted that the commission of this offense requires the existence of the specific intent either to injure the flesh or disfigure the body of a human being. In the absence of such an intent or if the act be done with an intent other than that specified in the statute the crime made punishable by Section 244 cannot be committed.

Administering Poison With Intent to Kill

"Every person who, with intent to kill, administers, or causes or procures to be administered, to another, any poison or other noxious or destructive substance or liquid, by which death is not caused, is punishable by imprisonment in the state prison for not less than ten years." (Penal Code, sec. 216.)

The word "poison" as here used includes any substance or liquid which, when applied to the human body externally or in any way introduced into the human system, without acting mechanically but by its own inherent qualities, is capable of destroying life. The words, "other noxious or destructive substance or liquid", refer to means which are not poisons but are capable of destroying life, such as pulverized glass or boiling water, when administered in sufficient quantities. The purpose of the statute is to provide punishment for attempts to kill and the means used must be capable of destroying life (People v. Van Deleer, 53 Cal. 147).

Causing a person to inhale chloroform is "administering" chloroform and is within the scope of the statute (People v. Tinnen, 49 Cal. App. 18).

Wilfully Poisoning, Food, Drink, Medicine or Water

"Any person who wilfully mingles any poison with any food, drink or medicine with intent that the same shall be taken by any human being to his injury, and every person who wilfully poisons any spring, well or reservoir of water, is punishable by imprisonment in the state prison for a term of not less than one nor more than ten years." (Penal Code, sec. 347.)

Throwing Object at Vehicle

Any person who, with intent to do great bodily injury, who maliciously and wilfully throws or projects any object capable of doing serious bodily harm at a vehicle or occupant thereof is guilty of a felony punishable by from 1 to 5 years in the state prison and all lesser throwing of objects at a vehicle or occupant thereof is guilty of a misdemeanor (Vehicle Code, sec. 604.2)

Discharging Firearm at Building

"Any person who shall maliciously and wilfully discharge a firearm at an inhabited dwelling house or occupied building, is guilty of a felony, and upon conviction shall be punished by imprisonment in the state prison for not less than one nor more than five years or by imprisonment in the county jail not exceeding one year." (Penal Code, sec 246).

Traumatic Injury Upon Wife or Child

"Any husband who inflicts upon his wife corporal injury resulting in a traumatic condition, and any person who wilfully inflicts upon any child any cruel or inhuman corporal punishment or injury resulting in a traumatic condition is guilty of a felony, and upon conviction thereof shall be punished by imprisonment in the State prison for not more than two years or in the county jail for not more than one year." Penal Code, sec. 273d, new section added in 1945.)

The term "traumatic condition" used in the statute means a bodily injury caused by the application of force (People v. Burns, 88 Cal. App. 2d 867).

Abandonment of Assault

Where the acts of a person have proceeded to the extent of amounting in law to an assault, the abandonment by the perpetrator of his purpose before he has accomplished the object for which the assault was committed does not free him from the consequences of his acts and he is guilty of the assault whether he voluntarily ceased his attack (People v. Jones, 112 Cal. App. 68; People v. Moore, 155 Cal. 237; People v. Johnson, 131 Cal. 511), whether he desisted because of the resistance of his intended victim (People v. Wilson, 119 Cal. 384; People v. Johnson, 131 Cal. 54; People v. Bier, 59 Cal. App. 2d 313), because of the approach of other parties permitting his victim to escape (People v. Stewart, 97 Cal. 238) or because the intended victim escaped. (People v. Singh, 59 Cal. App. 64; People v. Hunter, 71 Cal. App. 315.)

Assaults—Justification and Excuse

If the use of force, even though it involve an intent to commit physical injuries upon another, is lawful there is no assault. The use of force necessary to accomplish a lawful arrest, corporal punishment within lawful limits of a child by its parent, the lawful ejection of a trespasser or of a person disturbing the peace, or engaging in a lawful boxing contest would not constitute assaults but would become so if the application of force became unlawful.

Physical injuries inflicted by accident and misfortune in the doing of a lawful act by lawful means and without negligence or criminal intent could not be the basis of a charge of assault, for under these conditions the act would be neither unlawful nor would it bear the slightest resemblance to an attempt to inflict unlawful injury.

Justifiable Use of Force

The rights of self defense and of the defense of the person of another or in defense of property apply in defense to a charge of assault.

"Lawful resistance to the commission of a public offense may be made: 1. By the party about to be injured; 2. By other parties." (Penal Code, sec. 692.)

"Resistance sufficient to prevent the offense may be made by the party about to be injured; 1. To prevent an offense against his person, or his family, or some member thereof. 2. To prevent an illegal attempt by force to take or injure property in his possession." (Penal Code, sec. 693.)

"Any other person, in aid or defense of the person about to be injured, may make resistance sufficient to prevent the offense." (Penal Code, sec. 694.)

It is lawful for a person who is being assaulted and who has reasonable grounds for believing that he is in danger of bodily injury to defend himself from the attack and, in so doing, he may use all force and means reasonably necessary under the circumstances to prevent the injury which appears imminent. A person so assailed cannot set up his own standards of reasonableness of belief or of the amount of force necessary but is limited to that which the ordinary reasonable and prudent person, placed in the same position, would be warranted in considering reasonable and necessary.

While this right to resist exists when a person is being unlawfully assaulted he has no right to resist force with force where the force applied against him is lawful, as where an officer is lawfully endeavoring to place him under arrest. (People v. Giacobbi, 83 Cal. App. 12.)

Force Must Be Reasonable

And even though, under the circumstances, the lawful use of force in self defense is justified, such right may be exercised only to the extent of using such force as is reasonably necessary to prevent the injury threatened. The law does not justify the use of a greater degree of force than is reasonably necessary (People v. Alexander, 1 Cal. App. 2d 570) nor does it justify a person, who has been acting in self defense, in the infliction of further injuries upon his assailant after there is no longer any apparent danger. The use of excessive force in an endeavor to act in self defense is itself an assault and unlawful.

The general principles of self defense, of the person of another and of defense of property by force which will justify a homicide, apply where the force and circumstances fall short of justifying a homicide but still constitute the threatened unlawful use of force by one person in his attempt to unlawfully take or injure the person or property of another. The circumstances must be such as would induce in the mind of the ordinarily prudent person a reasonable belief that an unlawful injury is threatened and that force is necessary to resist and prevent the commission of the unlawful act, and the force used must not be more than is reasonably necessary to prevent the unlawful act threatened and the right to resist by force is justified whether it be actually or apparently necessary.

To justify the use of a deadly weapon in self defense the accused must have reasonably believed that he was in "great" bodily danger (People v. Lopez, 87 Cal. App. 2d 544).

Justification - Words of Abuse

Words of abuse, insult or reproach addressed to a person without any threat of injury or attempt to inflict injury will not justify an assault (People v. Mueller, 147 Cal. App. 2d 233, cases cited.

CHAPTER XVIII.

MAYHEM — *counted with Violent EW Jur?*

"Every person who unlawfully and maliciously deprives a human being of a member of his body, or disables, disfigures or renders it useless, or who cuts or disables the tongue, puts out an eye, or slits the nose, ear or lip, is guilty of mayhem." (Penal Code, sec. 203.)

"Mayhem is punishable by imprisonment in the state prison not exceeding fourteen years." (Penal Code, sec. 204.)

"An assault by the defendant upon the prosecuting witness is an essential element of the charge of mayhem" (People v. De Foor, 100 Cal. 150) and the injury inflicted must have arisen from an unlawful attempt to inflict a violent injury upon another. It is necessary to constitute mayhem that the act shall have been done "maliciously" and that word, as here used, means and imports "a wish to vex, annoy or injure another person, or an intent to do a wrongful act." (Penal Code, sec. 7, subd. 4.) Malice aforethought, such as exists in the crime of murder is not an element of the crime of mayhem nor does this offense require that the unlawful act shall have been the result of deliberation or premeditation. (People v. Wright, 93 Cal. 564; People v. Nunes, 47 Cal. App. 346.) It is not necessary that the accused shall have intended the particular injury suffered by the victim. The law being intended to prevent brutality, if one person attacks another, unlawfully and maliciously, and inflicts upon him one of the injuries specified in Section 203, even though he may not have intended that injury, the crime is nevertheless mayhem. (People v. Nunes, 47 Cal. App. 346; see also People v. Wright, 93 Cal. 565.)

While a "bite" does not necessarily amount to a "slit" (People v. De Masters, 105 Cal. 673), biting off a portion of the ear of a human being has been held to be mayhem. (People v. Golden, 62 Cal. 542; People v. Wright, 93 Cal. 565.) "What the statute obviously means by the expression or phrase 'put out the eye' is that the eye has been injured to such an extent that its possessor cannot use it for practical purposes of life." (People v. Nunes, 47 Cal. App. 346.)

FALSE IMPRISONMENT

"False imprisonment is the unlawful violation of the personal liberty of another." (Penal Code, sec. 236.)

"False imprisonment is punishable by fine not exceeding five hundred dollars, or by imprisonment in the county jail not more than one year, or by both. If such false imprisonment be effected by violence, menace, fraud, or deceit, it shall be punishable by imprisonment in the state prison for not less than one nor more than ten years.'' (Penal Code, sec. 237.)

Any act or threat of force by which another is deprived or restrained of his liberty and freedom of moving about or by which he is compelled to remain where he does not want to remain or to go where he does not wish to go is an imprisonment even though the defendant did not lay hands on the complainant. (People v. Agnew, 16 Cal. 2d 655.) If such imprisonment is unlawful, that is, if it is not authorized by law, it is false imprisonment. A bare false imprisonment is a misdemeanor, but if it is accomplished by the use of any violence or menace or fraud or deceit it is a felony.

"All that is necessary to make out a case of false imprisonment is that the individual be restrained of his liberty without any sufficient complaint or authority and it may be accomplished by words or acts which the individual fears to disregard. Temporary detention is sufficient and the use of actual physical force is not necessary'' (Ware v. Dunn, 80 Cal. App. 2d 936,943; Vandiveer v. Charters, 110 Cal. App. 347, 355).

In a prosecution for this crime it is not necessary to prove in the first instance that the imprisonment was unlawful since when it has been proven that there was an imprisonment the law presumes it to have been unlawful and the burden is cast upon the defendant to justify the imprisonment by proof that it was lawful (People v. McGrew, 77 Cal. 570; Monk v. Ehret, 192 Cal. 186; Peters v. Bigelow, 137 Cal. App. 135; People v. Agnew, 16 Cal. 2d 655; People v. Sagehorn, 140 Cal. App. 2d 138) but the defendant need not establish the lawfulness of the imprisonment by a preponderance of the evidence as he is entitled to an acquittal if the evidence on this point raises a reasonable doubt. (People v. Agnew, 16 Cal. 2d 655.)

Illustrative Cases

Forcibly removing a man from premises occupied by him by another who claimed the right of possession has been held to be false imprisonment. (People v. Wheeler, 73 Cal. 252; see also Ex parte Keil, 85 Cal. 309.) An arrest by a private citizen whereupon the prisoner is taken into custody by a peace officer who is present is an imprisonment even though no one laid hands on the prisoner. (People v. Agnew, 16 Cal. 2d 655.) Where an officer or private citizen who has made an arrest is guilty of unnecessary delay in taking his prisoner before a magistrate, the delay, being unlawful, constitutes a false imprisonment. (See Peckham v. Warner Bros., 36 Cal. App. 2d 214; Vernon v. Plumas Lbr. Co., 71 Cal. App. 112.)

Assault Crime   KIDNAPING *(outmoded crime)*

"Every person who forcibly steals, takes, or arrests any person in this state, and carries him into another country, state, or county, or into another part of the same county, or who forcibly takes or arrests any person, with a design to take him out of this state, without having established a claim, according to the laws of the United States, or of this state, or who hires, persuades, entices. decoys, seduces by false promises, misrepresentations, or the like, any person to go out of this state, or to be taken or removed therefrom, for the purpose and with the intent to sell such person into slavery or involuntary servitude, or otherwise to employ him for his own use, or to the use of another, without the free will and consent of such persuaded person; and every person who, being out of this state, abducts or takes by force or fraud any person contrary to the law of the place where such act is committed, and brings, sends or conveys such person within the limits of the state, and is afterwards found within the limits thereof, is guilty of kidnaping." (Penal Code, sec. 207.) — *209*

"Kidnaping is punishable by imprisonment in the state prison not less than one nor more than twenty-five years." (Penal Code, sec. 208.)

Section 207 enumerates a number of different acts, any one of which will constitute kidnaping, but it will be noted that in each instance the act, to constitute kidnaping, must be an unlawful act, and that the mere taking of a person from one place to another is not kidnaping.

Various Offenses Covered by Section 207

The first form of kidnaping described in section 207 is where the victim is forcibly and unlawfully taken out of the state or county or into another part of the county in which he is seized. There the offense is complete as soon as the victim has been taken to another part of the county. There is nothing in the law that requires that the victim be taken any particular distance before the kidnaping is accomplished and the moving of the victim for any distance, however short, is sufficient if the act be otherwise punishable under the statute. This form of kidnaping does not involve any specific intent and proof of the intent or purpose of the defendant is not essential to a conviction. (People v. Fick, 89 Cal. 144; People v. Bruno, 49 Cal. App. 372; People v. Sheasby, 82 Cal. App. 459; People v. Hunter, 49 Cal. App. 2d 243.) The act of forcibly and unlawfully moving of the victim from one place to another (People v. Hollowa, 138 Cal. App. 174) or the compelling of the driver of an automobile to drive and convey the defendant from one place to another (People v. Valdez, 3

Cal. App. 2d 700) will constitute kidnaping under this section. Unlawfully compelling another to enter an automobile would be a kidnaping. (People v. Brazil, 53 Cal. App. 2d 596; People v. Harris, 67 Cal. App. 2d 307.) Even though the victim originally entered an automobile voluntarily, if she is thereafter prevented from leaving the car when she desires to do so and is conveyed to another place against her will, such conveying constitutes kidnaping (People v. Trawick, 78 Cal. App. 2d 604).

The section next punishes as a crime the act of forcibly taking or arresting a person with a design to take him out of the state without legal authority. This provision is particularly directed to cases in which an officer, desiring to remove a person from this state to another jurisdiction for prosecution for a crime, instead of proceeding under the laws regulating extradition ignores such method of procedure and endeavors to accomplish his end by force without lawful authority.

The next portion of the section punishes the enticing or seducing another person to leave or be taken from the state for one of the specified unlawful purposes while the last part of the section punishes the person who, having kidnaped another outside of this state, causes the victim to be brought within this state.

Kidnaping for Extortion or Robbery

"Every person who seizes, confines, inveigles, entices, decoys, abducts, conceals, kidnaps or carries away any individual by any means whatsoever, with intent to hold or detain, or who holds or detains, such individual for ransom, reward or to commit extortion or to exact from relatives or friends of such person any money or valuable thing, or any person who kidnaps or carries away any individual to commit robbery, or any person who aids or abets any such act is guilty of a felony and upon conviction thereof shall suffer death or shall be punished by imprisonment for life without possibility of parole at the discretion of the jury trying the same in cases in which the person or persons subjected to such kidnaping suffers or suffer bodily harm, or shall be punished by imprisonment in the state prison for life with possibility of parole in cases where such person or persons do not suffer bodily harm." (Penal Code, sec. 209.) (Note: Section 190.1 of the Penal Code provides that the death penalty shall not be imposed upon any person who was under the age of eighteen years at the time of the commission of the crime and that the burden of proving age is upon the defendant.)

While in kidnaping under section 207 of the Penal Code the victim must be moved or caused to move from one place to another, it is sufficient in a prosecution under section 209 if the victim be "seized" although the victim is not moved. In other words the mere seizing of the victim with the specific intent required by the statute completes the commission of this form of kidnaping. (People v. Raucho, 8 Cal. App. 2d 665; People v. Dorman, 28 Cal. 2d 846) but if the object is robbery the victim must be moved for some distance which need not, however, be great; "It is the fact, not the distance, of forcible removal which constitutes kidnaping in this state" (see People v. Chessman, 38 Cal. 2d 166, 192 and cases cited), and the mere seizure or detention of the victim during the commission of the robbery does not constitute kidnaping under section 209 (People v. Taylor, 135 Cal. App. 2d 201; People v. Cluchey, 142 Cal. App. 2d 563). Whatever may have been the original motive of the kidnaping, if the kidnaper commits or attempts to commit extortion or robbery during the kidnaping, he "holds or detains" his victim "to commit extortion or robbery" within the meaning of section 209 (People v. Hernandez, 100 Cal. App. 2d 128). Where a kidnaping takes place after the actual perpetration of the robbery such kidnaping may be kidnaping for the purpose of robbery if it may be reasonably inferred that the transportation of the victim was for the purpose of effecting the escape of the robber or to remove the victim to another place where he might less easily sound an alarm (People v. Randazza, 132 Cal. App. 2d. 20).

The act of kidnaping need not precede or be coincident with the robbery to come within the scope of the statute. Thus, robbery followed by abduction for the primary purpose of escape during which the kidnaped person suffered bodily harm (People v. Christy, 4 Cal. 2d 504); where the defendant beat his female victim, dragged her around the house and attempted to rape her and ransacked the bureau drawers (People v. Dagger, 5 Cal. 2d 337); where defendant abducted a woman, raped her and then took her watch and automobile (People v. Brown, 29 Cal. 2d 555); taking a watch held to make the abduction kidnaping to commit robbery even though the original objective was rape and the robbery was an afterthought (People v. Knowles, 35 Cal. 2d 175); where, after robbing a man and his woman companion of his wallet and her purse, defendant forced the woman to walk to his car and commit an act in violation of section 288a of the Penal Code and took $5 from her purse (People v. Chessman, 38 Cal. 2d 166) are cases in which convictions were sustained. On the other hand, where there was a forcible abduction and attempted rape and the defendant took a package of cigarettes from the victim's purse but did not take the money which was in it, it was held that this was not kidnaping for the purpose of robbery (People v. Welsh, 7 Cal. 2d 209).

Specific Intent Required

A kidnaping under section 209 requires, as an element of the corpus delicti, that the act be done with the specific intent to hold or detain the victim for ransom or reward or to commit extortion either upon the victim or his relatives or friends or to commit robbery, and this intent may be deduced or inferred from the facts and circumstances attending the kidnaping, (People v. Fisher, 30 Cal. App. 135; People v. Raucho, 8 Cal. App. 2d 655; People v. Melendrez, 25 Cal. App. 2d 490) and the specific intent required by the statute is not necessarily disproved by the fact the perpetrator after kidnaping his victim committed a crime of a different character than that named in the section as being a necessary object of the kidnaper. Thus the fact that the female victim was ravished does not exclude the existence of an intent to rob her. (People v. Raucho, 8 Cal. App. 2d 655; People v. Melendrez, 25 Cal. App. 2d 490; People v. Hernandez, 100 Cal. App. 2d 128.) Where the female victim was robbed and then removed to another place and a sex crime was committed upon her it was held a question for the triers of the facts as to whether the kidnaping was for the purpose of robbery (People v. Chessman, 38 Cal. 2d 166, citing cases). It is not necessary that in a kidnaping for the purpose of robbery the kidnaping must precede the attempt to commit a robbery, although the crime would be complete if the kidnaping were committed with the intent to rob even though it were followed by no overt act toward the robbery. The offense is complete if the kidnaping is committed in the perpetration of the robbery. Forcing the bank employees into and locking them in the vault as an incident to a bank robbery is kidnaping. (People v. Johnson, 140 Cal. App. 729.) Where some convicts in the state prison entered the prison dining room and robbed members of the Board of Prison Terms and Paroles of jewelry and then compelled the members of the Board to accompany them in their flight, it was held that the robbery continued and still was in operation and progress at the time of the kidnaping. (People v. Kristy, 4 Cal. 2d 504.)

It is not necessary that the perpetrator shall have intended to commit extortion or robbery or to hold for ransom at the time of the original seizure or taking away of the victim. It is sufficient if the extortion, robbery or holding for ransom was committed or the intent to commit it occurred during the course of the abduction (People v. Brown, 29 Cal. 2d 555).

When Robbery Also Charged

Where the one act is basically a robbery in which the victim is seized or confined in a room to facilitate the robbery there is in law but one act and but one offense is committed and in such a case the conviction of robbery was reversed and the conviction for kidnapping which carried the greater penalty was affirmed (People v. Knowles, 35 Cal. 2d 175).

Penalty—Bodily Harm

In cases of kidnaping under section 209 where the victim suffers "bodily harm" the penalty is death or life imprisonment without possibility of parole in the discretion of the jury, or, if the trial be without a jury, or upon a plea of guilty, in the discretion of the trial judge. The term "bodily harm" has been defined as "any touching of the person of another against his will with physical force in an intentional, hostile and aggravated manner or the projection of such force against his person." (People v. Chessman, 38 Cal. 2d 166). Since every kidnaping involves some degree of bodily harm this provision of the statute obviously contemplates that the bodily harm which will bring a case within this penalty provision must be a degree of harm above and in addition to that necessarily involved in completing the corpus delicti of the crime (see People v. Jackson, 44 Cal. 2d 511). However, since the statute does not limit the bodily harm to that which is intentionally inflicted but merely that which the victim "suffers," the bodily harm which controls the possible penalty may not only be such as is intentionally inflicted but may also be such bodily harm as is caused by the manner in which the kidnaping is perpetrated or which is the proximate result thereof.

In the cases thus far decided our courts have held that binding the victim of kidnaping with intent to commit robbery to a chair and holding a burning magazine cover under his hands in an attempt to compel him to disclose the location of his money and binding another victim to a chair after she had been imprisoned in a close overheated closet and binding a victim to a chair were held examples of bodily harm justifying the application of one of the alternative penalties and in the earlier case a verdict carrying the death penalty was sustained. (People v. Tanner, 3 Cal. 2d 279; People v. Britton, 6 Cal. 2d 1, victims bound with wire and one of them

Jackson case— Now the law

struck on the head.) The forcible rape of the victim constitutes bodily harm (People v. Brown, 29 Cal. 2d. 555). Compelling the female to submit to rape or an act in violation of section 288a of the Penal Code is the infliction of bodily injury (People v. Chessman, 38 Cal. 2d. 166).

Where the victim's wrists and ankles were chained, ear plugs placed in his ears and adhesive tape over his mouth, made to lie down in his chained condition on a mattress throughout the night but his captors loosened the chains, the court questioned the definition in People v. Tanner, 3 Cal. 2d. 279 that "bodily harm" is "any touching of the person of another against his will and with physical force in an intentional, hostile and aggravated manner, or projecting of such force against his person" and inclined to the view that such injury as in an almost necessary incident to every forcible kidnaping is not such as would constitute the "bodily injury" contemplated by the statute (People v. Jackson, 44 Cal. 2d. 511).

Kidnaping—Attempt to Profit By Guilty of Felony

"Every person who for the purpose of obtaining any ransom or reward, or to extort or exact from any person any money or thing of value, poses as, or in any manner represents himself to be a person who has seized, confined, inveigled, enticed, decoyed, abducted, concealed, kidnaped or carried away any person, or who poses as, or in any manner represents himself to be a person who holds or detains such person, or who poses as, or in any manner represents himself to be a person who has aided or abetted any such act, or who poses as or in any manner represents himself to be a person who has the influence, power, or ability to obtain the release of such person so seized, confined, inveigled, enticed, decoyed, abducted, concealed, kidnaped or carried away, is guilty of a felony and upon conviction thereof shall be punished by imprisonment in the state prison during his natural life or for any number of years not less than five.

Nothing in this section prohibits any person who in good faith believes that he can rescue any person who has been seized, confined, inveigled, enticed, decoyed, abducted, concealed, kidnaped or carried away, and who has had no part in, or connection with such confinement, inveigling, decoying, abducting, concealing, kidnaping or carrying away, from offering to rescue or obtain the release of such person for a monetary consideration or other thing of value." (Penal Code, sec. 210.)

Statute Means What?

This cumbersomely worded statute evidently means that every person who, after a kidnaping in violation of section 209, "poses" as one of the kidnapers or as having the ability to obtain the release of the victim for the purpose of obtaining anything of value is guilty of this offense unless he falls within the exception applicable to one who in good faith offers to secure the return of the victim for a consideration. It would seem that the statute will apply to a person who, though having had no connection with the kidnaping, makes the false pretense that he was a principal therein and has the ability to obtain the return of the victim for a consideration or it could be applied where the person making the pretense was in fact one of the kidnapers against whom there was not sufficient evidence to convict him of the kidnaping but who by his conduct in endeavoring to obtain money or other consideration brought his conduct within the statute.

ABDUCTION

"Every person who takes any woman unlawfully, against her will, and by force, menace, or duress, compels her to marry him, or to marry any other person, or to be defiled, is punishable by imprisonment in the state prison not less than two nor more than fourteen years." (Penal Code, sec. 265.)

Taking Female for the Purpose of Prostitution
Or in Illicit Relation

"Every person who, within this state, takes any female person against her will and without her consent, or with her consent procured by fraudulent inducement or misrepresentation, for the purpose of prostitution, is punishable by imprisonment in the state prison not exceeding five years, and a fine not exceeding one thousand dollars." (Penal Code, sec. 266a.)

"Every person who takes any female person unlawfully, and against her will, and by force, menace, or duress, compels her to live with him in an illicit relation, against her consent, or to so live with any other person, is punishable by imprisonment in the state prison not less than two nor more than four years." (Penal Code, sec. 266b.)

Permitting Wife in House of Prostitution

"Every man who, by force, intimidation, threats, persuasion, promises, or any other means, places or leaves, or

Defiled—Seize & carry away by violence

procures any other person or persons to place or leave, his wife in a house of prostitution, or connives at or consents to, or permits, the placing or leaving of his wife in a house of prostitution, or allows or permits her to remain therein, is guilty of a felony and punishable by imprisonment in the state prison for not less than three nor more than ten years; and in all prosecutions under this section a wife is a competent witness against her husband." (Penal Code, sec. 266g.)

The last three quoted sections of the Penal Code, while not technically defining a form of abduction, describe crimes of a very similar character. Section 266g in addition to punishing the placing of a wife in a house of prostitution includes as an offense the act of a husband who allows or permits her to remain in such a house and he is guilty even though she remains there not as a prostitute, but in an innocent occupation, as, for example, a cook or seamstress. (People v. Conness, 150 Cal. 114.)

Abduction—Female Under Eighteen

"Every person who takes away any female under the age of eighteen years from her father, mother, guardian, or other person having the legal charge of her person, without their consent, for the purpose of prostitution, is punishable by imprisonment in the state prison not exceeding five years, and a fine not exceeding one thousand dollars." (Penal Code, sec. 267.)

The offense created by this section is complete when there is a taking for the purpose of prostitution. The actual placing in a house of prostitution is not an essential element of the crime. (People v. Lewis, 141 Cal. 543.) Neither the language nor the intent of the statute requires that the taking shall be by force (People v. Marshall, 59 Cal. 386; People v. De Mousset, 71 Cal. 611) and consent of the female is no defense. (People v. De Mousset, 71 Cal. 611.) Nor is it necessary that the defendant shall have declared his purpose either to the female or to the person having her legal custody (People v. Estrado, 88 Cal. 316), for the purpose may be deduced from the facts, as where the female is taken to a house of prostitution. (People v. Marshall, 59 Cal. 386; People v. Estrado, 88 Cal. 316; People v. Claudius, 8 Cal. App. 597.) Chastity of the female is not an element of this offense. "The law is intended to protect the chaste and reclaim the erring, to protect parents and guardians in their custody and care of minor females without regard to the character of the female for chastity." (People v. De Mousset, 71 Cal. 611; People v. Dolan, 96 Cal. 315.) And it is not a defense that the defendant did not know she was under age (People v. Fowler, 88 Cal. 136; People v. Dolan, 96 Cal. 317) or that the female was married. (People v. Newton, 11 Cal. App. 762.)

Purpose of Statute

While the purpose of the statute is to prevent young girls being lured away from their legal custodians, it does not apply to girls who have abandoned their homes and become common prostitutes. If a female under age who was a prostitute were taken from the custody of her parents under the circumstances prohibited by the statute the offense would be committed but if she were not in such charge the case would not fall within the provisions of section 267. A girl living separate from her parents and going about from place to place of her own volition, if taken under the other conditions of section 267, would not be taken from the custody of her parents within the meaning of section 267. (People v. Flores, 160 Cal. 766.)

CHILD STEALING

"Every person who maliciously, forcibly, or fraudulently takes or entices away any minor child with intent to detain and conceal such child from its parent, guardian, or other person having the lawful charge of such child, is punishable by imprisonment in the state prison not exceeding twenty years." (Penal Code, sec. 278.)

This offense is one against the parent or other legal custodian and not one against the child. (People v. Moore, 67 Cal. App. 2d. 789). The word "forcibly" does not necessarily imply the use of physical force. (People v. Hernandez, 100 Cal. App. 2d. 128; People v. Smith, 17 Cal. App. 2d. 468.) The word "maliciously" imports "a wish to vex, injure or annoy or injure another person, or an intent to do a wrongful act." (People v. Simmons, 12 Cal. App. 2d 329; People v. Smith, 17 Cal. App. 2d 468.) The word "entice" means "to instigate by inciting hope or desire; to lead astray." The minor may be enticed away without any domination over his or her will. The desire to do something promised by the abductor may alone suffice to lead astray the most self-willed boy or girl. (People v. Torres, 48 Cal. App. 606.) The word "detain" does not necessarily include the idea of force but includes delaying, hindering, retarding, etc. (People v. Moore, 67 Cal. App. 2d 789.)

In determining whether the offense has been committed the acts and conduct of the parties both before and after the act complained of should be taken into consideration (People v. Hernandez, 100 Cal. App. 2d. 128 and cases cited under this title).

Specific Intent

The vital essential element of this offense is the intent to conceal and detain the child from the person having lawful custody. The intent must be to both detain and conceal, and even though there be an intent to conceal the statute is not violated where there is no intent to detain. (People v. Black, 147 Cal. 426.) The intent to detain and conceal must be proven to establish the corpus delicti but it is not essential to this offense that such intent shall actually have been carried out (People v. Edenburg, 88 Cal. App. 558; People v. Annunzio, 120 Cal. App. 89), for actual concealment and detention are not elements of the crime. (People v. Simmons, 12 Cal. App. 2d 329; People v. Smith, 17 Cal. App. 2d 468.)

Consent of Child

In this offense consent of the child is immaterial and the fact that the child accompanied the defendant voluntarily is no defense. (People v. Gillespie, 104 Cal. App. 765; People v. Munoz, 84 Cal. App. 6; People v. Torres, 48 Cal. App. 606; People v. Smith, 17 Cal. App. 468.)

Once the child has been taken and enticed in the manner and form prohibited by the statute the crime is complete even though thereafter the child returns or is returned to his or her legal custodian. Where the defendant took and enticed the child and voluntarily released her after she had accomplished the felonious purpose of performing certain acts upon her a conviction was sustained as the crime was already complete when she released the child. (People v. Kocalis, 140 Cal. App. 566; see also People v. Mohr, 24 Cal. App. 2d 58, where defendant took a four year old child in his automobile and later released her after taking indecent liberties upon her, and People v. Palmer, 50 Cal. App. 2d 697, where the child was able to escape and return home.)

CHAPTER XIX.

RAPE

"Rape is an act of sexual intercourse, accomplished with a female not the wife of the perpetrator, under either of the following circumstances:

1. Where the female is under the age of eighteen years;
2. Where she is incapable, through lunacy or other unsoundness of mind, whether temporary or permanent, of giving legal consent;
3. Where she resists, but her resistance is overcome by force or violence;
4. Where she is prevented from resisting by threats of great and immediate bodily harm, accompanied by apparent power of execution, or by any intoxicating narcotic, or anesthetic, substance, administered by or with the privity of the accused;
5. Where she is at the time unconscious of the nature of the act, and this is known to the accused;
6. Where she submits under the belief that the person committing the act is her husband, and this belief is induced by any artifice, pretence or concealment practiced by the accused, with intent to induce such belief." (Penal Code, sec. 261.)

While the offense is listed in the statute under different classifications, rape is not divided into degrees. (People v. Rambaud, 78 Cal. App. 685.) One act of sexual intercourse can constitute but one offense of rape even though it comes within more than one of the subdivisions of section 261. (People v. Craig, 17 Cal. 2d 453; People v. Scott, 24 Cal. 2d 774.)

Where the information charges rape under one of the subdivisions of section 261 but the proof, while showing rape against the will and consent of the female, shows that the case comes under one of the other subdivisions of that section a conviction will be sustained (People v. Snyder, 75 Cal. 323, pleaded as "by force and violence" but the proof showed the act committed by the use of a narcotic or intoxicating substance; People v. Cassandras, 83 Cal. App. 2d 272, pleaded as "by force and violence" but the proof showed a case of the female being prevented from resisting by threats of bodily harm; see also People v. Blankenship, 103 Cal. App. 2d 60; People v. Craig, 17 Cal. 2d 453).

When Physical Ability Must be Proved

"No conviction for rape can be had against one who was under the age of fourteen years at the time of the act alleged, unless his physical ability to accomplish penetration is proved as an independent fact, and beyond a reasonable doubt." (Penal Code, sec. 262.)

Penetration

"The essential guilt of rape consists in the outrage to the person and feelings of the female. Any sexual penetration, however slight, is sufficient to complete the crime." (Penal Code, sec. 263; People v. Sheffield, 9 Cal. App. 130; People v. Lee, 119 Cal. 84.) The element of penetration may be proved by circumstantial as well as by direct evidence (People v. Vicencio, 71 Cal. App. 2d. 361; People v. Haywood, 131 Cal. App. 2d. 259). Testimony that when asked "did somebody rape you" the female answered in the affirmative, coupled with evidence of blood on her legs and clothing was held sufficient to prove penetration (Smith v. Sup. Ct., 140 Cal. App. 2d 863).

Penalty Sec. 261- under age of 18

"Rape is punishable by imprisonment in the state prison not less than three years except where the offense is under subdivision 1 of section 261 of the Penal Code, in which case the punishment shall be either by imprisonment in the county jail for not more than one year or in the state prison for not more than 50 years, and in such case the jury shall recommend by their verdict whether the punishment shall be by imprisonment in the county jail or in the state prison, provided that when the defendant pleads guilty of an offense under subdivision 1 of secton 261 of the Penal Code, the punishment shall be in the discretion of the trial court, either by imprisonment in the county jail for not more than one year or the state prison for not more than 50 years." (Penal Code, sec. 264).

In a prosecution for statutory rape under subdivision 1 a verdict is invalid unless it fixes the place of imprisonment (People v. Sachau, 76 Cal. App. 702; People v. Beck, 95 Cal. App. 257) and if the jury fixes the place of imprisonment as the county jail the court has no power to sentence the defendant to the state prison. (People v. Rambaud, 78 Cal. App. 685.)

No Corroboration Required

In a prosecution for rape a conviction may be had upon the uncorroborated testimony of the prosecutrix (People v. Frye, 117 Cal. App. 2d 101; People v. Soto, 155 Cal. App. 2d forcible rape). Section 1111 of the Penal Code does not apply since the female is not an accomplice (see Accomplice) nor does section 1108 of the code apply since that section applies only to cases of abortion and seduction for the purpose of prostitution (People v. Frye, supra).

Proof of Non-Marriage

In all prosecutions for rape the proof must show that at the time of the offense the female was not married to the defendant (People v. Gonzales, 6 Cal. App. 255; People v. Miles, 9 Cal. App. 312), but this element of the corpus delicti need not be established by formal proof and may be shown by circumstantial evidence. (People v. Meraviglia, 73 Cal. App. 402; People v. Bonzani, 24 Cal. App. 549; People v. Allison, 44 Cal. App. 118; People v. Truesdall, 124 Cal. App. 360; People v. Peters, 149 Cal. App. 2d 94).

The fact that at the time of the offense the prosecutrix was the wife of another is not a defense. (People v. Sheffield, 9 Cal. App. 130.)

Statutory Rape   *P.C. 261 - Sec. I*

The form of rape defined in subdivision 1 of section 261 is commonly referred to as statutory rape since, by statute, an act, which otherwise would amount only to fornication, is constituted rape where the female is under the age of eighteen years and is, under the law, incapable of consenting to the act. "From the disparity in the ages of the petitioner (defendant) and the victim the trial court could draw the inference that the victim was not the wife of the defendant" (Smith v. Sup. Ct., 140 Cal. App. 2d 862). Where, in the prosecution of her father for statutory rape, the victim was 13 years old at the time of the sexual act which resulted in the birth of a baby, lived with her parents under the same surname as her parents, responded when addressed as "Miss" Henry but refused to testify as to whether she had ever been married but testified that she was not married to the defendant, the court held that the corpus delicti had not been proved since there was no proof that she had not been married to the person responsible for her pregnancy (People v. Henry, 142 Cal. App. 2d 114).

It is wholly immaterial whether the accused knew that the girl was under the age of eighteen years and, if she was in fact under that age at the time of the act, the fact that she had represented herself to be over that age or had the appearance of being over that age (People v. Griffin, 117 Cal. 583; People v. Ratz, 115 Cal. 132) or that the defendant believed she was over eighteen (People v. Ratz, 115 Cal. 132) is no defense. The fact that the prosecutrix was not of previous chaste character, even though she had had acts of sexual intercourse with other men, does not affect the guilt of the accused. (People v. Derbert, 138 Cal. 467.)

While the failure to make outcry at the time of the offense or to make prompt complaint after the commission of the offense has an important bearing in cases of rape where consent would be a defense these matters have little significance in cases of statutory rape (People v. Williams, 24 Cal. App. 647; People v. McDonald, 167 Cal. 545) except in those cases in which the facts amounted to forcible rape or where the act was accomplished without the consent of the female. Consent is absolutely no defense, not even in a case where the defendant is younger than the prosecutrix and she has been the aggressor. (People v. Derbert, 138 Cal. 467.)

Female of Unsound Mind

In cases under subdivision 2 of section 261 the crime is made rape because the female is mentally incompetent and incapable of consenting. (People v. Boggs, 107 Cal. App. 492.) "In this species of rape neither force on the part of the man, nor resistance on the part of the woman, forms an element of the crime. If by reason of any mental weakness she is incapable of legally consenting, resistance is not to be expected any more than it is in the case of one who has been drugged into unconsciousness or robbed of her judgment by intoxicants. Nor will an apparent consent in such a case avail any more than in the case of a child who may actually consent but who by law is conclusively held incapable of legal consent. . . . It need but be said that legal consent presupposes an intelligence capable of understanding the act, its nature and its possible consequences." (People v. Griffin, 117 Cal. 583; People v. Peery, 26 Cal. App. 143.)

Where the prosecutrix was a moron who knew what constituted the physical act of sexual intercourse and that pregnancy might result therefrom, but had little conception of other serious consequences and gave a childish explanation as to why she had consented, a conviction was sustained. (People v. Boggs, 107 Cal. App. 492.) The belief of the defendant that the prosecutrix was capable of consenting and that she did consent is no defense; the test is whether she was capable of consenting and not what belief was entertained by the accused. (People v. Griffin, 117 Cal. 583.)

Forcible Rape

The form of rape covered by subdivision 3 of section 261 includes those cases wherein the act is committed by force and overcoming the resistance of the female.

Conviction on Circumstancial Evidence

A conviction may be had solely on circumstantial evidence. (see People v. Gulbrandsen, 35 Cal. 2d 514 wherein the prosecutrix did not testify but the evidence showed that she had been struck violently about the head and had suffered an act of sexual intercourse and, scantily dressed in a man's shirt and bloody and bruised went to a car which had stopped nearby and made complaint and her clothes and blood were found nearby and a conviction of forcible rape was sustained; see also People v. Peters, 149 Cal. App. 2d 94).

Degree of Resistance

The rule that the female must resist to the utmost is not recognized in California. As stated in People v. Cline, 117 Cal. App. 181, "The female need not resist as long as either strength endures or consciousness continues. Rather the resistance must be proportioned to the outrage, and the amount of resistance required necessarily depends upon the circumstances, such as the relative strength of the parties, the age and condition of the female, the uselessness of the resistance, and the degree of force manifested. Stated in another way, the resistance of the female to support a charge of rape need only be such as to make non-consent and actual resistance reasonably manifest (People v. Perkins, 80 Cal. App. 2d 68; People v. Ford, 81 Cal. App. 580; People v. Cassandras, 83 Cal. App. 2d 272; People v. Harris, 108 Cal. App. 2d 84; People v. Soewart, 109 Cal. App. 2d 334; People v. Nazworth, 152 Cal. App. 2d .... A.C.A. 836. The female need resist only until physical penetration occurs, when the crime is complete and her failure to resist after that is immaterial; and she need only resist until resistance becomes so useless as to warrant its cessation." (See also People v. Cook, 10 Cal. App. 2d 54; People v.

Burnette, 39 Cal. App. 2d 215; People v. Goldsmith, 130 Cal. App. 443; People v. Brown, 138 Cal. App. 748; People v. Perkins, 80 Cal. App. 2d 68.) Where, after being beaten and forcibly raped by two men, the victim was taken by them to the house of appellant and told to keep her mouth shut or she would be beaten again, was again raped by the two men and appellant had intercourse with her while one of the men held her, "her continued resistance was not, under such conditions essential to proof of forcible rape. She should not have resisted the crushing of her cranium or the further mutilation of her body to prevent the violation of her virtue." People v. Rivas. 92 Cal. App. 2d 663). Where the defendant placed a knife against the throat of the woman and in effect threatened to cut her throat, there was a reasonable explanation why she did not cry out, that she feared for her life and accepted the rape to avoid being killed (People v. Trapps, 152 Cal. App. 2d .... A.C.A. 454).

Forcible Rape by Threat or Drug

Where the offense comes under subdivision 4 of section 261 the characteristic is that the female is prevented from resisting by threats of great and immediate bodily harm or is incapable of resisting because of the effects of the administering of an intoxicating narcotic or anesthetic substance by or with the privity of the accused.

By Threat

Where the act is committed upon a female prevented from resisting by a threat of immediate and great bodily injury there is no requirement that the female resist. (People v. Raucho, 8 Cal. App. 2d 655.) Where at night defendant, entirely nude, came up behind the prosecutrix, grabbed her around the neck and struck her in the mouth, told her she had better not scream and dragged her onto a vacant lot and ravished her, it was held that the case came within the provisions of subdivision 4 of section 261. (People v. Rasmussen, 25 Cal. App 2d 399; see also to same effect, People v. Bouquet, 30 Cal. App. 2d 264.) A threat within subdivision 4 need not be expressed in words or through the exhibition of a weapon but may be expressed by acts and conduct. (People v. Flores, 62 Cal. App. 2d 700; People v. Cassandras, 83 Cal. App. 2d 272.) Fear of being shot by defendant, whom she believed to be armed with a pistol, he having displayed what appeared to be a real pistol but in fact was a toy pistol, by reason of which the female did not offer greater resistance, sufficiently establishes such violence as would characterize the enforced sexual act as rape. (People v. Coleman, 53 Cal. App. 2d 18.) Submission induced by the fear specified in the statute is not consent (People v. Cassandras, 83 Cal. App. 2d 272; People v. Peterman, 103 Cal. App. 2d 322).

The application of the latter half of subdivision 4 is shown by a case in which the defendant and the prosecutrix consumed intoxicants at a hotel and she was seen lying unconscious in the road with the defendant near by and she was unable to recall anything that had occurred after she left the hotel. The physical facts showed that someone had had sexual intercourse with her and other evidence and admissions showed the defendant to be the guilty person. The conviction was sustained. (People v. O'Brien, 130 Cal. 1.)

Rape—Unconscious Victim

Subdivision 5 of section 261 covers cases where the female "is at the time unconscious of the nature of the act, and this is known to the accused." The phraseology is not aptly chosen and has not yet been interpreted by our appellate courts. However, convictions have been sustained in other jurisdictions where a defendant accomplished the act by causing the female to believe that she was undergoing legitimate medical treatment and she was not aware of the true nature of the act and, there being no other provision in section 261 to cover a case where a man has an act of intercourse with a woman who is in a state of unconsciousness and without her consent, such a case might be held to come under the provisions of subdivision 5 for, if it does not, a woman in such condition would have no protection from such an attack.

Rape by Fraud

While there are but a handful of court decisions anywhere of cases which would come within the provisions of subdivision 6 of section 261 it has been held in this state that, where the defendant went through the form of marriage with the prosecuting witness, he knowing that the marriage was a mere sham and of no legal effect, whereas she believed it to be a valid marriage and permitted sexual intercourse under that belief, the defendant was held guilty of rape under this subdivision. (People v. McCoy, 58 Cal. App. 534.)

Rape—Who May Commit

Since the statute provides that ONE of the essential elements of the crime of rape is that the female must not be the wife of the perpetrator a husband cannot commit the crime upon his wife, but if he aids and abets another in the perpetration of rape he is guilty as a principal and the fact that the female victim is his wife is no defense. (In re Kantrowitz, 24 Cal. App. 203.) And similarly a woman who aids and abets a man in the commission of rape is equally guilty with the actual perpetrator. (People v. Bartol, 24 Cal. App. 659; People v. Anderson, 75 Cal. App. 365; People v. Young, 132 Cal. App. 770.)

Rape—Complaint by Prosecutrix   *Evidence ques.*

Evidence that the prosecutrix in a rape case made complaint of the attack shortly after it occurred is admissible as tending to corroborate her testimony that the act was against her will and without her consent, but the complaint must have been made within a reasonable time after the act (People v. Branch, 77 Cal. App. 384), and evidence of a complaint made three weeks after the alleged rape has been held inadmissible as not made within a reasonable time. (People v. Corey, 8 Cal. App. 720; People v. Brown, 71 Cal. App. 2d 669, two months.) What is a reasonable time always depends on the circumstances of the particular case, and while a delay until the victim has recovered from the immediate shock and has contacted some person to whom she could reasonably be expected to relate the experience would be reasonable, a failure to make complaint after ample opportunity and occasion to do so would generally be unreasonable.

Where Prosecutrix Does Not Testify

While it is the theory that evidence of prompt complaint by the prosecutrix is admissible as tending to corroborate and the general rule is that evidence of the fact of complaint is not admissible where she does not take the stand, this rule of exclusion does not seem to apply where the female is too young to become a witness (People v. Adams, 14 Cal. 2d 154, 158; People v. Figueroa, 134 Cal. 159, 162; People v. O'Bryan, 132 Cal. App. 496, 503; People v. Bianchino, 5 Cal. App. 633, 636) or where the prosecutrix is incapable, by reason of physical condition, to take the stand (People v. Gulbrandsen, 35 Cal. 2d 514, opinion discusses the point but leaves it rather open).

Evidence of Complaint

Evidence of complaint must be limited to proof merely that complaint was made (People v. Barney, 114 Cal. 554; People v. Baldwin, 117 Cal. 244; People v. Wilmot, 139 Cal. 103; People v. Branch, 77 Cal. App. 384) and evidence of what the prosecutrix said is inadmissible hearsay. (People v. Lambert, 120 Cal. 170; People v. Wilmot, 139 Cal. 103; People v. Porter, 48 Cal. App. 237; People v. Avila, 50 Cal. App. 228.) The authorities are not, however, in accord as to how far evidence of the fact of complaint may go. It has been held that the proof may show that the prosecutrix made complaint of an assault of the nature of that charged (People v. Branch, 77 Cal. App. 384; People v. Adams, 92 Cal. App. 6) and that it is not error to allow evidence that the prosecutrix made complaint naming the defendant (People v. Porter, 48 Cal. App. 237; People v. Adams, 92 Cal. App. 6; People v. Lopez, 33 Cal. App. 530), but other cases have held it error to allow proof that in making complaint the prosecutrix named the defendant. (People v. Wilmot, 139 Cal. 103; People v. Fernandez, 4 Cal. App. 314; People v. Avila, 50 Cal. App. 228; People v. Branch, 77 Cal. App. 384; People v. O'Bryan, 132 Cal. App 496.)

Note: Since evidence of the fact of complaint can be justified only where the complaint concerned the defendant and the act for which he is on trial it would seem in principle that it should be permissible to prove that the defendant was named and that the complaint concerned the subject of the offense for which the defendant is on trial and that the defendant should be permitted to prove, if such be the case, that he was not named or that the complaint was at variance with the crime charged. If proof is limited to the bare fact of complaint, the jury will naturally and justifiably assume that the complaint concerned the defendant and the offense for which he is on trial, an assumption which is not always warranted, since it does not follow that every complaint includes the unequivocal naming of the defendant or that the act complained of is the same as the act involved in the offense charged. Thus the prosecutrix in a rape case might make complaint of improper familiarities and of being embraced and kissed against her will but make no complaint of being subjected to an act of sexual intercourse and still, if the inquiry be limited to the mere fact of complaint, a question would be answered in the affirmative; the natural inference which the jury would draw from such an answer and the injustice resulting to the accused is obvious. (See People v. Adams, 92 Cal. App. 6.) It would seem also that evidence of complaint should be limited to cases in which the act was committed without the consent of the prosecutrix and wherein the outrage or pain and injury inflicted would naturally result in complaint but that in cases of statutory rape where the act was not without the consent of the prosecutrix and where the fact of complaint has no significance (People v. Jacobs, 16 Cal. App. 478; People v. McDonald, 167 Cal. 545; People v. Williams, 24 Cal. 647) neither the fact of complaint nor the failure to make complaint should be admitted for, if the act was not unwelcome, not only is the reason for permitting proof of complaint absent, there being no occasion to corroborate testimony that the act was against her will, but her failure to make complaint, which in a case of forcible rape might generate a doubt as to whether she had been outraged, would have no significance.

Chastity of Prosecutrix

Upon a charge of rape it is not a defense that the woman was of unchaste character or even that she was a common prostitute. In those cases, however, in which lack of consent is an element of the particular form of rape charged and cases in which the prosecutrix testifies that the act was accomplished by force and against her will, the defense may introduce evidence of her previous unchaste character as tending to show a greater likelihood of her having given consent. (People v. Degnen, 70 Cal. App. 567; People v. Biescar, 97 Cal. App. 205; People v. Benson, 6 Cal. 221; People v. Shea, 125 Cal 151; People v. Battalina, 52 Cal. App. 2d 685.)

In cases of statutory rape where the female testifies that the act was committed by force and against her will and consent, evidence of a lack of chastity is admissible to discredit her testimony that in accomplishing his purpose the defendant exerted force and violence. "It should be understood that the prior unchastity of the prosecutrix may not be put in issue in a statutory rape case except when force and violence is claimed to have been used in the commission of the offense." (People v. Pantages, 212 Cal. 237; People v. Griffin, 118 Cal. App. 18; People v. Vivian, 50 Cal. App. 2d 533.)

Proof of Unchastity

The evidence which may be introduced to prove the unchaste character of the prosecutrix must be such as will tend to prove her unchastity, such as lewd acts with other men or prior lewd acts with the defendant (People v. Degnen, 70 Cal. App. 567; People v. Benson, 6 Cal. 221), but evidence which does not tend to establish unchastity, such as that she habitually indulged in lewd conversations telling indecent stories, is not admissible to prove lack of chastity (People v. Kuches, 120 Cal. 566), nor should mere evidence of general reputation for unchastity be received for, considering the reason for admitting proof of unchastity, the great likelihood of an unchaste woman giving consent, the evidence should be limited to that which tends to prove actual unchastity. Evidence of general reputation has, however, been said to be admissible. (People v. Benson, 6 Cal. 221; see also California Criminal Evidence under Chastity of Prosecutrix).

Evidence in the Prosecution ~~provable by prosecution~~

Where the evidence in the prosecution of an offense involves proof of an act of sexual intercourse, and to corroborate testimony that such an act has taken place, the prosecution introduces evidence that the female became pregnant or suffered external or internal injuries, bruises or abrasions or contracted a venereal disease, the accused may not only prove that such condition was not caused by any act on his part but may show that the female had sustained sexual relations with other men to show further that her condition was not caused by him (People v. Kilfoil, 27 Cal. App. 29, 35), and such fact may be established either on the cross-examination of the prosecutrix or by independent evidence. (People v. Davidson, 23 Cal. App. 2d 116.) But the defendant is not entitled to introduce such proof unless the prosecution has first opened the door by the introduction of some evidence, other than and beyond the testimony that an act of sexual intercourse with the defendant had occurred, independently tending to prove that such an act had occurred. (People v. Currie, 14 Cal. App. 67; People v. Kilfoil, 27 Cal. App. 29; People v. Fong Chung, 5 Cal. App. 587.)

On the other hand the prosecution is not permitted to prove that the prosecutrix had never had an act of sexual intercourse with any other person prior to that had with the defendant (People v. Parish, 25 Cal. App. 314; People v. O'Brien, 130 Cal. 1) except, of course, in rebuttal of evidence that she had such prior experience.

Female Not Conscious of Nature of Act

There have been no decisions construing subdivision 5 of section 261 but in the light of decisions of other jurisdictions it applies to those cases in which sexual penetration is accomplished but the female does not know at the time that the act is one of sexual intercourse, not because of any mental defect or unconsciousness but because of a deception practiced upon her as where a physician or person purporting to be a physician under the representation that he is administering medical treatment to the sexual organs of the female actually has sexual intercourse with her.

Sexual Intercourse By Fraud _misrepresentation_

Section 266 of the Penal Code provides that "Every person who by any false pretenses, false representations or other fraudulent means procures any female to have sexual intercourse with any man is punishable by imprisonment in the state prison for not exceeding five years or by imprisonment in a county jail not exceeding one year or by a fine not exceeding one thousand dollars or by both such fine and imprisonment." While this section might in some cases come under the form of rape referred to in the preceding paragraph it will also apply to cases in which the female is aware of the fact that she is having sexual intercourse but her consent is obtained by fraud.

INCEST _not within family_

"Persons being within the degrees of consanguinity within which marriages are declared by law to be incestuous and void, who intermarry with each other, or who commit fornication or adultery with each other, are punishable by imprisonment in the state prison not less than one and not more than fifty years." (Penal Code, sec. 285.)

Section 59 of the Civil Code declares incestuous and void all marriages between parent and child, ancestors and descendants, brothers and sisters of the half or whole blood, uncles and nieces and aunts and nephews, whether the relationship is legitimate or illegitimate.

Fornication is voluntary unlawful sexual intercourse, and as such is not punishable in California, though when the act is committed under circumstances of aggravation as in adultery, incest or rape, or in violation of laws against prostitution, it is punishable as a separate offense under such special statute or ordinance.

CONSANGUINITY_Blood relationship
INCEST_cohabitation (live together as husband & wife)
between persons related within the degrees wherein
marriage is prohibited by law.

Consent of Both Parties

To constitute the offense of incest it is not necessary that both parties consent to the incestuous act. Thus, if the act of sexual intercourse is accomplished under such circumstances as would constitute either forcible or statutory rape, the offense is not the less incest because every element of the crime of rape is added to that of the relationship of the parties. (People v. Stratton, 141 Cal. 604; People v. Kaiser, 119 Cal. 456.)

If the act is with the consent of both parties they may both be prosecuted and upon the trial of one the other would, if called as a witness, be an accomplice whose testimony would not be sufficient to justify a conviction unless corroborated, (People v. Stratton, 141 Cal. 604) but a party who did not consent need not be corroborated (People v. Hall, 25 Cal. App. 2d 336), and where but one of the parties is guilty of the offense, as where the other by reason of age or other incapacity is incapable of committing the crime or where the act also amounts to forcible rape or the female is under the age of consent, the guilty party may be tried alone. (People v. Patterson, 102 Cal. 239.) Where the female is under the 18 year age of consent she is not an accomplice and is not guilty of incest (People v. Hamilton, 88 Cal. App. 2d 398).

Knowledge of Relationship

When the act charged was with the mutual consent of both parties and one had knowledge of their relationship and the other was ignorant of it, the former would be guilty but the other would not (People v. Patterson, 102 Cal. 239, 242; Penal Code sec. 26, subd. 4). The case of People v. Koller, 142 Cal. 621, merely holds that knowledge of the relationship need not be affirmatively pleaded.

Relationship

The word "child" as used in the statute means an immediate descendant and not an adopted child, a step-child or a son-in-law or daughter-in-law. (People v. Kaiser, 119 Cal. 456.)

SEDUCTION

"Every person who, under promise of marriage, seduces and has sexual intercourse with an unmarried female of previous chaste character, is punishable by imprisonment in the state prison for not more than five years or by a fine of not more than five thousand dollars, or by both such fine and imprisonment.'' (Penal Code, sec. 268.)

Prosecutrix Must Be Unmarried

This offense cannot be committed where the female is not unmarried. The fact that the prosecutrix is unmarried must be affirmatively proved and cannot be inferred from proof, for example, that she was referred to as "Miss" by the witnesses or her own testimony that she and the defendant had agreed to marry and had made arrangements for the marriage. (People v. Krusick, 93 Cal. 74.)

Under Promise of Marriage

An essential and vital element of the corpus delicti is that the seduction must have been accomplished "under promise of marriage," that the prosecutrix relied upon the promise to marry her and but for that promise would not have consented to the act of sexual intercourse. (People v. Krusick, 93 Cal. 74; People v. Wright, 18 Cal. App. 171.) To establish this fact the proof may be either by the statements and declarations of the parties or may consist of evidence of circumstances or a combination of both.

If the prosecutrix knew that the promise of marriage could not be carried out because of an obstacle, such as the fact that the accused was then a married man, she would not be warranted in relying upon the promise and if she consented upon the strength of such a promise the offense of seduction would not be committed even though she might have believed that the obstacle to marriage would be removed and the promise then kept. (People v. Wright, 18 Cal. App. 171; People v. Kehoe, 123 Cal. 224.) But if, though the accused was in fact married, the female did not know that he was married, but believed him to be free to carry out his promise to marry and she submitted in reliance upon such promise, the fact that he was married would neither excuse him or be a defense to the charge. (People v. Kehoe, 123 Cal. 224.)

Nature of Promise

The promise need not be such a legal promise as would support a civil action for breach of promise to marry, so long as it be such a promise to marry as would justify the female in relying upon it. Thus, if the accused be a boy of the age of sixteen years, though he be incapable of making a legal binding contract of marriage, he is not incapable of making a promise of marriage which in good faith it was his duty to perform and in such a case a prosecution for seduction will lie even though the girl knew his age. The distinction between such a case and one in which the female knew that the accused was married is that in the latter case the prosecutrix knows that the accused is legally incapable of marrying and is not justified in relying upon a promise which is necessarily conditional upon the death or putting away of his wife and so base a contract would not excuse her in law for surrendering her chastity in reliance thereon, while, in the case of the minor, the only conditional feature of the promise would be the lapse of time until he became of legal age to marry. (People v. Kehoe, 123 Cal. 224.)

It is not necessary that the promise to marry be the sole cause inducing the consent of the prosecutrix as it is sufficient if it be shown that the act of sexual intercourse would not have been consented to except for such promise. (People v. Wallace, 109 Cal. 611; People v. Zuvela, 191 Cal. 223.)

Distinction Must Be Drawn

A distinction must be drawn, however, between a promise to marry and a promise to marry the female only in the event of her becoming pregnant. In the latter instance, no prosecution would lie since there the promise to marry is made dependent upon pregnancy and not upon the consent to the illicit intercourse. (People v. Jensen, 15 Cal. App. 220.)

"It is sufficient if the circumstances be such as to warrant the jury in the deduction that the act of sexual intercourse would not have been accomplished without or in the absence of the promise (to marry)". (People v. Zuvela, 191 Cal. 223.)

Chastity of Prosecutrix

Another vital element of the offense is that it can only be committed where the prosecutrix is "an unmarried female of previous chaste character." (People v. Krusick, 93 Cal. 74.) Chastity within the view of section 268 "means, in the case of an unmarried female, simply that she is virgo intacta, and, though one woman may permit liberties or even indecencies at the thought of which another woman would blush, so long as that woman has not surrendered her virtue she is not put without the pale of the law," and she is considered to be of chaste character. The character for chastity involved in this offense is such character previous to the offense and the character of the prosecutrix for chastity thereafter, even though it be bad, is wholly immaterial and cannot be proved at the trial. (People v. Kehoe, 123 Cal. 224.) The statement in the cited case as to the female being virgo intacta must be limited, however, by the qualification that a female may be unmarried and of previous chaste character within the meaning of section 268 even though she had formerly been married and borne children of that marriage.

Previous character need not be proven by evidence given directly on that point but may be shown by circumstances (People v. Roderiges, 48 Cal. 9) and it has been held that a witness who had known the prosecutrix for several years may testify that he had never known of any improper conduct on her part (People v. Samonset, 97 Cal. 448), but the value of the latter decision as a precedent is doubtful.

Corroboration of Prosecutrix

While it might seem, at first blush, that section 1108 of the Penal Code may require that the testimony of the prosecutrix must be corroborated, that section has no application to a prosecution for seduction under section 268 and a conviction may be had upon her uncorroborated testimony. (People v. Wade, 118 Cal. 672; People v. Coffee, 161 Cal. 448; People v. Hough, 120 Cal. 538; People v. Votaw, 38 Cal. App. 715.) The corroboration required by section 1108 is in the case of a prosecution for seduction for the purposes of prostitution made punishable by section 266 of the Penal Code.

Good Faith of Accused

If under and by means of his promise of marriage, the defendant induced the prosecutrix to consent to an act of sexual intercourse and later refused to fulfill his promise, the offense is committed regardless of what his intentions as to keeping such promise may have been when such promise was made. (People v. Samonset, 97 Cal. 448.)

Subsequent Marriage

"The intermarriage of the parties subsequent to the commission of the offense is a bar to a prosecution for a violation of the last section; provided, such marriage takes place prior to the finding of an indictment or the filing of an information charging such offense." (Penal Code, sec. 269.)

While such marriage would be a bar to a prosecution, the woman is not required to marry her seducer and thus free him from the penalty of the law. Even though he be ready and willing, she may refuse to marry him and it is wholly immaterial whether the reasons for her refusal are good or bad, and when she has so declined, the road to a successful prosecution is free and undisturbed. The refusal of the accused to marry is not an element of the crime. (People v. Hough, 120 Cal. 538.)

CRIME AGAINST NATURE

"Every person who is guilty of the infamous crime against nature, committed with mankind or with any animal, is punishable by imprisonment in the state prison not less than one year." (Penal Code, sec. 286);

"Any sexual penetration, however slight, is sufficient to complete the crime against nature." (Penal Code, sec. 286; People v. Singh, 93 Cal. App. 32.)

This offense is variously named Sodomy, Bestiality or Buggery. These terms are not entirely synonymous but section 286 includes the offenses referred to by various authors and in the statutes of other states under these titles. (See People v. Erwin, 4 Cal. App. 394; People v. Battalina, 52 Cal. App. 2d 685; People v. Babb, 103 Cal. App. 2d 326.)

When committed with mankind the act must be per anum. (People v. Boyle, 116 Cal. 658.) The act when committed with a person's mouth is specially provided for in a separate section (288a) of the Penal Code and is not within the scope of section 286. (People v. Boyle, supra.) Both penetration and emission were necessary at common law, but by virtue of section 287, the crime is complete with penetration in any degree. Section 286, which does not define the act constituting the offense, must be construed as including those acts which at common law constituted the infamous crime against nature. When the offense is committed with an animal, any form of copulation is included and the scope of the statute is not limited to an act per annum (People v. Smith, 117 Cal. App. 2d 648).

In a prosecution for sodomy the fact of complaint by the victim is admissible the rule here being substantially the same as in cases of rape or violations of section 288 of the Penal Code. (People v. Brown, 71 Cal. App. 2d 669.)

LEWD AND LASCIVIOUS ACT WITH CHILD

"Any person who shall wilfully and lewdly commit any lewd or lascivious act including any of the acts constituting other crimes provided in part one of this code upon or with the body, or any part or member thereof, of a child under the age of fourteen years, with the intent of arousing, appealing to, or gratifying the lust or passions or sexual desires of such person or of such child, shall be guilty of a felony and shall be imprisoned in the state prison for a term of from one year to life." (Penal Code, sec. 288.)

Corpus Delicti

virtue of state of mind of accused

The corpus delicti of this crime consists of (1) any lewd or lascivious act upon any part of the body, (2) of a child under the age of fourteen years, (3) with intent of arousing, appealing to or gratifying the lust or passions or sexual desires of either the perpetrator or of such child. (People v. Bronson, 69 Cal. App. 83; People v. McCurdy, 60 Cal. App. 499; People v. Showers, 90 Cal. App. 2d 248; People v. Shields, 70 Cal. App. 2d 628.) Since the mere intent is all that the statute requires, it is not necessary that the passions of either party be actually aroused. (People v. Bronson, 69 Cal. 83; People v. Hunt, 17 Cal. App. 2d 284; People v. McCurdy, 60 Cal. App. 499.)

This offense does not in any manner depend upon, and it is not necessary for the prosecution to either plead or prove the sex of the child. (People v. Curtis, 1 Cal. App. 1; People v. Zuell, 2 Cal. App. 59.) It is not necessary to sustain a conviction to prove an attempt to commit rape or that the child attempted to resist (People v. Showers, 90 Cal. App. 2d 253 and cases cited and whether or not the child consented is immaterial.

Nature of Act

The act need not amount to an act of a sexual character nor need it be obscene (People v. Hobbs, 109 Cal. App. 2d 189) and may even be an act which under other circumstances would not be improper; it need only be of a lewd and lascivious character and performed with the specific intent set forth in the statute (People v. Bronson, 69 Cal. App. 83; People v. Kearney, 48 Cal. App. 2d 672; People v. Hyche, 52 Cal. App. 2d 661), but a mere lewd or licentious act without such specific intent is not sufficient. (People v. Stouter, 142 Cal. 146;

see also People v. Grinnell, 9 Cal. App. 238). Proof of an emission is not essential (People v. Coontz, 119 Cal. App. 2d 276.) To constitute an act within the prohibition of the statute it is not necessary that the naked body of the child be touched (People v. Dabner, 25 Cal. App. 630; People v. Schultz, 49 Cal. App. 2d 38; People v. Hartshorn, 59 Cal. App. 2d 285; People v. Ash, 70 Cal. App. 2d 583), and it need only be an act of a lascivious character (People v. Bronson, 69 Cal. App. 83), such as feeling the legs and breast of a female child (People v. McCurdy, 60 Cal. App. 449; People v. Adams, 7 Cal. App. 2d 743), feeling the legs (People v. Halistic, 69 Cal. App. 174; People v. Hyche, 52 Cal. App. 2d 661), pinching the breasts (People v. Epperson, 7 Cal. App. 2d 125), exposing his person and placing the child in a position indicating an indecent purpose (People v. King, 65 Cal. App. 306), placing the child's hand upon his private parts (People v. Anthony, 20 Cal. App. 586), placing his tongue in the child's mouth (People v. Ash, 70 Cal. App. 2d 583), bringing his head in contact with the child's legs (People v. Campbell, 80 Cal. App. 2d 798), or removing the panties of the child (People v. Lanham, 137 Cal. App. 737; People v. Pollock, 61 Cal. App. 2d 213.) An act of sexual intercourse may be a violation of section 288. (People v. Bush, 56 Cal. App. 2d 887; People v. Leete, 130 Cal. App. 2d 725).

Evidence

The crime may be proved by circumstantial evidence and, if so established, it is not even necessary that the child be called as a witness. (People v. Ewing, 71 Cal. App. 138; People v. Domenighini, 81 Cal. App. 484; People v. Mohr, 24 Cal. App. 2d 580.)

The corpus delicti of the offense may be proved circumstantially and without the testimony of the child. Thus where a four year old girl returned home in a hysterical condition and hardly able to walk and a medical examination disclosed a laceration of the external genitals and bleeding from the vagina which the doctor said could have resulted from the insertion of a part of an adult person, could not have been caused by a blow or a fall and could have been caused only by the insertion of some instrumentality into the vagina, it was held that the corpus delicti had been sufficiently established (People v. Smith, 100 Cal. App. 2d 166, holding also that the identity of the perpetrator is not an element of the corpus delicti). The mere fact that the child had a physical injury in the region of the private parts is not sufficient. Thus, where the only testimony was the testimony of a doctor that, upon examining the girl, he found a slight tear at the posterior of the genital organs, a laceration of the vagina, and the child testified that she did not know what, if anything, the defendant did to her and there was no evidence as to how the laceration was caused, it was held that this was insufficient to prove the corpus delicti or that the injury was received by unlawful means (People v. Schuber, 71 Cal. App. 2d 773).

Where the only testimony or evidence as to the age of the child is that which was elicited on the voire dire examination of the child as to her qualifications as a witness, she being under ten years of age, there was held to be no proof of her age to support the charge. The fact of age should have been elicited from the child after she had been qualified and sworn as a witness or established by other evidence. (People v. Adams, 7 Cal. App. 2d 743.)

Child Need Not be Corroborated *no other evidence needed than that of childs*

Since the offense can only be accomplished upon a person under the age of fourteen years the child victim of this offense is not an accomplice and his or her testimony does not require corroboration. (People v. Wilder, 151 Cal. App. 2d...... cases cited; People v. Ridout, 154 Cal. App. 2d........). (See also: ACCOMPLICE—who is not.)

Complaint by Child *— not competent witness*

The fact that, subsequent to the commission of the offense, the child made complaint of the occurrence may be proved by any witness who heard the complaint made (People v. Morcumb, 28 Cal. App. 2d 465; People v. Watrous, 7 Cal. App. 2d 7), but it is not permissible to give in evidence what the child said (People v. Guiterez, 126 Cal. App. 526; People v. Huston, 21 Cal. 2d 690) or that the child named the accused. (People v. Huston, 21 Cal. 2d 690, indicating, however, that it would be proper to identify the complaint "as being related to the matter under inquiry." Note:— See also comment under RAPE—Complaint by Prosecutrix.) A statement elicited from the child by a spanking is not a complaint and the rule permitting the proof of the fact of complaint does not apply. (People v. Ewing, 71 Cal. App. 138.)

Delay, on the part of the child, to make complaint goes only to the weight of her testimony (People v. Wilder, 151 Cal. App. 2d......).

In Connection With Other Offense

Where an act in violation of section 288 of the Penal Code precedes the commission of another sex offense the defendant may be convicted of either or both such offenses. (People v. Lind, 68 Cal. App. 575; People v. Bronson, 69 Cal. App. 83; People v. Parker, 74 Cal. App. 540; People v. Agullana, 4 Cal. App. 2d 34; see also FORMER JEOPARDY—Offenses Connected in Their Commission.)

Molesting Children

"Every person who annoys or molests any child under the age of 18 is a vagrant and is punishable upon first conviction by a fine of not exceeding five hundred dollars ($500) or by imprisonment in the county jail for not exceeding six months or by both such fine and imprisonment and is punishable upon a second and each subsequent conviction or upon the first conviction after a previous conviction under section 288 of this code by imprisonment in the state prison not exceeding five years." (Penal Code, sec. 647a).

The words "under the age of 18" mean "under the age of 18 years (People v. Pallares, 112 Cal. App. 2d 895).

The word "annoy" means to disturb or irritate, especially by continued and repeated acts. The word "molest" is generally a synonym for "annoy", conveys the idea of injury, injustice, hurt, inconvenience or damage and is also defined as meaning to trouble, disturb, annoy or vex. When these words are used in reference to offenses against children there is a connotation of abnormal sex motivation on the part of the offender although no specific intent is prescribed as an element of the offense (People v. Pallares, 112 Cal. App. 2d 895; People v. McNair, 130 Cal. App. 2d 696; People v. Carkaddon, 49 Cal. 2d......). The element of annoyance as provided in section 647a is not concerned with the state of mind of the child; it is the objectionable acts of the defendant which constitute the offense, and, if the conduct of the defendant is so lewd or obscene that the normal person would unhesitatingly be irritated by it, such conduct would "annoy or molest" within the meaning of the section (People v. McNair, 130 Cal.. App. 2d 696 People v. Carskaddon, 49 Cal. 2d........; People v. Moore, 137 Cal. App. 2d........). "The annoyance or molestation which is forbidden is in no sense a purely subjective state on the part of the child. The objectionable acts of a defendant constitute the annoyance or molestation contemplated by the statute'' (People v. Pallares, 112 Cal. App. 2d Supp. 895; People v. McNair, 130 Cal. App. 2d 696, defendant did not contact the child but displayed his nude body at a window in view of the child; People v. Moore, 137 Cal. App. 2d 197), defendant rubbed his body against that of the child, both being clothed).

Where defendant took a six year old girl into a park, bought her an ice cream bar and walked up the street and, when questioned by a police officer said that the girl was lost and he was taking her home but the girl said that defendant was not taking her home but was taking her down to the river the court held that there was nothing more than friendly non-criminal activity on the part of defendant (People v. Carskaddon, 49 Cal. 2d......).

A reading of the section as a whole indicates that the acts forbidden are those motivated by an abnormal or unnatural sexual interest with respect to children (People v. Pallares, supra; People v. Moore, supra).

Specific Intent

No specific intent is prescribed as an element of this offense (People v. Pallares, 112 Cal. App. 2d Supp. 895, 901; People v. McNair, 130 Cal. App. 2d 696; People v. Moore 137 Cal. App. 2d 197).

Indecent Exposure

''Every person who wilfully and lewdly. . . .

1. Exposes his person, or the private parts thereof, in any public place, or in any place where there are present other persons to be offended or annoyed thereby . . . is guilty of a misdemeanor . . . Upon a second and each subsequent conviction under subdivision 1 of this section, or upon a first conviction under subdivision 1 of this section after a previous conviction under section 288 of this code, every person so convicted is guilty of a felony and is punishable by imprisonment in the state prison for not less than one year.'' (Penal Code, sec. 311.)

SEX PERVERSIONS

''Any person participating in an act of copulating the mouth of one person with the sexual organ of another is punishable by imprisonment in the state prison for not exceeding 15 years, or by imprisonment in the county jail not exceeding one year; provided, however, whenever any person is found guilty of the offense specified herein, and it is charged and admitted, or found to be true that he is more than 10 years older than his coparticipant in such an act, which coparticipant is under the age of 14, or that he has compelled the other's participation in such an act by force, violence, duress, menace or threat of great bodily harm, he shall be punished by imprisonment in the state prison for not less than three years. The order of commitment shall expressly state whether a person convicted hereunder is more than 10 years older than his coparticipant and whether such coparticipant is under the age of 14. The order shall also state whether a person convicted hereunder has compelled participation in his act by force, violence, duress, menace or threat of great bodily harm." (Penal Code, sec. 288a).

This offense does not include as an element of the corpus delicti any specific intent, purpose or motive, (People v. Avanzi, 25 Cal. App. 301), both voluntary participants are guilty of the offense, (People v. Parsons, 82 Cal. App. 17) and the offense may be committed upon a person of either sex. (People v. Coleman, 53 Cal. App. 2d 18.) For discussion of the nature of this offense see:— People v. Angier, 44 Cal. App. 2d 417, distinguished in People v. Coleman, 53 Cal. App. 2d 18, which to an extent overrules the Angier case; see also People v. Owen, 68 Cal. App. 2d 617. A person is guilty of violating the statute when he has placed his mouth upon the genital organ of another, People v. Harris, 108 Cal. App. 2d 84 and penetration is not necessary People v. Bennett, 119 Cal. App. 2d 224. Any penetration of the mouth, however slight, is a violation of the section (People v. Milo, 89 Cal. App. 2d 705; People v. Hickok, 96 Cal. App. 2d 621; People v. Chamberlain, 114 Cal. App. 2d 192). In this offense it is not necessary that the person upon whom the act was committed be corroborated unless he was an accomplice. (People v. Coleman, 52 Cal. App. 2d 18.)

BIGAMY

"Every person having a husband or wife living, who marries any other person, except in the cases specified in the next section, is guilty of bigamy." (Penal Code, sec. 281.)

"Bigamy is punishable by a fine not exceeding five thousand dollars ($5,000) or by imprisonment in a county jail not exceeding one year or in the state prison not exceeding ten years." (Penal Code, sec. 283).

"The last section does not extend—

1. To any person by reason of any former marriage, whose husband or wife by such marriage has been absent for five successive years without being known to such person within that time to be living; nor,

2. To any person by reason of any former marriage which has been pronounced void, annulled, or dissolved by the judgment of a competent court." (Penal Code, sec. 282.) The foregoing exceptions are not exclusive (People v. Vogel, 46 Cal. 2d 798).

Corpus Delicti

The corpus delicti of bigamy consists of (1) a person going through a marriage ceremony (2) having a living lawful husband or wife (People v. LaMarr, 20 Cal. 2d 705; People v. O'Neal, 85 Cal. App. 2d 226). Section 282 enumerates exceptions constituting a defense. (See People v. Feilen, 58 Cal. 220; Ex parte Baker, 4 Cal. App. 25.) This crime does not include as one of its elements any specific intent; the only intent required is that of being a party to the second marriage. (People v. Hartman, 130 Cal. 491). The prosecution makes a prima facie case upon proof that the second marriage was entered into while the first spouse was still living (People v. Vogel, 46 Cal. 2d 798). "To make out a case on the part of the prosecution, the first and second marriages must be proved and it must also be proved that the former husband or wife was alive when the latter marriage was entered into" and this latter fact can no more be proved by the presumption of continuance of life or other presumption than can any other essential element of a crime. (People v. Feilen, 58 Cal. 218; Ex parte Baker, 4 Cal. App. 26; People v. Huntley, 93 Cal. App. 504.)

Belief of Accused

The earlier cases holding that it was immaterial whether the defendant believed that he was free to remarry are no longer the law and it is now the law that a defendant is not guilty of bigamy if he had a bona fide and reasonable belief that facts existed that left him free to remarry and evidence tending to show such belief is admissible (People v. Vogel, 46 Cal. 2d 798). Such defense, honest mistake of fact is predicated upon subd. Four, sec. 26 of the Penal Code.

Jurisdiction

"When the offense, either of bigamy or incest, is committed in one county and the defendant is apprehended in another, the jurisdiction is in either county." (Penal Code, sec. 785.)

"Upon a trial for bigamy it is not necessary to prove either of the marriages by the register, certificate, or other record evidence thereof, but the same may be proved by such evidence as is admissible to prove a marriage in other cases; and when the second marriage took place out of this state, proof of that fact, accompanied by proof of cohabitation thereafter in this state, is sufficient to sustain the charge." (Penal Code, sec. 1106.) Where the defendant entered into bigamous marriage in the state of Missouri and then lived with his bigamous wife in this state it was held that cohabitation, living together as husband and wife, (People v. Du Fault, 1 Cal. App. 2d 105) in this state was "a complete substitute for the second marriage in this state" under the provisions of the last clause of section 1106, and the conviction of bigamy was sustained. (People v. Ellis, 204 Cal. 39; also People v. Du Fault, 1 Cal. App. 2d 105.) People v. O'Brien, 97 Cal. App. 2d . . . bigamous marriage in England.

Proof of Marriage

As provided in section 1106 (supra), record of documentary proof of marriage is not necessary to proof of either the first or the bigamous marriage and either marriage may be proved as it would be in any other case in which proof of marriage is necessary, and proof that the parties cohabited and were generally reputed to be husband and wife is admissible. (People v. Hartman, 130 Cal. 487.) There must be proof at least prima facie that the person who performed the marriage had legal authority to do so (People v. Spitzer, 57 Cal. App. 593), but the form of the first marriage is immaterial as long as it is valid. (People v. Beevers, 99 Cal. 286.) Testimony by the wife that the marriage was solemnized by a minister of the gospel in the presence of two witnesses and that they cohabited and so far as she knew there had been no dissolution of the union is prima facie evidence of marriage. (People v. Jacobs, 11 Cal. App. 2d 1; Budd v. Morgan, 187 Cal. 741.) The presumption under section 1963 of the Code of Civil Procedure (which would be applicable by the express provision of section 1106 of the Penal Code as to how marriage may be proved) that a marriage will be presumed from general repute and the fact that the parties have conducted themselves as husband and wife is overcome where it appears that they were living together as the result of an illegal marriage. (People v. Spitzer, 57 Cal. App. 593.) A marriage performed in one county is valid though the license was issued in another county. (People v. Lininger, 22 Cal. App. 2d 440.)

Valid First Marriage—Presumptions—Burden of Proof

It is essential to guilt that there be a valid existing marriage of the defendant at the time of the alleged bigamous marriage. Thus if a person were to contract a second marriage it would be a defense if it were shown that the first marriage was void or had been terminated. When the prosecution has adduced evidence sufficient to establish a valid first marriage and the later marriage charged is bigamous, the burden is upon the defendant to show that the case comes under one of the exceptions of section 282 as such exceptions are matters of defense. (People v. Huntley, 93 Cal. App. 504; People v. Harlow, 9 Cal. App. 2d 643.) Where a former marriage is proved there is a rebuttable presumption of its validity and it is not necessary for the State to show that there were no impediments to it (People v. Van Wie, 72 Cal. App. 2d 227). The burden of proof is upon the defendant to establish the invalidity of a prior marriage proved by the state since, where such marriage is proved, there is a rebuttable presumption of its validity (People v. Van Wie, 72 Cal. App. 2d 227; People v. Huntley, 93 Cal. App. 2d 504; People v. Vogel, 46 Cal. 2d 798). Proof of a divorce as to the first marriage is rebuttable and not conclusive and a showing that it was a void (mail order) divorce would leave the first marriage valid and the second marriage bigamous. (People v. Harlow, 9 Cal. App 2d 643.) Also an effort to establish that the marriage proved by the prosecution as the first marriage was itself bigamous and void will not avail the defense if the evidence otherwise establishes that at the time of the final marriage charged as bigamous, the defendant was the lawful spouse of someone else even though not as to the marriage originally assumed to be a prior and valid marriage (People v. Lamarr, 20 Cal. 2d 705 and discussion of authorities therein, also see People v. Van Wie, 72 Cal. App. 2d 227).

Evidence that defendant's wife by a former marriage had, after defendant left her and while they were separated, lived with another man as husband and wife, would not in and of itself prove that her marriage to defendant had been dissolved (People v. Vogel, 46 Cal. 2d. ....).

Marriage to Person Already Married

''Every person who knowingly and willfully marries the husband or wife of another, in any case in which such husband or wife would be punishable under the provisions of this chapter, is punishable by a fine not less than five thousand dollars, or by imprisonment in the state prison not exceeding ten years.'' (Penal Code, sec. 284.)

Since only a person legally married can commit bigamy by entering into a second marriage, this section is intended to punish a person who enters into a bigamous marriage but who cannot be punished for bigamy because he or she is unmarried. The elements of this crime are substantially the same as those of bigamy except that to be guilty under section 284 the person must have known that the other party to the marriage was married and, notwithstanding this knowledge, joined in the marriage.

ABORTION

''Every person who provides, supplies or administers to any woman or procures any woman to take any medicine, drug or substance, or uses or employs any instrument or other means whatever, with intent thereby to procure the miscarriage of any woman, unless the same is necessary to preserve her life, is punishable by imprisonment in the state prison not less than two nor more than five years.'' (Penal Code, sec. 274.)

This section is constitutional (People v. Rankin, 10 Cal. 2d 198).

Specific Intent

This offense is one requiring a specific intent, the intent to procure a miscarriage, and to sustain a conviction this intent must be proved. (People v. Coltrin, 5 Cal. 2d 649; People v. Lee, 81 Cal. App. 49; People v. Murphy, 60 Cal. App. 2d 762; People v. Raffington, 98 Cal. App. 2d 455.) The requisite guilty intent cannot exist unless the defendant had actual knowledge or actually believed that the woman was pregnant since the intent must be to produce a miscarriage, but it is the belief and intent of the accused which is involved, not whether pregnancy in fact exists (People v. Wales, 136 Cal. App. 2d 846).

Nature of Offense

While this offense is commonly referred to as the crime of abortion the offense defined by the statute is actually no more than an attempt to produce a miscarriage and it is not required that a miscarriage shall have resulted from the prohibited acts to constitute the crime defined by section 274 (People v. Simon, 21 Cal. App. 88) and, since the former requirement of the section that the woman must be pregnant has been repealed (1935), it is immaterial whether in fact the woman is pregnant or not. (People v. Ramsey, 83 Cal. App. 2d 707; People v. Raffington, 98 Cal. App. 2d 455; People v. Crain, 102 Cal. App. 566; People v. Gallardo, 41 Cal. 2d 57) and it is not necessary to prove that the accused had either knowledge or belief that the woman was pregnant (People v. Ramsey, 83 Cal. App. 2d 707). It is not necessary that there be any proof of any agreement with the defendant to do anything or of what the female agreed to do or pay (People v. McKenney, 108 Cal. App. 700) nor is it necessary that any period of time shall have elapsed after conception (People v. Luckett, 23 Cal. App. 2d 539). It is not a defense that the woman may previously have attempted to bring about a miscarriage (People v. Green, 111 Cal. App. 2d 794.)

Necessity to Preserve Life

If the attempt to produce a miscarriage was in an effort to save the life of the woman the statute is not violated and to eliminate this exception it is incumbent upon the prosecution to negative the existence of such necessity by at least prima facie proof. (See People v. Balkwell, 143 Cal. App. 742; People v. Malone, 82 Cal. App. 2d 54; People v. Gallardo, 41 Cal. 2d 57.) Such proof may lie in the manner and circumstances attending the act (People v. Malone, 82 Cal. App. 2d 54; People v. Ramsey, 83 Cal. App. 2d 707), the declarations of the parties or other circumstances such as proof that the woman was in good health (People v. Brewer, 19 Cal. App. 742; People v. Smitherman, 58 Cal. App. 2d 121; People v. Gallardo, 41 Cal. 2d 57) or, where the woman died, that the defendant buried the body after covering it with acid and cutting it into parts. (People v. Thompson, 16 Cal. App. 742.)

Corroboration Required

"Upon a trial for procuring or attempting to procure an abortion, or aiding and assisting therein . . . the defendant cannot be convicted upon the testimony of the woman upon or with whom the offense was committed, unless she is corroborated by other evidence." (Penal Code, sec. 1108.)

The testimony of the abortee is sufficient to prove that an abortion was performed or attempted upon her and it is only her testimony as to the identity of the person who performed or attempted the abortion which must be corroborated (People v. Ames, 151 Cal. App. 2d......, cases cited).

The woman upon whom the abortion is performed is not an accomplice of the person performing the abortion (People v. Clapp, 24 Cal. 2d 835; People v. Wilson, 25 Cal. 2d. 341; People v. Alvarez, 73 Cal. App. 2d 528; People v. Raffington, 98 Cal. App. 2d 455; People v. Gallardo, 41 Cal. 2d 57; People v. Bowlby, 135 Cal. App. 2d 519) nor is she an accomplice where the prosecution is one against two or more other persons for conspiracy to commit abortions (People v. Buffum, 40 Cal. 2d 709) and the required corroboration of her testimony may be furnished by the testimony of an accomplice of the abortionist and the required corroboration of the testimony of the accomplice may be by the testimony of the woman and the corroboration required may be had in the statements and admissions of the defendant himself (People v. Wilson, 25 Cal. 2d 341, 347; People v. Gallardo, 41 Cal. 2d 57; People v. Tallent, 89 Cal. App. 2d 158; People v. Tibbitts, 35 Cal. App. 2d 669; People v. Raffington, 98 A.C.A. 651, 98 Cal. App. 2d 455, holding also that defendant's possession of instruments and substances customarily used to produce a miscarriage is substantial corroboration).

This section requires corroboration although the woman is not an accomplice. (People v. Clapp, 24 Cal. 2d 835; People v. Josselyn, 39 Cal. 393.) Such corroboration need not be in respect to every fact and detail, nor as to every material fact, but only to some of the material facts which constitute an element of the crime, such as the specific intent and "although more is required by way of corroboration than to raise a mere suspicion, yet the corroborating evidence is sufficient if it, of itself, tends to connect the defendant with the commission of the offense notwithstanding the corroboration be slight and of itself entitled to but little consideration," the rule here being virtually the same as that requiring the corroboration of the testimony of an accomplice. (People v. Lee, 81 Cali. App. 49; People v. Lorraine, 28 Cal. App. 2d 50; People v. Josselyn, 39 Cal. 393; People v. Garner, 60 Cal. App. 2d 63; People v. Murphy, 60 Cal. App. 2d 762; see also People

v. Richardson, 161 Cal. 552; People v. Malone, 82 Cal. App. 2d 54; People v. MacEwing, 45 Cal. 2d 218). Corroboration is sufficient if it tends to connect the defendant with the commission of the crime in such a way as may reasonably satisfy the jury that the woman is telling the truth" (People v. Gallardo, 41 Cal. 2d 57; People v. MacEwing 45 Cal. 2d 218; People v. Sherman, 127 Cal. App. 2d 230; People v. Davis, 43 Cal. 2d 661). The corroboration need not be as to the means used but "is sufficient if there is corroboration as to the criminal intent or as to the attempt to commit the crime by any means" and tending to connect the defendant with the commission of the offense (People v. Wah Hing, 15 Cal. App. 195; People v. Josselyn, 39 Cal. 393), and the corroboration may often be found in the testimony of the defendant (People v. Garner, 60 Cal. App. 2d 63; People v. Davis, 43 Cal. 2d 661) or that of an accomplice of the defendant (People v. Clapp, 24 Cal. 2d 835; People v. Wilson, 25 Cal. 2d 341; People v. Pierson, 69 Cal. App. 2d 285; People v. Emery, 79 Cal. App. 2d 226; People v. Collins, 80 Cal. App. 2d 526) or in the response of the defendant to an accusatory statement (People v. Davis, 43 Cal. 2d 661). "So long as corroborating evidence creates more than a suspicion of guilt it is sufficient even though it be slight and, when standing by itself entitled to but little consideration." People v. Wilson, 25 Cal. 2d 341; see also the subject of Corroboration of Accomplice to which the same principle applies). The possession by a defendant who is not a doctor of such instruments and drugs which could have been used to perform the abortion (People v. Morris, 110 Cal. App. 2d 469, 547) and false statements of defendant indicating consciousness of guilt (People v. Morris, supra) have been held to be corroborative evidence. The necessary corroboration may consist of inferences from the circumstances surrounding the criminal transaction (People v. Berger, 128 Cal. App. 2d 509; People v. Wilson, 25 Cal. 2d 341, 347).

The presence of the defendant in the house where the crime was committed, shown by independent witnesses, and his evasive and contradictory statements showing consciousness of guilt are sufficient corroboration (People v. Reimringer, 116 Cal. App. 2d 332). Where there are a number of counts, each charging a separate abortion, testimony relating to one count may be considered in corroboration of the testimony of the woman upon whom an abortion was alleged to have been committed in another count (People v. Reimringer, 116 Cal. App. 2d 332). Where the defendant is charged with several offenses of abortion "any one of the women upon whom an abortion is performed can act as a corroborating witness with respect to matters that are relevant to another count charging an abortion upon a different woman" (People v. Gallardo, 41 Cal. 2d 57; People v. Sherman, 127 Cal. App. 2d 230; People v. Davis, 43 Cal. 2d 661). "Although the testimony of one woman that a person performed an abortion upon her is not sufficient to corroborate the testimony of the second woman that the same person committed an abortion upon her, it has been held that there is sufficient corroboration if the independent testimony of the women shows that each abortion was committed in a similar manner" (People v. Gallardo, supra, and cases cited; People v. Davis, 43 Cal. 2d 661; People v. Bowlby, 135 Cal. App. 2d 519).

"The necessary corroboration may consist of inferences from the circumstances surrounding the criminal transaction" and "Whether the corroborating evidence by itself is as compatible with innocence as it is with guilt is a question for the trier of fact, not for the reviewing court" (People v. Berger, 128 Cal. App. 2d 509; People v. Wilson, 25 Cal. 2d 341).

The testimony of the woman upon whom the act is performed as to her good health does not require special corroboration. (People v. Kendall, 111 Cal. App. 2d 204; People v. Malone, 82 Cal. App. 2d 54). The corroboration is sufficient if, considered by itself, it tends to connect the defendant with the offense (People v. Malone, 82 Cal. App. 2d 54; People v. Miner, 96 Cal. App. 2d 43).

Unless the corroboration furnishes evidence tending to connect the defendant with the offense there is no legal and sufficient corroboration (People v. Crain, 102 Cal. App. 2d 566).

Corroboration—Conspiracy to Commit Abortion.

The requirement that the testimony of the woman upon whom the offense was committed must be corroborated applies also to the crime of conspiracy to commit abortion (People v. Buffum, 40 Cal. 2d 709; People v. MacEwing, 45 Cal. 2d 218).

Submitting to Attempt To Produce Abortion

"Every woman who solicits of any person any medicine, drug, or substance whatever, and takes the same, or who submits to any operation, or to the use of any means whatever, with intent thereby to procure a miscarriage, unless the same is necessary to preserve her life, is punishable by imprisonment in the state prison not less than one nor more than five years." (Penal Code, sec. 275.)

While the pregnant woman would not be an accomplice in a prosecution under section 274 (People v. Clapp, 24 Cal. 2d 835; People v. Wilson, 25 Cal. 2d 341), she is subject to prosecution under section 275. It should be noted, also, that it is not an element of the offense created by this section that the woman shall have been pregnant but specific intent to procure a miscarriage must exist.

Offering to Assist

One who, by any notice, advertisement or otherwise, offers his services to assist in the accomplishment of a miscarriage or abortion is guilty of a felony (sec. 601, Business and Professions Code).

Soliciting Woman to Submit to Operation etc

"Every person who solicits any woman to submit to any operation, or to the use of any means whatever, to procure a miscarriage, unless the same is necessary to preserve her life, is punishable by imprisonment in the county jail not longer than one year or in the state prison not longer than five years, or by fine of not more than five thousand dollars ($5,000). Such offense must be proved by the testimony of two witnesses, or one witness and corroborating circumstances." (Penal Code, sec. 276).

CHAPTER XX.

ARSON

"Any person who wilfully and maliciously sets fire to or burns or causes to be burned or who aids, counsels or procures the burning of any dwelling house, or any kitchen, shop, barn, stable or other outhouse that is parcel thereof, or belonging to or adjoining thereto, whether the property of himself or of another, shall be guilty of arson, and upon conviction thereof, be sentenced to the penitentiary for not less than two nor more than twenty years." (Penal Code, sec. 447a.)

While section 447a alone names the offense as "arson," other sections of the code describe other wilful and malicious burnings to which the general rules relative to arson apply, the real difference being only as to the subject of the burning, the other elements of the corpus delicti being the same. The offenses defined in sections 448a and 449a of the Penal Code have been commonly referred to as arson: (See In Re Bramble, 31 Cal. 2d 43.)

"Any person who wilfully and maliciously sets fire to or burns or causes to be burned or who aids, counsels or procures the burning of any barn, stable, garage or other building, whether the property of himself or of another, not a parcel of a dwelling house; or any shop, storehouse, warehouse, factory, mill or other building, whether the property of himself or of another; or any church, meeting house, courthouse, work house, school, jail or other public building or any public bridge; shall, upon conviction thereof, be sentenced to the penitentiary for not less than one nor more than ten years." (Penal Code, sec. 448a.)

"Any person who wilfully and maliciously sets fire to or burns or causes to be burned or who aids, counsels or procures the burning of any barrack, cock, crib, rick or stack of hay, corn, wheat, oats, barley or other grain or vegetable product of any kind; or any field of standing hay or grain of any kind; or any pile of coal, wood or other fuel; or any pile of planks, boards, posts, rails or other lumber; or any street car, railway car, ship, boat or other watercraft, automobile or other motor vehicle; or any other personal property not herein specifically named; (such property being of the value of twenty-five dollars and the property of another person) shall, upon conviction thereof, be sentenced to the penitentiary for not less than one nor more than three years." (Penal Code, sec. 449a.)

Burning Bridge or Thing Not Subject of Arson

"Every person who wilfully and maliciously burns any bridge exceeding in value fifty dollars ($50), or any structure, snow shed, vessel or boat, not the subject of arson, or any tent, or any stack of hay or grain or straw of any kind, or any pile of baled hay or straw, or any pile of potatoes, or beans, or vegetables or produce, or fruit of any kind, whether sacked, boxed, crated or not, or any fence, or any railroad car, lumber, cordwood, railroad ties, telegraph or telephone poles, or shakes, or any tule-land or peat-ground of the value of twenty-five dollars ($25) or over, not the property of such person, is punishable by imprisonment in the State prison for not less than one year nor more than 10 years." (Penal Code, sec. 600, as amended in 1945.)

Every person who wilfully and maliciously burns any growing or standing grain, grass or tree or any grass, forest, woods, timber, brush covered land or slashing, cut-over land, not the property of such person, is punishable by imprisonment in the state prison for not less than one year nor more than ten years (Penal Code, sec. 600.5).

As these sections, 600 and 600.5, were enacted after section 499a, and cover to a large extent the latter section, it would seem that they supersede that section to that extent and that prosecutions for the burning of property covered by sections 600 and 600.5 would have to be brought under the latter sections which, also, provide the penalties for such cases.

Corpus Delicti

Mere proof of the burning alone of a building does not establish the corpus delicti of arson (People v. Holman, 72 Cal. App. 2d 75).

This is one of the crimes in which the act must be done "maliciously" which word imports "a wish to vex, annoy or injure another person, or an intent to do wrongful act." (Penal Code, sec. 7, subd. 4.) In arson this means that the burning must have been intentional or of incendiary origin (People v. Nagy, 199 Cal. 235) and this is generally established by circumstantial evidence such as the finding of separate and distinct fires in various parts of the building (People v. Nagy, 199 Cal. 235 People v. Patello, 125 Cal. App. 480; People v. Sherman, 97 Cal. App. 2d 245) especially when there is evidence that inflammables and oil had been used. (People v. Weinberg, 5 Cal. App. 2d 191; People v. Sanders, 13 Cal. App. 743; or the setting of separate fires in inhabited territory endangering life and property People v. Freeman, 107 Cal. App. 2d 44; see also People v. Hiltel, 131 Cal. 577; People v. Jones, 123 Cal. 65; People v. Coulon, 138 Cal. App. 576; People v. Roganovich, 77 Cal App. 158; People v. Morhar, 78 Cal. App. 380.)

Setting Fire to or Burning Defined

To constitute the setting fire to or burning it is not necessary that the property in question shall have been destroyed. It is sufficient if fire is so applied as to destroy, even though it be to but a slight degree, any part of the property intended to be burned. (People v. Haggerty, 46 Cal. 354; People v. Simpson, 50 Cal. 304.) Maliciously setting fire to a structure which would naturally burn the building charged and which did burn is a burning of that building. (People v. Hiltel, 131 Cal. 577.)

Ownership

The rule prior to 1929, when the present statutes were adopted, that a person cannot be guilty of arson unless some person other than the defendant had an interest in or was in possession or occupancy of the property in question, no longer exists; section 452 of the Penal Code declaring this obsolete rule was repealed when the present statutes were enacted except as to the offense covered by section 449a. (q. v.)

Attempt To Burn

"Any person who wilfully and maliciously attempts to set fire to or attempts to burn or to aid, counsel or procure the burning of any of the buildings or property mentioned in the foregoing sections, or who commits any act preliminary thereto, or in furtherance thereof, shall upon conviction thereof, be sentenced to the penitentiary for not less than one nor more than two years or fined not to exceed one thousand dollars.

The placing or distributing of any flammable, explosive or combustible material or substance, or any device in any building or property mentioned in the foregoing sections in arrangement or preparation with intent to eventually wilfully and maliciously set fire to or burn same, or to procure the setting fire to or burning of same shall, for the purposes of this act, constitute an attempt to burn such building or property." (Penal Code, sec. 451a.)

Since an attempt to commit arson or any other felony was already punishable before section 451a was enacted, it must be assumed that this section was intended to create a new and additional public offense. This new element is that the section not only makes punishable the attempt to burn but also provides for the punishment of any person "who commits any act preliminary thereto, or in furtherance thereof," a provision which evidently makes punishable any act of preparation or any overt act toward the perpetration of an unlawful burning.

DESTROYING INSURED PROPERTY—FRAUDS ON INSURER

"Any person who wilfully and with intent to injure or defraud the insurer sets fire to or burns or causes to be burned, or who aids, counsels or procures the burning of any goods, wares, merchandise or other chattels or personal property of any kind, whether the property of himself or of another, which shall at the time be insured by any person or corporation against loss or damage by fire, shall upon conviction thereof, be sentenced to the penitentiary for not less than one nor more than five years." (Penal Code, sec. 450a.)

Section 450a is limited and applies only to destruction of property by burning and is applicable only to cases involving personal property. The reason for the adoption of this section is rather obscure since there already existed prior thereto an adequate provision, to the same effect but wider in its scope, in section 548 of the Penal Code:

"Every person who wilfully burns or in any manner injures, destroys, secretes, abandons, or disposes of any property which at the time is insured against loss or damage by fire, or theft, or embezzlement, or any casualty, with intent to defraud or prejudice the insurer, whether the same be the property or in the possession of such person or any other person, is punishable by imprisonment in the state prison for not less than one year and not more than ten years." (Penal Code, sec. 548.)

Section 548 apparently covers every method of simulating or causing a casualty to property, real or personal, against which it is insured and section 450a added nothing to the law existing at the time of its adoption. The gist of both sections is that the specific intent to defraud the insurer is an essential element of the crime created thereby. Where the property is destroyed or injured by burning, the act usually involves also the crime of arson or unlawful burning and in such an instance two separate crimes are committed and may be jointly charged and tried.

Corpus Delicti

In a prosecution under either section it is necessary to prove the intent to defraud the insurer and it follows that it is also necessary to show that the accused knew that the property was insured (People v. Ross, 38 Cal. App. 493; People v. Trim, 39 Cal. 75), but it is not necessary for the prosecution to show that the insurance policy was valid or that the assured could recover thereunder (People v. Morley, 8 Cal. App. 372; People v. Hughes, 29 Cal. 257) nor, if the intent to defraud exists, is it necessary that the accused would have benefited had the fraudulent scheme been successful. (People v. Morley, 8 Cal. App. 372.)

In a prosecution under section 450a of the Penal Code it must also be shown that the accused wilfully set fire to or burned the property in question or was a principal in such wilful act. While the section declares one who "aids" the actual perpetrator guilty of the offense, this word must be construed as the equivalent of "knowingly aids," since under the general rules of criminal law one who without criminal intent gives aid to another who perpetrates a crime is not guilty thereof. (See: PRINCIPALS AND ACCESSORIES—**Capacity to Commit Crime—Mistake of Fact.**) In a prosecution under section 548 it must be shown that the defendant wilfully injured, destroyed, secreted, abandoned or disposed of the property in pursuance of the intent to defraud. Mere proof that property was overinsured and that there was no apparent cause for the fire which destroyed it would fall far short of the proof necessary to sustain a conviction. (People v. Bispham, 26 Cal. App. 2d 216.)

FRAUDULENT CLAIM OR PROOF OF LOSS

"It is unlawful to:

a. Present or cause to be presented any false or fraudulent claim for the payment of a loss under a contract of insurance.

b. Prepare, make, or subscribe any writing with intent to present or use the same, or to allow it to be presented or used in support of any such claim.

Every person who violates any provision of this section is punishable by imprisonment in the state prison not exceeding three years, or by fine not exceeding one thousand dollars, or both." (Insurance Code, sec. 556, based on former Penal Code, sec. 549.)

Corpus Delicti

The gravamen of the offenses under this statute is the intent to defraud but it is not an element of the offense, nor is the prosecution required to prove that the contract of insurance imposed a liability upon the insurer. (People v. Grossman, 28 Cal. App. 2d 193.) It should be noted that the section punishes not only the fraudulent act when committed with reference to the usual proofs of claim for loss but includes and applies also to "any writing" such as a letter (People v. Grossman, 28 Cal. App. 2d 193) intended to be used in support of such a claim.

CHAPTER XXI.

THEFT

"Every person who shall feloniously steal, take, carry, lead or drive away the personal property of another or who shall fraudulently appropriate property which has been intrusted to him, or who shall knowingly and designedly, by any false or fraudulent representation or pretense, defraud any other person of money, labor, or real or personal property, or who causes or procures others to report falsely of his wealth or mercantile character and by thus imposing upon any person obtains credit and thereby fraudulently gets or obtains possession of money or property or obtains the labor or service of another is guilty of theft. In determining the value of the property obtained, for the purpose of this section, the reasonable and fair market value shall be the test, and in determining the value of services received the contract price shall be the test. If there be no contract price, the reasonable and going wage for the service rendered shall govern. For the purposes of this section any false and fraudulent representations made shall be treated as continuing, so as to cover any money, property or service received as a result thereof, and the complaint, information or indictment may charge that the crime was committed on any date during the particular period in question. The hiring of any additional employee or employees without advising each of them of every labor claim due and unpaid and every judgment that the employer has been unable to meet shall be prima facie evidence of intent to defraud." (Penal Code, sec. 484.)

Statute Interpreted

"Whenever any law or statute of this state refers to or mentions larceny, embezzlement or stealing, said law or statute shall hereafter be read and interpreted as if the word 'theft' were substituted therefor." (Penal Code, sec. 490a; See People v. Nahhas, 121 Cal. App. 428.)

"The effect of Section 484 of the Penal Code is that the former crimes of larceny, embezzlement and obtaining property by false pretenses are merged into the one crime of theft," (People v. Plum, 88 Cal. App. 575; People v. Stevenson, 103 Cal. App. 82; People v. Leaverton, 107 Cal. App. 51) and the term "theft" includes all or any one or two of the three said offenses. Thus, when a person is charged by complaint, indictment or information with the crime of theft in the form authorized by section 952 of the Penal Code ("that the defendant unlawfully took the labor or property of another") the effect is the same as if the criminal act had been charged in three separate counts as different statements of the same offense under the three theories, embezzlement, larceny and false pretenses. (People v. Bratton, 125 Cal. App. 337; People v. Bratten, 137 Cal. App. 658.) Where the criminal act may constitute either of two or three of the forms of theft, depending upon how the jury views the evidence, and the facts so warrant, the verdict of conviction can be sustained on either theory. (People v. Von Bodenthal, 8 Cal. App. 2d 404; People v. Miles, 19 Cal. App. 223; People v. Shepherd, 141 Cal. App. 2d 367). A defendant properly convicted on one theory cannot successfully urge that he is guilty of theft on some other theory. (People v. McCarthy, 140 Cal. App. 386).

What May Be the Subject of Theft

Theft can only be committed when the thing unlawfully taken is that which the law recognizes as property. Thus a winning lottery ticket is not recognized in law as property because of its inherent unlawful character and cannot be the subject of theft. (People v. Caridis, 20 Cal. App. 166; see also: People v. Gonzales, 62 Cal. App. 2d 274.) The fact, however, that the property is of such a character that its possession is, under certain conditions, unlawful, as, for example, intoxicating liquor (People v. Odenwald, 104 Cal. App. 209) or slot machines (People v. Walker, 33 Cal. App. 2d 18) does not affect the illegality of their being taken by theft, for, as stated in the Walker case, "Although it may be illegal to own or possess slot machines there yet exist certain rights in the individual who may possess such a contraband article as against anyone other than the state."

While at common law dogs were not property which could be stolen, in this state "Dogs are personal property and their value is to be ascertained in the same manner as the value of other property." (Penal Code, sec. 491.)

Real Property — Capable of being captured

Section 532 relating to the obtaining of property by false pretenses and which includes real property is valid (People v. Rabe, 202 Cal. 409,416; People v. Pugh, 137 Cal. App. 2d 226).

Real property may be the subject of embezzlement (People v. Roland, 134 Cal. App. 675; People v. Hart, 28 Cal. App. 335).

Fixtures

Property is also the subject of theft "where the thing taken is any fixture or part of the realty, and is severed at the time of the taking, in the same manner as if the thing had been severed by another person at some previous time." (Penal Code, sec. 495).

Instruments, Tickets, Deeds

"If the thing stolen consists of any evidence of debt, or other written instrument, the amount of money due thereon, or secured to be paid thereby, and remaining unsatisfied, or which in any contingency might be collected thereon, or the value of the property the title to which is shown thereby, or the sum which might be recovered in the absence thereof, is the value of the thing stolen." (Penal Code, sec. 492.)

"If the thing stolen is any passage ticket or other paper or writing entitling or purporting to entitle the holder or proprietor thereof to a passage upon any railroad or vessel or other public conveyance, the price at which tickets entitling a person to like passage are usually sold by the proprietors of such conveyance is the value of such paper, ticket or writing." (Penal Code, sec. 493.)

"All the provisions of this chapter apply where the property taken is an instrument for the payment of money, evidence of debt, public security or passage ticket a thing of and ready to be issued or delivered, although the same has never been issued or delivered by the maker thereof to any person as a purchaser or owner." (Penal Code, sec. 494.)

Deed, Subject of Theft

While a deed which has been delivered is a written instrument which may be the subject of theft, an undelivered deed is not, as a matter of law, a written instrument and its taking cannot be the basis of a charge of theft and does not come within the terms of either section 492 or 494. (People v. Dadmun, 23 Cal. App. 290.) Where deeds are obtained by fraud and hence there was no delivery and title did not pass, the deeds are worthless and cannot be made the basis of a charge of theft. (People v. Sewall, 90 Cal. App. 476; People v. Nye, 96 Cal. App. 186.) Delivery is not essential, however, to constitute an instrument for the payment of money, evidence of debt, public security, or passage ticket, completed value which may be the subject of theft. (See Penal Code, sec. 494, supra.)

Degrees of Theft

"Theft is divided into two degrees, the first of which is termed grand theft; the second, petty theft." (Penal Code, sec. 486.)

Grand Theft Defined

"Grand theft is theft committed in any of the following cases:

1. When the money, labor or real or personal property taken is of a value exceeding two hundred dollars; provided, that when domestic fowls, avocados, olives, citrus or deciduous fruits, nuts and artichokes are taken of a value exceeding fifty dollars provided further that where the money, labor, real or personal property is taken by a servant, agent or employee from his principal or employer and aggregates two hundred dollars ($200) or more in any 12 consecutive months period then the same shall constitute grand theft.

2. When the property is taken from the person of another.

3. When the property taken is an automobile, horse, mare, gelding, any bovine animal, any caprine animal, mule, jack, jenny, sheep, lamb, hog, sow, boar, gilt, barrow or pig." (Penal Code, sec. 487.)

"(a) Every person who shall feloniously steal, take, transport or carry the carcass of any bovine, caprine, equine, ovine or suine animal or of any mule, jack or jenny, which is the personal property of another or who shall fraudulently appropriate such property which has been entrusted to him, is guilty of grand theft.

"(b) Every person who shall feloniously steal, take, transport or carry any portion of the carcass of any bovine, caprine, equine, ovine or suine animal or of any mule, jack or jenny, which has been killed without the consent of the owner thereof, is guilty of grand theft" (Penal Code, sec. 487a).

"Theft in other cases is petty theft." (Penal Code, sec. 488.)

Every person who converts real estate of the value of fifty dollars ($50) or more into personal property by severance from the realty of another and, with felonious intent to do so, steals, takes and carries away such property is guilty of grand theft and is punishable by imprisonment in the state prison for not less than one year nor more than 14 years." (Penal Code, sec. 487b). If the value of the property is less than $50 the crime is petit theft and punishable by "imprisonment in the county jail for not more than one year, or by a fine not exceeding $1000, or by both such fine and imprisonment." (Penal Code, sec. 487c).

"Every person who feloniously steals, takes, and carries away or attempts to steal, take and carry from any mining claim, tunnel, sluice, undercurrent, riffle box, or sulfurate machine another's gold dust, amalgan or quicksilver is guilty of grand theft and is punishable by imprisonment in the state prison for not less than one year nor more than 14 years." (Penal Code, sec. 487d).

Value of Property

"Whenever in this code the character or grade of an offense, or its punishment, is made to depend upon the value of the property, such value shall be estimated exclusively in lawful money of the United States." (Penal Code, sec. 678).

In determining the value of the property the reasonable and fair market value is the test and in determining the value of services the contract price, or if there be no contract price the reasonable and going wage for such service is the test. (Penal Code, sec. 484; as to value of written documents and passage tickets see sections 492, 493 of the Penal Code, supra, under **What May Be the Subject of Theft.**)

In addition to proof of fair market value by expert testimony (People v. Mitchell, 80 Cal. App. 252; People v. Lizarraga, 122 Cal. App. 2d 406) the "owner of the property whether generally familiar with such values or not is competent to estimate its worth, the lack of knowledge going to the weight rather than the admissibility of the testimony, and this applies alike to real and personal property" (Kirstein v. Bekins Co., 27 Cal. App. 587; Willard v. Valley etc. Co., 171 Cal. 9; Hood v. Bekins Co., 178 Cal. 150; People v. Haney, 126 Cal. App. 473; People v. Burns, 128 Cal. App. 226; People v. More, 10 Cal. App. 2d 144, corporate stock; People v. Lenahan, 38 Cal. App. 2d 421 leases), but such methods of proving value are not exclusive and it may be established by proof of facts from which the inference of value may be drawn. (People v. Rose, 110 Cal. App. 648.) This is especially true where the article is not obtainable or salable in the open market.

The market value which is referred to in the law is that value at the time and at the place where the property was unlawfully taken (People v. Ciani, 104 Cal. App. 596; People v. Simpson, 26 Cal. App. 2d 223; see also People v. Robertson, 117 Cal. App. 1) and it is the total value of the property unlawfully taken and not the portion thereof which was received by a defendant which is the basis of determining whether the crime is grand or petty theft. (People v. Tenant, 32 Cal. App. 2d 1.)

Number of Offenses—Separate Takings

When the property of several persons is stolen at the same time from the same place there is but one taking and but one theft, but where the taking is from different persons at different places or where property is taken from the persons of different individuals at the same time or from different individuals by the same trick and device each transaction is a separate theft. (People v. Sichofsky, 58 Cal. App. 257.) Where, after receiving one sum of money by fraudulent means, constituting either larceny by trick and device or obtaining money by false pretenses, the accused later requested and received a further sum from the same person and upon the same fraudulent statement, each taking was held to constitute a separate offense. (People v. Henessy, 201 Cal. 568; People v. Serna, 43 Cal. App. 2d 106; People v. Caldwell, 55 Cal. App. 2d 238.)

Where, by false statement in his application for unemployment relief, the defendant obtained semi-monthly installments of $28.89 totalling $347.76, it was held that each separate receipt of money was a separate offense (People v. Sorna, 43 Cal. App. 2d 106; the defendant, before the receipt of each installment, was required to endorse upon each warrant a statement that he had correctly reported his status and was eligible for relief). In a similar case of Dawson v. Sup. Ct., 138 Cal. App. 2d 685, in which no such endorsement was required it was held that, since there was but one intention, one general impulse and plan, there was but one offense, the theft of the total amount received.

Where it was the intent of the thief to steal an entire lot of merchandise, the fact that, due to the circumstances, all of the property could not be taken at the same time but required a number of trips, but one theft, that of the total amount of property taken, is committed (People v. Dillon, 1 Cal. App. 2d 224; People v. Fox, 64 A. C. A. 81, not covered in decision of the Supreme Court) even though the trips were made on successive days (People v. Sing, 42 Cal. App. 385) and the same rule applies where separate takings were in pursuance of a single design. (People v. Yachimovitz, 57 Cal. App. 2d 375.) Where in embezzlement the accused received in his fiduciary capacity money in excess of two hundred dollars, but the individual receipts in no instance exceeded that amount, the embezzlement of the total sum received constituted but one crime, grand theft. (People v. Bratton, 125 Cal. App. 337; People v. Fleming, 220 Cal. 601.) If there is but one intention, one general impulse and one plan, even though there is a series of transactions, there is but one offense (People v. Howes, 99 Cal. App. 2d. 808, 818; People v. Lima, 127 Cal. App. 2d 29).

Where a person embezzles, on various occasions, funds with which he has been intrusted and there is nothing to show that there was ever any intent to take more than the amount taken on each occasion and each taking was with a separate intent, each taking is a separate embezzlement (People v. Hill, 132 Cal. App. 554; People v. Howes, 99 Cal. App. 2d 808) but if there be evidence that it was the intent of the accused to take a certain large sum of money, the fact that the taking and appropriation occurred on the instalment plan, on various occasions, here, there being but one intent, the combined acts constituted but one embezzlement of the total amount. (People v. Yachimovitz, 57 Cal. App. 2d 375). And in a similar case where, in pursuance of one design and purpose, defendant on various occasions took merchandise of his employer and sold it pocketing the proceeds, it was held that there was but one theft (held to be larceny) there being but one general intent and therefore but one offense (People v. Howes, 99 Cal. App. 2d 808). Where the defrauded person makes a series of payments to the embezzler, or the latter receives a series of payments in his fiduciary capacity, in connection with the same transaction and converts the entire amount, there is but one embezzlement (People v. Howes, 99 Cal. App. 2d 808; People v. Bratton, 125 Cal. App. 337; People v. Fleming, 220 Cal. 601) but if separate amounts are separately converted, separate offenses are committed (People v. Stanford, 16 Cal. 2d 247).

Possession of Stolen Property

Where, in the perpetration of a crime, personal property is stolen, evidence of the possession of such property by the defendant, charged with the crime in which the property was taken, is admissible as tending to show the identity of the perpetrator and to connect the defendant with the offense. The mere possession of stolen property is not, however, sufficient of itself to justify a conviction but is merely a circumstance tending to prove guilt (People v. Fierro, 140 Cal. App. 490; People v. White, 35 Cal. App. 2d 61; People v. Enriques. 39 Cal. App. 2d 160; People v. Taylor, 74 Cal. App. 2d 363; People v. Leary, 28 Cal. 2d 727). To sustain a conviction there must be, in addition to proof of the possession of the stolen property, other evidence tending to show guilt such as direct evidence of the commission of the offense by the accused or of incriminating circumstances such as flight (People v. Scott, 66 Cal. App 200; People v. Latham, 43 Cal. App. 2d 35), failure to explain the possession when the defendant could, if innocent, have done so (People v. Miller, 45 Cal. App. 494), refusal to explain the possession (People v. Blackburn, 65 Cal App. 2d 538), false or conflicting statements as to the possession (People v. Farrell, 67 Cal. App. 128; People v. Hunter, 59 Cal. App. 444; People v. Robertson, 117 Cal. App. 413; People v. Russell, 34 Cal. App. 2d 665) the sale of the property under a false name (People v. Cox, 29 Cal. App. 419; People v. Majors, 47 Cal. App. 374; People v. Morris, 124 Cal. App. 4020 or other circumstance tending to prove that the defendant was the one who committed the crime; People v. Buratti, 96 Cal. App. 447; People v. Shaw, 46 Cal. App. 2d 768; People v. Whisner, 99 Cal. App. 2d 845). The sale by the defendant about twelve hours after a burglary for $5 of stolen articles worth $100, giving a false name and address at the time and his explanation at the time of arrest that an unidentified friend had given them to him to sell would be sufficient to sustain a conviction (People v. Clark, 122 Cal. App. 2d. 342). Where the defendant has attempted to explain or account for the possession of the stolen property on a theory inconsistent with guilt the question of guilt is still one for the jury and the question as to whether he is telling the truth rests with the jury (People v. Howell, 126 Cal. App. 2d 780). An improbable explanation of the possession stands on the same footing with no explanation and the jury has the right to consider that the statement of the defendant that he received the property from an unknown person is in fact no explanation (People v. Melson, 84 Cal. App. 10; People v. Barber, 112 Cal. App. 2d 333). The term "unexplained possession" as used in the rule means the absence of an explanation sufficient to raise a reasonable doubt (People v. Barber, 112 Cal. App. 2d 333) and an improbable explanation stands on the same footing as no explanation (People v. Barber, supra). If an explanation of such possession is attempted by the accused it is for the trier of facts to judge of its truth and plausability (People v. Rutland, 120 Cal. App. 2d 798). A defendant's possession of stolen property immediately following the burglary, taken with false and misleading statements regarding his possession, his familiarity with the premises burglarized and the sale of the stolen goods for an inadequate price, is sufficient corroboration of the inference of guilt arising out of the possession of stolen property (People v. Conrad, 125 Cal. App. 2d 184). Where the defendant claims to have won the stolen check in a crap game, the question of whether he has told the truth rests solely with the jury or trier of facts and such trier of fact may disbelieve such story even though there is no direct contradiction of the attempted explanation and, if they so disbelieve such story, we have the corroborative circumstances of a false explanation of the possession and the conviction will be sustained (People v. Nelson, 126 Cal. App. 2d 453).

Where, in a case of burglary, the defendant sold some of the stolen property using a name other than his own, a false statement that he had received the property from his father and defendant moved his place of residence because he had been told that a police officer was looking for him, in connection with his purchase of an automobile under another name, the possession of the stolen property was sufficiently corroborated to sustain the conviction (People v. Citrino, 46 Cal. 2d 284). Where, in the commission of the burglaries charged, safes were broken into by punching out the tumblers and in one case the building was entered by cutting a hole in a wall with a torch and torches, acetylene tanks and tools such as might have been used and part of the stolen property were found in defendant's room and defendant said, "I guess they are mine" and that he had rented the apartment under a false name and made false and inconsistent statements, the conviction was sustained (Peo. v. Gregor, 141 Cal. App. 2d 711).

"Among the circumstances which, coupled with the possesion of stolen property, have been held to connect the defendant with the crime and to sustain his conviction are flight, false statements showing consciousness of guilt; false statements as to how the property came into the defendant's possession; assuming a false name and an inability to find the person from whom the defendant claimed to have received the property; sale of the property under a false name and at an inadequate price; sale of the property with marks of identity removed and failure to account for its possession and giving false testimony and an effort to throw away the stolen property" (People v. Russell, 120 Cal. App. 622, 625 and extensive citations; People v. Harrison, 129 Cal. App. 2d 197, a deliberate intent to cause a lie detector test to be inaccurate; People v. McClure, 133 Cal. App. 2d 631, aiding another in removing the stolen goods from the scene of the crime, attempting to conceal them sufficient to convict defendant of burglary).

While these rules relate to stolen property they apply not only to cases in which a theft is charged but also to cases in which a theft was committed in connection with the crime charged (People v. Russell, 120 Cal. App. 622) such as murder (People v. Peete, 54 Cal. App. 333; People v. Perkins, 8 Cal. 2d 502), driving an automobile without the consent of the owner (People v. Zabriskie, 135 Cal. App. 169), burglarly (People v. Howard, 58 Cal. App. 340; People v. Murphy, 91 Cal. App 530; People v. Montgomery, 145 Cal. App. 2d 121), robbery (People v. Smith, 74 Cal. App. 510) and all cases in which the evidence of the possession of personal property unlawfully acquired tends to connect the defendant on trial with the crime charged or tends to prove that crime. "Where goods have been taken by means of a burglary and they are immediately or soon thereafter found in the possession of a person who gives a false account or refuses to give any account of the manner in which he came into their posession, proof of such possession and guilty conduct is evidence, not only that he stole the goods but that he made use of the means by which access to them was obtained" (People v. Corral, 60 Cal. App. 2d 66, 72 and cases cited; People v. Howell, 126 Cal. App. 2d 780).

The element of time between the unlawful taking of the property and the finding of the property in the possession of the defendant goes to the weight rather than to the admissibility of the evidence (People v. Arbaugh, 82 Cal. App. 2d 971).

Possession Defined

Within the meaning of the law a person is in possession of an article of personal property when it is under his dominion and control and, to his knowledge, either is carried on his person or is in his presence and custody, or, if not on his person or his presence, the possession thereof is immediate, accessible and exclusive to him. Two or more persons may have possession of such property if jointly and knowingly they have the dominion, control and exclusive possession such as exists where but one person has possession (Caljic No. 41 and cases cited; see also Possession under Narcotics, infra).

Property Stolen Outside of this State and
Brought into this State

"Every person who, in another state or country, steals or embezzles the property of another, or receives such property knowing it to have been stolen or embezzled, and brings the same into this state, may be convicted and punished in the same manner as if such larceny, or embezzlement, or receiving, had been committed in this state." (Penal Code, sec. 497.) This section punishes as larceny, embezzlement or receiving stolen property the bringing into this State of property so unlawfully obtained in another state or country and the pleading and penalty is the same as if such original offense had been committed wholly within this state (People v Case, 49 Cal. 2d ....). Under this statute a person could be convicted of larceny, as if the unlawful taking had occurred in this state if he brought property in this state which he had taken by larceny in Canada (People v. Black, 122 Cal. 73), Mexico (People v. Barnes, 57 Cal. App. 495), or Arizona (People v. Staples, 91 Cal. 23; between Alaska and Oregon ,49 Cal. 2d........), and jurisdiction would be in any county into or through which the property was taken. (Penal Code, sec. 789).

Penalty

"Petty theft is punishable by fine not exceeding five hundred dollars, or by imprisonment in the county jail not exceeding six months, or both." (Penal Code, sec. 490.)

"Grand Theft is punishable by imprisonment in the county jail for not more than one year or in the state prison for not less than one nor more than ten years or in the county jail for not more than one year." (Penal Code, sec. 489).

"If the embezzlement or defalcation is of the public funds of the United States, or of this state, or of any county or municipality within this state, the offense is a felony, and is punishable by imprisonment in the state prison not less than one nor more than ten years; and the person so convicted is ineligible thereafter to any office of honor, trust, or profit in this state." (Penal Code, sec. 514.) In such a case the crime is a felony regardless of the amount involved.

defalcation—misappropriation of money by one who has it in his trust.

Petit Theft After Felony Conviction

"Every person who, having been convicted of any felony either in this state or elsewhere, and having served a term therefor in any penal institution, commits petty theft after such conviction, is punishable therefor by imprisonment in the county jail not exceeding one year or in the state prison not exceeding five years." (Penal Code, sec. 667.)

A county jail is a "penal institution" within the meaning of this section (People v. James, 155 Cal. App. 2d ......).

It is not necessary that the defendant shall have served the full term of imprisonment for his prior offense; service of a part of his sentence is sufficient (People v. James, 155 Cal. App. 2d ......).

"Any person sentenced to a state prison under section 667 of this code shall be subject to parole as a first term prisoner." (Penal Code, sec. 3051.) A conviction under section 667 carries only a maximum penalty of five years in state prison and, even though the accused had three prior felony convictions, the habitual criminal law (Penal Code, sec. 644) does not apply (In re Boatwright, 216 Cal. 677) and the penalty is uninfluenced by any prior conviction.

Petit Theft as Prior Conviction

"Every person who having been convicted of petit larceny or petit theft and having served a term therefor in any penal institution or having been imprisoned therein as a condition of probation for such offense commits any crime after such conviction, is punishable therefor as follows:

1. If the offense of which such person is subsequently convicted is such that, upon a first conviction, an offender could be punished by imprisonment in the state prison for any term exceeding five years, such person may be punished by imprisonment in the state prison for the maximum period for which he might have been sentenced if such offense had been his first offense, but in no case less than five years.

2. If the subsequent offense is such that upon a first conviction the offender would be punishable by imprisonment in the state prison for five years, or any less term, then the person convicted of such subsequent offense is punishable by imprisonment in the state prison not exceeding ten years.

3. If the subsequent conviction is for petit theft then the person convicted of such subsequent offense is punishable by imprisonment in the county jail not exceeding one year, or in

the state prison not exceeding five years." (Penal Code, sec. 666.)

This section has no application unless the prior conviction of petit larceny or petit theft was followed by the actual service of a term of imprisonment under a sentence imposed. Where a person convicted of an offense is required as a condition of probation to spend a period of time in jail this is not the serving of a term of imprisonment. (People v. Wallach, 8 Cal. App. 2d 129; In re Martin, 82 Cal. App. 2d 16 and cases cited.)

Effect of Theft Statutes on Prior Statutes

The passage of the theft statutes (Penal Code, 484, 490a) merely merged the offenses of larceny, embezzlement and obtaining property by false pretenses and the statutes and rules specially applicable to these offenses as they existed prior to 1927 are still in effect, except where they have been repealed or amended, and the distinction between these offenses is still of importance, not only in determining whether the facts are sufficient to sustain a conviction and, in the case of obtaining property by false pretenses, to apply the rule requiring corroboration, but in the decision of cases such as burglary, robbery and receiving stolen property. For this reason the various forms of theft will be considered separately.

Restitution No Defense

Restoration or reimbursement of property taken or appropriated is no defense to a charge of theft (People v. Pond, 44 Cal. 2d 665).

EMBEZZLEMENT

Embezzlement is the fraudulent appropriation of property by a person to whom it has been intrusted. (Penal Code, secs. 484, 503 to 508 inclusive.)

Elements of Embezzlement

The elements necessary to embezzlement are:

1. Fiduciary relation between the defendant and complainant.

2. That the property came into the defendant's possession as the property of complainant.

3. That the accused received the property in the course of his employment, and

4. That the defendant appropriated the property to his own use or some use not within the purpose of his trust, with intent to deprive the owner thereof. (People v. Hemple, 4 Cal. App. 125; People v. Rowland, 121 Cal. 17.)

"A distinct act of taking is not necessary to constitute embezzlement." (Penal Code, sec. 509.)

Who May Commit

Further amplifying the provisions of sections 484 and 503, and to more particularly define the character of the relationship in which a person may commit embezzlement, specific provision has been made by statute that every public officer, his deputy, agent and servant (Penal Code, secs. 424, 504), every carrier or other person having property under his control for the purpose of transportation for hire, every banker, trustee, merchant, broker, attorney, assignee in trust, executor, administrator or collector or any other person otherwise intrusted with or having in his control property for the use of any other person (Penal Code, sec. 506), every person acting in any capacity in connection with a business for the purpose of collecting accounts or debts (Penal Code, sec. 506a); every bailee, tenant, lodger or attorney in fact (Penal Code, sec 507); every insurance agent (sec. 1730 Ins. Code), and every clerk, agent or servant (Penal Code, sec. 508) who fraudulently appropriates property intrusted to him in such capacity, shall be guilty of embezzlement.

Fiduciary Capacity

The receipt of the property in a fiduciary capacity is an essential element of embezzlement. (People v. O'Brien, 106 Cal. 104; People v. Gordon, 133 Cal. 328; People v. Goodrich, 142 Cal. 216.) Where the defendant received the money as a loan there could be no embezzlement. (People v. Kirkpatrick, 77 Cal. App. 104.) While a servant may commit embezzlement if he fraudulently appropriates "any property of another which has come into his control or care by virtue of his employment as such . . . servant," a mere caretaker of the house, whose duty it was to keep it clean and see that nobody took anything out of it, and who removed therefrom silverware and other property was held guilty of larceny and not embezzlement since he did not have possession of the stolen articles with any duty of trust in relation to them, but was merely a custodian or guard without any duty to perform with the articles in question. (People v. Kawananakoa, 37

Cal. App. 433.) Where the defendant with the idea of preparing a souvenir program for an agricultural fair secured the approval of the local Chamber of Commerce which was to receive a fee of $300 for the use of their name as sponsors and the defendant collected money from advertisers for advertising in such program, it was held that there was no relation of principal and agent between the defendant and the Chamber of Commerce and that the defendant could not be guilty of embezzlement of the money collected (People v. Petrin, 122 Cal. App. 2d 578).

Possession of Property

To constitute embezzlement it is not necessary that the perpetrator have actual possession of the property and it is sufficient, where the accused was not in actual possession, to show that the property was under his control, direction and management (People v. Hess, 104 Cal. App. 2d 642; People v. Knott, 15 Cal. 2d 628).

Aider and Abettor

A person not occupying the fiduciary capacity essential to embezzlement may be convicted of this offense where he has aided and abetted the actual embezzler (People v. Hess, 104 Cal. App. 2d 642; People v. Hess, 107 Cal. App. 2d 407).

Intent

The intent essential to embezzlement is the intent to fraudulently appropriate the property to a use and purpose other than that for which it was intrusted, the intent to deprive the owner of his property, but, the other elements of the offense being committed, the crime is committed even though it was intended to deprive the owner of his property only temporarily and to eventually return it. (People v. Jackson, 138 Cal. 462; People v. Harris, 100 Cal. App. 78; People v. Talbot, 220 Cal. 3; People v. Braiker, 61 Cal. App. 2d 406; People v. McClain, 140 Cal. App. 2d 899; Penal Code, sec. 512). Mere conversion of the property is not sufficient; the conversion must have been with intent to defraud (People v. Whitney, 121 Cal. App. 2d 515).

Personal Benefit to Accused

"Any diversion of funds held in trust constitutes embezzlement, whether there is direct personal benefit or not, as long as the owner is deprived of his money" (People v. Pierce, 110 Cal. App. 2d 598, 609; People v. Talbot, 220 Cal. 3; People v. Braiker, 61 Cal. App. 2d 406; People v. Schmidt, 147 Cal. App. 2d ......).

What Property May Be Subject of Embezzlement

Penal Code, Sec. 510—"Any evidence of debt, negotiable by delivery only, and actually executed, is the subject of embezzlement, whether it has been delivered or issued as a valid instrument or not."

The property which may be the subject of embezzlement may be money, goods, chattels, things in action or evidence of debt (People v. Hart, 28 Cal. App. 335), or real property. (People v. Roland, 134 Cal. App. 675; Penal Code, sec. 484.)

Transmuted Property

Where an agent is authorized to transmute property from one form to another—as where he sells the property of his principal and receives the proceeds or where exchanges the property for other property—he holds the transmuted property in trust for his principal in its new form (People v. Martin, 153 Cal. App. 2d ...... A.C.A. 300).

Illustrative Cases

Where the secretary of a corporation was given a check, payable in blank, to pay a specific indebtedness, but inserted his own name as payee and secured the money thereon and converted the same to his own use, he was guilty of embezzlement. "If an agent obtains money of his principal in the capacity of agent, but in a manner not authorized, and converts the same to his own use with intent, etc., it is money received in the course of his employment as agent." (People v. Gallagher, 100 Cal. 466, 470. See also Ex parte Hedley, 31 Cal. 108.) Where a fiduciary relation does in fact exist the mere fact that, in rendering an account of moneys, the agent rendered a statement listing "receipts" and "disbursements" or "credits" and "debits," does not change the fiduciary relationship to that of debtor and creditor. (People v. Hatch, 163 Cal. 382.) Even though an agent may have authority to sell the property of his principal and convert the same into cash for the use and benefit of his principal such agent would be guilty of embezzlement if he fraudulently converted the property or money to his own use or for some use other than that for which he had been authorized. (People v. Stafford, 81 Cal. App. 159; People v. Coyle, 81 Cal. App. 671.) A dealer, receiving a piano upon consignment for the purpose of sale, the contract reserving title to the property and the proceeds in the consignor, who sells such piano and converts the proceeds to his own use, is guilty of embezzlement. (In re Cantua, 57 Cal. App. 346; People v. Maljan, 34 Cal. App. 384.) The fact that the money was intrusted to the accused for an illegal purpose is no defense to a charge of embezzlement. (People v. Ward, 134 Cal. 309; People v. Martin, 102 Cal. 558.) Where a person holds bonds or other articles of value as security for a loan made to the complainant and converts such securities to his own use by pledging them for an obligation of his own after the debt is fully paid, he is guilty of embezzlement. (In re Tambara, 185 Cal. 604; People v. Tambara, 192 Cal. 236.) While there is in a sense an agency of a partner it is the general rule that a partner cannot be guilty of embezzling the assets of the copartnership because of his ownership interest therein. (Ex parte Cirro, 76 Cal. App. 142; People v. Brody, 29 Cal. App. 2d 6.) Where, however, the defendant and four others formed an association with an agreement that no member should receive any compensation for work done for the club, and the defendant converted to his own use part of the money received by the club from the sale of tickets for a show, it was held that the defendant, who had exclusive charge of securing the entertainment and the sale of tickets through solicitors was neither a partner nor engaged with the four others in a joint venture but an agent for the club and hence was guilty of embezzlement. (People v. Foss, 7 Cal. 2d 669.) Defendant received money under an agreement that a corporation was to be formed and defendant was to turn stock in the corporation over to complainant but the corporation was never formed and the money was never returned and defendant used the money for his own purposes. Held a case of embezzlement. (People v. Fewkes, 214 Cal. 142.) Where defendant hired a horse in San Diego to drive to Sunnyside and thereafter formed the intent to and went on to Los Angeles he was guilty of embezzlement. (People v. Jackson, 138 Cal. 462.) An employer who secures from an employee property to hold as security for the faithful performance of his duties and refuses upon termination of the employment to return the property is guilty of embezzlement. (People v. Ward, 14 Cal. App. 143.) A person who holds property as a bailee or pledgee of the property of another and, without authority so to do, pledges such property as security on a personal obligation of his own is guilty of embezzlement. (People v. Rose, 110 Cal. App. 648; People v. Fleming, 220 Cal. 601.) Where a person dealing with a defendant puts up a sum of money as a bond to guarantee faithful performance by him of the contract, such money not to be used by the defendant and to be returned upon a thirty-day written notice with interest or within thirty days after the expiration of the agreement and the money is used by the defendant in his business, the crime of theft by embezzlement has been committed (People v. Pierce, 110 Cal. App. 2d 598; see also People v. Bratten, 125 Cal. App. 337; People v. Keefer, 146 Cal. App. 2d 726). One who receives shares of stock from another for a purpose which does not include their sales is guilty of embezzlement if he sells the securities and uses the money even though he intended to later buy back such stock. (People v. Peterson, 120 Cal. App. 197; see also People v. Wyatt, 121 Cal. App. 180; People v. Schneider, 3 Cal. App. 2d 1). An officer or agent of a corporation which is intrusted to him or which comes into his possession by virtue of his office or agency and use it, even temporarily, for his personal benefit and avoid criminal responsibility by calling it a loan. The fact that he had done this on other occasions when the money was returned or that the practice was prevalent is no defense. (People v. Talbot, 22 Cal. 3). Where a police officer, to save it for the owner, removed property from premises in the path of a brush fire his possession of the property was lawful and if he thereafter withheld the property and did not return it to the owner he was guilty of embezzlement. (People v. Coon, 38 Cal. App. 2d 512). Where a public officer customarily received funds from recreational facilities and paid them to the city treasurer a fraudulent appropriation of such money is an embezzlement even though the handling of such funds was not pursuant to any statutory duty. (People v. Kirk, 47 Cal. App. 2d 136). Defendant visited a used car lot and stated that he wanted to buy a certain car there and requested permission to take the car promising to return it the following Wednesday and signed an installment contract which provided that the deal was to be completed on his wife's approval, otherwise the contract to be void, the contract not to become binding unless accepted in writing by the seller. Defendant did not return the car on the Wednesday or at all, never executed a conditional sales contract or made any payment whatever and the car was finally recovered from defendant's possession eight months, later, bearing stolen license plates and the motor number having been altered. A conviction of theft was sustained (People v. Gerundo, 112 Cal. App. 797).

Section 405 of the Labor Code, providing that property put up by an employee or applicant as a bond shall not be used for any purpose other than liquidating accounts between such person and the employer or to return the same and shall not be mingled with the property of the employer and that one who does so is guilty of theft, is constitutional (People v. McEntyre, 32 Cal. App. 2d Supp. 752 People v. Pond, 44 Cal. 2d 665; People v. Vandersee, 139 Cal. App. 2d 388).

Where a contractor to construct a building received a payment on the contract in trust and as bailee for the express purpose of paying all labor and material furnished to date in the construction of the building, the use of part of the money for purposes other than the building, without paying for the labor and material, constituted embezzlement (People v. Clemmons, 136 Cal. App. 2d 529).

Assuming to Act as Agent

Where a defendant has secured possession of property by representing himself as being the agent or bailee of another he cannot defend a charge of embezzling such property on the ground that he was not such agent or bailee. "If the defendant assumed to act as agent or bailee and by so assuming to act was intrusted with property, it does not lie in his mouth to say that he was not really the agent or bailee, but that he merely assumed to act as such. If he assumed to act as agent or bailee and by this means was intrusted with the property, he was such agent." (People v. McLean, 138 Cal. 306; People v. Treadwell, 69 Cal. 226; People v. Pyle, 44 Cal. App. 130; People v. Jones, 87 Cal. App. 482; People v. Robertson, 6 Cal. App. 514.) Where a defendant has received money as and in the capacity of an agent or trustee, he cannot in defense of his act of appropriating it to his own use raise the question of title as between others (People v. Hedderly, 43 Cal. 2d 476), nor will he be permitted to say that he was not authorized to receive the money or property or that the person for whom he received the property was not entitled to it (People v. Royce, 106 Cal. 173; see also People v. Blackmore, 87 Cal. App. 222).

Partnerships—Joint Funds

Because of the fact that a partner is a joint owner of the partnership assets he is not guilty of embezzlement if he appropriates such assets to his personal use (People v. Hotz, 85 Cal. App. 450; People v. Cravens, 72 Cal. App. 2d. 658; People v. Foss, 7 Cal. 2d. 669), but this rule applies where the funds or property taken are those of the partnership. The same rule seems to apply where funds are appropriated out of a joint bank account upon which the accused has the right to draw (People v. Cravens, 79 Cal. App. 2d. 658).

Where, though ostensibly a partnership, the truth is that no partnership in fact existed, a pseudo-partner may be convicted of the embezzlement of funds contributed by himself and others (People v. Skeen, 93 Cal. App. 2d 489).

Where, however, a person is induced to part with his money by false pretenses and promises, his funds to go into an existing partnership of which the defendant is a member and complainant is to become a member of such partnership and such money is paid into the funds of the partnership, the crime of theft by false pretenses has been committed and the fact that the money was not turned over to the defendant personally does not make it any the less a crime the gist of which is that of depriving the victim of his property by false pretenses with intent to defraud (People v. Jones, 36 Cal. 2d 373).

Where the same trickery, as that used to perpetrate the theft, was used to create an alleged partnership, no partnership would be created (People v. Reinschreiber, 141 Cal. App. 2d 688 case of larceny by trick and device).

Claim of Title as a Defense

"Upon any indictment for embezzlement, it is a sufficient defense that the property was appropriated openly and avowedly, and under a claim of title preferred in good faith, even though such claim is untenable. But this provision does not excuse the unlawful retention of the property of another to offset or pay demands held against him." (Penal Code, sec. 511; see People v. Crane, 34 Cal. App. 760; People v. Doane, 77 Cal. 560.) Where the defendant was authorized to sell the property of the complainant for $1150 but actually sold it for $1450 and kept $300 openly and avowedly and in good faith believing that he was entitled to the amount over $1150 as compensation, he was held not guilty of embezzlement. (People v. Lapique, 120 Cal. 25.)

To maintain a defense under section 511 it is not sufficient to show that the property was appropriated openly and avowedly (People v. Talbot, 220 Cal. 3), for it must also be shown that the appropriation was made "under a claim of title preferred in good faith" and the mere belief of the defendant that he was acting legally is not sufficient. (People v. Holmes, 13 Cal. App. 212; People v. Clemmons, 136 Cal. App. 2d 529; People v. Clemmons, 136 Cal. App. 2d 529). The circumstances themselves must be indicative of good faith (People v. Martin, 153 Cal. App. 2d ...... A.C.A. 300). Section 511 does not apply to a case where the defendant withheld funds of the complainant to offset or pay demands against him. (People v. Hill, 2 Cal. App. 2d 141).

Demand For Property

There is nothing in the definition of embezzlement which requires that a demand be made for the return or delivery of the property and proof of a demand is not necessary where the evidence otherwise shows the fraudulent appropriation by the defendant. (People v. Royce, 106 Cal. 173; People v. Hatch, 163 Cal. 368; People v. Blair, 19 Cal. App. 688; People v. Kirk, 94 Cal. App. 378; People v. Hill, 2 Cal. App. 2d 141; People v. Ahern, 31 Cal. App. 2d 655.) The circumstances, however, may be such as to require proof of such demand and the failure of accused to return or deliver the property. This is true in cases where there is no evidence as to what the accused has done with the property, and the circumstances are such that the duty of the agent or bailee to deliver the property would not arise until a demand was made, as, for example, where money is delivered to an agent to purchase property for the principal whenever such property can be located or found or where the duty to be performed by the agent is to be done, not within any specific time, but merely within a reasonable time. In such cases it must be assumed that the failure of the agent is merely a neglect to return the property or to perform a duty and proof of demand would be necessary to show the felonious conversion. (People v. Crane, 102 Cal. 557; People v. Wyman, 34 Cal. App. 599; People v. Ward, 134 Cal. 301; People v. Ephraim, 77 Cal. App. 29.) If, however, the time for the delivery or return of the property is fixed by the agreement between the owner of the property and the person holding the property as a fiduciary, no demand is necessary where such time has elapsed and the property has not been returned or delivered. Thus, where an agent's duty requires him to pay over funds at a definite time and he fails to do so (Ex parte Vice, 5 Cal. App. 153; People v. Fisher, 16 Cal. App. 271; People v. Hall, 55 Cal. App. 2d 386), he is guilty of embezzlement and this is also the case if he fails to turn over the funds of his employer upon the termination of his employment. (Ex parte Vice, 5 Cal. App. 153.)

What is Not a Defense

The fact that the defendant intended to restore the property embezzled or even if he actually returned it after he had embezzled it is no defense (Penal Code, secs. 512, 513; People v. Kay, 34 Cal. App. 2d 691; People v. Colton, 92 Cal. App. 2d 704) nor is it a defense to a charge of embezzlement that the money had been intrusted for an illegal purpose (People v. Ward, 134 Cal. 301) or that the money had been paid by complainant to a third party where such payment was at the request of the defendant. (People v. Fewkes, 214 Cal. 142.)

Removal and Disposal of Leased Property

"Every person who shall fraudulently remove, conceal or dispose of any goods, chattels or effects, leased or let to him by any instrument in writing, or any personal property or effects of another in his possession, under a contract of purchase not yet fulfilled, and any person in possession of such goods, chattels, or effects knowing them to be subject to such lease or contract of purchase who shall so remove, conceal or dispose of the same with intent to injure or defraud the lessor or owner thereof, is guilty of embezzlement." (Penal Code, sec. 504a.)

This provision is intended to punish as embezzlement those cases in which the vendor reserves title in himself until the property is paid for and the purchaser fraudulently removes, conceals and disposes of the property and covers an offense which is not of necessity covered by the other sections defining embezzlement. (See In re Angelo, 78 Cal. App. 550.)

Embezzlement by Public Officer

"Each officer of this state, or of any county, city, town or district of this state, and every other person charged with the receipt, safekeeping, transfer, or disbursement of public moneys, who either:

1. Without authority of law, appropriates the same, or any portion thereof, to his own use, or to the use of another; or

2. Loans the same, or any portion thereof; makes any profit out of, or uses the same for any purposes not authorized by law; or

3. Knowingly keeps any false account, or makes any false entry or erasure in any account of or relating to the same; or

4. Fraudulently alters, falsifies, conceals, destroys or obliterates any such account; or

5. Wilfully refuses or omits to pay over, on demand, any public moneys in his hands, upon the presentation of a draft, order, or warrant drawn upon such moneys by competent authority; or

6 Wilfully omits to transfer the same, when such transfer is required by law; or

7. Wilfully omits or refuses to pay over to any officer or person authorized by law to receive the same any money received by him under any duty imposed by law so to pay over the same:

Is punishable by imprisonment in the state prison for not less than one nor more than ten years, and is disqualified from holding any office in this state." (Penal Code, sec. 424.)

Moneys received by a public officer in his official capacity are "public moneys" within the meaning of section 424 of the Penal Code (People v. Crosby, 141 Cal. App. 2d 172, holding also that a public administrator is a public officer and that to keep money in a safe deposit box or elsewhere is not to "use" it).

Any record required by law to be kept by a public officer or which he keeps as necessary or convenient to the discharge of his official duties is a public record (People v. Marquis, 153 Ca. App. 2d ......).

It will be noted that section 424 makes punishable some acts which would not come under the forms of embezzlement previously discussed and which do not have the same corpus delicti as embezzlement. (People v. Dillon, 191 Cal. 1.)

Where a county assessor used funds received for taxes, which he had failed to turn over to the county treasurer as required by law, to repay money to a taxpayer after a reduction of his assessment a conviction was sustained. The court held that it was unnecessary that the accused should have any wrongful intent to defraud the county and that the intentional failure to turn over the public funds was of itself a violation of section 424. (People v. Johnson, 14 Cal. App. 2d 373.) A county assessor who was delinquent in his payments to the county treasurer for one year paid the delinquency out of moneys received by him for taxes of the following year. Held a violation of subdivision 2 of section 424. (People v. Moulton, 116 Cal. App. 552.) A deputy county treasurer who loaned county funds to his codefendant taking the latter's check as security was held guilty under section 424. (People v. West, 3 Cal. App. 2d 568.)

Embezzlement By Public Officer or Employee.

"Every public officer of this state, or of any county, city and county, or other municipal corporation or subdivision thereof, and every deputy, clerk or servant of any such officer who fraudulently appropriates to any use or purpose not in the due and lawful execution of his trust any property which he has in his possession, or under his control by virture of his trust, or secretes if with fraudulent intent to appropriate it to such use or purpose, is guilty of embezzlement." (Penal Code, sec. 504).

This section includes not only cases of those who have possession of the property but also those who have control thereof (People v. Knott, 15 Cal. 2d 628).

The use by a city councilman of stationery, furnished him by the city for use in his official capacity, for the purpose of promoting his campaign for election and not for any official use, is a violation of this section (People v. Nathanson, 134 Cal. App. 2d 43).

CHAPTER XXII.

LARCENY

Larceny is the felonious stealing, taking, carrying, leading or driving away of the personal property of another. (Penal Code, sec. 484; see People v. Myers, 206 Cal. 480.) The corpus delicti of larceny consists of (1) the asportation, (2) of the personal property of another, (3) with the specific intent of permanently depriving the owner of his property.

Taking or Asportation

To constitute the taking or asportation essential to larceny the taker must not only move or remove the personal property involved but he must secure dominion or control over the property. Thus where a thief, intending to steal an overcoat from a clothing dummy in front of a store, removed the coat from the dummy but was unable to carry it away because it was fastened to the dummy by a chain, there was no larceny; not having obtained dominion or control over the coat there was no asportation. (People v. Myer, 75 Cal. 383.) Where, however, dominion or control over the property is secured and there be any movement of the property from the place it occupied to another place, even though the distance it was moved is only a matter of inches, asportation is complete. Merely grasping the handle of a suitcase with intent to steal would not be asportation but merely an attempt, but once the thief has raised or moved the suitcase from its place the asportation and the larceny is complete. Unlawfully killing a bovine animal of another by shooting and then removing its carcass is larceny (People v. Wilcoxin, 69 Cal. App. 267; People v. Faust, 137 Cal. App. 549; People v. Davis, 76 Cal. App. 2d 701), such circumstances constituting the asportation. It is not necessary that the asportation go to the extent of removing the stolen property from the premises upon which it was stolen (People v. Arnest, 133 Cal. App. 114) and the asportation "need be only for an appreciable time be it ever so short." (People v. Dukes, 16 Cal. App. 2d 105; People v. Quiel, 68 Cal. App. 2d 674). Once there is asportation the voluntary return of the property does not affect the guilt of the thief (People v. Post, 76 Cal App. 2d 511).

Property of Another

Larceny is committed only when property to the thing taken is in another but the ownership of such other need not

266

be complete or absolute. A person rightfully in possession of personal property has such ownership therein as may be the subject of larceny. (People v. Hayes, 72 Cal. App. 292; People v. Sampson, 99 Cal. App. 306.) Thus a bailee or other person having lawful possession of property has such a property right therein as to make its stealing from the possession of such person amount to larceny. (People v. Buelna, 81 Cal. 135.) If the owner of property, which is in the lawful possession of a bailee, takes such property from the possession of such bailee, with the intent of holding the bailee liable for the loss of such property, the owner is guilty of larceny even though he was the owner, for the bailee has a property right and right to the possession. (People v. Stone, 16 Cal. 369; People v. Thompson, 34 Cal. 671; Jones v. Jones, 71 Cal. 92; People v. Cain, 7 Cal. App. 163; People v. Photo, 45 Cal. App. 2d 345.)

Since all that the law requires is that the thing taken be the property ''of another'' it would be no defense to a charge of larceny that the defendant had taken the property from the person of one who had found it (People v. Beach, 62 Cal. App. 2d 803) or of one who had himself stolen it, since the property was still that of the owner from whom it had been stolen. While at common law the husband and wife were considered one person and neither could steal from the other, in this state either party may commit larceny by stealing the separate property of the other. (People v. Graff, 59 Cal. App. 706; People v. King, 77 Cal. App. 434.) The taking of community property which is subject to the husband's control and which was handed to the accused by the wife and the removal of the property, with intent either to steal it from both parties or the husband alone, is larceny. (People v. Swalm, 80 Cal. 46.)

Possession by an express company would be sufficient proof of ownership (People v. Oldham, 111 Cal. 648) and proof that property was stolen from the pocket of another is sufficient proof that he owned it (People v. Nelson, 56 Cal. 77) even in the absence of the testimony of the person from whom it was taken. (People v. Davis, 97 Cal. 194.) The fact that the defendant stole articles of clothing from hangers on racks in a store is sufficient to show possession in the store and no further proof of ownership is necessary. (People v. Corral. 60 Cal. App. 2d 66.) Where the testimony of eyewitnesses showed that a pocketbook was taken from the person of an unidentified victim who was not a witness at the trial it was

Asportation - Intent - Same

held that the fact that the pocketbook was in the possession of the victim was sufficient evidence of ownership in her (People v. Davis, 97 Cal. 194). (For cases where the defendant claims that the property was his, lost in gambling, see: Ownership of Property under ROBBERY.)

The retaking of personal property by the seller under the terms of a conditional sales contract is not larceny (People v. Novelli, 140 Cal. App. 2d 438).

Intent

To constitute larceny there must exist in the mind of the perpetrator, at the time of the taking, the specific intent to permanently deprive the owner of his property. A taking with the intention of returning the property or a taking without the intent to permanently deprive the owner of his property will not amount to larceny even though the perpetrator, after gaining possession of the property, formed that intent. (See People v. Tucker, 104 Cal. 440; People v. Brown, 105 Cal. 66; People v. Marino, 85 Cal. 515; People v. Devine, 95 Cal. 227; People v. Pillsbury, 59 Cal. App. 2d 107.) Where a person hired a horse, promising to return it by evening, but never did so and never returned, the offense is not larceny unless it appears from the evidence that he intended to steal the animal at the time it came into his possession. (People v. Jersey, 18 Cal. 337; People v. Smith, 23 Cal. 280.) If one in good faith takes the property of another believing it to be legally his own or that he has a legal right to its possession he is not guilty of larceny since the specific intent necessary to constitute larceny, to-wit, the specific intent to permanently deprive the owner of his property, is absent. (People v. Photo, 45 Cal. App. 2d 345.) Where the defendant, charged with the theft of an automobile, had, after the taking, purchased sixteen gallons of gasoline, it was held that the evidence was sufficient to establish the required specific intent (People v. Crawford, 115 Cal. App. 2d 838).

Consent

To constitute larceny the taking must be unlawful and without the consent of the owner. Larceny can only exist where the accused intended to permanently deprive the owner of his property without his consent where the owner at no time had the intent that the accused should become the owner of the property. If the owner consents it is a complete defense so far as the crime of larceny is concerned but there must be real consent. It is not part of the offense that there be, and the prosecution is not required as part of its case to prove, lack of consent (People v. Davis, 97 Cal. 194) and in the absence of proof to the contrary the taking will be assumed to have been without the owner's consent. (See also discussion, infra, of the difference between larceny, embezzlement, and obtaining property by false pretenses.)

From the Person

Where the property is taken by theft from the person of another the fact alone that it is so taken makes the offense grand theft regardless of the value of the property taken. (People v. Fiegelman, 33 Cal. App. 2d 100; People v. Crenshaw, 63 Cal. App. 2d 395.) To constitute a taking from the person the property must be either on the body or in the clothing being worn or in a receptacle carried by such person. If in the attempt to pick the pocket of his victim the effort caused the purse of the latter to fall to the ground and then defendant picked it up the larceny is from the person. (People v. Carroll, 20 Cal. App. 41.) But where the money was stolen from the trousers which were under the owner's pillow while he slept, this is not a larceny from the person. (People v. McElroy, 116 Cal. 583.)

Property Delivered By Mistake

Where a person delivers money or property by mistake to a person not entitled to receive the same and the receiver, knowing that a mistake is being made and with intent to take advantage thereof and to keep it as his own, carries it away, he is guilty of larceny and this rule applies to a case wherein the receiver was entitled to receive a certain sum of money but by mistake was paid a larger amount. Where, however, the mistake is mutual, the receiver not knowing that he had received something to which he was not entitled until after he had taken the property away, there is no larceny, for here there was no intent to steal at the time he came into possession of the property. If, by mistake, a bank credits the account of a depositor with a sum of money to which he is not entitled and the depositor, knowing this to be the fact, draws out of his account the money credited to him by such mistake, he is as guilty of the larceny of the money as if he had stolen it out of the bank's cash drawer. (People v. Tullos, 57 Cal. App. 2d 233.)

Lost Property

"One who finds lost property under circumstances which give him knowledge of or means of inquiry as to the true owner, and who appropriates such property to his own use, or to the use of another person not entitled thereto, without first making reasonable and just efforts to find the owner and to restore the property to him, is guilty of theft." (Penal Code, sec. 485; see also People v. Buelna, 81 Cal. 137.) To invoke the application of section 485 the property must have been lost and the accused must have been the finder (People v. Devine, 95 Cal. 227).

Here the distinction must be made between property that has been lost and property which is merely mislaid, or forgotten, as where the owner intentionally places property in a place and forgets it, or property which has been abandoned. It is only when the property is lost that the statute applies. Property abandoned is, so far at least as theft is concerned, property without an owner and one who finds and takes it can not be guilty of its theft even though he took it with intent to steal, for there can be no theft except where the property taken is that of some other person. Where, however, propert is lost, mislaid or forgotten and even though it has been stolen from the owner, the property still has an owner and can be the subject of larceny.

Section 485 applies only to cases in which the property was first lost and then found by one who took it, not as a thief, but as the finder of lost property. In such a case the finder is not guilty when he takes the property into his possession. His guilt arises when, having the means of inquiry as to the true owner, he appropriates the property to his own use without making reasonable efforts to find the owner and restore the property to him.

Section 485 does not declare or create a kind of theft or larceny which would not otherwise be included in the offense of theft or larceny but merely declares a rule of evidence which, being fulfilled, constitutes the crime as defined and included in the general section 484 of the Penal Code. (People v. Buelna, 81 Cal. 135.)

Larceny by Trick and Device

Larceny by trick and device, more commonly referred to as a "bunco" or "confidence" game, differs from the more ordinary form of larceny, in which the taking is in secret or by stealth, in that it is a form of swindle in which by trick, device, fraud or artifice, most often by false and fraudulent representations, there is held out to the victim the promise of financial or other gain much to be desired, and often appealing to his cupidity, while in other instances the appeal is by false and fraudulent representations which appeal to the sympathy or emotions or desires of the victim. Whatever may be the form of the trick and device used, it is the intent and purpose of the swindler to steal the money or other property which will come into his possession as the result of the fraud which he has practised. The victim, on the other hand, believing things to be what the swindler has induced him to believe them to be, is induced to turn over to the possession of the swindler his money or property, never intending that the defendant will receive and keep as his own the money or property, but solely intending that it shall and will be devoted or turned over by the defendant to the uses and purposes contemplated by the speculation, venture or enterprise which, due to the false and fraudulent representations, he believes has an actual existence. Larceny by trick or device is characterized by the fact that the defendant intends to steal the property at the time it comes into his possession and that the owner never intends that title shall pass to the defendant so that he may use the property as he may see fit. It differs from embezzlement in which the defendant receives the property without any intent to steal it and from obtaining property by false pretenses in which the owner intends that title to the property shall pass to the defendant. (People v. Schwartz, 43 Cal. App. 696; People v. Raschke, 73 Cal. 378; People v. Tomlinson, 102 Cal. 23; People v. Kelley, 81 Cal. App. 398; People v. Johnson, 91 Cal. 265; People v. Shaughnessy, 110 Cal. 602; People v. Delbos, 146 Cal. 736; People v. Miles, 19 Cal. App. 223; People v. Rial, 23 Cal. App. 713; People v. Sichofsky, 58 Cal. App. 257; In re Clark, 34 Cal. App. 440; People v. Sing, 42 Cal. App. 385; People v. Hutchings, 56 Cal. App. 397; People v. Edwards, 72 Cal. App. 102; People v. Robertson, 26 Cal. App. 507; People v. Barnett, 31 Cal. App. 2d 173; People v. Watson, 35 Cal. App. 2d 587; People v. White, 124 Cal. App. 548; People v. Weber, 7 Cal. App 2d 620; People v. Cook, 10 Cal. App. 2d 54; People v. Harden, 14 Cal. App. 2d 489; People v. Henessy, 201 Cal. 568; People v. Post, 76 Cal. App. 2d 511.)

Illustrative Cases

In addition to the illustrative cases last cited convictions have been sustained on this theory of larceny:—where defendant went through the semblance of buying property but received the property with intent to steal the same and without intent to pay therefor (People v. Sing, 42 Cal. App. 385; People v. Miller, 64 Cal. App. 330); fraudulently obtaining complainant's signature to a promissory note by misrepresenting that it was merely a recommendation as to defendant's reputation (People v. Cichetti, 107 Cal. App. 631); buying property for complainant but obtaining a larger sum from complainant by representing that the property had cost such larger price (People v. Delbos, 146 Cal. 734; People v. Harold, 17 Cal. App. 426); defendant obtaining money by falsely representing that he could obtain a parole for the son of complainant (People v. Meadows, 108 Cal. App. 67); pretending to have found a wallet and inducing victim to turn over money as an evidence of good faith so she could share in the contents of the wallet (People v. Watson, 35 Cal. App. 2d 587); money received on representation it was to be paid to blackmailers to prevent a criminal prosecution of complainant (People v. Robertson, 26 Cal. App. 507); "handkerchief game" (People v. Perrin, 67 Cal. App. 612); "Pay off" game (People v. Berry, 191 Cal. 109); false and fraudulent spiritual manifestations (People v. Arnold, 20 Cal. App. 35); and where a loan was obtained upon the representation that the money was to be used for paying an obligation of defendant but this was purely fictitious (People v. Rae, 66 Cal. 423; In re Clark, 34 Cal. App. 440; People v. Brennan, 41 Cal. App. 2d 143; People v. Alba, 46 Cal. App. 2d 859; People v. Cook, 10 Cal. App. 2d 54; People v. Reed, 113 Cal. App. 2d 339); defendant, an automobile dealer obtained money for the purpose of paying freight on automobiles with the preconceived design to use the money for other purposes (People v. Reinschreiber, 141 Cal. App. 2d 688). dishonest card game (People v. Solano, 48 Cal. App. 2d 126); secret formula for treating cotton seed (People v. McCabe, 60 Cal. App. 2d 492); making a promise which the defendant did not intend to perform (People v. Mason, 86 Cal. App. 2d 445); obtaining money to bet upon an alleged fixed horse race when in fact the defendant knew there was no such race (People v. Owens, 117 Cal. App. 2d 121); defendant obtained from complainant a sum of money as the result of his false representations that a certain woman needed money to save her home and that complainant would receive a bonus when the loan was repaid but never turned the money over to the woman but used it himself (People v. Bartges, 126 Cal. App. 2d 763).

Where the defendants pretended to have found some money, which they offered to divide with the victim who was induced

to put up a sum of money, allegedly in case the alleged loser of
the money claimed it within three months, and one of the defendants left with the victim's money and never returned, a
conviction was sustained (People v. Shepherd, 141 Cal. App.
2d 367). Where in the drawing of what appeared to be the
winning ticket at a theatre "bank night" the person making
the drawing purportedly drew the winning ticket but in fact
drew out a ticket which he had palmed and the prize money
was collected from the theatre, a conviction of larceny by trick
and device was sustained (People v. Carpenter, 141 Cal. App.
2d 884). Where the defendant represented that he had a tried
system by which he could win at roulette and that those who
gave him money for that purpose would receive 30% monthly
profit on their investment and it appeared that the defendant
did not intend to make good on his promises and had appropriated the funds to his own use, the conviction was sustained
on the theory of larceny by trick and device and also on the
theory of having made false pretenses with intent not to perform the promises made (People v. Gilliam, 141 Cal. App. 2d
749).

Fraudently obtaining money or property by "three card
monte" or any other game or device, sleight of hand, preten-
sions to fortune telling, trick, betting or game is punishable
as in case of the theft of property of like value (sec. 332, Penal
Code).

Where the elements of the crime are present it is no defense
that the victim was influenced in part by the statement of a
third party that he would see that complainant would suffer
no loss. (People v. Hennessy, 201 Cal. 568).

No Corroboration Required

While this form of larceny resembles the obtaining of property by false pretenses the provision of section 1110 of the
Penal Code requiring corroboration does not apply where the
offense committed is larceny by trick and device. (People v.
Edwards, 133 Cal. App. 335; People v. Santora, 51 Cal. App.
2d 707; People v. Stanley, 58 Cal. App. 2d 310; People v. Beilfuss, 59 Cal. App. 2d 83; People v. Reed, 113 Cal. App. 2d 339;
People v. Theodore, 121 Cal. App. 2d 17; People v. Bartges,
126 Cal. App. 2d 763; People v. Reinschreiber, 141 Cal. App.
2d 688).

Obtaining Property by Fraudulent Game or Trick

"Every person who by the game of "three car monte",
so-called, or any other game, device, sleight of hand, preten-

tious to fortune telling, trick, or other means whatever, by use of cards or other implements or instruments, or while betting on sides or hands of any such play or game, fraudulently obtains from another person money or property of any description, shall be punished as in the case of larceny of property of like value''. (Penal Code, sec. 332.) (For typical case of fraudulent poker game see People v. Mendoza, 103 Cal. App. 2d 113).

Restitution No Defense

The fact that the owner of the property has been reimbursed for his loss, even though the restitution was made voluntarily, is not a defense to a charge of larceny. (People v. Alba, 46 Cal. App. 2d 859.) The same rule applies where, after the theft, the thief returns the stolen property to the victim (People v. Post, 76 Cal. App. 2d 511).

OBTAINING PROPERTY BY FALSE PRETENSES

The crime of obtaining property by false pretenses is included in section 484 defining theft and is more specifically defined:—

"Every person who knowingly and designedly, by any false or fraudulent representation or pretense, defrauds any other person of money, labor, or property, whether real, or personal, or who causes or procures others to report falsely of his wealth or mercantile character, and by thus imposing upon any person obtains credit, and thereby fraudulently gets possession of money or property, or obtains the labor or service of another, is punishable in the same manner and to the same extent as for larceny of the money or property so obtained.'' (Penal Code, sec. 532.)

"There is no inconsistency between sections 484 and 532 of the Penal Code and the applicable provisions of the former have in effect repealed the identical provisions of the latter.'' (People v. Jackson, 24 Cal. App. 2d 182; People v. Carter, 131 Cal. App. 177; People v. Breyer, 139 Cal. App. 547.)

Real Property.

The provision of section 532 that real property may be the subject of theft is valid (People v. Rabe, 202 Cal. 409, 416; People v. Pugh, 137 Cal. App. 2d 226).

Corpus Delicti

To constitute this offense, four things must concur:

1. There must be an intent to defraud; *Animus Furandi*
2. There must be actual fraud committed;
3. False pretenses must be used for the purpose of perpetrating the fraud; and
4. The fraud must be accomplished by means of the false pretenses made use of for the purpose; viz.: They must be the cause which induced the owner to part with his property. (People v. Wasservogel, 77 Cal. 173; People v. Rose, 42 Cal. App. 540; People v. Carpenter, 6 Cal. App. 231; People v. Alston, 139 Cal. App. 575; People v. Frankfort, 114 Cal. App. 2d 680.)

convincing victim

Intent to Defraud—Knowledge

Get something that isn't yours by trick.

Obtaining property by false pretenses has as an essential element the specific intent to defraud and this, of necessity, implies that the accused must know that his representation was false. If a person makes a statement under a justifiable belief in its truth, such statement, though in fact false, will not sustain a charge of obtaining property by false pretenses since in such case there would be no intent to defraud. (People v. Griffith, 122 Cal. 212.) A statement or representation made recklessly and without information justifying a belief that it is true is tantamount to knowledge of the falsity of the representation (People v. Cummings, 123 Cal. 269; People v. Daener, 96 Cal. App. 2d 827).

Fraud

Actual fraud

Deception, deliberately practiced for the purpose of gaining an unfair advantage over another, is fraud and goods obtained by such practices are obtained by fraud. (People v. Wieger, 100 Cal. 356; People v. Bryant, 119 Cal. 595; People v. Moore, 82 Cal. App. 165.) "If a person is induced to part with his property by reason of fraudulent pretenses and misrepresentations he is thereby defrauded of the property so parted with even though he may eventually make himself whole in some mode not then contemplated. It is not necessary to show that the property has been absolutely lost to him to sustain the charge" (People v. Bryan, 119 Cal. 595; People v. Moore, 82 Cal. App. 165) nor is it a defense that the property received was worth what the complainant gave or paid for it (People v. Raines, 66 Cal. App. 2d 960); "financial loss is not a necessary element of the crime" (People v. Talbott, 65 Cal. App.

2d 654). Even if the property is worth the consideration paid therefor, this is not a defense when there is substantial evidence that the defendant knowingly made false representations with intent to defraud and with the purpose and the effect of inducing the prosecuting witness to part with his property when otherwise he would not have done so (People v. Pugh, 137 Cal. App. 2d 226) nor is it a defense that in the end he suffered no loss or even gained a profit. The crime is complete when the complainant's property has been obtained in the manner and by the means made punishable by the statute and reimbursement or even a profit to the complainant will not erase the crime already perpetrated. While no crime is perpetrated where the complainant gets exactly what he bargained for "it cannot be said that a person get what he bargains for although he gets the same article, if the article is of a value less than for which he bargained." (People v. Ingles, 117 Cal. App. 22.) "Money may be obtained by false pretenses through acts otherwise legal as well as those that are illegal" (People v. Bianco, 84 Cal. App. 2d 281).

Causal Connection

Even though a false representation is made and property obtained by the person making the representation, no prosecution will lie where the complainant parted with his property to the accused from some cause other than such false representation since to constitute this offense the representation must have been a material element in proximately causing the complainant to part with his property and without which he would not have done so. (People v. Kahler, 26 Cal. App. 452; People v. Hass, 28 Cal. App. 182; People v. Canfield, 28 Cal. App. 792; People v. Wasservogel, 77 Cal. 173; People v. Rose, 42 Cal. App. 540; People v. Tufts, 167 Cal. 266; People v. Seeley, 75 Cal. App. 2d 525). While the false prestenses must have materially influenced the owner to part with his property it is not necessary that such pretense be the sole inducing cause (People v. Ashley, 42 Cal. 2d 246).

What Constitutes a False Pretense

To constitute a false pretense a representation must be a statement as to a past or present fact (People v. Reese, 136 Cal. App. 657; People v. Walker, 76 Cal. App. 192; People v. Ames, 61 Cal. App. 2d 523) and not a mere expressing of an opinion or a promise to do something in the future. (People v. Reese, 136 Cal. App. 657; People v. Downing, 14 Cal. App. 2d

392; People v. Jackson, 24 Cal. App. 2d 182.) However, a promise, if unconditional, and made without present intention of performance, will constitute actionable fraud (People v. Gordon, 71 Cal. App. 2d 606; People v. Mason, 86 Cal. App. 2d 445; People v. Jones, 36 Cal. 2d 373; see also Statements as to the Future, infra). The representation must be knowingly false and made with the specific intent to defraud; it must be relied upon and believed by the person to whom it is made and must cause such person to part with his property, with the intention of parting with title thereto to the accused, or to someone designated by the accused, because of such representation.

The characteristics of a case of obtaining property by false pretenses are that it resembles a legitimate transaction, usually in the nature of an exchange, transfer or sale of property in which, in order to induce the complainant to part with his property as his part of the transaction, the defendant knowingly and with intent to defraud misrepresents that which the complainant is to receive and the complainant, believing and relying upon the representation as being a true state of facts, and because thereof, parts with the title to his property though he would not have done so had he known the true state of affairs.

It has been held that the statutes which prescribe punishment for false representations were intended to protect persons against those who report falsely with respect to their earthly and material possessions and that a prosecution can not be predicated upon the representations of a person claiming the possession of exceptional spiritual power or knowledge. (People v. Blackburn, 214 Cal. 402.)

Examples of False Pretenses

Among the false pretenses involved in cases coming before our appellate courts are found the following:—Representations of the present condition of the affairs of a partnership (People v. Bianchi, 56 Cal. App. 579); that the defendant had credit with a certain firm (People v. Wasservogel, 77 Cal. 173); that the accused had bonds which he would use to raise money (People v. Bowman, 24 Cal. App. 781); that a certain mortgage was a first mortgage (People v. Henninger, 20 Cal. App. 79); that a judgment had been secured against the complainant (People v. Martin, 102 Cal. 558); that the accused had a certain amount of capital and that his liabilities did not exceed a certain amount (People v. Wieger, 100 Cal. 352; People v. Mace, 71 Cal. App. 10); that the defendant had a specified sum in the bank (In re James, 47 Cal. App. 205); that certain barrels contained whiskey when in fact they contained colored water (People v. Abbott, 65 Cal. App. 51); that a certain business had an income of a certain specified amount (People v. Helminger, 69 Cal. App. 139); that a certain bill had been paid (People v. Pearson, 69 Cal. App. 524; People v. Hand, 127 Cal. App. 484); selling conditional sales contracts which did not represent any actual transaction (People v. Leaverton, 107 Cal. App. 51; People v. Cordish, 110 Cal. App. 486); as to the ownership of property (People v. Hamilton, 108 Cal. App. 621); as to value of property (People v. Ingles, 117 Cal. App. 22); that a restaurant was doing a certain volume of business (People v. Foster, 117 Cal. App. 252); that certain stock could not be purchased because of its tremendous earnings (People v. Lesser, 123 Cal. App. 489); that an apartment house was occupied by permanent tenants (People v. Reid, 72 Cal. App. 611); representation by a contractor that all bills incurred had been paid (People v. Hand, 127 Cal. App. 484); and a conviction was sustained where defendant manipulated the books of three business trusts to show that they were earning larger profits than were in fact earned and either caused or permitted his agents to sell interests in these trusts upon the representations that the false book profits were actual. (People v. Ferguson, 134 Cal. App. 41.) Where the complainant was induced by false pretenses to pay money to a copartnership and become a member of the copartnership the conviction was sustained (People v. Jones, 36 Cal. 2d 373). Where a building contractor obtained money as one of the progress payments under the building contract through affidavits that all labor and material had been paid when in fact such was not the case the conviction was sustained (People v. Gloster, 102 Cal. App. 2d 872.)

Where the defendant represented that certain electric and electronic machines used by him would respectively diagnose from a blood specimen and cure various ailments including cancer and there was expert evidence that the machines were not capable of so doing, the conviction of conspiracy to commit theft in the nature of false pretenses was sustained and the defense argument that there was expert testimony contrary to that of the People's experts was without merit (People v. Schmitt, 155 Cal. App. 2d........).

While ordinarily a loan transaction creates only civil rights and obligations, the evidence may actually establish the offense of obtaining property by false pretenses or larceny by trick and device, more likely the latter (see People v. Lauten-schlager, 56 Cal. App. 2d 615; People v. Reed, 113 Cal. App. 2d 339).

A concealment of a material fact may amount to a false pretense when the circumstances are such that the victim is, under the circumstances, led to believe that such fact did not exist and would not have entered into the transaction but for his induced belief that it did not exist. Thus where, under the circumstances, honesty and fair dealing required that the defendant make a full and fair disclosure of his financial condition and made a list of his debts, such statement implied that he had no debts other than those listed and was in effect a statement that he had no other debts (People v. Mace, 71 Cal. App. 10, 21).

Matters of Opinion (are not false pretenses)

Statements which amount to no more than an expression of opinion are not false pretenses. (People v. Walker, 76 Cal. App. 192; People v. Reese, 136 Cal. App. 657; People v. Downing, 14 Cal. App. 2d 392; People v. Jackson, 24 Cal. App. 2d 182; People v. Daniels, 25 Cal. App. 2d 64.) Thus a representation that the land and mortgage were good and sufficient security for the money obtained on a promissory note was held a mere matter of opinion and not a false pretense. (People v. Gibbs, 98 Cal. 661.)

The line between the statement of an opinion and a statement of fact is not always clear and what may be an opinion under one statement of facts could under other conditions be a false pretense. Thus if in a case like People v. Gibbs, supra, it could be shown that the person who made the statement as to the value of the security knew that in fact the land was valueless the statement would be a false pretense, for then it would no longer be an opinion but the making of a statement contrary to an existing known fact, and a statement as to the value of property if made as a statement of an existing fact may be a false pretense. (People v. Schwarz, 78 Cal. App. 561; People v. Ingles, 117 Cal. App. 122.) Thus, also, a statement by a physician, declared as a fact, that a person had a certain fatal disease which he declared he could cure, would, if knowingly false, be such a false pretense as is contemplated by the statute. (People v. Arberry, 13 Cal. App. 749.)

Statements as to the Future

The crime of obtaining property by false pretenses cannot be predicated upon a representation or promise as to a matter in the future, no matter how unwarranted such statement may be. (People v. Woods, 190 Cal. 513; People v. Wasservogel, 77 Cal. 173; People v. Walker, 76 Cal. App. 192; People v. Daniels, 25 Cal. App. 2d 64; People v. Downing, 14 Cal. App. 2d 392; People v. Jackson, 24 Cal. App. 2d 182.) In a recent case, involving an agreement of the defendant for the future care and support of the complainant for life the court said, "If one of the parties entertains a present intention of not performing her part of such a contract when it is made, and falsely represents to the other that she will give him a home and care for life and has no present intention of performing, and obtains money or property from the other while he relies on the truth of such false representations, then they relate to a present fact and are not merely predictions of the occurrence of future events or the expressions of an opinion concerning them." People v. Ames, 61 Cal. App. 2d 523; see also: People v. Gordon, 71 Cal. App. 2d 606; People v. Mason, 86 Cal. App. 2d 445; People v. Jones, 36 Cal. 2d 373; People v. Frankfort, 114 Cal. App. 2d 680; People v. Staver, 115 Cal. App. 2d 711). In other words, if a person states that he has now in mind the intent to do a particular thing in the future, that is a statement of a present fact even though the carrying out of the intent is left to the future. A promise made with the intent not to perform it is a "false or fraudulent representation" within the meaning of section 484 of the Penal Code, the intent not to perform being shown by evidence that, under the circumstances, the defendant must have known that he could not keep the promise made (People v. Ashley, 42 Cal. 2d 246; People v. Weitz, 42 Cal. 2d 338; People v. Rocha, 130 Cal. App. 2d 656), but proof of nonperformance is not sufficient to prove that an intent not to perform existed at the time the promise was made (People v. Ashley, supra).

Form of Pretense

The false pretense while usually an oral statement may be in writing or by the act or silence of a person, or by a person knowingly allowing his agents to make the false statement. (People v. Ferguson, 134 Cal. App. 41.) A statement on the price tag of an article as to its quantity or weight or the material of which it is made, if false, may be a false pretense and one who wears a uniform which he has no right to wear is by such act representing that he has such right. While there is a specific statute punishing a person who, with intent to defraud, cashes his personal check without having sufficient funds or credit to meet the same upon presentation at the drawee bank, such act would also constitute the offense of obtaining money by false pretenses, the act of presenting and passing the check being the equivalent of an express declaration that the check was good and that the amount of the check was then in the bank, subject to draft. (People v. Wasservogel, 77 Cal. 173. See also People v. Bercovitz, 163 Cal. 636.)

Written Contract, Effect of

Where a written contract was entered into by the defendant and the complainant, the prosecution is not bound by it and is at liberty to show the true nature of the transaction even though it varies from the written agreement (People v. Frankfort, 114 Cal. App. 2d 680; 114 A.C.A. 825).

Tricks of the Trade—"Puffing"

The law does not contemplate as punishable what are known as tricks of the trade, or "puffing" statements, where, without any false representation as to the character, quality or quantity of merchandise sold or disposed of, false and exaggerated statements are made to induce a sale. Thus statements by a merchant that, by reason of low expenses he could sell goods 25 per cent cheaper than anyone else, when in fact his prices were higher than the same goods could be bought for elsewhere, do not amount to false pretenses. As our supreme court has said, "Customers are presumed to have sound knowledge of the value of what they purchase," and that if such representations are criminal "a crime is paraded in numerous show windows in every city." (People v. Morphy, 100 Cal. 84.)

False Pretense Must Be Relied Upon

To constitute this crime it must also appear that the complainant relied upon the false pretense and parted with his property by reason of his reliance upon the truth of one or more of the false representations of the accused. While it must appear that the complainant relied upon the false pretense. it is not necessary that he specifically so testify it being sufficient if an inference to that effect may be drawn from the evidence (People v. Frankfort, 114 Cal. App. 2d 680). If the complainant knew that the representations were false or did not rely upon them or part with his property by reason thereof, or if in parting with his property he was actuated by some cause other than such representations, the offense is not committed. It is not necessary, however, that the complainant make any investigation to ascertain the truth of the representation and he is under no obligation to do so. (People v. Cummings, 123 Cal. 269; People v. Smith, 3 Cal. App. 62; see also People v. Breyer, 139 Cal. App. 547) and the rule of caveat emptor does not apply (People v. Bellew, 90 Cal. App. 2d 801). While the victim of the offense must part with his property because of the false pretense it is not necessary that the false representation was the sole cause of the owner parting with his property (People v. Staver, 115 Cal. App. 2d 711).

The express testimony of a victim of false pretenses that he was induced to part with his property by the fraudulent statements of the accused is not essential to the successful prosecution for theft by false pretenses but it is sufficient if the inference of his reliance could have been drawn from all of the evidence (People v. Adams, 137 Cal. App. 2d 660; People v. Schmidt, 147 Cal. App. 2d 222).

One False Pretense Sufficient

Even though the transaction was accompanied by the making of a number of false pretenses, it is not necessary that all of such pretenses and their falsity be proved. It is sufficient to sustain a conviction if, the other elements of the offense being established, but one of the false pretenses is established. (People v. Cory, 26 Cal. App. 735; People v. Smith, 3 Cal. App. 62; People v. Griesheimer, 176 Cal. 44; People v. Revley, 67 Cal. App. 553; People v. Walker, 76 Cal. App. 192; People v. Fraser, 81 Cal. App. 281; People v. White, 85 Cal. App. 241.)

Accused Need Not Personally Receive Property Obtained

In this offense it is not necessary that the accused shall have himself received the property involved in the theft or even that he shall have profited by his fraud, but it is sufficient if, induced by his false representations, the property is delivered to another, either for the benefit of that other or for his own benefit. (People v. Coffelt, 140 Cal. App. 444; People v. Rabe, 202 Cal. 409; People v. Cheeley, 106 Cal. App. 2d 748; People v. Ashley, 42 Cal. 2d 246; People v. Schmidt, 147 Cal. App. 2d 222).

Corroboration Required *[handwritten: Supportive — Prove that false pretense was made.]*

"Upon a trial for having, with intent to cheat or defraud another designedly, by any false pretense, obtained the signature of any person to a written instrument, or having obtained from any person any labor, money or property, whether real or personal, or valuable thing, the defendant cannot be convicted if the false pretense was expressed in language unaccompanied by a false token or writing, unless the pretense, or some note or memorandum thereof is in writing, subscribed by or in the handwriting of the defendant, or unless the pretense is proven by the testimony of two witnesses, or that of one witness and corroborating circumstances; but this section does not apply to a prosecution for falsely representing or personating another, and, in such assumed character, marrying, or receiving any money or property." (Penal Code, sec. 1110.)

This section, like section 1111 governing the corroboration required of the testimony of an accomplice (q. v.), refers to proof "upon a trial" and, as in the application of section 1111, corroboration would not be required at a preliminary examination to justify a magistrate in holding the accused to answer to the superior court. (See Ex parte Schwittala, 36 Cal. App. 511.)

Upon a trial, however, the corroboration required by section 1110 must be present to justify a conviction. (People v. Curran, 24 Cal. App. 2d 673; People v. Fawver, 29 Cal. App. 2d 775; People v. Leach, 106 Cal. App. 442; People v. Carter, 131 Cal. App. 177) and, while section 1110 was in force before the crime of obtaining property by false pretenses was included in the crime of theft, it applies where the prosecution is under the theft statute. (People v. Leach, 106 Cal. App. 442; People v. Carter, 131 Cal. App. 177; People v. Beilfuss, 59 Cal. App. 2d 83.)

The corroboration required is not for the purpose of bolstering up the testimony of a witness but to show by evidence of either another witness or corroborating circumstances that the false pretense was made (People v. Beilfuss, 59 Cal. App. 2d 83), the original theory of requiring corroboration being that a conviction should not be had solely upon the testimony of the complaining witness as to matters of conversation which might easily have been misunderstood or misinterpreted at the time or which, with the lapse of time and contributing factors, might be remembered differently when related at a trial.

Where the false pretense or some note or memorandum thereof is in writing, either subscribed by or in the handwrit-

[handwritten at bottom: Abortion— a. that it was committed]

ing of the accused, no corroboration is required. Nor is corroboration required where the false pretense is oral but is accompanied by a false token or writing.

Form of Corroboration   *Re-Read*

(For section 1110 Penal Code, which requires corroboration see preceeding subtitle).

"It is not necessary that the 'corroborating circumstances' required by section 1110 of the Penal Code . . . shall of themselves be sufficient to establish guilt. If reasonably and fairly they may be said to **tend** to show the guilt, then, as corroborating circumstances, they respond to the requirement of the statute. . . . As employed then, in section 1110 of the Penal Code, the phrase 'corroborating circumstances' means that the circumstances must be such as to serve to strengthen the direct testimony of a witness as to the false pretense, or to render it more probable or such as may serve to impress a jury with the belief of the truth of the fact to be corroborated." (People v. Mace, 71 Cal. App. 10). The inclusion of obtaining money by false pretenses in the definition of theft did not affect the rule of section 1110 requiring corroboration but it is only the pretense which must be corroborated (People v. Reinschreiber, 152 Cal. App. 2d ...... A.C.A. 797).

The necessary corroboration may be furnished by any evidence, direct or circumstantial, which corroborates, to the degree required, the making of the false pretense and may be by proof of the admission or confession of the accused (People v. Mace, 71 Cal. App. 10; People v. Smith, 3 Cal. App. 62) or may consist of proof that the defendant made, to other persons, representations similar and to the same effect as those made to the complaining witness. (People v. La France, 28 Cal. App. 2d 152; People v. Munson, 115 Cal. App. 694; People v. Whiteside, 58 Cal. App. 33; People v. Wymer, 53 Cal. App. 204; People v. Helminger, 69 Cal. App. 139; People v. Jones, 36 Cal. 2d 373). The circumstances connected with the transaction, the entire conduct of the defendant and his declarations to other persons may be looked to to furnish the required corroboration (People v. Frankfort, 114 Cal. App. 2d 680 and cases cited).

False Token

A false token is a thing or an object which is used as a means to defraud and which is of such character that, were it not false it would commonly be accepted as what it obviously appears and purports to be and which, though false, is apparently what it purports to be; People v. Cheeley, 106 Cal. App. 2d 748. A false measure used in the sale of a commodity, a false bank note and a false trade-mark are examples of false tokens.

Where a false contract was used for the purpose of fraudulently obtaining money it was held that such contract was a false token. (People v. Fleshman, 26 Cal. App. 788.) Where the false pretense was the statement that a certain lumber bill had been paid and the accused had displayed to complainant a receipted bill from the lumber company, which receipt he had obtained by the delivery of a worthless check, the court held that the receipted bill constituted a false token. (People v. Pearson, 69 Cal. App. 524.) A bank check may be a false token where the maker passed it for value knowing he had neither funds nor credit at the bank to insure its payment upon presentation. (People v. Donaldson, 70 Cal. 116.) Where the defendant without authority from the owner sold a quantity of the latter's hay, giving the buyer a memorandum of the sale which he signed, the memorandum was a false token. (People v. Payton, 36 Cal. App. 2d 41.) A promissory note bearing fictitious names as makers and used in connection with the representations is a false token (People v. Beilfuss, 59 Cal. App. 2d 83) but a genuine writing which contains no false statements is not. (People v. Beilfuss, supra.) Where the defendant obtained the complainant's automobile and gave his promissory note therefor, the note was held not to be a false token (People v. Carter, 131 Cal. App. 177), for in such case the note was in fact what it purported to be. Conditional sales contracts, apparently representing but in fact not representing any actual transactions, and used as security for loans, are false tokens. (People v. Wynn, 44 Cal. App. 2d 723.)

Actual Loss Not Necessary

In cases of this kind it is not necessary that the victim suffered any actual loss of money or property (People v. Schmidt, 147 Cal. App. 2d 222, cases cited).

Question of Fact for Jury

Whether the representations of the accused were material inducements to the obtaining of the property and whether they were made honestly or with intent to deceive and defraud are questions of fact for the jury (People v. Schmitt, 155 Cal. App. 2d ....).

Restitution No Defense

When once the crime of obtaining property by false pretenses has been completed by the obtaining of the property "the defendant is not purged of culpability even by subsequent restoration, restitution or repayment." (People v. Wynn, 44 Cal. App. 2d 723; People v. Jones, 36 Cal. 2d 373; People v. Cheeley, 106 Cal. App. 2d 748.) Neither is it a defense that it would have been unlawful to have completed the transaction. (People v. Raines, 66 Cal. App. 2d 960.)

Offenses Similar to False Pretenses

Special provision is made in the Penal Code for Marrying Under False Personation (sec. 528), Personating Another in Private or Official Capacity (sec. 529); Receiving Money or Property in a False Character (sec. 530), Making False Statement of Financial Condition (sec. 532-a), Selling Land Twice (sec. 533), Married Person Selling Lands Under False Representations (sec. 534), issuing a check without sufficient funds or credit (sec. 476a), and other offenses closely resembling obtaining property by false pretenses.

Selling or Transferring Mortgaged Property

Section 538 of the Penal Code provides that any person who, after mortgaging personal property, with intent to defraud, removes, sells, transfers or destroys the same, unless in case of and prior to the sale, transfer or further incumbrance thereof he informs the person to whom such sale, transfer or incumbrance is made and also the prior mortgagee of the intended sale, transfer or incumbrance in writing, is guilty of theft. In such a case the fact that the mortgage was ultimately paid is immaterial (People v. Iden, 24 Cal. App. 627). The intent to defraud is an element of the offense of selling mortgaged property without giving the mortgagee prior notice in writing (People v. Farmer, 47 Cal. 2d 479). Where the property is sold with the consent of the mortgagee, prior written notice is not required and no offense is committed (People v. Farmer, supra).

Presenting False Claims

"Every person who, with intent to defraud, presents for allowance or for payment to any state board or officer, or to any county, town, city, district, ward or village board or officer, authorized to allow or pay the same if genuine, any false or fraudulent claim, bill, account, voucher, or writing, is guilty of a felony." (Penal Code, sec. 72). The penalty for this offense is imprisonment in the state prison for a term not exceeding five years nor less than six months (Penal Code, secs. 18, 18a).

Where the official or officials to whom a claim is presented could in no way allow the claim, even though it be allowed and paid, an essential element of the corpus delicti is missing (People v. Lanterman, 9 Cal. App. 674; People v. Butler, 35 Cal. App. 357). The general rule that allowance by a board of supervisors of a claim is final, if the claim is on its face properly chargeable and payable by the county, does not apply in a criminal case under this section (People v. Knott, 15 Cal. 2d 628). The later enactment of section 101 (a) of the Unemployment Insurance Act supersedes, as to cases coming within its provisions, section 72 (People v. Haydon, 106 Cal. App. 2d 105).

Embezzlement, Larceny and Obtaining Property by False Pretenses Distinguished

Although the consolidation of the three offenses into the one crime of theft has simplified the manner in which they are charged and prosecuted, they still retain their individual characteristics and the ability to distinguish which offense is shown by a given state of facts is often of vital importance. Thus a case tried on the theory of larceny by trick and device may result in the conviction being reversed if the case is in fact one of obtaining money by false pretenses and there was not the corroboration required by law. Viewed as obtaining property by false pretenses a set of facts may seem to present no case because the fraudulent statements do not in law amount to false pretenses when a proper appraisal of the facts might show that a conviction could be secured on the theory of larceny. The distinction between the three offenses lies in the fact that there is a distinct difference in the corpus delicti of each of the offenses from the corpus delicti of the other two, each has one or more elements necessary to constitute that particular crime which are not elements of the other two.

Embezzlement Distinguished—

Embezzlement is most easily distinguished by the fact that when the property came into the possession of the accused he received it honestly upon a trust or bailment and charged with the duty to do with the property only those things for which it had been intrusted. No criminal act is committed until this duty and trust is violated and the property is fraudulently converted to some use or purpose other than that for which it was intrusted. It is this act of violating his trust and doing with the property as he chooses and not what his duty requires that constitutes the theft. Where the original taking of the property into the possession of the defendant was not felonious and there were no false or fraudulent representations inducing the owner to turn the property over to the defendant and the property came into and was in the possession of the defendant lawfully, the offense can not be larceny or obtaining property by false pretenses and the only form of theft possible is embezzlement. (People v. Stanford, 16 Cal. 2d 247; see also People v. Sichofsky, 58 Cal. App. 257; People v. Knox, 32 Cal. 158; and cases under **Embezzlement.**)

Larceny Distinguished

Larceny is distinguished from embezzlement in that, while in embezzlement the property comes into the possession of the agent or trustee lawfully and without any unlawful intent on his part, he who perpetrates larceny intends, at the very moment the property comes into his possession, to permanently deprive the owner of his property. That form of larceny in which the taking is in secret and without the knowledge of the owner is easily identified, but larceny by trick and device and obtaining property by false pretenses are frequently so similar in the modus operandi employed by the swindler that, depending upon the conclusion which may be formed as to the intent of the parties, the crime may be viewed as either larceny or obtaining property by false pretenses and a verdict of conviction of either offense may be sustained. (People v. Von Bodenthal, 8 Cal. App. 2d 404; People v. Miles, 19 Cal. App. 223.) In both offenses the victim is deceived into parting with his property by the fraud and deceit practiced by the defendant. If the false representations do not relate to the past or present or are mere matters of opinion or promise the possibility of the crime being obtaining property by false pretenses is eliminated. The basic test, however, is found in the intent of the owner. In false pretense cases the owner of the property turns it over to the defendant intending that the defendant shall become the unconditional and unrestricted owner thereof. In larceny by trick and device, however, the owner never intends that the property shall belong to or become the property of the defendant; he never intends to part with title to the defendant but merely turns the possession of the property to the defendant to be used by the latter in accordance with and for the purposes expressed in the conversations and agreement between the parties. The expression in some opinions that in larceny the owner never intends to part with title to the property is not strictly accurate; the rule is that he does not intend to part with the title **to the defendant** but this is not affected by the fact that he usually does intend that title to his property shall pass according to the plan or scheme proposed by the defendant and which he believes will be carried out. The larcenist, having obtained possession of the property by representing a purely fictitious or misrepresented venture as real, at all times intends to steal the property for himself. (People v. Rae, 66 Cal. 423; People v. Raschke, 73 Cal. 378; People v. Tomlinson, 102 Cal. 23; People v. Shaughnessy, 110 Cal. 602; People v. Schwartz, 43 Cal. App. 696; People v. Evanoff, 45 Cal. App. 108; People v. Arnold, 20 Cal. App. 35; People v. Miles, 19 Cal. App. 228; People v. Campbell, 127 Cal. 278; People v. Delbos, 146 Cal. 734; People v. Edwards, 72 Cal. App. 102; People v. Solomon, 75 Cal. App. 9; People v. Beilfuss, 59 Cal. App. 2d 83; People v. Pillsbury, 59 Cal. App. 2d 107; People v. Barnett, 31 Cal. App. 2d 173.) Where an employee takes the merchandise of his employer with intent to sell it and pocket the proceeds and carries out this intent the crime is theft by larceny (People v. Howes, 99 Cal. App. 2d 808).

CHAPTER XXIII.

ROBBERY

"Robbery is the felonious taking of personal property in the possession of another, from his person or immediate presence, and against his will, accomplished by means of force or fear." (Penal Code, sec. 211.)

Corpus Delicti

Robbery, being a compound larceny, contains all of the elements of larceny (People v. Sheasby, 82 Cal. App. 459) and therefore an essential element of robbery is the specific intent to permanently deprive the owner of his property. The larceny involved in robbery is, however, limited to the taking from the person or immediate presence of the owner and against his will (see People v. Jones, 53 Cal. 58; People v. Nelson, 56 Cal. 77) but, like all larceny, robbery must include asportation. (See **Asportation** under **Larceny**.) "Proof of motive or conspiracy to commit the robbery is not essential to a conviction for neither deliberation nor premeditation is made an element of the crime." (People v. Thomas, 45 Cal. App. 2d 128.)

Proof By Circumstantial Evidence

Robbery may be proved by circumstantial evidence. Thus where a person is assaulted and rendered unconscious and some of the property which he had on his person is missing when he regains consciousness the facts warrant the conclusion that the victim was robbed by the person who committed the assault and a conviction is sustained by the evidence (People v. Hubler, 102 Cal. App. 2d 689).

Intent

What has been said heretofore under Larceny concerning the specific intent is applicable to robbery. This intent is usually evident from the circumstances but further proof may show that the intent to permanently deprive the owner of his property was absent. Thus it may be that, while the property was taken, it was taken only with the intent of temporarily depriving the owner of his property and then returning it or the taking may be lawful as where one in self defense forcibly takes from his assailant the deadly weapon with which the attack is being made. Again it would not be robbery if the property taken belonged to him who took it or if in good faith he believed that the property he was taking was his own in which latter case the mistake of fact would be a defense. Where the seller under a conditional sales contract took the property from the vendee by the use of force a conviction of robbery was reversed as there was not any intent to steal. (People v. Sheasby, 82 Cal. App. 459.)

It is not the original intent with which the incident started but the intent with which the taking was accomplished that determines whether the crime is robbery. Thus where the original plan was to commit extortion but the victim refused to give the defendants the money they demanded and they then took the money against his will by force and fear the crime of robbery was committed. (People v. Courtney, 132 Cal. App. 198, 204.)

Asportation — *unlawful taking Need not be permanent (Sec. only)*

An attempt to commit a robbery does not become a robbery until there has been an asportation of some property from the person or immediate possession of another. Here again the rules of Larceny (q. v.) apply. Once the property has been taken and the asportation accomplished, the crime of robbery, the other elements of the offense being present, is complete. Thus where, in a bank robbery, one of the robbers had taken some of the money in the vault and was then knocked unconscious by some of the bank employees, the crime of robbery was complete even though the money was never taken out of the presence of the bank employees from whose possession it was taken. (People v. Beal, 3 Cal. App. 2d 251; People v. Clark, Cal. App. 2d 132.)

The taking or asportation may also be accomplished where the victim, under the menace of force or fear, is compelled to turn property in his possession over to a person other than the defendant. Thus where the defendant under the menace of a gun forced a taxicab driver to pay for the rental of two rooms in an auto court a conviction of robbery was sustained. (People v Headlee, 42 A. C. A. 266, but case reversed on another point by Supreme Court.)

Where, under menace of a gun and the order of the robber, the victim threw his wallet upon the ground, there was sufficient asportation and the crime of robbery was consummated even though the robber did not pick up the wallet (People v. Quinn, 77 Cal. App. 2d 734) and where the bartender victim,

asportation was complete

convert to own use — make anothers property yours

on demand of the armed defendant, laid the money from the cash register on the bar, at which time the defendant was struck down and captured by a patron, a conviction of robbery was sustained (People v. Wellman, 141 Cal. App. 2d 101).

Person or Immediate Presence

In robbery the taking must be either from the person or from the immediate presence of another. To take property from the person of another the property must be taken from the body, clothing or some receptacle carried and in the actual physical possession of another. (See subhead **From the Person** under LARCENY.) Where the prosecutrix after accepting an offer of the defendant to take her to her place of employment was taken to an unfrequented road where defendant attempted familiarities with her and she jumped out of the car and fell down whereupon defendant drove away and she later missed her handbag, containing her money, and a companion of defendant testified he and defendant later found the purse and divided the money it was held that the offense amounted only to larceny as the evidence did not warrant the conclusion that the property was taken from either the person or immediate possession of the prosecutrix (People v. Sylvis, 72 Cal. App. 632.) Where defendant under menace of a gun was forced to participate in a dice game in which he lost all the money he had a conviction of robbery was sustained. (People v. Unipeg, 118 Cal. App. 485.)

The provision of the statute that the taking must be from the "immediate presence" of the victim does not mean that the victim must have been actually present and able to observe the actual taking. A person perpetrating a robbery cannot avoid conviction of that charge by first removing his victim to another location before he takes the property and contending that the taking was not in the immediate presence of the owner. Where the defendant held up the watchman and janitor and, after tying him up, went into another room and stole the money of the theatre from the safe it was held that the crime of robbery had been committed. (People v. Dean, 66 Cal. App. 602; followed under similar facts by People v. Lavender, 135 Cal. App. 582.) Where the defendant held up a theatre cashier and she ran out of the box office and then defendant took the money and ran (People v. Davis, 100 Cal. App. 179) and where, after stealing the money, the owner came up to the defendant who made his escape with the money, preventing the owner from resisting by menacing him with a gun (People v. Perhab, 92 Cal. App. 2d 663) convictions were sustained.

Force or Fear

To constitute the crime of robbery it is necessary that the act of taking be accomplished by means of force or fear. It is sufficient if the taking is by either force or fear and it is not necessary that there be both force and fear. (People v. Ferrara, 31 Cal. App. 1.) Without proof of the use of either force or fear to accomplish the taking the crime can not be robbery. (People v. Welch, 7 Cal. 2d 209.)

Force

To constitute robbery the force used must be more than the force which, under the circumstances, is necessary to accomplish the asportation. While "purse snatching," where the only force used is that necessary to take the purse from the possession of the owner, amounts only to larceny, "where property is snatched from the person of another or procured by threats of bodily harm or under circumstances reasonably creating grave apprehension on the part of the owner of receiving bodily injury at the hands of the thief the crime is robbery." (People v. Jefferson, 31 Cal. App. 2d 562; People v. Church, 116 Cal. 300.) Where the defendant knocked a strong box out of the victim's arm and, upon the victim catching it, made another effort which succeeded and he then grabbed the box and made off with it, it was held that the force used was in excess of that incident to a mere larceny and that the crime was robbery. (People v. Clayton, 89 Cal. App. 405.)

Since the perpetration of a robbery includes not only the initial taking but the asportation which continues until after the perpetrator departs from the place where he seized the property (People v. Wallace, 36 Cal. App. 2d 1) it follows that the use of force or fear to accomplish the asportation at any time up to the departure from the scene would make the crime robbery rather than larceny.

Fear

"The fear mentioned in the last section (i. e., section 211) may be either:

1. The fear of an unlawful injury to the person or property of the person robbed, or of any relative of his or member of his family; or

2. The fear of an immediate and unlawful injury to the person or property of any one in the company of the person robbed at the time of the robbery.'' (Penal Code, sec. 212.)

It will be noted that the second subdivision of this section refers to the fear of unlawful injury to the person or property of some person, in the company of the person robbed, who is not a relative or member of the family of the person whose property is taken and the fear in a case under this subdivision must be a fear of an immediate injury. Where, however, the injury is threatened to the person or property of the person whose property is taken or of any relative of his or member of his family, the injury threatened need not be immediate and a threat of injury in the future would be sufficient to form a basis for the element of fear. While instances of robbery accomplished by means of fear induced by a threat of injury to property are comparatively rare such a threat, as for example to set fire to a building or otherwise destroy property or to kill an animal, would be sufficient to furnish this element of robbery.

Where no force is used and the property is taken by fear, it is not necessary that the victim be shaken with fear or deprived of the ability to resist if he were foolish enough to take the risk. A victim who is not afraid as long as he complies with the demands of the robber and who complies because of the injury which might be inflicted if he did not comply is in fear within the meaning of the law of robbery. (People v. Borrea, 123 Cal. App. 482.)

Ownership of Property - Sufficient - claim of possession - Does not have to be owned by you

In robbery, as in larceny, the property taken must be that of some person other than the one who takes it. It is not necessary that the person from whom the property is taken be the sole and unconditional owner with complete title thereto and it is sufficient if he be in possession of the property and that the property be not that of the robber. (People v. Shuler, 28 Cal. 490; People v. Hicks, 66 Cal. 103; People v. Oldham, 111 Cal. App. 648; People v. Downs, 114 Cal. App. 2d 758; see also cases in subhead **"Property of Another"** under LARCENY.)

A servant or employee left in sole occupation of the premises or particular part thereof by the owner has sufficient possession under the robbery statute (People v. Downs, 114 Cal. App. 2d 758).

Where the owner of property takes it from another by force and fear and against the will of the holder, the crime of robbery is not committed. (People v. Vice, 21 Cal. 344.) When money is lost in an illegal gambling game it remains the property of the loser and it cannot be robbery or larceny for him to take it back. (People v. Rosen, 11 Cal. 2d 147.) In the case last cited the court further said that it is not incumbent to such a defense that the accused prove that the money reclaimed was the identical money won from him but that he must intend in good faith to retake his own property. This case is not authority for the proposition that such a defense could be maintained where the accused took from the one to whom he lost it an amount of money equal to that which he had lost merely to make good his loss where he knew that the money he was taking was not the identical money he had lost or had no reason to believe it was the identical money. And in a case in which the accused contends he was merely retaking his own money which he had lost at illegal gambling the defendant may be convicted if the evidence warrants the conclusion that the defendant did not intend to merely retake the money he had lost but to take all of the money the winner had in his possession (People v. Lain, 57 Cal. App. 2d 123) or if, in addition to money he also took the victim's watch. (People v. Beard, 36 Cal. App. 2d 35.)

Value of Property

The crime of robbery does not in any degree depend upon the amount or value of the property taken and, the other elements of the offense being present, the crime of robbery is made out even though the property taken be of slight value. (People v. Stevens, 141 Cal. 488; People v. Ferlito, 100 Cal. App. 355; People v. Factor, 125 Cal. App. 618; People v. Thomas, 45 Cal. App. 128; People v. Simmons, 28 Cal. 2d 699.)

Degrees of Robbery

"All robbery which is perpetrated by torture or by a person being armed with a dangerous or deadly weapon is robbery in the first degree. All other kinds of robbery are of the second degree." (Penal Code, sec. 211a.)

Torture

While the question has not as yet come before our appellate courts it would seem, following the rule in those murder cases where the killing is perpetrated by means of torture (q. v.), that cases of robbery which are of the first degree because perpetrated by torture include not only cases wherein the perpetrator intentionally caused pain and anguish to the victim to compel him to surrender his property or to disclose the hiding place of his property but also those cases in which the force used upon the victim in perpetrating the robbery amounts to torture, even though such force was not necessary to accomplish the robbery.

Armed With a Dangerous or Deadly Weapon *[capable] of being used as one*

Robbery perpetrated by a person "armed with a dangerous or deadly weapon" is robbery of the first degree. (Penal Code, sec. 211a.) There is nothing in this section which requires that such weapon must be used in order to make the robbery one of the first degree; it is only required that the perpetrator be so armed (People v. Jones, 114 Cal. App. 91; People v. Palumbo, 127 Cal. App. 703; People v. Kiser, 22 Cal. App. 2d 435; People v. Seaman, 101 Cal. App. 302) and "once the character of the instrumentality is established as a 'dangerous or deadly weapon' it is immaterial whather such weapon is used or even exposed to view." (People v. Raleigh, 128 Cal. App. 105.)

Where a robbery is committed by several persons and one of them is armed with a deadly or dangerous weapon, all of such persons are guilty of robbery in the first degree (People v. Perkins, 37 Cal. 2d 62; People v. Silva, 143 Cal. App. 2d 162).

Since a robbery is not at an end the moment the stolen property comes into the possession of the perpetrator but continues during the asportation and his departure from the scene (see subhead "In the perpetration" of a Felony under MURDER) a robber who arms himself with a dangerous or deadly weapon after the theft and uses the weapon to prevent his being captured or followed is guilty of first degree robbery (People v. Wallace, 36 Cal. App. 2d 1) and, under the authorities above cited it would not be necessary that the weapon be used to make the robbery one of first degree.

"Dangerous or deadly weapons" may be divided into two classes: (1) those instrumentalities which are weapons in the strict sense of the word, having been manufactured and designed for the purpose of their being used as weapons, and so constructed as to be the efficient means of inflicting great bodily injury, such as firearms, dirks, daggers, blackjacks, slungshots and metal knuckles, and which may be said as a matter of law to be dangerous or deadly weapons; and (2) instrumentalities not originally intended to be used as weapons, such as ordinary razors, pocket knives, hat pins, canes, hammers, hatchets and other sharp or heavy objects which are not weapons in the strictest sense of the word nor dangerous in the use for which they were originally intended and which cannot be said as a matter of law to be dangerous or deadly weapons but which, if capable of being used to inflict great bodily injury and carried by the possessor with the intent to use the same should occasion require as a weapon of offense or defense in the perpetration of a robbery, thereby become dangerous or deadly weapons. (People v. Raleigh, 128 Cal. App. 105.) The words "armed with a dangerous or deadly weapon" mean furnished or equipped with a weapon of offense or defense and mere possession thereof at the time of the robbery is sufficient even if it is not used or exposed. (People v. Hall, 105 Cal. App. 358.) The definition of the term "deadly weapon" as used in connection with the law concerning the crime of assault with a deadly weapon does not apply to the law relating to the offense of robbery. (People v. Raleigh, 128 Cal. App. 105.)

The term "armed with" contemplates that the weapon be either carried or that it at least be readily available for immediate use should occasion require. Where a defendant has possession of a weapon under circumstances where he could not avail himself of it should he desire to do so he is not "armed with" such weapon within the meaning of the statute (People v. Calderone, 84 Cal. App. 2d 513; weapon in glove compartment of the automobile parked outside of the building in which the robbery was attempted).

Whenever the perpetrator of a robbery is armed with a weapon in the first class, an instrumentality which was originally in its manufacture intended to be used as a weapon with which to inflict bodily injuries, he is guilty of robbery of the first degree as a matter of law. If a robbery is perpetrated by a person who carries with him an instrument of the second class, an object not originally designed for use as a weapon, and the object is capable of being used as a dangerous or deadly weapon, and was carried by the robber with intent to use it as such in the perpetration of the robbery if the occasion should require, then the character of the instrumentality is established as a dangerous or deadly weapon and it is robbery of the first degree. (People v. Raleigh, 128 Cal. App. 105.)

A rifle, loaded with ammunition of a kind for which it was not intended, which could probably be discharged but which

might misfire was held to be a deadly weapon. (People v.
Ekstrand, 28 Cal. App. 2d 1.)   Where a robber is unarmed,
merely simulating a gun, but arms himself by taking a gun
from his victim during the robbery the crime is robbery of the
first degree.   (People v. Wallace, 36 Cal. App. 2d 1.)   Proof
that the victim of the robbery was unconscious from a blow
by the robber for a considerable period of time warrants the
conclusion that a deadly weapon was used.   (People v. Sampson, 99 Cal. App. 307.)   Where two or more persons commit a
robbery and one of them is armed with a dangerous or deadly
weapon, they are all guilty of robbery of the first degree.
(People v. Jones, 114 Cal. App. 91; People v. Palumbo, 127 Cal.
App. 703; People v. Kiser, 22 Cal. App. 2d 435.)

Proof that a firearm was pointed at a human being, within
firing distance and with the threat, express or implied, that it
might be used to shoot with, or of other circumstances which
justify and warrant the conclusion that the gun was loaded,
establishes   prima   facie   that   the   firearm   was   loaded
and a verdict of first degree robbery is justified.   (People v.
Eberle, 72 Cal. App. 414; People v. Hall, 87 Cal. App. 634;
People v. Milburn, 89 Cal. App. 526; People v. Newman, 102
Cal. App. 2d 302.)

The fact that a dangerous or deadly weapon was used may
be established by circumstantial evidence.   Thus, where the
victim was attacked from behind and could not see what hit
him but he testified that it was a hard object and that the
blow rendered him semi-unconscious for some seven minutes,
this justified the inference that a dangerous weapon was used
(People v. Lopez, 118 Cal. App. 2d 235; People v. Sampson,
99 Cal. App. 306; see also Assault With Deadly Weapon).

Unloaded Firearm

It is not necessary, however, that a gun be loaded to constitute it a dangerous or deadly weapon and where the perpetrator of a robbery is shown to have been carrying, at the time
of the offense, a revolver or firearm such fact will justify the
conclusion that he was armed with a dangerous weapon, even
though it was not loaded, and he is guilty of first degree robbery.   (People v. Egan, 77 Cal. App. 279; People v. Schaffer,
81 Cal. App. 752; People v. Freeman, 86 Cal. App. 374; People
v. Barnett, 87 Cal. App. 243; People v. Ward, 84 Cal. App. 2d
357; People v. Raner, 86 Cal. App. 2d 107.)   ''It is a matter of
common knowledge that in committing robbery pistols are frequently used as bludgeons rather than as firearms. The fact,

therefore, that a person perpetrating such crime is armed with a pistol is enough to justify the conclusion that the pistol is a dangerous weapon within the meaning of said section 211a of the Penal Code, even though it be not loaded." (People v. Egan, 77 Cal. App. 279.) The fact that a gun is loaded may be established by circumstantial evidence (People v. Ash, 88 Cal. App. 2d 819).

Toy Pistol

Where the robber displayed what appeared to be an automatic pistol but which was merely a toy cap pistol weighing about a pound and about six inches long a conviction of first degree robbery was sustained on the theory that it was capable of being used as an instrument to produce bodily harm when used as a club. (People v. Coleman, 53 Cal. App. 2d 18; People v. Ward, 84 Cal. App. 2d 357, a toy .32 automatic weighing half a pound.)

Other Weapons

Where the robber carried a small hammer in his hip pocket the question of whether the defendant was armed with a dangerous or deadly weapon was held to be one of fact for the jury and a first degree conviction was sustained (People v. McKinney, 111 Cal. App. 2d 690).

Return of Property

Once the act of asportation has occurred the crime is complete and it is no defense that the property taken was returned, not even if the restitution occurred directly after the taking. (People v. Strauss, 75 Cal. App. 447; People v. James, 20 Cal. App. 2d 88; People v. Tipton, 96 Cal. App. 2d 840.)

Penalty

"Robbery is punishable by imprisonment in the state prison as follows:

1. Robbery in the first degree for not less than five years;

2. Robbery in the second degree, for not less than one year." (Penal Code, sec. 213.)

The maximum penalty for robbery of either degree is life imprisonment and the period of imprisonment may be for any period of years not less than the minimum prescribed by section 213. (Penal Code, sec. 671.)

EXTORTION

"Extortion is the obtaining of property from another, with his consent, or the obtaining of an official act of a public officer, induced by a wrongful use of force or fear, or under color of official right." (Penal Code, sec. 518.)

"Fear, such as will constitute extortion, may be induced by a threat, either:

1. To do an unlawful injury to the person or property of the individual threatened or of a third person.

2. To accuse him, or any relative of his, or member of his family, of any crime; or,

3. To expose, or impute to him or them any deformity or disgrace; or,

4. To expose any secret affecting him or them." (Penal Code, sec. 519.)

The law does not require that the fear induced by the threat must be a fear that the alleged extortioner would himself carry out the injury threatened and a threat that the injury would be inflicted by some other person is sufficient (People v. Hopkins, 105 Cal. App. 2d 708).

Penalty

"Every person who extorts any money or other property from another, under circumstances not amounting to robbery, by means of force, or any threat such as is mentioned in the preceding section is punishable by imprisonment in the state prison for not less than one nor more than ten years." (Penal Code, sec. 520.)

Distinguished from Robbery

Extortion is distinguished from robbery in that while it is the taking of property by means of force or fear, or under color of official right, the taking, when accomplished, does not amount to larceny and is with the consent of the victim. Extortion in some jurisdictions is called blackmail.

Consent

To constitute consent on the part of the victim of extortion it is not necessary that the turning over of his property shall have been entirely voluntary on his part, but the consent is in the nature of a choice on his part between turning over his property or of refusing to do so and thereby incurring the possible consequences threatened by the extortioner. The force or fear in extortion is not such as would leave to the victim no choice or which would compel him to allow the taking of his property against his will, for that would be robbery and not punishable as extortion. In a legal sense money or property is obtained from a person with his consent if he with apparent willingness turns it over to another with the understanding that he will be thereby saved from some personal calamity or injury, turning over his property as the lesser of two unpleasant alternatives, notwithstanding that he may mentally protest against the circumstances which compel the choice. (People v. Peck, 43 Cal. App. 638.)

Force or Fear

The force contemplated by the law of extortion differs from the force which is an element of robbery in that it is not such as compels the victim to turn over his property as the only alternative.

To constitute extortion the force or fear must be the operating or inducing cause which produces the consent and results in the property being obtained by the extortionist. If some other cause is the primary and controlling cause for the consent to the property being turned over there is no extortion. (People v. Williams, 127 Cal. 212; People v. Beggs, 178 Cal. 79.) If a person were to endeavor to commit extortion but the intended victim, not actuated by fear but with the desire to detect and prosecute the blackmailer, turned over the property in the presence of concealed witnesses, there would be at most only an attempted extortion. And where there is no threat but merely an offer, following an arrest, that upon the payment of a certain sum of money the charges would be dismissed there is no extortion. (People v. Anderson, 75 Cal. App. 365.)

Obtaining

To obtain property by means of extortion it is not necessary that the defendant personally receive the property and, the other elements of the offense being present, the offense is committed if the property, at defendant's request, is turned over to some third person. (People v. Peppercorn, 34 Cal. App. 2d 603.)

Threats

The words "unlawful injury" in subdivision 1 of section 519 include only such injuries which, if committed, would constitute such a wrong as might be the basis of a civil action. (People v. Schmitz, 7 Cal. App. 330; In re Nichols, 82 Cal. App. 73; People v. Sanders, 188 Cal. 744; People v. Swan, 188 Cal. 759.) But a threat by a person to do that which he has an absolute legal right to do is not a threat to do an unlawful injury. (In re Nichols, 82 Cal. App. 73.) A threat to cause bodily harm to others and to inflict damage upon their property is a threat to do an unlawful injury within the meaning of the statute. (People v. Peppercorn, 34 Cal. App. 2d 603.)

Subdivision 2 of section 519 as to a threat to accuse another of a crime is not limited to false accusations. One who threatens the thief who has stolen his property with criminal prosecution, unless he makes good the loss suffered, and thereby obtains property from the thief is, without reference to good faith in exacting that which is justly due, guilty of extortion. (People v. Beggs, 178 Cal. 79.) And a threat to accuse a person or his relative or member of his family of a criminal offense is a threat within subdivision 2 even though such a person is guilty thereof (People v. Powell, 50 Cal. App. 436; People v. Choynski, 95 Cal. 640; Morrill v. Nightingale, 93 Cal. 452; People v. Franquelin, 109 Cal. App. 2d 777) and this rule is not affected by the fact that the threat is to accuse of an offense under the Federal statutes. (People v. Sexton, 132 Cal. 37; Sexton v. United States, 189 U. S. 319; People v. Sanders, 188 Cal. 744; People v. Swan, 188 Cal. 759.)

Where the defendant sent a letter to complainant in which he stated that, unless the complainant withdrew an appeal in certain civil cases, he would make public certain affidavits which would injure the reputation of complainant it was held that this was a threat to expose a person to disgrace within subdivision 3 of section 519 of the Penal Code. (People v. Cadman, 57 Cal. 562.)

Where the threat is to expose a secret under subdivision 4 of section 519 the secret must be such as to affect the person threatened in some way so unfavorable to his reputation or interests as to be likely to induce him through the threat to pay money or turn over property to avoid disclosure. (People v. Lavine, 115 Cal. App. 289. For case of conviction for operating the "badger game" see People v. Turner, 22 Cal. App. 2d 186.)

Attempted Extortion

"Every person who attempts, by means of any threat, such as is specified in section 519 of this code, to extort money or other property from another is punishable by imprisonment in the county jail not longer than one year or in the state prison not exceeding five years, or by fine not exceeding five thousand dollars, or by both such fine and imprisonment." (Penal Code, sec. 524.)

Obtaining Signature by Threat

"Every person who, by any extortionate means, obtains from another his signature to any paper or instrument, whereby, if such signature were freely given, any property would be transferred, or any debt, demand, charge, or right of action created, is punishable in the same manner as if the actual delivery of such debt, demand, charge, or right of action were obtained." (Penal Code, sec. 522.)

Sending Threatening Letters

"Every person who, with intent to extort any money or other property from another, sends or delivers to any person any letter or other writing, whether subscribed or not, expressing or implying, or adapted to imply, any threat such as is specified in section 519, is punishable in the same manner as if such money or property were actually obtained by means of such threat." (Penal Code, sec. 523.)

Under this section the letter must be adapted to imply one or more of those threats specially mentioned in section 519 or the offense is not committed, and the truth or falsity of the charge forming the basis of the threat is immaterial. (People v. Choynski, 95 Cal. 640.) Under section 523 the offense is complete as soon as such a letter is sent or delivered and it is not necessary that any money or property be turned over as the result of the threatening letter.

"Every person who knowingly and willfully sends or delivers to another any letter or writing, whether subscribed or not, threatening to accuse him or another of a crime, or to expose or publish any of his failings or infirmities, is guilty of a misdemeanor." (Penal Code, sec. 650.)

This section is intended to cover those cases of threatening letters in which the intent to extort money or property is absent and the gist of the offense is the threat communicated by letter or other writing.

Sending When Complete

"In the various cases in which the sending of a letter is made criminal by this code, the offense is deemed complete from the time when such letter is deposited in any post-office or any other place, or delivered to any person, with intent that it shall be forwarded." (Penal Code, sec. 660.)

CHAPTER XXIV.

BURGLARY

"Every person who enters any house, room, apartment, tenement, shop, warehouse, store, mill, barn, stable, outhouse or other building, tent, vessel, railroad car, trailer coach as defined by the Vehicle Code, vehicle as defined by said code when the doors of such vehicle are locked, aircraft as defined by the Harbor and Navigation Code, mine, or any underground portion thereof, with intent to commit grand or petit larceny or any felony is guilty of burglary." (Penal Code, sec. 459.) By virtue of section 490a of the Penal Code the word "larceny" in section 459 must be read and interpreted as if the word "theft" had been used. (People v. Myers, 206 Cal. 480; People v. Bayne, 136 Cal. App. 341; People v. Corral, 60 Cal. App. 2d 66.)

(A "trailer coach" is a vehicle without motive power designed for human habitation and for carrying persons and property (Sec. 52 Vehicle Code). "Aircraft" includes any contrivance used or designed for flying except a parachute or other contrivance used primarily for safety (sec. 1940 Harbors and Navigation Code).

Corpus Delicti

The corpus delicti of burglary consists of (1) the entry; (2) of a building or one of the other places listed in the statute; and (3) with the specific intent, at the time of the entry, to commit grand or petit theft or any felony. Where these elements exist the crime of burglary is complete the moment the entry has been made (People v. Shaffer, 81 Cal. App. 752) and it is not necessary that the entry be followed by any other unlawful act. (People v. McGowan, 127 Cal. App. 39; People v. Rhodes, 137 Cal. App. 137; People v. Piner, 11 Cal. App. 542; People v. Hall, 94 Cal. 545.) Where the entry is made with the required burglarious intent the crime is complete even though it develops that the intent to steal cannot be carried out because there is no property which can be stolen (People v. Shaber, 32 Cal. 36) or even though, after the entry, the burglar voluntarily abandons his unlawful purpose. (People v. Novo, 12 Cal. App. 2d 525; see also People v. McFarlane, 138 Cal. 481.)

Circumstantial Proof of Intent

Burglary being one of those crimes which are usually committed in secret, the proof of the corpus delicti generally must rest on circumstantial evidence alone. Where a person is found within a building without having been invited and without permission or right the evidence establishes prima facie that the entry was unlawful and the intent to commit a theft or a felony may also be inferred from the circumstances such as his having entered the room of a stranger in the building and examining the clothing of the occupant (see People v. Swenson, 28 Cal. App. 2d 636) or resorting to violence and threats of great bodily harm when discovered or while attempting to leave. (People v. Hawkins, 129 Cal. App. 720.) Quite commonly the corpus delicti is established by proof that property was stolen from a building or dwelling in the absence of the owner (People v. Willison, 116 Cal. App. 157; People v. Russell, 120 Cal. App. 622; People v. Harris, 114 Cal. 575) or while the owner was asleep (People v. Reynolds, 130 Cal. App. 754) or from a place of business closed for the night. (People v. Reed, 68 Cal. App. 19.) Proof that defendant entered a dwelling in the nighttime and seized a girl who was sleeping on a couch and choked her and ran away when she screamed and her mother came to the doorway is sufficient to establish a burglary with intent to commit rape (People v. Nanez, 84 Cal. App. 2d 778). The burglarious intent can reasonably and justifiably inferred from an unlawful and forcible entry alone (People v. Stewart, 113 Cal. App. 2d 687).

Intent

The gist of the crime of burglary is the burglarious intent, the intent to commit either grand or petit theft or any felony after the entry has been effected. This requisite intent must exist at the time of the entry. If a person enters a building without any burglarious intent but, after the entry is complete, forms the intent to and does commit a theft or a felony, the crime of burglary has not been committed. (People v. Lowen, 109 Cal. 381; People v. Gibson, 107 Cal. App. 76.) Where there is an entry without permission or other right the commission, after the entry, of a theft or felony generally warrants the conclusion that the entry was made with the intent to commit such offense. (People v. De Soto, 33 Cal. App. 2d 478.) If no crime be committed after the entry the circumstances, such as flight when being hailed by an occupant of the building (People v. Noon, 1 Cal. App. 44), the entry of a dwelling house through a window (People v. Soto, 53 Cal. 415) or gaining admission through a locked doorway (People v. Sturman, 56 Cal. App. 2d 173; People v. Dreyer, 71 Cal. App. 2d 181) without any reasonable explanation of his entry, will warrant the conclusion that the entry was made with the intent to steal. Where the defendant entered and hid himself in the attic of a tavern about midnight and, when the police came an hour later, did not answer when called to but, when the officer shone a light in his face and ordered him to come out, complied, the evidence supported the inference that the defendant hid in the attic with intent to commit larceny after the tavern closed (People v. Terry, 152 Cal. App. 2d ......). Where the defendant removed his shoes and entered an apartment and ran when the owner approached, there was sufficient evidence of the specific intent to steal (People v. Franklin, 153 Cal. App. 2d........). Where the defendant was found in a market crouched behind some packing cases with a revolver, a rope, a mask and goggles and wearing gloves the evidence was held sufficient to sustain a conviction (People v. Kramer, 103 Cal. App. 2d 35). One common form of burglary is that in which the perpetrator enters a hotel or rooming house and is detected entering one or more of the rooms, sometimes is observed in acts such as going through the clothing or closets of the occupants, and when detected offers the explanation that he was looking for a person whom he knew but is either unable to give any description of his alleged friend or gives a false description; here the circumstances warrant the conclusion that the intent to steal existed. (See People v. Swenson, 28 Cal. App. 2d 636.) But, even though the entry be unlawful or unauthorized, if there existed no intent to commit grand or petit theft or a felony, there is no burglary even though the intent be the doing of an unlawful act. (People v. Brown, 105 Cal. 66.)

The theft of merchandise in a store during business hours is not sufficient to establish the offense of burglary but where it is shown that a short time previous the defendant had committed another similar theft in the same store and that he wore a belt specially adapted to the purposes of a shoplifter the conclusion that he entered the store with intent to steal, and that he is guilty of burglary, is justified. (People v. Corral, 60 Cal. App. 2d 66; People v. Vitos, 62 Cal. App. 2d 157.)

Where the defendant entered a dwelling and the wife of the occupant was awakened by the defendant pulling at the bedclothes who was then leaning over the foot of the bed and, upon her awakening, he started for the door and broke into a run when she screamed and the information charged that the entry was with the intent to commit the crimes of theft and rape, the court said, ''The evidence and the reasonable inferences therefrom justify the conclusion that the defendant entered the house with the intent to commit larceny and rape'' (People v. Kittrelle, 102 Cal. App. 2d 149, 156). Where a person entered a store, equipped with a large package with a trapdoor at one end so that articles could be pushed inside after which the door closed and was not noticeable, and stole merchandise and placed it in the package and left the store, a conviction of burglary was sustained since the facts supported the theory that the intent to steal existed at the time of entering the store (People v. De Nava, 119 Cal. App. 2d 82). Where a beer tavern was locked about midnight and shortly thereafter an officer observed that the lock was missing and defendant standing inside and defendant said that he had entered to urinate, the bent lock was found lying on the floor inside the building and a screwdriver, not belonging to the owner, was found stuck in the wall, the evidence was sufficient to establish the crime of burglary and that the defendant was the one who had made the forcible entry (People v. Daniels, 145 Cal. App. 2d 615). Evidence that, prior to the entry, the defendant had made plans for the disposal of the property taken proved the burglarious intent (People v. Morris, 143 Cal. App. 2d 531). Where defendants, in pursuance of a common plan and similar modus operandi, entered a food market and stole moneys by a ''short change'' trick worked upon the cashiers, convictions of burglary were sustained (People v. Stone, 155 Cal. App. 2d.......).

Where the charge and the evidence are predicated upon the theory that the entry was with intent to commit theft by larceny it is necessary that there be, at the time of the entry, the specific intent to permananently deprive the owner of his property (People v. Garrow, 130 Cal. App. 2d 75). Among the cases in which the specific intent was to commit a crime other than theft are People v. Novo, 12 Cal. App. 2d 525, rape; People v. Denningham, 82 Cal. App. 2d 117, sec. 288a Penal Code; People v. Shields, 70 Cal. App. 2d 628, sec. 288, Penal Code).

The entry of a building with intent to commit an assault with a deadly weapon is burglary (People v. Laya, 123 Cal. App. 2d 7; People v. Clifton, 148 Cal. App. 2d 276).

Where the person who makes the entry resorts to theft when discovered in the building, this will sustain the implied finding that the entry was made with the intent to commit the crime charged (People v. Crisel, 137 Cal. App. 2d 275, entry with intent to commit theft).

The Entry

The rule at common law and in some jurisdictions that the entry must be by "breaking" does not exist in California and any entry is sufficient. (People v. Ferns, 27 Cal. App. 285; People v. Barry, 94 Cal. 481.) A thief who enters a store or other place of business during business hours (People v. Brittain, 142 Cal. 8; People v. Barry, 94 Cal. 481; People v. Descheneau, 51 Cal. App. 437; People v. Corral, 60 Cal. App. 2d 66; People v. Jollett, 60 Cal. App. 2d 245; People v. Vitos, 62 Cal. App. 2d 157) or a church open to the public (People v. Head, 9 Cal. App. 2d 647) is guilty of buglary if, at the time of entering he had the intention of committing theft therein. The entry of a building with intent to commit murder or a felonious assault is burglary as soon as the entry is made (People v. Schwab, 136 Cal. App. 2d 280). Where the entry is made with the intent to commit theft, the offense is complete as soon as the entry is made even though, after the entry, the burglar abandons his purpose (People v. Stewart, 113 Cal. App. 2d 687) and the rule would be the same in the case of any other burglarious intent. In People v. Descheneau, 51 Cal. App. 437, the defendant, intending to steal property within a storage warehouse, made the entry by concealing himself in a specially constructed trunk which was delivered to and carried into the building by the warehouseman as the result of arrangements made by the defendant. It was held that the defendant was guilty of burglary and that the fact that the owner of the warehouse had learned of the scheme before the trunk was taken into the warehouse and did nothing to prevent the defendant from carrying out his scheme had no effect upon the guilt of the defendant. Another unusual burglary was one in which the defendant, who was a salesman in a store, devised a scheme in pursuance of which he procured other persons to buy merchandise from him below the regular price and appropriated to his own use the money so received and as additional inducement to such purchasers they were given other merchandise without charge. The court held that a purchaser who joined with the defendant in this scheme to obtain the property of the employer by theft entered the store with the intent to commit theft and was guilty of burglary and that the defendant was a coprincipal in such burglary. (People v. Sparks, 44 Cal. App. 2d 748.)

Where a person enters a building, or one of the places covered by the burglary statute, in pursuance of an invitation of the proprietor, if he nevertheless enters with the intent to commit a theft or any felony, he is guilty of burglarly (People v. Garrow, 130 Cal. App. 2d 75 and cases cited, also cases in preceding paragraph).

Reaching Through Window

It is not necessary to constitute an entry of a building that the entire body or any part thereof should actually enter the building. Reaching into a room through an open window or door with the arm or hand (People v. Pettinger, 94 Cal. App. 297) or even by the use of a stick with a hook at the end for the purpose of stealing or committing a felony would be burglary. (People v. Allison, 200 Cal. 404.) Where two men entered a box car with intent to steal hams therein and handed hams out to another person standing outside of the car the court said, ''If he reached up into the car, as he must have done to take the hams from the persons inside, his reaching in was an entry, coupled with the intent to abstract the hams, sufficient to constitute the crime of burglary. Or even if it be argued that the evidence does not prove the actual introduction of his arm into the car, nevertheless, it is clear that whenever he took a ham from his confederate inside, his arm was extended by the length of the ham to its contact with the hand of the other within the car and, under the authorities . . . this too would be deemed an entry coupled with the specific intent to constitute the crime of burglary.'' (People v. Allison, 200 Cal. 404.)

The Place Entered

A house or building within the meaning of the burglary statute must be a structure with walls on all sides and covered by a roof. (People v. Stickman, 34 Cal. 242; People v. Coffee, 52 Cal. App. 118.) The building need not be one intended as a habitation for human beings; a chicken house (Brooks v. Sessagissimo, 139 Cal. App. 679), even if it be on skids so it may be moved from place to place (People v. Stickman, 34 Cal. 242), is included in the term ''building.'' A popcorn stand on wheels located on a city lot, its lighting equipment connected with the city power lines, is a building. (People v. Burley, 26 Cal. App. 2d 213.) Where a shoe store was conducted in the basement of a building, showcases along the walls and sides of the stairway which was under the roof were held to be part of the store and an entry of the showcases followed by the theft of shoes therein was held to be the burglary of a building (People v. Franco, 79 Cal. App. 682) and a showcase, containing merchandise and cemented to the floor of a store entrance and within the property line and sheltered by the roof and sidewalls of the building was held to be a place the entry of which could be burglary. (People v. Jackson, 131 Cal. App. 605.) A telephone booth fastened to a building, on the outside of the building, and having a roof, walls on three sides and a glass door on the fourth side, is a building which can be the subject of burglary (People v. Miller, 95 Cal. App. 2d 631). A powder magazine dug in the side of a hill, the rear, sidewalls and roof being formed by the natural earth and rock, held in place by planks, and the front closed by a solid door has been held to be a building (People v. Buyle, 22 Cal. App. 2d 143), but a bin having three sides with the top covered by a floor of the building but open on the fourth side was held not to be a structure which could be the subject of a burglary. A roofed garage having walls on three sides, the fourth side being a door, is a building within the law of burglary even though at the time of the entry the door was open (People v. Picaroni, 131 Cal. App. 2d 612). (People v. Gibbons, 206 Cal. 112.) While a railroad caboose may be the subject of a burglary it is not a building. (People v. Jones, 78 Cal. App. 683.)

Burglary of a Mine

The burglary of a mine is rather a novel offense, for the entry of that portion of a mine above ground including the equipment used in the operation of the mining plant is an entry within the law of burglary and, where some men stole gasoline from a storage tank, located above ground and forming part of the mine equipment, they were held guilty of burglary (People v. Silver, 16 Cal. 2d 714) although, but for the tank being part of the mine, there would have been no burglary.

Burglary of Vehicle

Where the place entered is a vehicle, section 459 adds an additional element to the corpus delicti, viz. that the doors of such vehicle must have been locked. Thus where there was no evidence that the doors of the vehicle had been locked it was held that the evidence was insufficient to sustain a conviction and that the mere fact that the glass in the door had been broken was not sufficient to sustain the inference that the doors had been locked (People v. Burns, 114 Cal. App. 2d 566).

Where the doors and trunk compartment of an automobile were locked and the windows closed, the entry of the trunk compartment with intent to steal property therein constitutes a burglary within the statute, the court also holding that the hinged top of the trunk compartment is a "door" within the term "door" used in the statute (People v. Toomes, 148 Cal. App. 2d 465).

Possession of Stolen Property.

For the effect and significance of possession by the defendant of property stolen in the burglary see Possession of Stolen Property under THEFT.

Burglary—Degrees

"1. Every burglary of an inhabited dwelling house, trailer coach as defined by the Vehicle Code, or building, committed in the night time, and every burglary whether in the day time or in the night time, committed by a person armed with a deadly weapon, or who while in the commission of such burglarly arms himself with a deadly weapon, or who while in the commission of such burglary assaults any person, is burglary of the first degree.

"2. All other kinds of burglary are of the second degree.

"3. This section shall not be construed to supersede or affect section four hundred sixty-four of the Penal Code." (Penal Code, sec. 460.) (Note:—Section 464 relates solely to the separate crime of Burglary with Explosives.)

"The phrase 'night-time,' as used in this chapter, means the period between sunset and sunrise." (Penal Code, sec. 463.)

The word "inhabited" in section 460 applies to both "dwelling house" and "building." (People v. Clinton, 70 Cal. App. 262; People v. Black, 73 Cal. App. 13.) Where a building is customarily used as a dwelling house it is an inhabited building and the temporary absence of its occupants, as on a vacation, does not change the status of the building. The burglary of such a dwelling in the night-time is first degree burglary even though the building is temporarily unoccupied. (People v. Allard, 99 Cal. App. 591; People v. Hann, 104 Cal. App. 492; People v. Stewart, 113 Cal. App. 2d 687.) The fact that a part of a building is inhabited does not impress that character on the rest of the building; hence a store in a building, the upper floor of which is used as a hotel, is not an inhabited building. (People v. Warwick, 135 Cal. App. 476.)

Deadly Weapon

The term "deadly weapon" includes not only those instrumentalities which by their nature and the purpose for which they were manufactured are naturally deadly weapons, such as firearms, dirks and blackjacks, but also those instrumentalities with which a burglar arms himself with the intention of using the same as a weapon of offense or defense should the occasion arise and which are capable of being used as weapons to inflict great bodily harm. (See discussion under Robbery, subhead **Armed with Dangerous or Deadly Weapon.**)

The mere fact that a burglar steals a deadly weapon as a part of his loot is not sufficient to make the burglary one of the first degree as the mere act of stealing is not the same as arming one's self. (People v. Black, 73 Cal. App. 13.) For a burglar to arm himself while in the commission of the burglary he must not only take into his possession a deadly weapon but he must also do so with the intention of using the same as a weapon of offense or defense if the occasion of using a weapon should arise. To be armed with a deadly weapon under section 460 of the Penal Code it is sufficient that the perpetrator had it in his possession available for immediate use (People v. Moore, 143 Cal. App. 2d 333), defendants carried the pistol with them into a burglarized store in a suitcase which they there opened).

Penalty

"Burglary is punishable as follows:

1. Burglary in the first degree: by imprisonment in the state prison for not less than five years.

2. Burglary in the second degree: by imprisonment in the county jail not exceeding one year or in the state prison for not less than one year or more than fifteen years." (Penal Code, sec. 461.)

Burglary With Explosives

"Any person who, with intent to commit crime, enters, either by day or by night, any building, whether inhabited or not, and opens or attempts to open any vault, safe or other secure place by use of acetylene torch or electric arc or nitroglycerine, dynamite, gunpowder, or any other explosive, is guilty of burglary with explosives.

"Any person duly convicted of burglary with explosives shall be deemed to be guilty of a felony and shall be punished by imprisonment in the state prison for a term of not less than ten years nor more than forty years." (Penal Code, sec. 464.)

It is sufficient specific intent to constitute this crime if it be the intent of the perpetrator to open a safe and steal its contents. (In re Wilson, 196 Cal. 515.) Evidence showing that defendants entered a safe by the use of an oxy-acetylene torch was held sufficient to bring a burglary within section 464. (People v. Wilson, 46 Cal. App. 2d 218.)

RECEIVING STOLEN PROPERTY

Receiving or Concealing Stolen or Extorted Property

·1. Every person who buys or receives any property which has been stolen or which has been obtained in any manner constituting theft or extortion, knowing the same to be so stolen or obtained, or who conceals, withholds or aids in concealing or withholding any such property from the owner is punishable by imprisonment in a state prison for not more than 10 years or in a county jail for not more than one year." (Penal Code, sec. 496).

"Any person who buys or receives any property which has been stolen or which has been obtained in any manner constituting theft or extortion, from a person under the age of 18 years shall be presumed to have bought or received such property knowing it to have been so stolen or obtained, unless such property is sold by such minor at a fixed place of business carried on by the minor or his employer. This presumption may, however, be rebutted by proof." (Penal Code, sec. 496.) (Note: Other subdivisions of this section are hereinafter discussed under the subhead Presumptions and Burden of Proof.)

Corpus Delicti

The corpus delicti of receiving stolen property under section 496 consists of:

1. The property must have been obtained by theft or extortion;

2. The defendant must have bought, received, concealed or withheld such property from the owner;

3. The defendant must have known at the time he committed one of the acts specified in subdivision 2 (above) that the property had been obtained by theft or extortion. (People

v. Rossi, 15 Cal. App. 2d 180; People v. Gould, 111 Cal. App. 2d 1; People v. Scaggs, 153 Cal. App. 2d ...... A.C.A. 368).

Under this section it is not necessary that the acts constituting the offense should be done with any specific intent.

Since larceny is included in the crime of robbery, the receiving of property obtained by robbery is the same as receiving property by means of theft. (People v. Warren, 36 Cal. App. 2d 278.)

Value of Property

In the crime of receiving stolen property the value of the property involved is immaterial and need not be proved or set forth in the indictment or information. (People v. Rice, 73 Cal. 221; People v. Fitzpatrick, 80 Cal. 538.)

Property from Several Takings

Since it is the act of receiving or buying which is the gist of this offense the receiving or buying at the same time of the products of two or more thefts constitutes but one crime of receiving stolen property. (People v. Willard, 92 Cal. 482; People v. Smith, 26 Cal. 2d 854.)

Identity of Thief

While it is necessary to show that the property was the product of theft or extortion it is neither necessary to plead nor to prove the identity of the person who so obtained the property. (People v. Avila, 43 Cal. 196; People v. Ribolsi, 89 Cal. 496; People v. Grable, 67 Cal. App. 183.)

Ownership

Proof of the ownership involved in a prosecution for this offense is material only in so far as it is necessary to establish the identity of the property and that it was obtained by theft or extortion. (People v. Mitchell, 109 Cal. App. 116.)

Receiving

In addition to evidence of delivery of the property to the accused proof of constructive delivery of the property to the accused is sufficient to prove that he received the property. (People v. Silvas, 34 Cal. App. 638.) Proof that the property in question was concealed on the defendant's premises by others with his knowledge or consent is sufficient proof of the element of receiving. (People v. Rossi, 15 Cal. App. 2d

180.) Mere proof, however, that the property was found on his premises, without proof that he had knowledge that it was there would not be sufficient. (People v. Jolley, 35 Cal. App. 2d 159.)

Concealing

Where property comes into the possession of a person and he then learns that such property has been stolen and conceals or withholds it, section 496 has ben violated (People v. Scott, 108 Cal. App. 2d 231; People v. Scaggs, 153 Cal. App. 2d ...... A.C.A. 368).

Knowledge

One of the essential elements of the crime of receiving stolen property is knowledge on the part of the accused that the property has been unlawfully obtained by either some form of theft or by extortion. (People v. Juehling, 10 Cal. App. 2d 527; People v. Rossi, 15 Cal. App. 2d 180.) While this is readily established where there is available an eye witness to the occasion when the accused received the property, knowledge may also be shown circumstantially as by proof that the property was purchased at a price far below its value, buying from a known criminal or irresponsible person or from a person who would not be likely to have property of that character in his lawful possession either as to its kind or in the quantity offered, buying under circumstances which would indicate to the ordinary individual that the property was unlawfully obtained, hiding and concealing the property or making false or evasive statements concerning the possession of the property, failing to keep a record required by law or other circumstances tending to prove that the receiver must have known that the property was unlawfully obtained. (People v. Clausen, 120 Cal. 381; People v. Mercado, 59 Cal. App. 69; People v. Levison, 16 Cal. 98; People v. Silvas, 34 Cal. App. 638; People v. Carrow, 207 Cal. 366; People v. DeVaughn, 136 Cal. App. 746; People v. Moore, 137 Cal. App. 130; People v. Hansen, 137 Cal. App. 725; People v. Juehling, 10 Cal. App. 2d 527; People v. Rossi, 15 Cal. App. 2d 180; People v. Bausell, 18 Cal. App. 2d 15; People v. Lima, 25 Cal. 2d 573.) As said in People v. Clausen, supra, "That which a man in defendant's position ought to have suspected he must be regarded as having suspected." Evidence of the known questionable character of the person from whom the stolen goods were obtained is admissible for such bearing as it may have upon the issue of the defendant's knowledge that they were stolen (People v. Bruback, 152 Cal. App. 2d .... A.C.A. 427).

Statements made to the police giving different versions of how he came into possession of the stolen property, the first of which was absolutely false, will justify the inference that the property was received with knowledge that it was stolen (People v. Lopez, 126 Cal. App. 2d 274). Evidence that the property was stolen by the sons of the defendant, who returned to defendant's residence and awakened the defendant who came out of the house and looked at the property a part of which was put into defendant's cellar in his presence, and a week later defendant gave an accomplice of his sons an automobile and sold part of the property, is sufficient to show knowledge on the part of the defendant that the property was stolen (People v. Morrow, 127 Cal. App. 293). The purchase of the stolen machines for an amount far less than their value and paying the seller for signing a paper that he had never sold anything to the defendant would justify the jury in finding that the defendant knew that the machines were stolen (People v. Bycel, 133 Cal. App. 2d 596). The sale by defendant of stolen diamonds for half their value, alteration of a stolen necklace by removing some of the diamonds and possession of cutting pliers with gold, silver and platinum traces, indicating that they had been used on the stolen jewelry and possession of loose diamonds held sufficient to show the element of knowledge (People v. Malouf, 135 Cal. App. 2d 697). Possession of stolen property accompanied by no explanation of the possession or an unsatisfactory explanation of the possession will justify an inference that the goods were received with knowledge that they had been stolen (People v. Lopez, 126 Cal. App. 2d 274, 278; People v. Malouf, 135 Cal. App. 2d 697). Possession of stolen property shortly after it was stolen, accompanied by no explanation or an unsatisfactory explanation or false and evasive answers or by suspicious circumstances, justify the inference that the goods were received with knowledge that they were stolen (People v. Reynolds, 149 Cal. App. 2d 290).

"Although guilty knowledge of the fact that the property was stolen is an essential fact to be proved in a prosecution for receiving stolen property, such knowledge need not be that actual and positive knowledge which is acquired from personal observation of the fact. It is not necessary that the defendant be told directly that the property was stolen. Knowledge may be circumstantial and deductive.'' (People v. Boinus, 153 Cal. App. 2d ......).

Presumptions and Burden of Proof

"2. Every person whose principal business is dealing in or collecting used or second hand merchandise or personal property, and every agent, employee or representative of such person, who buys or receives any property which has been stolen or obtained in any manner constituting theft or extortion, under such circumstances as should cause such person, agent, employee or representative to make reasonable inquiry to ascertain that the person from whom such property was bought or received had the legal right to so sell or deliver it, without making such reasonable inquiry, shall be presumed to have bought or received such property knowing it to have been so stolen or obtained. This presumption may, however, be rebutted by proof.

"3. When in a prosecution under this section it shall appear from the evidence that the defendant's principal business was as set forth in the preceding paragraph, that the defendant bought, received or otherwise obtained, or concealed, withheld or aided in concealing or withholding from the owner, any property which had been stolen or obtained in any manner constituting theft or extortion, and that the defendant bought, received, obtained, concealed or withheld such property under such circumstances as should have caused him to make reasonable inquiry to ascertain that the person from whom he bought, received or obtained such property had the legal right to sell or deliver it to him, then the burden shall be upon the defendant to show that before so buying, receiving or otherwise obtaining such property, he made such reasonable inquiry to ascertain that the person so selling or delivering the same to him had the legal right to so sell or deliver it.'' (Penal Code, sec. 496.)

Mere inquiry by the defendant of the seller does not meet the requirements of sudivisions of sections 2 and 3 of section 496 as to inquiry whether the seller has the legal right to sell the property in question. (People v. Seerman, 43 Cal. App. 2d 506.) While the nature of the inquiry necessary depends upon the facts and circumstances of each case a "reasonable inquiry" should go at least to the extent of satisfying any doubt or suspicion which would be aroused in the mind of the ordinary honest and prudent individual under the same circumstances.

Receiving From a Minor

"Any person who buys or receives any property which has been stolen or which has been obtained in any manner constituting theft or extortion, from any person under the age of 18 years, shall be presumed to have bought or received such property knowing it to have been so stolen or obtained, unless such property is sold by such minor at a fixed place of business carried on by the minor or his employer. This presumption may, however, be rebutted by proof." (Penal Code, sec. 496.) (Note: It is very doubtful whether this provision is constitutional. The mere purchase or receiving of property from a minor, while a circumstance which can be considered, seems wholly insufficient to warrant the presumption that the receiver knew that the property was stolen or unlawfully obtained.) It has, however, been held that the quoted portion of the statute is applicable (People v. Lopez, 126 Cal. App. 2d 274) but this case does not decide the question of constitutionality).

Unlawful Taking is Separate from Receiving

The offense of receiving stolen property is separate and distinct from the unlawful taking; it is subsequent to the taking and by a person other than the taker. (People v. Hawkins, 34 Cal. 181.) Thus the person who directly commits a theft and takes the property into his possession cannot receive from himself the fruits of his crime (People v. Jacobs, 73 Cal. App. 344) and is not an accomplice of one who is prosecuted for receiving from him the stolen property. (See: ACCOMPLICE.) However one who was a principal or co-conspirator in the commission of theft or extortion but who did not personally take the property from the victim of the crime is guilty of receiving stolen property if he receives the property from one of his co-principals. (People v. Taylor, 4 Cal. App. 2d 214; People v. Warren, 36 Cal. App. 2d 278; People v. Stoddard, 48 Cal. App. 2d 86; People v. Lima, 25 Cal. 2d 573) but is not guilty of receiving stolen property unless he actually receives it (People v. Ferguson, 152 Cal. App. 2d.........).

CHAPTER XXV.

FORGERY

"Every person who, with intent to defraud, signs the name of another person, or of a fictitious person, knowing that he has no authority so to do, to, or falsely makes, alters, forges, or counterfeits, any charter, letters-patent, deed, lease, indenture, writing obligatory, will, testament, codicil, bond, covenant, bank bill or note, postnote, check, draft, bill of exchange, contract, promissory note, due-bill for the payment of money or property, receipt for money or property, passage ticket, power of attorney, or any certificate of any share, right, or interest in the stock of any corporation or association, or any controller's warrant for the payment of money at the treasury, county order or warrant, or request for the payment of money, or the delivery of goods or chattels of any kind, or for the delivery of any instrument of writing, or acquittance, release, or receipt for money or goods, or any acqittance, release or discharge of any debt, account, suit, action, demand or other thing, real or personal, or any transfer or assurance of money, certificate of shares of stock, goods, chattels, or other property whatever, or any letter of attorney, or other power to receive money, or to receive or transfer certificates of shares of stock or annuities, or to let, lease, dispose of, alien, or convey any goods, chattels, lands, or tenements, or other estate, real or personal, or any acceptance or indorsement of any bill of exchange, promissory note, draft, order, or any assignment of any bond, writing obligatory, promissory note, or other contract for money or other property; or counterfeits or forges the seal or handwriting of another; or utters, publishes, passes, or attempts to pass, as true and genuine, any of the above-named ₁alse, altered, forged, or counterfeited matters, as above specified and described, knowing the same to be false, altered, forged, or counterfeited, with intent to prejudice, damage, or defraud any person; or who, with intent to defraud, alters, corrupts, or falsifies any record of any will, codicil, conveyance, or other instrument, the record of which is by law evidence, or any record of any judgment of a court or the return of any officer to any process of any court, is guilty of forgery." (Penal Code, sec. 470.)

Penalty

"Forgery is punishable by imprisonment in the state prison for not less than one year nor more than fourteen years, or by

imprisonment in the county jail for not more than one year.''
(Penal Code, sec. 473.)

This section makes both the act of forgery and the uttering
of a forgery (in some jurisdictions two separate offenses) but
one offense and it is the common practice to charge both the
making and the uttering of the forgery in one count and the
jury may convict upon proof of either violation of the statute.
(People v. Whitaker, 127 Cal. App. 452; People v. Lucas, 67
Cal. App. 452; People v. Frank, 28 Cal. 507; People v. Mitchell,
92 Cal. 590.)

Corpus Delicti—Proof by Circumstantial Evidence

The corpus delicti may be established by circumstantial
evidence and inferences that may be drawn therefrom (People
v. Sheeley, 151 Cal. App. 2d ......).

Intent to Defraud

To constitute forgery it is necessary that the act be committed with the intent to defraud, but it is not necessary that
any person be actually defrauded or suffer any loss. (People
v. Baender, 68 Cal. App. 49; People v. Webber, 44 Cal. App.
120.) Where the act involved is the making of a forgery the
crime is complete when the act of forging is committed with
the intent to defraud and it is not necessary that the forgery
be used. Thus where a check is forged it is not essential to
a completed crime of forgery that the check be presented for
payment and the fact that the check was not presented to the
bank or otherwise uttered or passed is no defense. (People v.
West, 34 Cal. App. 2d 55; People v. Breuer, 15 Cal. App. 2d
745; In re Harper, 17 Cal. App. 2d 446; People v. Escalera, 36
Cal. App. 212.) It is sufficient if it appear that, if the evident intent of the accused had been carried out, damage or
detriment would or might have followed. (People v. Kuhn,
33 Cal. App. 319; People v. Webber, 44 Cal. App. 120; People
v. Baender, 68 Cal. App. 49; People v. Turner, 113 Cal. 278;
People v. Horowitz, 70 Cal. App. 2d 675.) The fact that no
person was actually injured or defrauded is no defense (People
v. Weitz, 42 Cal. 2d 338). The fact that money earned by a wife
during her marriage is community property would not give
her husband the right to sign his wife's name to checks on
her personal individual bank account in which such earnings
were deposited but, if he does so, he would not be guilty of
forgery unless he acted with intent to defraud and such
intent cannot be inferred from the mere fact that he had so

signed her name (People v. Crowder, 126 Cal. App. 2d 578; People v. Valdez, 155 Cal. App. 2d ......). When a person signs the name of another as endorser of a check without authority, that is evidence of an intent to defraud (People v. Epperson, 134 Cal. App. 2d 413).

What May Be the Subject of Forgery

The subject of forgery need not be written in the sense of being written by hand with a pen or pencil but may be an instrument or document or other paper which is typewritten or printed. The question as to whether a particular paper, document or instrument may be the subject of forgery is generally answered by the statute itself which lists many of the subjects of forgery but this list is not exclusive and the test as to whether a particular paper, document or instrument is the subject of forgery is whether it is of apparent legal efficacy and which, if genuine, would be capable of affecting the personal or property rights of some other person. (People v. Somsky, 46 Cal. App. 377; People v. Di Ryana, 8 Cal. App. 333.) "The test is whether upon its face it will have the effect of defrauding one who acts upon it as genuine." (People v. McKenna, 11 Cal. 2d 327; People v. Morgan, 140 Cal. App. 2d 796). Even though the instrument on its face does not create a liability but is one capable of being used to defraud, it may be the subject of forgery. (People v. McGlade, 139 Cal. 66).

Where it appears from the face of the instrument that it cannot possibly be said to be of apparent legal efficacy it cannot be the subject of forgery. Thus, if the document is one obviously void on its face it would not be the subject of forgery. If, however, the instrument is merely one which in its present state is ineffective but may be made so, as, for example, an instrument which required a revenue stamp to make it valid, it may be the subject of forgery. The mere fact that the instrument is against public policy, such as an assignment of the unearned salary of a public school teacher (People v. Munroe, 100 Cal. 664) does not prevent its being a forgery for the test is not whether the instrument in question, if genuine, would create a legal liability or have any legal effect (People v. Cline, 79 Cal. App. 2d 11) but whether or not it is possible to defraud by reason of the forgery thereof (People v. Brown, 101 Cal. App. 2d 740) and even a document against public policy may upon its face present an appearance that if genuine might injure another and such a

document satisfies the test which the courts have laid down.
(People v. Munroe, 100 Cal. 664; People v. Collins, 9 Cal. App.
622; People v. Gayle, 202 Cal. 159, a contract for the sale of
land in an unrecorded tract and therefore unenforceable; see
also People v. Remsberg, 92 Cal. App. 615; People v. Thorn,
138 Cal. App. 714; People v. McKenna, 11 Cal. 2d 327, a deed
which conveyed no title.)

Examples of Forgery

Among the writings which have been held the subjects
of forgery are:—a letter which might pass as a binding declaration against interest (People v. McKenna, 11 Cal. 2d
327); a certificate of recordation of a deed (People v. Turner,
113 Cal. 278); the seal and signature of a notary to the acknowledgment of a deed (People v. Webber, 44 Cal. App.
120); an affidavit of birth (In re Parker, 57 Cal. App. 2d 388;
People v. Weiskopf, 60 Cal. App. 2d 214); proof of loss under
an insurance policy (People v. Di Ryana, 8 Cal. App. 333); certification of a check (People v. Somsky, 46 Cal. App. 377);
a clearing house certificate (People v. Collins, 9 Cal. App.
622); a contract which had been signed in blank forged by
filling it out to represent a sale when there had been no sale
(People v. Remsberg, 92 Cal. App. 615); erasing the body of
a letter and writing in its place a contract of employment
(People v. Staigers, 92 Cal. App. 628); altering escrow instructions (People v. Jones, 100 Cal. 550); changing the name
of the grantee in a deed (People v. Hall, 55 Cal. App. 2d
343); a prescription for narcotics (People v. Brown, 113 Cal.
App. 492); a will (People v. Davidian, 20 Cal. App. 2d 720);
an assignment of real or personal property (People v. Mc-
Kenna, 11 Cal. 2d 327); certified copy of decree of divorce
(Ex parte Finley, 66 Cal. 262); an order of the trustees of
a school district upon the county superintendent of schools
for a requisition upon the county auditor for a county warrant (People v. Bibby, 91 Cal. 470); and an order for the
delivery of five gallons of beer (People v. James, 110 Cal.
155) writing a will above the signature of the alleged testator
which signature had been written upon a piece of blank paper.
(People v. Horowitz, 70 Cal. App. 2d 675.) Where the defendant, without the consent or knowledge of the maker, takes
a check signed by the latter in blank, fills it out and then
cashes it, he is guilty of forgery (People v. Bartages, 126 Cal.
App. 2d 763).

Forgery by Alteration

It is not necessary to constitute the crime of forgery that the entire instrument be forged since it is likewise forgery to alter an instrument by adding, erasing or changing a part thereof. Such alteration must, however, be of a material part of the instrument resulting in a change in its apparent legal effect. (People v. Brotherton, 47 Cal. 388; Union Tool Co. v. Farmers and Merchants Bank, 192 Cal. 40; People v. Jones, 100 Cal. App. 550). The alteration of a document without authority with the intent to defraud may constitute a forgery and such alteration may consist of the insertion of matter in the document in question, without the consent of the signor, after it had been signed and which inserted matter materially changed the rights or obligations of the signor (People v. McKenna, 11 Cal. 2d 327; People v. Jones, 100 Cal. App. 550; People v. Nesseth, 127 Cal. App. 2d 712).

Signature Obtained by Fraud

The procuring of a genuine signature by fraudulent representations constitutes forgery (People v. Nesseth, 127 Cal. App. 2d 712, purchase order contained larger amount due than had been agreed upon).

Forgery of Endorsement

Forgery may also be committed by falsely signing the name of the payee, or other person whose signature is necessary to its negotiability, upon a check, bill of exchange or other negotiable instrument. In this instance the forgery is that of an endorsement and must be both pleaded and prosecuted as such and not as the forgery of the instrument, for the endorsement is not a part of the instrument. (People v. Cole, 130 Cal. 13; People v. Thornburgh, 4 Cal. App. 38.) To constitute the forgery of an endorsement the name forged must be the name of the payee or other person whose signature is essential to negotiability and the writing of another name would not constitute a forgery of endorsement. (In re Valencia, 84 Cal. App. 26.)

Authority To Sign

Since there would not be a forgery if the writing of a signature is authorized it is essential upon a trial for forgery that there be proof that the defendant acted without authority (People v. Whiteman, 114 Cal. 338; People v. Lundin, 117

Cal. 124; People v. McGlade, 139 Cal. 66; People v. Laird, 118 Cal. 291; People v. Maoli, 135 Cal. App. 205) and knowing that he had no authority to do so. Lack of authority may be shown either by the testimony of the person whose name has been forged or by circumstantial evidence that authority was not or could not have been given (People v. Cullen, 99 Cal. App. 2d 468), but the fact that by agreement between the depositor and the bank only a certain person or persons may sign checks against the account does not establish lack of authority, so far as forgery is concerned, to draw checks against the account. (People v. Maoli, 135 Cal. App. 205.) The absence of authority of the defendant to sign the name of another to a check was in one instance established by proof that, prior to the forgery, the defendant had murdered the person whose name he later forged. (People v. Sanders, 114 Cal. 216.) Where the forgery is that of an actual person proof of lack of authority for defendant to sign such name is necessary to prove the falsity of the instrument; if the person whose name is signed is fictitious, proof of this fact is likewise proof of the falsity of the instrument (People v. Porter, 136 Cal. App. 2d 461).

The fact that a person has authority to sign the name of another to checks or other instruments does not give him any right to act in excess of that authority. An agent who has the authority to sign the name of his principal, in the course of his employment, would be guilty of forgery if, with intent to defraud, he signed a check which was not within the authority given him. (See People v. Rittenhouse, 56 Cal. App. 541.) Proof that the defendant wrote the forgery charged is however insufficient, even though the handwriting be simulated or disguised, unless there is in addition proof of lack of authority.

Signature by Purported Agent

Since the making or altering of the instrument must be false to constitute a forgery, it is not a forgery for a person to sign his own name, or execute an instrument, as the agent of another, although in fact he was not the agent of such person and had no authority to sign the instrument. To constitute the forgery of a signature, it must be made as the signature of a person other than the accused and must purport to be what it is not. (People v. Bendit, 111 Cal. 274; People v. Cole, 130 Cal. 13.)

Identity of Defendant's Name With Name Forged

While it is not forgery if a person sign his own name to an instrument thus making the instrument his own, even though he acted with intent to defraud, it would be forgery, all the other elements of the offense being present, if we were to write as the forgery a name identical with his own (People v. Rushing, 130 Cal. 449) or a name which he has assumed for the purpose of perpetrating the fraud in which the forgery is involved. It is forgery if the name signed is intended to be the name of another or that of a fictitious person. Where it was intended to create a false power of attorney of one E. Geddes and the defendant did so by having the power of attorney signed by a person whose real name was E. Geddes but who was not the one whose power of attorney the instrument purported to be, the crime of forgery was committed as fully as though defendant himself had done the writing. (People v. Rushing, 130 Cal. 449.)

Forgery of Fictitious Name

Prior to the amendment of section 470, the signing of the name of a fictitious person could not be forgery (People v. Elliott, 90 Cal. 586) but the section now expressly declares it to be forgery whether the name signed be the "name of another person, or of a fictitious person." (See People v. Jones, 12 Cal. App. 129; People v. Lucas, 67 Cal. App. 452; People v. Gayle, 202 Cal. 159; People v. Cohen, 113 Cal. App. 260; People v. Carmona, 80 Cal. App. 159.)

It is not necessary to allege nor to prove and it is immaterial whether the signature forged is that of a real or fictitious person if the elements of the offense of forgery are otherwise established. (People v. McDonald, 16 Cal. App. 2d 687; People v. Bernard, 21 Cal. App. 56; People v. Whittaker, 68 Cal. App. 7; People v. Williamson, 134 Cal. App. 775; People v. Gayle, 202 Cal. 159.)

Where a person forges a check using the name of a fictitious person as both maker and payee it is not a defense that he had assumed and used the same fictitious name in opening an account at the bank. (People v. Ryan, 74 Cal. App. 125). In such a case the intent to defraud distinguishes it as not within the rule that a person may, without court proceeding, change his name by assuming another if it involves no unlawful intent.

The fact that the name forged is that of a fictitious person also establishes that the signing of such name was without authority. Evidence that there was no account in the bank on which the check was drawn in the name appearing as the drawer of a check is prima facie evidence that the name is fictitious. (People v. Eppinger, 105 Cal. 36; People v. Thal, 61 Cal. App. 48; People v. Roche, 74 Cal. App. 556; People v. Carmona, 80 Cal. App. 159; People v. Reed, 84 Cal. App. 685; People v. Cohen, 113 Cal. App. 260; People v. Menne, 4 Cal. App. 2d 91; In re Harper, 17 Cal. App. 2d 446; People v. Schneider, 36 Cal. App. 2d 292; People v. Slattery, 59 Cal. App. 2d 451). Evidence that the check had been uttered and passed as genuine when there was no account in the drawee bank in the name of the drawer and no such name appeared in the register of voters or the local directory has been held prima facie proof of the corpus delicti of forgery (People v. Felt, 98 Cal. App. 2d 137).

Unusual Cases

Where a husband and wife have a joint checking account at the bank it is forgery for a third person to draw a check on the account, with intent to defraud, forging the wife's name and then the husband's name as though the latter had signed the wife's name and it is no defense that this had been authorized by the husband since the husband himself could not legally sign his wife's name to such a check and hence could not authorize another person to do so. (People v. Russell, 90 Cal. App. 266.) The fact that the defendant had misspelled the name of the person which he intended to forge is no defense. (People v. Alden, 113 Cal. 264.) A forgery of a check is complete, other elements of the crime being present, even though the name of the payee is left blank. (People v. Gorham, 9 Cal. App. 341.) One who has committed a forgery is not relieved of criminal responsibility by the fact that he intended ultimately to make good any loss suffered by reason of the forgery (People v. Morris, 33 Cal. App. 2d 677) or, if he has forged the check of his employer, by charging himself on the books of the employer with the amount of the check. (People v. Rittenhouse, 56 Cal. App. 541.) While a partner is not guilty of embezzlement or theft if he wrongfully appropriates partnership funds to his own use still, if the partnership funds in a bank are subject to withdrawal only upon the signatures of both parties, a partner who, without authority and with intent to defraud, draws a check on the account signing his own name and that of his partner, is guilty of forgery. (People v. Van Skander, 20 Cal. App. 2d 284.)

Uttering a Forged Instrument

Section 470 also punishes, under the title of Forgery, the uttering, publishing, passing or attempt to pass a forged instrument as genuine. To constitute this form of forgery, the instrument must be uttered, published, passed or attempted to be passed as true and genuine with intent to defraud and with knowledge that the instrument is a forgery. (People v. Smith, 103 Cal. 563.)

To "utter" or "publish" a forged instrument is to declare or assert, directly or indirectly by words or actions, or both, that the instrument is genuine. To utter a forged instrument there must be an attempt to make use of it with intent to defraud. Actual passing of the instrument is not essential; offering to pass the same would constitute an uttering. Thus, presenting a check to a teller at a bank for payment would constitute an uttering. (People v. Harrold, 84 Cal. 567; People v. Rodway, 77 Cal. App. 738.)

The gist of uttering a forged instrument is that to constitute this form of forgery a person must utter, publish, pass or attempt to pass, as true and genuine, an altered, forged or counterfeited matter, knowing that it was so false, altered, forged or counterfeited, with the specific intent to defraud. As examples of uttering may be cited the attempt to cash a forged check at a bank (People v. Rodway, 77 Cal. App. 738, 783) and the filing of a forged lease for record. (People v. Driggs, 14 Cal. App. 507.)

Where upon a first attempt to pass the forged check the defendant learned that there was no such account in the drawee bank and thereafter defendant and his companion went to another place where the companion, at defendant's suggestion cashed the forged check and defendant accepted part of the proceeds a conviction of forgery was sustained (People v. Felt, 98 Cal. App. 2d 137).

To Constitute an Uttering

To constitute an uttering there must be at least an attempt to pass or put the forged instrument into circulation. If a principal delivers to his agent a forged instrument with the intent and directions that the agent shall utter and put it into circulation, the crime of uttering or attempting to pass the instrument is not complete until the agent has committed an overt act amounting to such an attempt; until such overt act the forgery is still within the control of the principal and if the agent were to destroy the instrument without doing anything else with it no crime of forgery by uttering is committed. (See People v. Compton, 123 Cal. 403; People v. Davis, 124 Cal. 42.) A person may be guilty of uttering a forgery by passing it with intent to defraud even though there was no intent to defraud at the time the writing was fabricated. (Ex parte Finley, 66 Cal. 262.)

The uttering or passing at the same time and to the same person of two or more forged instruments is but one act and constitutes but one offense (People v. Gayle, 202 Cal. 159) but the making and forging of a number of forged instruments constitutes as many crimes of forgery as there are forged instruments, each forged instrument being the product of a separate crime. (People v. Gayle, 202 Cal. 159; People v. Cline, 79 Cal. App. 2d 11).

Special Statutes Allied to Forgery
Possessing or Receiving Forged Bill or Note

"Every person who has in his possession, or receives from another person, any forged promissory note or bank bill or bills, for the payment of money or property, with the intention to pass the same, or to permit, cause, or procure the same to be uttered or passed, with the intention to defraud any person, knowing the same to be forged or counterfeited, or has or keeps in his possession any blank or unfinished note or bank bill made in the form or similitude of any promissory note or bill for payment of money or property, made to be issued by any incorporated bank or banking company, with intention to fill up and complete such blank and unfinished note or bill, or to permit, or cause, or procure the same to be filled up and completed in order to utter or pass the same, or to permit or cause, or procure the same to be uttered or passed, to defraud any person, is punishable by imprisonment in the state prison for not less than one nor more than fourteen years." (Penal Code, sec. 475.)

Documents Relating to Vehicles

Section 239 of the Vehicle Code makes a special provision for the forging or uttering of a forgery certificate of ownership, registration cards and license with the same penalties as other forgeries.

Forging Records

"Every person who, with intent to defraud another, makes, forges or alters any entry in any book of records, or any instrument purporting to be any record or return specified in the preceding section (sec. 470) is guilty of forgery." (Penal Code, sec. 471.)

Public Records—Altering, Falsifying, Destroying, Stealing

Provisions specially covering public records provide:—

"Every officer having the custody of any record, map or book, or of any paper or proceeding of any court, filed or deposited in any public office, or placed in his hands for any purpose, who is guilty of stealing, wilfully destroying, mutilating, defacing, altering or falsifying, removing or secreting the whole or any part of such record, map, book, paper or proceeding, or who permits any other person so to do, is punishable by imprisonment in the state prison not less than one nor more than fourteen years." (Government Code, sec. 6200.)

"Every person not an officer such as is referred to in the preceding section, who is guilty of any of the acts specified in that section, is punishable by imprisonment in the state prison not exceeding five years, or in a county jail not exceeding one year, or by a fine not exceeding one hundred dollars, or both." (Government Code, sec. 6201.)

The filing of a document imports that it is thereby placed in the custody of a public officer to be preserved by him for public use and it is no less a public document or record if it is excluded from public gaze by reason of its confidential nature (People v. Pearson, 111 Cal. App. 2d 9). A public record embraces any document or record which may properly be kept by an officer in connection with the discharge of his official duties (People v. Purcell, 22 Cal. App. 2d 126; People v. Pearson, 111 Cal. App. 2d 9). One who is not such an officer but who aids and abets such officer in the commission of such acts is a principal in and guilty of such offense (People v. Thompson, 122 Cal. App. 2d 567). Where the defendant surreptitiously removed a superior court file from the custody of the county clerk and it was found several days later on a counter in the clerk's office and it was discovered that the file contained papers differing in content from those originally in the file, some changes had been made on defendant's typewriter by adding pages substituted for those originally in the pleading filed and some filing dates had been changed, a conviction under section 6201 was sustained (People v. McKenna, 116 Cal. App. 2d 207, holding also that each document in the file which had been altered constituted a separate offense and that the fact that the pleadings changed were those of the defendant did not relieve her of responsibility as they had become public records by having been filed in the clerk's office).

In one of the early cases it appeared that the defendant had erased his first name as grantee in a deed and inserted the name of his wife and then had the deed recorded. Later the defendant informed the recorder, before whom the deed had been acknowledged, of what he had done and requested him to change the deed and the record so that both would speak the truth with respect to the transaction. After obtaining the consent of the grantor and the wife of the defendant the recorder erased the name of the wife in the deed and in the record and inserted defendant's name instead. The conviction was sustained, the court holding that the statute had been violated and that "it was not necessary in making out the offense to prove any fraudulent intention on the part of the defendant." (People v. O'Brien, 96 Cal. 171, 179; see also Newby v. Times Mirror Co., 173 Cal. 388; People v. Tomalty, 14 Cal. App. 224.) The words "filed or deposited" in section 6200 are equivalent to "on file or on deposit" and when records or books become and are records of an office they are on file and on deposit in such office. (People v. Tomalty, 14 Cal. App. 224.) In the offenses described in sections 6200 and 6201, "the intent is immaterial" and "Even a laudable defacement of the record is a violation" and "The act itself without intent other than that of doing it constitutes the offense regardless of the object." (Newby v. Times Mirror Co., 173 Cal. 388, 392, 393, holding that the striking out of a satisfaction of a judgment, the entry of which had been obtained by fraud, was a violation of the statute.)

However, where a record has been made which does not speak the truth it is not a violation of the section for a person charged with making a true record to change it in good faith to make it speak the truth as such an alteration would be wholly lacking in criminal intent. (People v. McAtee, 35 Cal. App. 2d 329.) Such an alteration is distinguishable from that in Newby v. Times Mirror Co., supra, for there the record was correct when made.

Offering False or Forged Instrument for Record

"Every person who knowingly procures or offers any false or forged instrument to be filed, registered or recorded in any public office within this state, which instrument, if genuine, might be filed, or registered, or recorded under any law of this state or of the United States, is guilty of a felony." (Penal Code, sec. 115.)

In a prosecution under this section it is immaterial whether the certificate of acknowledgment of such instrument is fatally defective. (People v. Webber, 44 Cal. App. 120.) The section simply seeks to cover the various classes of instruments entitled to be recorded without regard to whether the particular instrument is defective in form or certification. (People v. Webber, 44 Cal. 120.) The recording of a false deed in which the grantors' names were forged is a violation even though such grantors never had title to the land involved. (People v. Baender, 68 Cal. App. 49.)

Section 115 does not require that there be any intent to defraud or that anyone be actually defrauded (People v. Standley, 126 Cal. App. 739; People v. Horowitz, 70 Cal. App. 2d 675) and it is only necessary that the act prescribed by the statute be done knowingly, with knowledge that the instrument is false or forged. Nor is it necessary that the instrument be one which by its recording will result in a fraud. Thus if a forged will is procured or offered to be recorded with the county clerk the crime is committed whether the decedent named died with or without an estate. (People v. Davidian, 20 Cal. App. 2d 720; People v. Horowitz, 70 Cal. App. 2d 675.)

The section applies however only to a false or forged "instrument" and this term means an agreement expressed in writing, signed and delivered by one person to another, transferring title to or creating a lien on property or giving the right to a debt or duty and therefore the filing of a false birth certificate, giving the names of the persons who were not the parents, is not an act within the scope of section 115. (People v. Fraser, 23 Cal. App. 82.) The section also requires that the instrument must be one which, if genuine, was entitled to be filed, registered or recorded in the office where it is offered and the offering of, for example, a forged assignment of letters patent for record to an office where it is not entitled to be recorded is not within the statute. (People v. Harrold, 84 Cal. 567.)

Forgery of Public and Corporate Seals

"Every person who, with intent to defraud another, forges or counterfeits the seal of this state, the seal of any public officer authorized by law, the seal of any court of record, or the seal of any corporation, or any other public seal authorized or recognized by the laws of this state, or of any other state, government, or country, or who falsely makes, forges or counterfeits any impression purporting to be an impression of any seal, or who has in his possession any such counterfeited seal or impression thereof, knowing it to be counterfeited, and wilfully conceals the same, is guilty of forgery." (Penal Code, sec. 472.)

Forging of Telegram or Telephone Message

"Every person who knowingly and wilfully sends by telegraph or telephone to any person a false or forged message, purporting to be from a telegraph or telephone office, or from any other person, or who wilfully delivers or causes to be delivered to any person any such message falsely purporting to have been received by telegraph or telephone, or who furnishes, or conspires to furnish, or causes to be furnished to any agent, operator or employee to be sent by telegraph or telephone, or to be delivered, any such message, knowing the same to be false or forged, with the intent to deceive, injure or defraud another, is punishable by imprisonment in the state prison not exceeding five years, or in the county jail not exceeding one year, or by fine not exceeding five thousand dollars, or by both such fine and imprisonment." (Penal Code, sec. 474.)

This offense involves the specific "intent to deceive, injure or defraud." The words "intent to deceive" are broader than "intent to defraud" and are not limited to an act whereby one does or may suffer a financial loss (People v. Norwoods, 100 Cal. App. 2d 281; People v. Reed, 113 Cal. App. 2d 339).

Fictitious Bills, etc.

"Every person who makes, passes, utters or publishes, with intention to defraud any other person, or who, with the like intention, attempts to pass, utter or publish, or who has in his possession, with like intent to utter, pass or publish, any fictitious bill, note, or check, purporting to be the bill, note or check, or other instrument in writing for the payment of money or property of some bank, corporation, copartnership, or individual when in fact, there is no such bank, corporation, copartnership or individual in existence, knowing the bill, note, check or instrument in writing to be fictitious, is punishable by imprisonment in the county jail for not more than one year, or in the state prison for not more than fourteen years." (Penal Code, sec. 476.)

This section creates an offense, very similar to forgery, which has as its elements the intent to defraud and, as to uttering or possession with intent to utter, requires knowledge as to the fictitious character of the instrument but this section is limited to fictitious instruments for the payment of money and in addition to punishing the making or uttering also punishes the possession with intent to utter such instrument. Where the instrument is the subject of forgery a fictitious instrument may be prosecuted as forgery or under section 476. (For discussion of fictitious checks see **Forgery of Fictitious Name** under FORGERY.) The forgery of a fictitious instrument other than a bill, note, check or other instrument for the payment of money or property can only be prosecuted under the forgery statute.

CHAPTER XXVI.

ISSUING CHECK OR DRAFT WITH INTENT TO DEFRAUD

"(a) Any person who for himself or as the agent or representative of another or as an officer of a corporation, willfully, with intent to defraud, makes or draws or utters or delivers any check or draft or order upon any bank or depositary, or person, or firm, or corporation, for the payment of money, knowing at the time of such making, drawing, uttering or delivering that the maker or drawer or the corporation has not sufficient funds in, or credit with said bank or depositary, or person, or firm, or corporation, for the payment of such check, draft or order, and all other checks, drafts or orders upon such funds then outstanding, in full upon its presentation, although no express representation is made with reference thereto, is punishable by imprisonment in the county jail for not more than one year, or in the state prison for not more than fourteen years.

"(b) However, if the total amount of all such checks, drafts or orders that the defendant is charged with and convicted of making, drawing or uttering does not exceed $50, the offense is punishable only by imprisonment in the county jail for not more than one year except that this subdivision shall not be applicable if the defendant has previously been convicted of a violation of section 470, 475 or 476 of this code, or of this section of this code or of the crime of petty theft in a case in which defendant's offense was a violation also of section 470, 475 or 476 of this code or of this section, or if the defendant has previously been convicted of any offense under the laws of any other state or of the United States which, if committed in this State, would have been punishable as a violation of Section 470, 475 or 476 of this code or of this section of this code or if he has been so convicted of the crime of petty theft in a case in which, if the defendant's offense had been committed in this State, it would have been a violation also of Section 470, 475 or 476 of this code, or of this section."

"(c) Where such check, draft or order is protested, on the ground of insufficiency of funds or credit, the notice of protest thereof shall be admissible as proof of presentation, non-payment and protest and shall be presumptive evidence of knowledge of insufficiency of funds or credit with such bank or depository or person or firm or corporation."

335

"(d) The word 'credit' as used herein shall be construed to mean an arrangement or understanding with the bank or depositary or person or firm or corporation for the payment of such check, draft or order . . ." (Penal Code, sec. 476a).

Where a defendant has previously been convicted of any one of the offenses mentioned in paragraph "b" of section 476a that paragraph, so far as making a violation of the section a misdemeanor, is inapplicable (People v. Long, 152 Cal. App. 2d ...... A.C.A. ....).

Corpus Delicti

The essential elements of this offense are (1) the intent to defraud, (2) the making, drawing, uttering or delivering (3) of a check, draft or order for the payment of money (4) upon a bank or other person, (5) a lack of sufficient funds or credit with the drawee at the time the check, draft or order is made or uttered and (6) knowledge on the part of the accused of such lack of funds or credit.

When a person with intent to defraud makes, draws or utters a check on a bank knowing at the time that he has not sufficient funds or credit at least equal to the amount of the check he is guilty of a violation of Section 476a of the Penal Code regardless of what he or someone else may do thereafter (People v. Cortze, 108 Cal. App. 111; People v. Williams, 69 Cal. App. 169) for the offense, if committed at all, is committed at the time the check is made, drawn or uttered as the case may be. (In re Scott, 85 Cal. App. 170; People v. Schneider, 120 Cal. App. 749), and it is not necessary that the check be presented at the bank upon which it was drawn (People v. Ekberg, 94 Cal. App. 2d 613). The offense is complete when the check is issued with intent to defraud even though no one is defrauded thereby (People v. Freedman, 111 Cal. App. 2d 611).

If all the necessary elements of the offense are present, one may be guilty of the offense whether he acts for himself or as the agent or representative of another (People v. Weiss, 123 Cal. App. 2d 487, check signed by the general manager of a copartnership).

Intent To Defraud

It is the intent to defraud which is the gist of the offense and which makes it a felony to do what, without such specific intent, would amount merely to an overdraft. Proof of the intent to defraud and the knowledge that there were not, at the time of the commission of the offense, sufficient funds or credit to pay the check or draft in full were it immediately presented to the drawee are essential to a conviction. (People v. Wilbur, 33 Cal. App. 511; People v. Frey, 165 Cal. 140; People v. Owens, 57 Cal. App. 84; People v. Leuschen, 134 Cal. App. 312.) When it has been proved that the defendant issued his check, without a sufficient balance in the bank to cover it and without having credit in the bank, and obtained the property of another by delivering the check to him and that the check had been dishonored, a prima facie case has been made out for the element of fraudulent intent can be inferred from that evidence (People v. Yrigoyen, 45 Cal. 2d 46). But, while there must be an intent to defraud, it is not necessary that any person shall have been defrauded or shall have suffered a loss, for the offense is complete as soon as the intent to defraud is coupled with and accompanies the making, drawing, uttering or delivering of the check or draft, the other elements of the offense being present. (People v. Khan, 41 Cal. App. 393; People v. Sherman, 100 Cal. App. 587; People v. Fisher, 11 Cal. App. 2d 232; People v. Cortze, 108 Cal. App. 111; People v. Oliver, 115 Cal. App. 677.) Where appellant owed complainant money on account of work performed and, the debt being due and payment demanded, appellant issued his check in payment though he knew he had neither funds nor credit in the bank and appellant contended that there was no intent to defraud since the check was for a past due debt, the court said: "To our minds the fraudulent intent here was shown when it was made to appear that the appellant gave the check, representing thereby that it was good and valid and that it was given and received with the intent that it should pay appellant's debt. It seems to us immaterial as to whether the acceptance of the worthless check had the effect of extinguishing the debt." (People v. Khan, 41 Cal. App. 393; see also People v. Williams, 69 Cal. App. 169; People v. Boyce, 87 Cal. App. 2d 828.) "The intent of the person who issued the check, contrary to the provisions of section 476a of the Penal Code, cannot be made to depend upon the success of the enterprise. When the check has been drawn, issued and delivered to the payee with intent to defraud, and there is no money in the bank with which to pay the same, and the drawer has knowledge of such want of funds, the crime is complete, even though the person to whom such check is delivered is not thereby disadvantaged or placed in any worse position than formerly existed. . . . If a consideration were necessary, it is evident that the delay occasioned by the issuance of such spurious paper would furnish the same." (People v. Williams, 69 Cal. App. 169.)

Where it had been the custom of the bank, when he overdrew his account, to notify the defendant when funds were needed to cover checks constituting an overdraft and defendant had always covered and paid his former checks, it was held that this showed a lack of intent to defraud and overcame the prima facie case of the prosecution. (In re Leuschen, 134 Cal. App. 312) but this might be overcome by other evidence showing that, nothwithstanding these facts, an intent to defraud did exist as to a particular check.

(As to Fraud see also Obtaining Property By False Pretenses).

Intent As Affected by Knowledge of Payee

Where, at the time of the delivery of the check, the person receiving the check was informed that there were not then sufficient funds in the bank to pay the check, there is no deception and no intent to defraud, for the receiver fully knew there were no funds against which it could be drawn, and the fact that the person giving the check promised to place funds in the bank to meet the check upon its presentation, a promise which was not kept, does not establish that, at the time the check was delivered, there was an intent to defraud. (People v. Wilkins, 67 Cal. App. 758; In re Griffin, 83 Cal. App. 779; People v. Burnett, 39 Cal. 2d 556.) The check in such a case is in effect merely a promissory note. Where the defendant asked the person to whom he gave the check to hold it for a stated period of time, this in effect was a statement that the check was not then good or cashable at the bank and there is no intent to defraud but, where such a request is made and the person who is to receive it refuses to hold it any length of time and the defendant nevertheless concludes the transaction, such conduct on his part removes the effect of the prior request that the check be held and in effect declares that the check is then good and backed by sufficient funds or credit at the bank and the proof shows the intent to defraud. (People v. Thompson, 114 Cal. App. 258). Where the defendant gave a check as a down payment on a car and requested that the receiver of the check should not deposit it for several days because he did not want his wife to know about it but also showed his bank deposit book which he had altered so that it showed that he had

sufficient funds on deposit when in fact he had not, there was
ample evidence of intent to defraud (People v. Whisenhunt,
155 Cal. App. 2d.........). There can be no conviction under section
476a if the payee is informed by the maker at the time of
the delivery that that there are insufficient funds in the bank
to pay the check (People v. Burnett, 39 Cal. 2d 556).

Knowledge

To sustain a conviction of this offense the proof must show
that, at the time of the drawing, uttering or delivering of the
check, draft or order, the defendant knew that he did not have
funds or credit with the corporation, firm or person, upon whom
such order was drawn, sufficient to pay the same. This may
be shown by circumstantial evidence (People v. Magladdery,
40 Cal. App. 2d 643) as where a person, having but a small
balance in the bank, draws and cashes a check for a much
larger amount and his balance was later overdrawn (People
v. Rose, 9 Cal. App. 2d 174) or where the check is drawn on
a bank in which the drawer never had any account or arrangement for credit. An honest mistake of fact, the drawer honestly believing that his account was sufficient to pay his check
in full, would be a good defense even though in fact his balance was less than the amount of the check.

Funds or Credit

If at the time of drawing or uttering the check, draft or
order there are sufficient funds or credit with the bank or
person on whom the order is drawn to pay the same in full
if it were immediately presented the statute is not violated
even though thereafter, and before such order is presented
for payment, the funds or credit have, by other draft, been reduced to an amount insufficient to pay such order. The lack
of funds or an arrangement with the bank for payment of the
check or draft is an essential element of the offense. (People
v. Frey, 165 Cal. 140; People v. Owens, 57 Cal. App. 84.) But
to constitute funds or credit the funds must be such as to be
subject to the check upon which the charge is based or, in the
case of credit, it must be an arrangement for the payment of
a check such as that upon which the prosecution is based. Thus
it would not be a defense to a charge under Section 476a that
the defendant had sufficient cash in his safe deposit box or
in a savings or other non-checking account unless the bank
or depositary had the authority to use the same to pay the
check or draft of the accused. Also, if the accused had an

account that only such of his checks would be paid by the
arrangement with the bank with reference to his checking
bank as bore a certain mark, a check on such account which
did not bear such an identifying mark would be as much a
check without funds or credit as if there were no account
at all. (People v. Kahn, 41 Cal. App. 393.)

Effect of Deposit for Collection

Where a person opens an account at a bank by the deposit
of a check under the express condition that he can not draw
against the account until the bank has a report from the bank
on which such check deposited for collection was drawn or until such check has been paid, such deposit creates no funds or
credit and, if the depositor makes a purchase or obtains cash
with a check drawn on such account before such bank report
has been received or the deposited check has been cashed,
Section 476a is violated. (People v. Routh, 182 Cal. 561; People
v. Bowles, 100 Cal. App. 464.)

Check on Branch Bank

Where a person draws a check on a branch of a bank
in which he has to his knowledge no funds or credit, it is
wholly immaterial whether he had funds or credit in another
branch of the same bank. (People v. Eppstein, 108 Cal. App.
72.)

Post-Dated Check

Where all the elements of the offense exist the crime is
committed even though the check or draft be one which is post-
dated. But, if the recipient knows that the check or draft is
post-dated at the time he receives it, the circumstances warrant the inference that he was thereby informed that the
check or draft was not intended to be good until the arrival
of the date it bears and the transaction will be considered in
the same light as though at the time of its delivery he had been
informed that the check or draft was not then protected by
funds or credit then with the drawee, but that it would be
so protected upon the date on its face. (People v. Bercowitz,
163 Cal. 636; see also People v. Weaver, 96 Cal. App. 1; People
v. Lane, 144 Cal. App. 2d 87). Where the maker claims that
the check was post dated and was given with the understanding that it was to be held until a future time, the fact of post
dating is evidence of such understanding (People v. Burnett,
39 Cal. 2d 556).

What Is No Defense

The fact that no actual loss resulted from the passing of the check or that the merchandise received thereby was recovered is no defense. (People v. Sherman, 100 Cal. App. 587.) It is not a defense that the check was drawn on a bank which had no existence; such fact even tends to prove the offense. (People v. Silverman, 33 Cal. App. 2d 1.) A check drawn by the defendant to his own order is not excepted from the operation of the statute. (People v. Wilbur, 33 Cal. App. 511.) It is wholly immaterial whether the offender draws his personal check or draws a check in the name of a company, partnership or association and where a defendant has neither funds nor credit to cover the check he has drawn, it is immaterial whether the check was drawn upon company funds or was intended to be his personal check. (People v. Newell, 192 Cal. 659.) The fact that overdrafts on former occasions had been paid by the bank is no defense where such payment was the result of bank employees having corruptly cooperated with the defendant to pay checks in excess of funds or credit in violation of their duties as employees of the bank; in such instance a defendant cannot claim that he believed the bank would pay subsequent overdrafts. (People v. Zimmer, 23 Cal. App. 2d 518.) Where all the elements of the offense exist it is not a defense that the defendant had money coming to him which he intended to deposit on the day following the giving of the check. (People v. King, 63 Cal. App. 674. The case of People v. Becker, 137 Cal. App. 349, seems to hold to the contrary inferentially deciding that the intention of the defendant to open an account in the bank on the Monday following the Saturday on which the check was given so that the check would be paid on presentation would be a defense. The decision, reversing the conviction because the defendant was not allowed to testify to his intent to open such account, overlooks the fact that defendant obtained a watch by giving for it a check on the bank in which he had no account or credit whereby the seller of the watch was defrauded and the fact that the defendant intended to make the check good by thereafter opening an account is no more a defense than if he intended in some other manner to reimburse the vendor. Evidence of the intent of the accused is, however, admissible even though it fails to establish a defense. See also People v. Gaines, 106 Cal. App. 2d 176. While the testimony of a defendant that he had intended to deposit money in the bank sufficient to cover the check on presentation tends to rebut proof of an intent to defraud, the jury is not obliged to believe such testimony (People v. Burgess, 147 Cal. App. 2d 780). If in fact a fraud is perpetrated upon the receiver of the check and the elements of the corpus delicti are present, the fact that the defendant intended to make a deposit in the bank to meet the check or that he intended in some other manner to make the check good or to reimburse the receiver no more purges him of guilt than in the case of the thief who returns or makes restitution for the property he has stolen. Basically the offense defined in section 476a is merely a form of obtaining property by false pretenses, one of the forms of theft).

Where the defendant testified that he believed that one H had deposited funds to defendant's account, this was immaterial where the defendant also testified that he wrote the checks charged without any reliance upon such deposit (People v. Brown, 141 Cal. App. 2d 299).

(Note: The statement in People v. Griffith, 120 Cal. App. 2d 873 that, "In negotiating a check the maker does not necessarily represent that he then has in the bank funds out of which it will be paid; but he only represents, by the act of passing the check, that it is a good and valid order for its amount and that the existing state of facts is such that in the ordinary course of business it will be paid on presentation" is not supported by any cited authority. Since a check is a bill of exchange payable on demand the receiver has the right to present it to the drawee bank for payment immediately after he receives it and the giver of the check by his act and conduct represents that the receiver can do this and will receive the amount of the check from the bank and, if in fact there are neither funds nor credit with the bank at the time the check is given, the giver has materially misrepresented the facts).

Check Under Fictitious Name

Where a person, with intent to defraud, makes and cashes a check, signing not his own name but that of a fictitious person, he may be convicted under section 476a, if it also appears that there was no account or credit with the drawee bank in the name used in the signing of the check. In fact in such a case it would be immaterial whether the name was that of a real or a fictitious person. (People v. Hamby, 55 Cal. App. 37.)

Check Signed By Another Person As Maker

Where a defendant wrote a check payable to his order and signed it with the name of another and there was no account in the drawee bank under either name the conviction was sustained. "Defendant could be convicted of violating section 476a if the jury found the intent to defraud whether it found that he actually wrote the maker's signature on the check or passed it knowing that the maker (his brother) had no funds in or credit with the bank." (People v. Porter, 99 Cal. App. 2d 506).

Restitution

An offer of restitution or restitution itself is no defense (People v. Porter, 99 Cal. App. 2d 506).

CHAPTER XXVII

BRIBERY

Bribery, generally speaking, is the asking, giving, receiving or agreeing to receive any valuable consideration for the purpose of corruptly influencing a person or official in the performance or failure to perform a public duty within the scope of his office or position.

"The word 'bribe' signifies anything of value or advantage, present or prospective, or any promise or undertaking to give any, asked, given or accepted, with a corrupt intent to influence, unlawfully, the person to whom it is given, in his action, vote or opinion, in any public or official capacity." (Penal Code, sec. 7, subd. 6; People v. Glass, 158 Cal. 650, 676; see also People v. McGee, 107 Cal. App. 56).

Of Executive Officer

"Every person who gives or offers any bribe to any executive officer of this state with intent to influence him in respect to any act, decision, vote, opinion, or other proceeding as such officer, is punishable by imprisonment in the state prison not less than one nor more than fourteen years, and is disqualified from holding any office in this state." (Penal Code, sec. 67.) The phrase "any executive officer of this state" is not synonymous with "state officer" but refers to any executive officer in this state and includes a county executive officer. (Singh v. Superior Court, 44 Cal. App 64), a district attorney or a city executive officer (People v. Hallner, 43 Cal. 2d 715, president of the board of police commissioners, city attorney and assistant city attorney). A police officer of the city of Los Angeles is an "executive officer" within the scope of section 67 (People v. Mathews, 124 Cal. App. 2d 67).

Of Ministerial Officer or Employee

"Every person who gives or offers as a bribe to any ministerial officer, employee or appointee of the State of California, county or city therein or political subdivision thereof, any thing the theft of which would be petty theft is guilty of a misdemeanor; if the theft of the thing so given or offered would be grand theft the offense is a felony." (Penal Code, sec. 67½.)

344

By Executive or Ministerial Officer or Employee

"Every executive or ministerial officer, employee or appointee of the State of California, county or city therein, or political subdivision thereof, who asks, receives, or agrees to receive, any bribe, upon any agreement or understanding that his vote, opinion, or action upon any matter then pending, or which may be brought before him in his official capacity, shall be influenced thereby, is punishable by imprisonment in the state prison not less than one nor more than fourteen years; and, in addition thereto, forfeits his office, and is forever disqualified from holding any office in this state." (Penal Code, sec. 68.)

Of Member of Legislature

"Every person who gives or offers to give a bribe to any member of the legislature, or to another person for him, or attempts by menace, deceit, suppression of truth, or any corrupt means, to influence a member in giving or withholding his vote, or in not attending the house or any committee of which he is a member, is punishable by imprisonment in the state prison not less than one nor more than ten years." (Penal Code, sec. 85.)

By Member of Legislature

"Every member of either of the houses composing the legislature of this state who asks, receives, or agrees to receive any bribe upon any understanding that his official vote, opinion, judgment, or action shall be influenced thereby, or shall be given in any particular manner, or upon any particular side of any question or matter upon which he may be required to act in his official capacity, or gives, or offers, or promises to give any official vote in consideration that another member of the legislature shall give any such vote, either upon the same or another question is punishable by imprisonment in the state prison not less than one nor more than fourteen years, and upon conviction thereof shall, in addition to said punishment, forfeit his office, be disfranchised, and forever disqualified from holding any office or public trust." (Penal Code, sec. 86.)

Section 85 includes more than the giving or offering of a bribe and covers any attempt to influence a member of the state legislature in the casting of his vote or to remain away from the house or any committee of which he is a member. Section 86 also includes the additional offense of vote trading or "log rolling."

Of Judges, Jurors, Referees, etc.

"Every person who gives or offers to give a bribe to any judicial officer, juror, referee, arbitrator, or umpire, or to any person who may be authorized by law to hear or determine any question or controversy, with intent to influence his vote, opinion, or decision upon any matter or question which is or may be brought before him for decision, is punishable by imprisonment in the state prison for not less than one nor more than ten years." (Penal Code, sec. 92.)

By Judges, Jurors, Referees, etc.

"Every judicial officer, juror, referee, arbitrator, or umpire, and every person authorized by law to hear or determine any question or controversy, who asks, receives, or agrees to receive, any bribe, upon any agreement or understanding that his vote, opinion, or decision upon any matters or question which is or may be brought before him for decision, shall be influenced thereby, is punishable by imprisonment in the state prison not less than one nor more than ten years." (Penal Code, sec. 93.)

Attempt to Influence Juror

"Every person who corruptly attempts to influence a juror, or any person summoned or drawn as a juror, or chosen as an arbitrator, or umpire, or appointed a referee, in respect to his verdict in, or decision of any cause, or proceeding, pending, or about to be brought before him, either:

1. By means of any communication, oral or written, had with him except in the regular course of proceedings;

2. By means of any book, paper, or instrument exhibited, otherwise than in the regular course of proceedings;

3. By means of any threat, intimidation, persuasion, or entreaty; or,

4. By means of any promise, or assurance of any pecuniary or other advantage; is punishable by fine not exceeding five thousand dollars, or by imprisonment in the state prison not exceeding five years." (Penal Code, sec. 95.)

Corruption of Juror

"Every juror or person drawn or summoned as a juror, or chosen arbitrator or umpire, or appointed referee, who either:

One—Makes any promise or agreement to give a verdict or decision for or against any party; or

Two—Wilfully and corruptly permits any communication to be made to him; or receives any book, paper, instrument, or information relating to any cause or matter pending before him, except according to the regular course of proceedings, is punishable by fine not exceeding five thousand dollars, or by imprisonment in the state prison not exceeding five years.'' (Penal Code, sec. 96.)

Of City Councilmen, Supervisors, etc.

"Every person who gives or offers a bribe to any member of any common council, board of supervisors, or board of trustees of any county, city and county, city, or public corporation, with intent to corruptly influence such member in his action on any matter or subject pending before, or which is afterward to be considered by, the body of which he is a member, and every member of any of the bodies mentioned in this section who receives, or offers, or agrees to receive any bribe upon any understanding that his official vote, opinion, judgment, or action shall be influenced thereby, or shall be given in any particular manner or upon any particular side of any question or matter, upon which he may be required to act in his official capacity, is punishable by imprisonment in the state prison not less than one nor more than fourteen years, and upon conviction thereof shall, in addition to said punishment, forfeit his office, and forever be disfranchised and disqualified from holding any public office or trust." (Penal Code, sec. 165.)

Classes of Bribery

Bribery may be divided into those cases in which an outsider either gives or offers the bribe, those in which the public officer or employee asks or offers to receive a bribe, those in which he agrees to receive a bribe and those in which the bribe is received by the public officer or employee.

Giving and Offering a Bribe

A charge of giving a bribe requires that the bribe be delivered to either the person being bribed or to some person or other agency for him and, except in those cases in which the officer is a member of the legislature, the proof of delivery to an intermediary must show not only that the bribe was delivered "to another person for him" but that such other person was authorized by the officer or employee in question to receive the same. In the cases involving a member of the legislature the offense is complete if the bribe is given or offered "to another person for him'' even though such legislator is unaware of the transaction or any of the negotiations leading up to it.

In the offense of offering a bribe it is not necessary that any particular language or formula be used by the intending corruptor, it only being required that the language or conduct used, viewed in the light of the attending circumstances, will fairly sustain the inference that a bribe was being offered. Where an officer had arrested a woman motorist on a charge involving the driving of an automobile while she was intoxicated and was approached by the defendant who stated that he was a friend of the husband of the woman and that if the officer in testifying at the trial would say nothing about the subject of liquor being involved ''everything will be fixed up for you,'' the court said that ''this evidence was sufficient to prove the offer of something of value or advantage, with a corrupt intent to influence unlawfully the person to whom the promise was made.'' (People v. McGee, 107 Cal. App. 56.) ''It is not necessary to the completion of the crime of offering to give a bribe that the thing offered as a bribe should have a present existence or a definite and ascertained value,'' (People v. Vincilione, 17 Cal. App. 513; People v. McGee, 107 Cal. App. 56) and the offer need not go to the extent of an actual tender of the bribe. (People v. Ah Fook, 62 Cal. 493; People v. Hurley, 126 Cal. 351.)

Where the briber does not act in person but the offer is conveyed to the officer sought to be bribed by a third person not only is the instigator who furnishes the bribe guilty but the third person who conveys the offer is also guilty even though the bribe does not come out of his pocket. (People v. Northey, 77 Cal. 618, 634; see also Accomplice; Principal and Accessory.)

Asking and Offering to Receive a Bribe

The asking of a bribe and the offering to receive a bribe are virtually the same; in either instance the bribe is solicited and no specific words or formula need be used by the bribe seeker and the asking of a bribe may be established by proof of words, acts or conduct unmistakably importing that a bribe is being asked (People v. Elliott, 103 Cal. App. 329) and it is not necessary that a bribe shall have been suggested or offered by another for the soliciting of the bribe may be solely the idea of the defendant. (People v. Hurley, 126 Cal. 351.) In this form of bribery it is not necessary that the person approached should consent to give the bribe nor is it necessary that the defendant shall have made any effort to carry out the corrupt purpose by attempting to perform the act which was to be the consideration for the bribe (People v. Squires, 99 Cal. 327) for the crime is complete if the accused was ready and willing to enter into the corrupt agreement that his conduct should be influenced by the bribe when he asked or solicited the bribe. (People v. Powell, 50 Cal. App. 436; People v. Fitzpatrick, 78 Cal. App. 37.)

It is not necessary that the bribe be asked concerning one of the regular statutory duties of the officer. Thus, where the secretary of the Governor asked and agreed to receive a bribe to approve and obtain from the Governor a pardon for a person who had been convicted of a crime the court said, "It is sufficient to charge that the subject matter upon which the bribe was to operate existed and could be brought before the public officer in his official capacity. The fact that the duty is not specifically conferred upon the officer by statute is immaterial." (People v. Megladdery, 40 Cal. App. 2d 748; People v. Silver, 75 Cal. App. 2d 1.)

Agreeing to Receive a Bribe

The offense of agreeing to receive a bribe does not contemplate or require that there shall have been an agreement or meeting of the minds of the person who is to give and the person who is to receive the bribe to the extent of constituting an agreement or contract between the parties. A mere offer of a public official to accept a bribe without any feigned or actual acceptance of the offer and without any promise or agreement on the part of such official that, if the bribe were paid, he would perform the act which was the consideration for the bribe, does not constitute agreeing to receive a bribe. (People v. Weitzel, 201 Cal. 116.) Where, however, the official does agree with one of whom he has asked the bribe that he will perform a certain duty of his office in a particular way if such bribe is paid the offense of agreeing to accept a bribe is complete and this is true even though the person of whom he asked the bribe acted without corrupt intent but was, after the first overtures were made to him, acting under the directions of the law enforcement officers for the purpose of entrapment. (People v. Fitzpatrick, 78 Cal. App. 37.) The terms of the statute are met if the defendant agrees or intends in his own mind to receive the bribe. (People v. Kerns, 9 Cal. App. 2d 72; People v. Vollman, 73 Cal. App. 2d 769.)

Receiving a Bribe

Receiving a bribe is an offense even though the act for which the bribe was given was one which the officer was authorized to perform and which was not itself corrupt for it is the corrupt intent which induces the bribery that is the gist of the offense. The acceptance by a traffic officer of a hundred dollars, in consideration of which he accepted bail from a person whom he had arrested on misdemeanor charges, is an act in his official capacity and his official action was corruptly influenced, and, even though the practice of accepting bail by officers existed with the permission of the city recorder, the acceptance of the check constituted bribery. (People v. Fraser, 80 Cal. App. 464).

Illustrating the breadth of section 86, it has been held that a member of the legislature who accepted money, he being a member of a legislative committee appointed to investigate building and loan associations, upon his promise to keep certain companies out of the investigation, is guilty of bribery. (In re Bunkers, 1 Cal. App. 61; People v. Bunkers, 2 Cal. App. 197.)

Police Officer

Since it is the corrupt receiving of the bribe which constitutes the offense a police officer who receives a bribe in consideration of his promise not to arrest any one of a certain class of persons for the violation of a particular law, such as the law against gaming, is guilty even though no occasion thereafter arose for the making of such an arrest, as this is the receiving of a bribe "in a matter which may be brought before him in his official capacity," (People v. Markham, 64 Cal. 157; People v. Mechler, 75 Cal. App. 181; People v. Finkelstein, 98 Cal. App. 2d 545) and the same rule applies if the agreement is that of a city police officer that he will not make an arrest for a specified violation of a federal law. (Harris v. Superior Court, 51 Cal. App. 15.) A police officer is an executive officer (People v. Finkelstein, 98 Cal. App. 2d 545; People v. Mathews, 124 Cal. App. 2d 67). "It is not essential to the crime of bribery that the officer's action is with actual authority so long as it falls within the general scope of his duties and he is purporting to act in his official capacity" (People v. Longo, 119 Cal. App. 2d 416 and cases cited).

Deputy Sheriff

A deputy sheriff arresting a fugitive from justice from another jurisdiction under the order and direction of his superior officer is acting in his official capacity (People v. Lips, 59 Cal. App. 38) and such an arrest is as to a "matter then pending" regardless of whether a proper charge had been filed against the prisoner in the foreign jurisdiction. (People v. Anderson, 62 Cal. App. 222.) "The legality of the arrest or the power of the officers to make the arrest, or thereafter to detain the men arrested, is not a matter of controlling importance in cases of this character. It is sufficient if the officers assumed to act under legal authority in arresting and detaining their prisoners and thereafter accepted a bribe upon the condition that they would release them and not further prosecute the charges against them." (People v. Anderson, 75 Cal. App. 365; People v. Lips, 59 Cal. App. 381; People v. Fraser, 81 Cal. App. 281.)

Bribery of a Witness

"Every person who gives or offers or promises to give to any witness or person about to be called as a witness, any bribe upon the understanding or agreement that such a person shall not attend upon any trial, or every person who attempts by means of any offer of a bribe to dissuade any such person from attending upon any trial, is guilty of a felony." (Penal Code, sec. 136½.)

"Every person who gives or offers, or promises to give, to any witness, or person about to be called as a witness, any bribe, upon any understanding or agreement that the testimony of such witness shall be thereby influenced, or who attempts by any other means fraudulently to induce any person to give false or withhold true testimony, is guilty of a felony." (Penal Code, sec. 137.)

An essential requirement of section 137 is that there must be an understanding or agreement that the testimony of the witness will be influenced (People v. Terry, 44 Cal. 2d 371).

"Every person who is a witness, or is about to be called as such, who receives, or offers to receive, any bribe, upon any understanding that his testimony shall be influenced thereby, or that he will absent himself from the trial or proceeding upon which his testimony is required, is guilty of a felony." (Penal Code, sec. 138.)

To Constitute an Offense

To constitute an offense under the above quoted sections of the Penal Code, the person sought to be bribed must be, at the time of the commission of the alleged offense, under subpoena as a witness or one who is "about to be called as a witness" and this includes one who has knowledge that he will be called as a witness. A person who has merely sworn to a complaint is not, by that act alone, a witness within the terms of the statute but a person who has been told that he will be called as a witness is a witness within the statute in a prosecution against him for receiving a bribe. (People v. McGee, 24 Cal. App. 563.) It is not necessary to the commission of an offense under these sections that the case in which the person is to be a witness shall have been filed at the time of the bribery (People v. McAllister, 99 Cal. App. 37; People v. Martin, 114 Cal. App. 392) for a person who is a material witness to the issues of a cause of action falls within the phrase "about to be called as a witness." (Cases last cited.)

In a charge of offering a bribe to a person about to be called as a witness it is not necessary that such witness consent or accept the offer or agree that his testimony will be influenced. (People v. Schultz, 18 Cal. App. 2d 485.) While guilt of the offense prescribed by section 137 does not depend upon the intention of the witness to testify as required, the giving, offering or promising of the bribe must still be upon an understanding or agreement that the testimony of the witness will be influenced thereby and where the offer made is rejected by the witness the crime is not consummated. (In re Jang, 25 Cal. App. 2d 529) and the act will amount at most to an attempt.

The offense of bribery to influence the testimony of a witness must be distinguished from the crime of preventing or dissuading a witness from attending upon a trial as a witness and where money is offered to a witness to leave the state and to remain away from the trial the case falls within section 136½ of the Penal Code. (In re Johnson, 119 Cal. App. 57.)

Bribery of Players

The giving, offering or attempt so to do, of a bribe to a participant in athletic or sporting event, to influence the result is punishable by not to exceed five years in the state prison, a fine not exceeding $5000, or both such fine and imprisonment (Penal Code, sec. 337b; see People v. Phillips, 76 Cal. App. 2d 515).

CHAPTER XXVIII

PERJURY

"Every person who, having taken an oath that he will testify, declare, depose, or certify truly before any competent tribunal, officer or person, in any of the cases in which such an oath may by law be administered, wilfully and contrary to such oath, states as true any material matter which he knows to be false, and every person who testifies, declares, deposes, or certifies "under penalty of perjury" in any of the cases in which such testimony, declarations, depositions, or certification is permitted by law under "penalty of perjury" and wilfully states as true any matter which he knows to be false, is guilty of perjury." (Penal code, sec. 118).

Perjury is the willful testifying and assertion as to a material matter of fact, opinion or knowledge, made under oath or affirmation in a judicial proceeding or before any competent tribunal, public officer or person in any case in which such oath may by law be administered, where such statement is known by the person making it to be false, or where such statement is an unqualified declaration of that which the person making it does not know to be true, but as to which he claims knowledge. Perjury is not limited to sworn statements given by a witness in the course of a trial, but includes false statements by witnesses before a grand jury, upon a preliminary examination, in the making of a deposition or affidavit, authorized or required to be made in the course of legal proceedings, as well as an oath made in pursuance of law, a sworn application for a marriage license, verification of a document required by law, etc.

"It is no defense to a prosecution for perjury that the accused was not competent to give the testimony, deposition, or certificate of which falsehood is alleged. It is sufficient that he did give such testimony or make such deposition or certificate." (Penal Code, sec. 122. See Ex parte Carpenter, 64 Cal. 267.)

"It is no defense to a prosecution for perjury that the accused did not know the materiality of the false statement made by him; or that it did not, in fact, affect the proceeding in or for which it was made. It is sufficient that it was material, and might have been used to affect such proceeding." (Penal Code, sec. 123.)

"An unqualified statement of that which one does not know to be true is equivalent to a statement of that which one knows to be false." (Penal Code, sec. 125; See People v. Agnew, 77 Cal. App. 2d 748).

Penalty

"Perjury is punishable by imprisonment in the state prison not less than one nor more than fourteen years." (Penal Code, sec. 126.)

"Every person who, by willful perjury or subornation of perjury procures the conviction and execution of any innocent person, is punishable by death." (Penal Code, sec. 128.)

Corpus Delicti

"To establish the corpus delicti in the crime of perjury it must be proven that the defendant took an oath that he would testify, declare, depose or certify truly before a competent tribunal, officer or person; that such oath was taken in a case in which such oath may by law be administered; and, finally that, wilfully and contrary to such oath, the defendant stated as true a material matter which he knew to be false." (People v. Macken, 32 Cal. App. 2d 31; In re Blache, 40 Cal. App. 2d 687.) In every case perjury must be knowingly false (People v. Dixon, 99 Cal. App. 2d 94). The intent to swear falsely is the specific intent that must be shown to establish the crime of perjury (People v. Rodley, 131 Cal. 240, 260) and the statements in People v. Pustau, 39 Cal. App. 2d 407 and People v. Tolmachoff, 58 Cal. App. 2d 824, are not in conflict with the rule as stated in the Rodley case (People v. Guasti, 110 Cal. App. 2d 456). The word "wilfully" simply means that the witness made the perjured statement knowing it was false, or not knowing that it was true, and with intent to have it received as true. (People v. Tolmachoff, 58 Cal. App. 2d 815.) To sustain a charge of perjury it is not necessary that the false statement be made for the purpose of injuring another. (People v. Darcy, 59 Cal. App. 2d 342.)

Where the alleged perjury consists of testimony given before a court or other tribunal it is necessary that such tribunal have jurisdiction of the cause in which the testimony is given (People v. Howard, 111 Cal. 655; but see People v. De Carlo, 124 Cal. 462) and testimony given upon a trial under a complaint which wholly fails to charge a criminal offense would not amount to perjury. (In re Clark, 54 Cal. App. 57.)

To constitute perjury it is essential that the statements be made wilfully. There is no criminal intent and no wilfulness where the statement is made under an honest mistake and under a justifiable belief in its truth and a statement so made cannot be perjury even if untrue. (People v. Von Tiedeman, 120 Cal. 128; People v. Turner, 122 Cal. 679; People v. Wong Fook Sam, 146 Cal. 114.)

The word "false" in the statute means that the statement was false in fact. (People v. Wong Fook Sam, 146 Cal. 114.)

Conviction On One Of Several Assignments

Where the indictment or information is based upon testimony given before a court or other tribunal the pleading may, in one count, set forth a number of assignments of perjury based upon two or more alleged false statements and the defendant may be convicted upon proof of any one of such assignments. (People v. Follette, 74 Cal. App. 178; People v. Low Ying, 20 Cal. App. 2d 39; People v. Mizer, 37 Cal. App. 2d 148; People v. Gray, 52 Cal. App. 2d 620.)

Federal Jurisdiction

Perjury committed before a federal tribunal or officer is not subject to prosecution in the state courts. (People v. Kelly, 38 Cal. 145.)

The Oath

"The term 'oath,' as used in the last two sections, includes an affirmation and every mode authorized by law of attesting the truth of that which is stated." (Penal Code, sec. 119.)

"It is no defense to a prosecution for perjury that the oath was administered or taken in an irregular manner, or that the person accused of perjury did not go before, or was not in the presence of, the officer purporting to administer the oath, if such accused caused or procured such officer to certify that the oath had been taken or administered." (Penal Code, sec. 121.)

Even though all the other elements of perjury are present there can be no conviction unless the person who administered the oath had the power and authority to administer that particular oath. (People v. Simpton, 133 Cal. 367; People v. Cohen, 118 Cal. 74.) Thus in People v. Cohen, supra, where the alleged perjury was committed before a judge of the Superior Court sitting as a committing magistrate it was held that, since the defendant was there sworn as a witness by the county clerk, who had no authority to administer an oath in such cases, there was no perjury.

It will not avail a defendant charged with perjury that a mere irregularity existed in the form of administering or taking the oath if it was so administered and taken that the witness can be said to have known that he was being placed under oath and that any testimony or statement given by him would be under the pains and penalty of perjury if he falsified therein. (People v. Collins, 6 Cal. App. 492; Ex parte Carpenter, 64 Cal. 267; People v. Rodley, 131 Cal. 240; People v. Parent, 139 Cal. 602; People v. Cohen, 118 Cal. 74; People v. Swist, 136 Cal. 520; Fairbanks Morse Co. v. Getchell, 13 Cal. App. 458; People v. Brown, 125 Cal. App. 2d 83).

To constitute perjury the oath must be one "in any of the cases in which such an oath may by law be administered" (Penal Code, sec. 118) and there can be no perjury when there is no provision of law providing for the statement to be made under oath. (People v. White, 122 Cal. App. 2d 551, and cases cited). Where a person supported his application for financial relief from the county by an affidavit but the alleged false statement therein was not one which was required to be under oath, no charge of perjury could be predicated thereon, even though the ordinance required a written verified statement before such aid could be given. (People v. French, 134 Cal. App. 694.) It is not necessary, however, that the requirement of an oath be by state statute and it is sufficient if such oath be required by local ordinance. (People v. Ziady, 8 Cal. 2d 149.)

Perjury cannot be predicated upon the verification of an answer to a complaint in a civil action where the law does not require that such answer be verified. (People v. Millsap, 85 Cal. App. 732.) If, however, a complaint be verified under a statute providing that such a complaint may or may not be verified, a false statement therein may be charged as perjury as it is a case in which an oath "may by law be administered." (People v. Godines, 17 Cal. App. 2d 721; People v. Agnew, 77 Cal. App. 2d 748.)

If a person wilfully swears to a belief in the existence of a fact which he knows does not exist, he is as guilty of perjury as if he had sworn directly to the existence of a fact which he knew did not exist (People v. Agnew, 77 Cal. App. 2d 748; People v. Sagehorn, 140 Cal. App. 2d 138), and perjury may be predicated upon an answer by a witness that he does not recall the matter referred to in the question when in fact he does remember it (People v. Guasti, 110 Cal. App. 2d 456; People v. Sagehorn, 140 Cal. App. 2d 138).

Materiality

No false statement under oath, though made knowingly and with evil intent, can constitute perjury unless it is a statement as a matter material to the proceeding in which it is made. (People v. McDermott, 8 Cal. 288; People v. Perrazo, 64 Cal. 106; People v. Ah Sing, 95 Cal. 657.) Testimony is material "when it can be said that the testimony could have properly influenced the tribunal before whom the case was being heard upon the issues involved." (People v. Pustau, 39 Cal. App. 2d 407; People v. Lem You, 97 Cal. 224; People v. Dunstan, 59 Cal. App. 574.) "The matter sworn to need not be directly and immediately material. It is sufficient if it be so connected with the facts directly in issue as to have a legitimate tendency to prove or disprove such facts, by giving weight or probability to the testimony of a witness testifying thereto or otherwise" and "it is material also when contradicting part of the testimony given by another witness which is material, or if going to the credit or discredit of another witness." (People v. Low Ying, 20 Cal. App. 2d 39; People v. Senegrim, 27 Cal. App. 301; People v. Patterson, 64 Cal. App. 223; People v. Phillips, 56 Cal. App. 291; People v. Albert, 91 Cal. App. 774; People v. Chand, 75 Cal. App. 459.) "Any testimony which is relevant in the trial of a given case is so far material to the issue as to render a witness who knowingly and wilfully falsifies in giving it guilty of the crime of perjury." (People v. Chand, 75 Cal. App. 459; People v. Guasti, 110 Cal. App. 2d 456.) The test of materiality is whether the testimony could have influenced the final decision or verdict and any statement made for the purpose of affecting the ultimate determination of the matter being heard is material (People v. Dunstan, 59 Cal. App. 574.)

Materiality—Illustrative Cases

As examples of statements held to be material see: People v. Prather, 134 Cal. 436, evidence having a tendency to weaken the evidence going to the identification of stolen property; People v. Green, 54 Cal. 592, testimony which adds to or detracts from the weight of other and material evidence in the case; People v. Lee Fat, 54 Cal. 527, testimony as to the identity of the perpetrator of a crime; People v. Clementshaw, 59 Cal. 385, testimony before a coroner as to how deceased came to his death; People v. Platt, 67 Cal. 21 and People v. Naylor, 82 Cal. 607, omission of property from a verified petition in insolvency; People v. Brilliant, 58 Cal. 214, and People v. Barry, 63

Cal. 62, an answer to a question concerning a former statement of the witness; People v. Reitz, 86 Cal. App. 791, testimony in a divorce action as to non-cohabitation of the parties; People v. Lem You, 97 Cal. 224, testimony contradicting other material testimony; People v. Metzler, 21 Cal. App. 80, impeaching testimony; People v. Dunstan, 59 Cal. 574, testimony affecting the credibility of another witness; People v. Paden, 71 Cal. App. 247, denial of prior felony conviction; People v. McGee, 103 Cal. App. 149, testimony supporting a false alibi; People v. Rosen, 20 Cal. App. 2d 445, false testimony on a hearing on an order to show cause; Ex parte Carpenter, 64 Cal. 267, false statement under oath before a notary public by one impersonating the grantor in a deed; People v. Waite, 102 Cal. 251, false affidavit for registration; People v. Darcy, 59 Cal. App. 2d 342, false statement as to name and place of birth in registering as a voter; People v. Hitchcock, 104 Cal. 482, false statement as to matter admitted by the defense; People v. Kelly, 59 Cal. 372, and People v. Torterice, 66 Cal. App. 115, giving false age or other material false statement (People v. Brown, 125 Cal. App. 2d 83) in an application for a marriage license; People v. Von Tiedeman, 120 Cal. 128, testimony identifying a photograph; People v. Rodley, 151 Cal. 240, testimony of a witness to a will; People v. Phillips, 57 Cal. App. 291, testimony as to a belief in a fact the witness knew did not exist.

A false statement by a juror on voire dire that if chosen as a juror he would try the case solely upon the evidence and the court's instructions on the law will constitute perjury but in such a case it must be shown that the answer was false at the time it was made. (In re De Martini, 47 Cal. App. 228; People v. De Martini, 50 Cal. App. 109; People v. Raymond, 87 Cal. App. 510.)

A false statement by a person qualifying as a surety on a bail bond for the appearance of another on a charge of grand larceny is not perjury where the charge against such other person is not grand larceny but robbery. (People v. Strassman, 112 Cal. 683.)

Need Not Affect Decision

Materiality does not depend upon whether the alleged false testimony had in fact any effect or influence upon the judge or jury who tried the cause in which it was given. (People v. Macken, 32 Cal. App. 2d 31.) The fact that the alleged perjured statement was not considered in the rendering of the decision in the matter in which it was given or that such statement was intentionally disregarded or was so incredible as to be unworthy of credence does not affect the question of its materiality. Also it would not be a defense to a person charged with perjury upon his former trial on a criminal charge that he was there acquitted. (People v. Housman, 44 Cal. App. 2d 627.)

Upon the trial for perjury the materiality of the matter assigned as perjury is a question of law for the court and not one of fact for the jury. (People v. Senegrim, 27 Cal. App. 303; People v. Phillips, 56 Cal. App. 291; People v. Macken, 32 Cal. App. 2d 31; People v. Brophy, 49 Cal. App. 2d 15; People v. Sagehorn, 140 Cal. App. 2d 138) and it is the province of the court to instruct the jury thereon (cases 1st cited).

Opinion

Testimony of a witness that the speed of his automobile was between 20 and 30 miles per hour when in fact he was going 50 miles per hour constitutes perjury and the fact that he couched his testimony in the form of an opinion does not relieve him from guilt (People v. Dixon, 99 Cal. App. 2d 94).

False Affidavits

"Any person who, in any affidavit taken before a person authorized to administer oaths, swears, affirms, declares, deposes, or certifies that he will testify, declare, depose, or certify before any competent tribunal, officer, or person, in any case then pending or thereafter to be instituted, in any particular manner, or to any particular fact, and in such affidavit willfully and contrary to such oath states as true any material matter which he knows to be false, is guilty of perjury. In any prosecution under this section, the subsequent testimony of such person, in any action involving the matters in such affidavit contained, which is contrary to any of the matters in such affidavit contained, shall be prima facie evidence that the matters in such affidavit were false." (Penal Code, sec. 118a.)

"The making of a deposition, affidavit or certificate is deemed to be complete, within the provisions of this chapter, from the time when it is delivered by the accused to any other person, with the intent that it be uttered or published as true." (Penal Code, sec. 124.)

The word affidavit in the foregoing section includes a deposition. (People v. Robles, 117 Cal. 681.)

To constitute an offense where the charge of perjury is based upon an affidavit, deposition or certificate it is necessary that the accused must have made use of such statement or that it shall have passed out of his possession in connection with the matter with reference to which it was made. (People v. Robles, 117 Cal. 681; People v. Maxwell, 118 Cal. 50; People v. John, 137 Cal. 220; People v. Teixeira, 59 Cal. App. 598.) Thus perjury in the making of false statements in the petition and schedules in insolvency proceedings is complete when the papers are filed with the court. (People v. Maxwell, 118 Cal. 50.)

Corroboration Required

"Perjury must be proved by the testimony of two witnesses, or of one witness and corroborating circumstances." (Penal Code, sec. 1103a; to same effect, Code Civ. Proc. 1968.) This rule dates back to the common law, the reason for the rule originally being that at that time the defendant in a criminal case was not permitted to testify in his own behalf. (People v. Todd, 9 Cal. App. 2d 237.)

A conviction of perjury cannot be based upon the uncorroborated testimony of a single witness (People v. Davis, 61 Cal. 536) or upon evidence that is wholly circumstantial. (People v. Burcham, 69 Cal. App. 614.) The direct evidence required by the law "means that there must be direct evidence only as to the falsity of the testimony charged as perjury." (People v. Rodley, 137 Cal. 240.)

Where, to prove that the defendant had committed perjury in stating that he was in the Long Beach jail on a certain date when he was in fact in the Los Angeles jail on that date, the prosecution depended upon the records of the two jails, the evidence was held insufficient since the falsity of the statement must be proved by the testimony of two witnesses or one witness and corroborating cihcumstances and circumstantial evidence, the jail records, alone, will not support a conviction (People v. O'Donnell, 132 Cal. App. 2d 840).

Satisfying Statute

"The statute respecting the quantum of evidence necessary in perjury cases will be satisfied if there be testimony of one witness to the facts that are absolutely incompatible with the innocence of the accused corroborated by circumstances which, of themselves, and independently of such directly inculpatory evidence, tend, with a reasonable degree of certitude, to show that the accused is guilty as charged." (People v. Casanova, 54 Cal. App. 439; People v. Pustau, 39 Cal. App. 2d 407.) The corroboration need not, however, be such as is absolutely incompatible with defendant's innocence. (People v. Housman, 44 Cal. App. 2d 619.) The "corroborating circumstances" specified by the statute relates to evidence of circumstances which tend to corroborate the facts as to the falsity of the alleged perjured statements (People v. Galbraith, 66 Cal. App. 761; People v. Woodcock, 52 Cal. App. 412), but must be more than tending to prove that the testimony was given. "The law governing the character of corroborative circumstances in a case of perjury is the same as that governing the character of corroborative circumstances in a case where the guilt of an accused is sought to be established by the testimony of an accomplice, and that being so, the corroborative evidence need not be strong, nor even be sufficient in itself without the aid of other evidence to establish the fact. The circumstances legally sufficient to sustain a conviction may consist of the extrajudicial statements, declarations and admissions of the accused; his silence in the face of accusatory statements, or where he voluntarily becomes a witness in his own behalf, and it may be gathered from his testimony." (People v. Todd, 9 Cal. App. 2d 237; see also People v. Follette, 74 Cal. App. 178; People v. Housman, 44 Cal. App. 2d 627; People v. Sagehorn, 140 Cal. App. 2d 138).

Subornation of Perjury

"Every person who willfully procures another person to commit perjury is guilty of subornation of perjury, and is punishable in the same manner as he would be if personally guilty of the perjury so procured." (Penal Code, sec. 127.)

To constitute subornation of perjury it is necessary that some person shall have committed the crime of perjury and that the perjury was committed through the procurement of the person charged with its subornation and that the accused knew that the testimony given was untrue. If the evidence fails to establish that the person who gave the testimony did not in fact commit perjury, as where he gave the testimony in a sincere belief in its truth and under an honest mistake, he is not guilty of perjury and his testimony cannot be the basis of a charge of subornation of perjury.

CHAPTER XXIX

ESCAPE

An escape is the unlawful voluntary departure of a prisoner from lawful custody. (People v. Quijada, 53 Cal. App. 39.)

While there are special statutes governing escapes and attempts to escape from a state prison (Penal Code, secs. 4530, 4531), a public training school or reformatory or county hospital (Penal Code, secs. 107, 109), California Vocational Institution (Penal Code, sec. 2042), or furnishing the means for such an escape (Penal Code, sec. 110) and escapes from state hospitals (Welfare and Institutions Code, sec. 6721), most escapes are from local officers and places of detention and are covered by the statute:

(a) "Every prisoner formally charged with or convicted of a misdemeanor who is confined in any county or city jail or prison or industrial farm or industrial road camp or who is engaged on any county road or other county work or who is in the lawful custody of any officer or person, who escapes or attempts to escape from such county or city jail, prison, industrial farm or industrial road camp or from the custody of the officer or person in charge of him while so engaged on or going to or returning from such county work or from the custody of any officer or person in whose lawful custody he is, is guilty of a felony; and if such escape or attempt to escape was not by force or violence, is punishable by imprisonment in the state prison for not less than six months nor more than five years, regardless of any prior conviction, or in the county jail for not exceeding one year; provided, however, if such escape or attempt to escape is by force or violence, such person is guilty of a felony and is punishable by imprisonment in the state prison not exceeding 10 years, or in the county jail not exceeding one year; provided that when said second term is to be served in the county jail, it shall commence from the time such prisoner would otherwise have been discharged from said jail."

"A conviction of violation of this subdivision, not by force or violence, shall not be charged as a prior felony conviction in any subsequent prosecution for a public offense" (see People v. Lavendera, 151 Cal. App. 2d ......).

(b) "Every prisoner charged with or convicted of a felony who is confined in any county or city jail or prison or industrial farm or industrial road camp or who is engaged on any

362

county road or other county work or who is in the lawful
custody of any officer or person, who escapes or attempts
to escape from such county or city jail, prison, industrial
farm or industrial road camp or from the custody of the
officer or person in charge of him while so engaged on or
going to or returning from such county work or from the
custody of any officer or person in whose lawful custody he
is, is guilty of a felony and is punishable by imprisonment in
the state prison not exceeding 10 years, or in the county jail
not exceeding one year; provided, that when said second term
of imprisonment is to be served in the county jail it shall
commence from the time such prisoner would otherwise have
been discharged from said jail.'' (Penal Code, sec. 4532).

Section 4532 includes the escapes of misdemeanor prisoners
as well as prisoners in custody under a charge of felony. (In
re Halcomb, 21 Cal. 2d 126; In re Haynes, 21 Cal. 2d 891; In re
Petrie, 21 Cal. 2d 132; People v. Smillie, 55 Cal. App. 2d 381.)
This section covers a large variety of escapes since it includes
the escape or attempt to escape ''from the custody of any
officer or person in whose lawful custody he is.''

Where a person, charged with an offense punishable by
either imprisonment in the state prison or the county jail,
escapes, he may be sentenced to the state prison since that
charge is a felony (People v. Segura, 134 Cal. App. 2d 552).

Youth Authority Escape

Any person committed to the Youth Authority who escapes
or attempts to escape from the institution in which he is confined is guilty of a misdemeanor (W. & I. Code, sec. 1768.7).

Imprisonment Must Be Legal

To constitute a punishable escape, the imprisonment or
restraint must have been lawful since, if it be unlawful, the
prisoner cannot be punished for exercising his lawful right to
liberty. (People v. Ah Teung, 92 Cal. 431; People v. Clark,
69 Cal. App. 520.) However, while in such a case the escape
is lawful, it may have been committed in such a manner as to
constitute a separate offense as, for example, that created by
section 606 infra. Where, however, the process is merely irregular in form or the statute under which the prisoner is confined
is unconstitutional the escape is unlawful (cases cited in People
v. Scherbing, 93 Cal. App. 2d 736).

The fact that the conviction would have been reversed on
appeal, the judgment being voidable but not void, or that the

defendant had not been accorded his constitutional rights, will not render his escape from custody, lawful. To justify the escape and render it lawful the case must be one in which the prisoner is at the time clearly entitled to his absolute freedom. If the imprisonment is merely unlawful, based on error or irregularity, the prisoner who understakes to free himself instead of pursuing his remedy through the courts is guilty of an escape (People v. Hinze, 97 Cal. App. 2d 1; People v. Ganger, 97 Cal. App. 2d 11).

Where a warrant had been issued for defendant's arrest on a charge of robbery and an officer, knowing of but not then being in possession of the warrant but knowing of the robbery by the defendant, saw defendant in front of his house and told him he was wanted and that a felony warrant for his arrest was at the police station and defendant ran into the house and the officer followed and again told defendant that he was under arrest and to give himself up and defendant grabbed a knife and the officer drew his gun and defendant's sister intervened and telephoned defendant's lawyer who told her to tell the defendant to go with the officer which she did and defendant asked time to change his shoes, went into a bedroom and escaped by a back entrance, the evidence sustained the conviction (People v. Torres, 152 Cal. App. 2d ...... A.C.A. ....).

When a prisoner is delivered to the warden of San Quentin prison and thereafter transferred to Folsom penitentiary, he is "committed to" the latter prison within the meaning of section 4531 and if he escapes from a convict road camp to which he was transferred from the latter prison, he is guilty of an escape. (People v. French, 61 Cal. App. 275; People v. Warren, 68 Cal. App. 803.)

Where the prisoner, having been made a trusty and been permitted to go outside of the jail, ran away, a conviction of escape was sustained (People v. Hinze, 97 Cal. App. 2d 1).

The term "while being conveyed to prison" applies to the original delivery of the prisoner to prison and also to his transfer from prison to a road camp or from one prison to another. (People v. Upton, 67 Cal. App. 445.)

A prisoner who is legally arrested and booked on "Suspicion" of forgery in a city jail is in legal custody charged with a felony and the form of the booking is no defense to a charge of escape. (People v. Serrano, 123 Cal. App. 339.) Mere irregularity of process (People v. Clark, 69 Cal. App. 520) or insanitary conditions or fear of inhuman punishment will not justify or excuse an escape. (People v. Whipple, 100 Cal. App. 261.)

A person lawfully imprisoned who secures his release by means not authorized by law is guilty of at least a technical escape (Ex part Vance, 90 Cal. 208).

A person serving a term of imprisonment in a state prison is a prisoner therein as well when at work outside under the surveillance of guards as when confined within its walls (Bradford v. Glenn, 188 Cal. 350; People v. Leslie, 118 Cal. App. 2d 700, escape from forestry camp, and cases cited).

"A prisoner committed to the county jail for trial or for examination or upon conviction for a public offense, must be actually confined in the jail until he is legally discharged; and if he is permitted to go at large out of the jail, except by virtue of legal order or process, it is an escape . . ." (Penal Code, sec. 4004). See **Liability of Persons Other Than Prisoner**, infra.)

The defendant was, by order of the trial judge, transferred to the county hospital for treatment, to be kept there during the period of treatment without guard and to be returned to the custody of the sheriff upon recovery and was placed in a locked room with the window covered with a heavy mesh grating locked with a padlock. The defendant sprung the padlock and escaped through the window. Held that the phrase "without guard" relieved the sheriff of the duty of furnishing a guard for the defendant at the hospital but that the hospital authorities had the duty to keep the defendant who was guilty of escape (People v. Priegel, 126 Cal. App. 2d. 587).

Injuring Public Jail

"Every person who wilfully and intentionally breaks down, pulls down, or otherwise destroys or injures any place of confinement, is punishable by fine not exceeding ten thousand dollars, and by imprisonment in the state prison not exceeding five years, except that where the damages or injury to any city, city and county or county place of confinement is determined to be two hundred dollars ($200) or less, he is guilty of a misdemeanor." Section 4600 of the Penal Code has the same provisions but limits its operation to jails or prisons. (Penal Code, sec. 606).

The crime provided for by this section is not included within the crime of escape. Therefore, even if the injury to the place of confinement be an incident to an escape, the prisoner is punishable under this section without regard to or in addition to such punishment as he may incur for the escape. (People v.

Sheldon, 68 Cal. 434.) Though the injury to the jail may consist in various acts—digging a hole in the floor, removing bricks or stones, pulling down or breaking a door, etc.—if committed in pursuance of one intent and purpose, the several acts constitute but one injury and one offense though any one of the acts by itself would constitute the crime. (People v. Sheldon, supra.)

Liability of Persons Other Than Prisoner

"Every keeper of a prison, sheriff, deputy sheriff, constable, or jailer, or person employed as a guard, who fraudulently contrives, procures, aids, connives at, or voluntarily permits the escape of any prisoner in custody, is punishable by imprisonment in the state prison not exceeding ten years, and fine not exceeding ten thousand dollars." (Penal Code, sec. 4533.)

"If the sheriff does voluntarily permit him (such a prisoner) to go at large outside, either with or without escort, the sheriff himself is guilty of permitting an escape." (Pedersen v. Superior Court, 149 Cal. 389.)

"Any person who wilfully assists any paroled prisoner whose parole has been revoked, any escape, any prisoner confined in any prison or jail, or any inmate of any public training school or reformatory, or any person in the lawful custody of any officer or person, to escape, or in an attempt to escape from such prison or jail, or public training school or reformatory, or custody, is punishable as provided in section 4533 of the Penal Code." (Penal Code, sec. 4534.)

One cannot be guilty of assisting a prisoner to escape unless his act of assistance accompanies an actual attempt of the prisoner to escape. If the defendant's act preceded and merely made possible the subsequent escape by the prisoner it is not an escape in which the defendant assisted. An attempt to free a prisoner without any effort on the part of the prisoner is an attempt to rescue and not the offense of assisting an escape and may come within the scope of section 4535 of the Penal Code. (People v. Murphy, 130 Cal. App. 408.)

"Every person who rescues or attempts to rescue or aids another person in rescuing or attempting to rescue any prisoner from any prison, or prison road camp or any jail or county road camp or from any officer or person having him in lawful custody, is punishable as follows:

1. If such prisoner was in custody upon a conviction of a felony punishable with death: By imprisonment in the state prison not less than one nor more than fourteen years;

2. If such prisoner was in custody otherwise than as specified in subsection 1 hereof: By imprisonment in the state prison not to exceed five years, or by imprisonment in the county jail not to exceed one year.'' (Penal Code, sec. 4550).

Taking Aids to Escape Into Jail or Prison

"Every person who carries or sends into a prison or jail anything useful to aid a prisoner or inmate in making his escape, with intent thereby to facilitate the escape of any prisoner or inmate confined therein, is guilty of a felony and shall be imprisoned in the State prison not less than one year.'' (Penal Code, sec. 4535.)

Taking Deadly Weapons Into Jails or Prisons

"Any person not authorized by law, who brings into any State prison or prison road camp or any jail or any county road camp in this State, or within the grounds belonging or adjacent to any such institution, any firearms, deadly weapons or explosives is guilty of a felony and punishable by imprisonment in the State prison for not less than one year.'' (Penal Code, sec. 4574.)

CHAPTER XXX

DANGEROUS WEAPONS CONTROL LAW

Possession of Certain Weapons Prohibited

"Any person in this State, who manufactures or causes to be manufactured, imports into this State, keeps for sale, or offers or exposes for sale, or who gives, lends, or possesses any instrument or weapon of the kind commonly known as a blackjack, slung shot, billy, sandclub, sandbag, or metal knuckles, or who carries concealed upon his person any explosive substance other than fixed ammunition, or who carries concealed upon his person any dirk or dagger, is guilty of a felony, and upon conviction shall be punishable by imprisonment in the county jail not exceeding one year or in a state prison for not less than one year nor more than five years." (Penal Code, sec. 12020).

Elements of Offense

The offense defined by this section does not involve any specific intent. Merely manufacturing, importing, keeping or exposing for sale or possession alone of a black-jack, slungshot, billy, sand-club or metal knuckles constitute the offense and it is immaterial whether the purpose of the accused was good or bad. (People v. Cannizzaro, 138 Cal. App. 28; People v. McKinney, 9 Cal. App. 2d 523.) And it is not necessary that the accused shall have carried the weapon on his person if the weapon be one of those above listed (People v. Voss, 2 Cal. App. 2d 188; People v. Quinones, 140 Cal. App. 609), nor does the law require that the accused shall have been the owner of the weapon. (People v. McKinney, 9 Cal. App. 2d 523.) Where one of these prohibited weapons is found under circumstances justifying the conclusion that it is in the possession of someone, as where it is found in a suitcase in a room occupied by several persons, this is sufficient to establish the corpus delicti of the offense and the admission of the defendant that he is the owner of the weapon will make the evidence sufficient to sustain a conviction. (People v. McKinney, 9 Cal. App. 2d 523.) The trend of the decisions is clearly in the direction of holding that a weapon falls within the terms of the statute if it substantially meets the description in the statute even though it be crudely made and not of the usual form of such weapon. A club 14½ inches long, thicker at one end than the other, with

368

nails driven into the larger end and covered with tape has been held a "billy" or "blackjack." (People v. Canales, 12 Cal. App. 2d 215.) A large number of metal washers strung upon a rawhide thong, the washers forming two parallel masses about three inches long and the excess of the thong forming a loop at the end opposite the knot at the lower end of the washers with ends of the rawhide which could be looped over the wrist was held to be a slungshot or blackjack within the meaning of the statute. (People v. Mulherin, 140 Cal. App. 212.) In another case the defendant had in his possession a flat steel wrench six inches long and weighing five ounces and a looped leather strap about twelve inches long so contrived by means of wire and leather thongs as to allow the wrench to be placed in a pocket at one end while the other end of the strap formed a loop which could be slipped over the wrist of the user and held in the hand. The court held this to be a blackjack or slungshot and that the fact that, when found, the leather device and the wrench were not assembled did not change the character of the weapon. (People v. Williams, 100 Cal. App. 149.) A contrivance made of alternate strips of sheet lead and adhesive tape making a set of knuckles somewhat in the shape of a bracelet and of a size to fit over four finger knuckles is within the term "metal knuckles" as used in the statute and its nature is not altered by the fact that material other than metal went into its construction. (People v. Quinones, 140 Cal. App. 609.)

Where the alleged weapon is in fact an article manufactured, not for use as a weapon but for a lawful and proper use, it is not prima facie a deadly weapon within the terms of the Act even though it could be used as a weapon and, if made to be used as such, would be a weapon under the Act (People v. Golden, 76 Cal. App. 2d 769, a weight on the end of a piece of rope used on shipboard).

Possession—What Constitutes

A person is in possession of an article of personal property when it is under his dominion and control and, to his knowledge, is carried on his person or, if not on his person, the possession thereof is immediate, accessible and exclusive to him or to himself and one or more other persons jointly (see Caljic #41 and cases cited and **Possession of Narcotics**, infra). The one basic essential to possession is that the person have knowledge of the fact that he has possession (People v. Patterson, 102 Cal. App. 2d 675 and cases under **Possession of Narcotics**).

Defining Billy, Bludgeon, Blackjack

The giving of an instruction to the jury defining a "billy" as "a bludgeon, as one for carrying in the pocket, a policeman's club" and defining a "blackjack" as "a short bludgeon consisting of a heavy head as of metal, on an elastic shaft or with a flexible handle" was approved in a case in which an instruction that "Under the law a blackjack is a leather covered billy or club weighted at the head and having a flexible shaft" was held properly refused (People v. Mulherin, 140 Cal. App. 212) for the reason that it is not necessary to constitute a weapon a blackjack that it be covered with anything. The fact that metal knuckles or any of the weapons listed in section 1 are heirlooms, mementos or curios is not a defense to a charge under this section of unlawfully having possession thereof. (People v. Ferguson, 129 Cal. App. 300. Note: The court, however, expressly refrained from expressing an opinion as to whether the statute was applicable to museum keepers.)

That portion of the section applicable to explosives or a dirk or dagger has an additional element in that the prohibited weapon must be carried concealed upon the person. A British bayonet with a portion filed off, which could be worn on the body, has been held a dagger within the definition "any straight knife to be worn on the person which is capable of inflicting death except what is commonly called a pocket knife," the court also holding that the terms "dirk" and "dagger" are used synonymously and may consist of any straight stabbing weapon fitted primarily for stabbing and that the word "dagger" is a generic term covering the dirk, dagger, poniard, stiletto, etc. (People v. Ruiz, 88 Cal. App. 502.)

Possession of Firearms by Aliens, Exconvicts and Narcotic Addicts

"Any person who is not a citizen of the United States and any person who has been convicted of a felony under the laws of the United States, of the State of California, or any other state, government or country, or who is addicted to the use of any narcotic drug, who owns or has in his possession or under his custody or control any pistol, revolver, or other firearm capable of being concealed upon the person is guilty of a public offense, and shall be punishable by imprisment in the state prison not exceeding five years, or in a county jail not exceeding one year or by a fine not exceeding five hundred dollars ($500), or by both." (Penal Code, sec. 12021.)

In cases of possession of a firearm by an ex-convict the penalty provided by this section is not affected or increased by reason of any one or more prior felony convictions (In re Rodgers, 121 Cal. App. 370). This section is constitutional (People v. Cordero, 50 Cal. App. 2d 140; People v. Garcia, 97 Cal. App. 2d 733; see also People v. Wells, 68 Cal. App. 2d 476).

Possession by State Prisoner

Where the offender is a prisoner in the custory of state prison officials and has in his possession any of the weapons mentioned in section 12020 or any firearm, the offense is punishable by not less than five years in the state prison (Penal Code, sec. 4502). The intention with which the weapon is possessed is not an element of the offense (People v. Marcus, 120 Cal. App. 2d. 347; People v. Marcus, 133 Cal. App. 2d. 579).

Capable of Being Concealed Upon the Person

The terms "pistol", "revolver", and "other firearms capable of being concealed upon the person" as used in the Dangerous Weapons Control Law "apply to and include all firearms having a barrel less than twelve inches in length." (Penal Code, sec. 12001.)

Illustrated Cases

Section 12021 punishes the mere ownership, possession, custody or control of a pistol, revolver or other firearm capable of being concealed upon the person, i.e., having a barrel less than twelve inches in length, by a person who has been convicted of a felony, or who is not a citizen of the United States or who is a narcotic addict. The term "convicted of a felony" applies to every person who by plea or upon a trial is found guilty of a felony regardless of whether he served a term of imprisonment for such offense or whether he was granted probation. (See **Felony and Misdemeanor Distinguished**.) Mere possession of a prohibited firearm by an alien, a narcotic addict or one who has been convicted of a felony is sufficient to constitute the offense and the offense does not include in its corpus delicti any specific intent (People v. Gonzales, 72 Cal. App. 626; People v. Cannizzaro, 138 Cal. App. 28), nor is it necessary that the accused have the weapon concealed on his person. (People v. Voss, 2 Cal. App. 2d 188.) The fact that the firearm was out of repair, not capable of striking the primer of an old shell with sufficient force to discharge it and that the trigger had to be reset by hand after each shot was held not to bring it within the exception of being an antique. (People v. McCloskey, 76 Cal. App. 227.) The fact that the firearm was disassembled into two or more parts does not take it out of the operation of the statute (People v. Ekberg, 94 Cal. App. 2d 613).

In a prosecution for the possession of a dangerous weapon by a person who has been convicted of a felony, the conviction of the defendant in another state of an offense which is a felony in that state brings the defendant within the statute and those of our California statutes which consider prior felony convictions as an element of penalty (such as Penal Code section 668) have no application (People v. Domenico, 121 Cal. App. 2d 124).

The fact that the defendant is an unnaturalized alien and not a citizen of the United States may be established by circumstantial evidence. (People v. Bedoy, 80 Cal. App. 783.)

Where the evidence shows that the defendant is an alien, in this case a native of the Philippine Islands, the burden is upon him to prove citizenship. (People v. Cordero, 50 Cal. App. 2d 146.)

The statute prohibiting the possession of weapons by aliens, narcotic addicts and ex-convicts is a proper exercise of the police power and constitutional (People v. Cordero, 50 Cal. App. 2d 146; People v. Garcia, 97 Cal. App. 2d 733). Ownership of the weapon is not essential mere possession being a violation of the law (People v. Garcia, 97 Cal. App. 2d 733).

Where a person falling within the prohibited class has in his possession at the same time two or more firearms the possession of which is made unlawful by the statute there is but one offense but if it can be shown that after having possession of one such weapon he subsequently came into the possession of another such weapon there would be two possessions and two separate offenses. (People v. Pupillo, 100 Cal. App. 559.)

Excepted Persons

Persons not prohibited from possessing firearms under the provisions of section 12021 may own and possess such firearms under the provisions of section 12026 and those persons to whom section 12025 does not apply are listed in section 12027 of the Penal Code.

"Nothing in this chapter prohibits police officers, special police officers, peace officers, or law enforcement officers from carrying any wooden club, baton, or any equipment authorized for the enforcement of the law or ordinance in any city or county." (Penal Code, sec. 12002).

Concealed Weapon

"Except as otherwise provided in this chapter, any person who carries concealed upon his person or within any vehicle which is under his control or direction any pistol, revolver, or other firearm capable of being concealed upon the person without having a license to carry such firearm as provided in this chapter is guilty of a misdemeanor, and if he has been convicted previously of a felony or of any crime made punishable by this chapter, is guilty of a felony.

"Firearms carried openly in belt holsters are not concealed within the meaning of this section, nor are knives which are carried openly in sheaths suspended from the waist of the wearer." (Penal Code, sec. 12025.)

In view of the use of the word "knives" in this section this rule does not apply to a "dirk" or "dagger", especially since the words are not synonymous.

The mere fact that a firearm is carried in an automobile is not a violation of the law if it is not concealed. (People v. Frost, 125 Cal. App. 794.)

Tampering With Marks on Firearms

"Any person who changes, alters, removes or obliterates the name of the maker, model, manufacturer's number, or other mark of identification, including any distinguishing number or mark assigned by the State Bureau of Criminal Identification and Investigaton, on any pistol or revolver without first having secured written permission from the bureau to make such change, alteration or removal shall be punished by imprisonment in the state prison for not less than one year nor more than five years." (Penal Code, sec. 12090).

"Possession of any pistol or revolver upon which the name of the maker, model, manufacturer's number or other mark of identification has been changed, altered, removed or obliterated, shall be presumptive evidence that the possessor has changed, altered, removed or obliterated the same." (Penal Code, sec. 12091). Held constitutional (People v. Scott, 24 Cal. 2d 774).

Committing Felony While Armed—Penalty

"Any person who commits or attempts to commit any felony within this state while armed with any of the weapons mentioned in section 12020 or while armed with any pistol, revolver, or other firearm capable of being concealed upon the person, without having a license or permit to carry such firearm as provided in this chapter, upon conviction of such felony or of an attempt to commit such felony, shall in addition to the punishment prescribed for the crime of which he has been convicted, be punishable by imprisonment in a state prison for not less than five nor more than 10 years. Such additional period of imprisonment shall commence upon the expiration or other termination of the sentence imposed for the crime of which he is convicted and shall not run concurrently with such sentence.

"Upon a second conviction under like circumstances the additional period of imprisonment shall be for not less than 10 years nor more than 15 years, and upon a third conviction under like circumstances the additional period of imprisonment shall be for not less than 15 nor for more than 25 years, such additional imprisonment to run consecutively.

"Upon a fourth or subsequent conviction under like circumstances the person so convicted may be imprisoned for life or for a term of not less than 25 years, within the discretion of the court in which the fourth or subsequent conviction was had." (Penal Code, sec. 12022.)

This section of the Dangerous Weapons Control Law does not create a separate offense but merely imposes an additional penalty in cases where the perpetrator of a felony was armed with any one of the prohibited weapons at the time the offense was committed. The section is mandatory that such additional penalty shall be consecutive to the term imposed for the felony itself and the court has no discretion such as it ordinarily has under section 669 of the Penal Code under which the court may order sentences to run either concurrently or consecutively. (People v. Shull, 23 Cal. 2d 745.)

Section 12022 does not, however, apply to a case in which the element of being armed with the particular weapon is an essential element of the corpus delicti. In other words if the fact of being so armed is necessarily used in making up the crime charged, the fact of being armed can not again be used to bring the case within section 12022 and the infliction of the additional penalty therein provided. Thus upon a conviction of assault with a deadly weapon, wherein the possession of the weapon standing alone would be a violation of the Dangerous Weapon Control Act, section 12022 does not apply. (People v. Shull, 23 Cal. 2d 745.)

Prima Facie Evidence of Intent

Section 12022 also provides: "In the trial of a person charged with committing or attempting to commit a felony against the person of another while armed with any of the weapons mentioned in section 12020, or while armed with any pistol, revolver, or other firearm capable of being concealed upon the person, without having a license or permit to carry such firearm as provided by this chapter, the fact that he was so armed shall be prima facie evidence of his intent to commit the felony." (Penal Code, sec. 12023.)

This section has been held violative of the due process of law clause of the Constitution and the giving of an instruction in the language quoted is reversible error. (People v. Murguia, 6 Cal. 2d 194; see also People v. Delgado, 28 Cal. App. 2d 665.)

Machine Guns

Under the Machine Gun Law (Penal Code, section 12200, 12201, 12220, 12230) every person who "sells, offers for sale, possesses or knowingly transports any firearm of the kind commonly known as a machine gun" is punishable by imprisonment in the state prison for not exceeding five years or by a fine not exceeding five thousand dollars or both such fine and imprisonment. The law excepts police, sheriffs, marshals, military and naval forces, defines what constitutes a machine gun and provides for permits where good cause for their issuance exists. The mere fact of possession of a firearm which is a machine gun is a violation of the statute and knowledge of the defendant of the fact the weapon is a machine gun within the law is not an essential element of the offense (People v. Daniels, 118 Cal. App. 2d 340).

CHAPTER XXXI

FELONIES UNDER CALIFORNIA VEHICLE CODE

Revocation of Driver's License

The California Vehicle Code makes special provision for felonies involving the operation or use of an automobile and also provides that the Department of Motor Vehicles shall immediately revoke the license and privilege to operate a motor vehicle of any person convicted of any of such felonies or of any felony in the commission of which a motor vehicle was used and such privilege cannot be renewed until the expiration of one year after the date of revocation. (Sec. 304, C.V.A.) This latter provision is practically an increase or addition to any penalty imposed upon the conviction of a defendant of any felony in the perpetration of which an automobile was used, (In re Von Perhacs, 190 Cal. 364; People v. O'Rourke, 124 Cal. App. 752) and such license may be revoked without notice and solely upon the fact of such conviction. (Cases last cited.)

DRIVING UNDER INFLUENCE OF LIQUOR

"Any person who, while under the influence of intoxicating liquor, drives a vehicle and when so driving does any act forbidden by law or neglects any duty imposed by law in the driving of such vehicle, which act or neglect proximately causes bodily injury to any person other than himself, is guilty of a felony and upon conviction thereof shall be punished by imprisonment in the State prison for not less than one year nor more than five years or in the County jail for not less than 90 days nor more than one year and by fine of not less than two hundred fifty dollars ($250) nor more than five thousand dollars ($5000)." (C.V.A. sec. 501).

To constitute a violation of section 501 it is not necessary that the driver of the vehicle be "drunk" or "intoxicated" but only that he be "under the influence of intoxicating liquor," which clause has been thus defined: "If intoxicating liquor has so far affected the nervous system, brain or muscles of the driver of an automobile as to impair to an appreciable degree his ability to operate his car in the manner that an ordinarily prudent and cautious man, in the full possession of his faculties, using reasonable care, would operate or drive a similar vehicle under like conditions, then such

376

driver is 'under the influence of intoxicating liquor' within the meaning of the statute.'' (People v. Dingle, 56 Cal. App. 445; People v. Ekstromer, 71 Cal. App. 239; People v. McKee. 80 Cal. App. 200.) This rule is approved in People v. Haeussler, 41 Cal. 2d 252, and the dictum of Taylor v. Joyce, 4 Cal. App. 2d 612 and People v. Lewis, 4 Cal. App. 2d (Supp.) 725 that ''under the influence of intoxicating liquor'' is synonymous with ''intoxicated'' is disapproved, the court holding, however, that they are correct in so far as they hold that a person who is intoxicated also is under the influence of intoxicating liquor.

Unlawful Driving Necessary

To constitute the crime it is essential that while driving the vehicle under the influence of intoxicating liquor the driver shall do some act forbidden by law or shall neglect to perform some duty imposed by law in the driving of such vehicle and thereby proximately cause bodily injury to some person (People v. Levens, 28 Cal. App. 2d 455), such as running into a disabled car stopped on the highway and injuring a mechanic between such car and the car which had been towing it (People v. Dawes, 37 Cal. App. 2d 44) or driving on the wrong side of the road causing a collision with a motorcycle and injuring the rider (People v. Trantham, 24 Cal. App. 2d 177) driving an automobile on the wrong side of a highway and striking another car (People v. Hill, 116 Cal. App. 2d 212) driving with a dirty windshield (People v. Graybehl, 67 Cal. App. 2d 210).

It is not sufficient, however, that, in addition to driving a vehicle while under the influence of intoxicating liquor, the driver did some act forbidden by law or neglected some duty imposed by law unless such act or neglect was the proximate cause of bodily injury to another. (In re Ryan, 61 Cal. App. 2d 310.)

Proximate Cause

The proximate cause of an injury is that cause which, in natural and continuous sequence, unbroken by any efficient intervening cause, produces the injury, and without which the result would not have occurred. It is the efficient cause—the one that necessarily sets in operation the factors that accomplish the injury. (BAJI, 3rd ed., 104.)

This does not mean that the law seeks and recognizes only one proximate cause of an injury, consisting of only one factor, one act, one element of circumstances, or the conduct of only one person. To the contrary, the acts and omissions of two or more persons may work concurrently as the efficient cause of an injury, and in such case, each of the participating acts or omissions is regarded in law as a proximate cause. (BAJI, 3rd ed., 104A.)

The element of the corpus delicti that the driver of the vehicle was under the influence of intoxicating liquor may be established by proof that all of the occupants of the vehicle were in such condition (People v. Ellena, 67 Cal. App. 683), but before a defendant can be convicted it must be shown that he was the driver of the vehicle and proof which goes no further than to show that the defendant, even though he was the owner of the vehicle, was in the car is not sufficient proof that he was driving it. (People v. Kelly, 27 Cal. App. 2d 771.) The condition of the driver may be shown by proof of the manner in which he operated the vehicle. (People v. Fellows, 139 Cal. App. 337.)

Section 501 is not limited to cases in which the vehicle was driven upon a public highway. (People v. Stanley, 13 Cal. App. 2d 559; People v. Knight, 35 Cal. App. 2d 472.)

Contributory negligence on the part of the person injured or of some other person is not a defense to a prosecution under section 501. (People v. Fator, 14 Cal. App. 2d 403.)

DRIVING BY NARCOTIC ADDICT OR UNDER INFLUENCE OF A DRUG

"(a) It is unlawful for any person who is addicted to the use, or under the influence, of narcotic drugs or amphetamine or any derivative thereof to drive a vehicle upon any highway. Any person convicted under this subsection shall be guilty of a felony and upon conviction thereof shall be punished by imprisonment in the State prison for not less than one year nor more than five years or in the county jail for not less than 90 days nor more than one year or by a fine of not less than two hundred dollars ($200) nor more than five thousand dollars ($5000) or by both such fine and imprisonment.

"(b) It is unlawful for any person under the influence of any drug, other than a narcotic or amphetamine or any derivative thereof to a degree which renders him incapable of safely driving a vehicle, to drive a vehicle upon any highway. Any person convicted under this subsection shall be guilty of a misdemeanor and shall be punished by imprisonment in the county jail not to exceed one year or by a fine of not to exceed five hundred dollars ($500) or both.

"(c) The fact that any person charged with a violation of this section is or has been entitled to use such drugs or amphetamin or any derivative thereof under the laws of this state shall not constitute a defense against any violation of this section." (C.V.A. sec. 506).

"Under the Influence of"

The phrase "under the influence of narcotic drugs" means almost the same as the phrase "under the influence of intoxicating liquor" used in section 501 of the California Vehicle Code, the only difference being that under the latter section the condition described results from the use of intoxicating liquor while under section 506 such condition must be the result of the use of a narcotic drug.

Section 506 does not, as does section 501, require that the vehicle be driven in an unlawful manner or that any injury to either person or property shall result from the driving of the vehicle.

No Unlawful Driving

This section makes the mere driving of a vehicle a felony if the driver be a narcotic addict and, where the driver is a narcotic addict, the law is violated even though the use of the drug had no effect upon his ability to drive such vehicle. (People v. Berner, 28 Cal. App. 2d 392.) The section is, however, applicable only when the driving is upon a public highway.

Subdivision b of the section covers those cases in which the driver is under the influence of a drug other than a narcotic.

Driving While Under the Influence of Dangerous Drugs

"Any person who, while knowingly under the influence of any dangerous drug, other than a narcotic, to a degree which renders him incapable of safely driving a vehicle and when so driving does any act forbidden by law or neglects any duty imposed by law in the driving of such vehicle, which act or neglect proximately causes bodily injury to any person other than himself is guilty of a felony and upon conviction thereof shall be punished by imprisonment in the state prison for not less than one year nor more than five years or in the county jail for not less than 90 days nor more than one year or by fine of not less than two hundred dollars ($200) nor more than five thousand dollars ($5000) or by both such fine and imprisonment.

"Any person who commits any of the acts specified in this section, while under the influence of any dangerous drug, other than a narcotic, to a degree which renders him incapable of safely driving a vehicle, shall be presumed to have knowledge that he is under the influence of such drug. This presumption may be rebutted." (Vehicle Code sec. 506.1).

FAILURE TO STOP AFTER ACCIDENT

"The driver of any vehicle involved in an accident resulting in injury to any person other than himself or death of any person shall immediately stop such vehicle at the scene of such accident and shall fulfill the requirements of Section 482 (a) hereof and any person failing to stop or to comply with said requirements under such crcumstances is guilty of a public offense and upon conviction thereof shall be punished by imprisonment in the State prison for not less than one year nor more than five years or in the county jail for not to exceed six months or by a fine of not to exceed five hundred dollars ($500) or by both." (C.V.A. sec. 480.)

"The driver of any vehicle involved in an accident resulting in injury to or death of any person shall also give his name, address and the registration number of the vehicle he is driving, the name of the owner, and shall upon request and if available exhibit his operator's or chauffeur's license to the person struck or the driver or occupants of any vehicle collided with or shall give such information and exhibit such license to any traffic or police officer at the scene of the accident and shall render to any person injured in such accident reasonable assistance, including the carrying or the making arrangements for the carrying of such person to a physician, surgeon or hospital for medical or surgical treatment if it is apparent that such treatment is necessary or if such carrying is requested by the injured person. In the event of death of any person resulting from an accident, the driver of any vehicle involved must, after fulfilling the requirements of Section 480 of this code and the foregoing requirements of this subsection, and if there be no traffic or police officer at the scene of the accident to whom to give the information required by this subsection shall, without delay, report such accident to the nearest office of the California Highway Patrol or office of a duly authorized police authority and submit

with such report the information required by this subsection."
(C. V. A. sec. 482, subd. a.)

Failure To Do Any One Act Sufficient

The failure to do any one of the things required by the statute is a crime under these sections (People v. Scofield, 203 Cal. 703; People v. Huber, 64 Cal. App. 352) but the jury must be unanimous as to the one or more of these duties which the defendant failed to perform before they can convict. (People v. Scofield, 203 Cal. 703.)

These sections include not only a case in which a pedestrian or occupant of another vehicle involved in the accident but also a case in which a person riding in the car of the defendant is injured. (People v. Kinney, 28 Cal. App. 2d 232.)

Since the statute formerly applied to "the driver of any vehicle which strikes any person or collides with any other vehicle" but was changed to apply to "the driver of any vehicle involved in an accident" the present statute must be held to apply not only to the driver of a car which is the colliding force but to any case in which the vehicle is involved in an accident. Also the statute applies whether the accident was due to the negligence or unlawful act of such driver or of some other person, the concurrent negligence of two or more persons or whether the accident was unavoidable. (People v. Scofield, 203 Cal. 703.) The duties required by the law are not limited to the performance of the required acts toward pedestrians or occupants of other vehicles who are injured but must also be performed by the driver where an occupant of his car is injured (People v. Kinney, 28 Cal. App. 2d 232).

This crime does not include a specific intent as one of the elements of the offense. (People v. Henry, 23 Cal. App. 2d 155.)

"Involved In An Accident"

The words "involved in an accident" are not limited to cases involving the striking of a pedestrian or other car or object but include all machines involved in accidents of any nature in which another individual is injured or killed (People v. Green, 96 Cal. App. 2d 283, passenger fell out of a moving car and was injured; People v. Kinney, 28 Cal. App. 2d 232, car overturned while being driven and a passenger was injured; People v. Sell, 96 Cal. App. 2d 521, where the act of the defendant was the proximate cause of the accident his car having sideswiped another car which collided with a third car the personal injuries resulting from such collision).

Knowledge of Injury

It is essential to a violation of sections 480, 482a, that the driver must have known that the vehicle he was driving was involved in an accident resulting in personal injuries to another (People v. Ely, 203 Cal. 628; People v. Bowlin, 19 Cal. App. 2d 397; People v. Rallo, 119 Cal. App. 393; People v. Wallace, 2 Cal. App. 2d 238) and the absence of such knowledge is a complete defense. While the accused is the only person who could state whether or not he had such knowledge, his mere denial of such knowledge is not conclusive and the jury is not bound to accept his denial and may, upon the evidence of the circumstances, conclude that he had such knowledge (People v. Henry, 23 Cal. App. 2d 155). Such knowledge may be proved by the circumstances attending and following the accident, such as the conduct of the defendant, the manner of his driving at the time of the accident or leaving the scene, the location and nature of the injuries to his vehicle, as well as by his subsequent conduct or declarations. (People v. De Vries, 69 Cal. App. 201; People v. Pahner, 10 Cal. App. 2d 294; People v. Henry, 23 Cal. App. 2d 155; People v. Roche, 49 Cal. App. 2d 459; People v. Moody, 93 Cal. App. 2d 66.)

"Shall Immediately Stop"

The phrase "shall immediately stop such vehicle at the scene of the accident" means that the driver shall promptly stop at the scene of the accident for the purpose of rendering necessary aid to the person injured and to give the information required by the law. The word "immediately" does not mean "instantly" and the law does not require the performance of that which is impossible. Where the driver stops as promptly as is reasonably possible under the circumstances he has complied with the duty to stop imposed by the statute. (People v. Odom, 19 Cal. App. 2d 64; People v. Steele, 100 Cal. App. 639.)

The word "immediately" applies to the word "stop" but is not to be construed as limiting or modifying the words of the statute setting forth the duties to be performed in the giving of the required information and the rendering of aid. A driver might have a valid excuse or justification for not stopping immediately but, if such be the case, it would not relieve him from complying with the further requirements of the law and, if though not stopping immediately after the accident, there was still sufficient time for the driver to return and give the information and render the assistance required by the law his failure so to do is a violation of the statute. (People v. Steele, 100 Cal. App. 639, wherein defendant, the owner of the car, took the wheel from the person who had been driving at the time of the accident when the latter stopped the car four blocks from the scene of the collision and then drove in a direction away from the victim and the conviction was sustained.)

Must Stop in All Cases

The duty imposed upon the driver of an automobile who has knowledge that his vehicle has been involved in an accident is a duty which he must perform in all cases regardless of whether the accident was unavoidable or, if due to carelessness or unlawful act, regardless of who may have been responsible for causing the accident. (People v. Graves, 74 Cal. App. 415; People v. Campridon, 204 Cal. 701; People v. Leutholtz, 102 Cal. App. 493.)

Even though the person injured is killed or so seriously injured that assistance is no longer necessary and the information which the law provides and requires can not be given the driver must still stop and stand ready to comply with the provisions of the law. (People v. McKee, 80 Cal. App. 200.) Merely stopping and then driving on is not a compliance with the law (People v. Halbert, 78 Cal. App. 598) even though the driver upon stopping is told that the victim is dead. (People v. McIntyre, 213 Cal. 50.)

Where Information Can Not Be Given

Where the driver of a vehicle involved in an accident can not under the circumstances give the information required by the statute to the injured party his failure to do so is not in violation of the section (People v. Scofield, 203 Cal. 703) and where the injured person is killed (People v. Reid, 106 Cal. App. 616) or where the necessary assistance is being given to a victim of the accident by other persons (People v. Scofield, 203 Cal. 703) the driver is relieved of the duty of rendering aid.

Owner May Be Deemed Driver

"The owner of a machine who is riding therein, having control of its operation at the time of the accident, may be deemed to be the driver thereof for the purpose of this section, even though another person may be actually at the steering wheel." (People v. Rallo, 119 Cal. App. 393; People v. Odom, 19 Cal. App. 2d 641.)

Aiding and Abetting

Where the driver of a vehicle violates this section by failing to stop, a passenger riding with him who urges him to drive on is a principal and may be convicted by reason of such aiding and abetting. (People v. Graves, 74 Cal. App. 415.)

Failure to Report Accident

Where the deceased fell or jumped from an automobile in which she was riding as a passenger and was killed and defendant the driver failed to report the accident as required by the latter portion of section 482, subd. a, a conviction was sustained (People v. Donald, 139 Cal. App. 2d 855).

UNLAWFUL TAKING OF A VEHICLE

"Any person who drives or takes a vehicle not his own, without the consent of the owner thereof and with intent to either permanently or temporarily deprive the owner thereof of his title to or possesion of such vehicle, whether with or without intent to steal the same, or any person who is a party or accessory to or an accomplice in any such driving or unauthorized taking or stealing is guilty of a felony, and upon conviction thereof shall be punished by imprisonment in the State prison for not less than one year nor more than five years or in the county jail for not more than one year or by a fine of not more than five thousand dollars ($5000) or by both such fine and imprisonment. The consent of the owner of a vehicle to its taking or driving shall not in any case be presumed or implied because of such owner's consent on a previous occasion to the taking or driving of such vehicle by the same or a different person." (C. V. A. sec. 503.)

Distinguished from Larceny

This offense differs from the larceny of an automobile in that the intent to permanently deprive the owner of his property, a necessary element of the corpus delicti of larceny, is not essential and it is sufficient if the intent be merely to temporarily deprive the owner of the possession of his vehicle. (People v. Zervas, 61 Cal. App. 2d 381; People v. Orona, 72 Cal. App. 2d. 478).

To constitute this offense there must be some moving or asportation of the vehicle but any such moving or asportation, however slight, is sufficient. (People v. White, 71 Cal. App. 2d 524, car pushed twenty feet.)

What Constitutes the Offense

Where officers observed the defendant driving the car several hours after it had been unlawfully taken, without the consent of the owner, and in the car was found a stolen license plate and defendant failed to testify or offer any evidence the conviction was sustained (People v. Holland, 82 Cal. App. 2d. 310).

The asportation may be proved by circumstantial evidence and proof that defendant was seen getting out of the car several hours after it was taken, his glove was found on the back seat of the car, no other persons were in the vicinity and the motor was left running is sufficient to show the commission of the offense (People v. Ragone, 84 Cal. App. 2d. 476).

Proof that a car was taken without the consent of the owner and five hours later the defendant was found seated back of the steering wheel, the car then being parked a mile from where it was taken, the ignition on but the engine not running, and that the car was not parked there shortly before it was discovered, will sustain a conviction (People v. Valdez, 14 Cal. App. 2d. 580).

On the other hand the mere fact that the defendant was seated in a car which had been unlawfully taken and that his fingerprint was found on the rear vision mirror (People v. Flores, 58 Cal. App. 2d. 764) or that the defendant had ridden as a passenger (People v. Lewis, 81 Cal. App. 2d. 119) is not sufficient.

CHAPTER XXXII

NARCOTIC FELONY OFFENSES
(Division 10, Health and Safety Code)

"Narcotics" as used in this division of the Health and Safety Code means any of the following: (a) Cocaine, (b) Opium. (c) Morphine. (d) Codiene. (e) Heroin. (f) Alpha eucaine. (g) Beta eucaine. (h) All parts of the plant Cannabis sativa L. (commonly known as marihuana), whether growing or not; the seeds thereof; the resin extracted from any part of such plant; and every compound, manufacture, salt, derivative, mixture, or preparation of such plant, its seeds or resin; except as otherwise provided by law. (i) Isonipecaine. (j) Amidone. (k) Any substance decreed to be a narcotic as provided in section 11002.1 which provides that the chief of the Narcotic Division may add new narcotics to those enumerated in sections 11001 and 11002. (l) All parts of the plant of the geni Lophophora whether growing or otherwise; the buttons thereof; the alkaloids extracted from such plant; and every compound, salt, derivative, mixture or preparation of such plant. (m) Dromoran. (n) Nisentil. (o) Ketobemidine. (sec. 11001. Note: Technical chemical definitions included in the above paragraph have been omitted).

" 'Narcotics,' as used in this division, also means any of the salts, derivatives, or compounds of a narcotic or any preparation or compound containing a narcotic or its salts, derivatives, or compounds." (sec. 11002.) (See People v. Nordeste, 125 Cal. App. 2d. 462, sale of a derivative of morphine sustained.)

" 'Cannabis sativa' as used in this division, means the male and female of any species commonly known as cannabis sativa, hemp, Indian hemp, or marihuana." (sec. 11003.)

The foregoing definitions of the word "narcotic" apply only to that term as used in the provisions of Division 10 of the Health and Safety Code which does not cover other narcotics not included in the definitions. Other sections of our laws using the word "narcotic" in the definition of crimes thereunder are not affected by the limited definition of the Health and Safety Code.

Giving, Selling, Possessing, etc.

"Except as otherwise provided in this division, no person shall possess, transport, import into this state, sell, furnish, administer or give away, or offer to transport, import into this state, sell, furnish, administer or give away, or attempt to transport or import into this state, a narcotic except upon the written prescription of a physician, dentist, chiropodist or veterinarian licensed to practice in this State." (sec. 11500.)

This section is constitutional (People v. Mistriel, 110 Cal. App. 2d 110).

The words "no person" in this section mean exactly what they say and physicians, dentists, chiropodists and veterinarians are not excluded and are as liable for violations of this section as any other person unless the case comes within one of the exceptions or exemptions provided for in the Health and Safety Code (People v. Jackson, 106 Cal. App. 2d 114).

Prescription—Burden of Proof

The burden of proving the defense that the defendant had a lawful prescription for the narcotic is upon the defendant and in the absence of such proof it must be assumed that the defendant had no such prescription (People v. Moronati, 70 Cal. App. 17; People v. Bill, 140 Cal. App. 389).

Growing Marihuana

"No person shall plant, cultivate, harvest, dry or process any Cannabis sativa, also known as indian hemp or marihuana, or any part thereof, or any of the geni of the Lophophora, also known as peyote, or any of the parts thereof." (sec. 11530).

Maintaining Place for Disposal of Narcotics

"It is unlawful to open or maintain any place for the purpose of unlawfully selling, giving away or using any narcotic." (sec. 11557), (see People v. Cannon, 148 Cal. App. 2d 163 A.C.A. 163).

Penalties—Possession, etc.

"Any person convicted under this division for having in possession any narcotic, or of violating the provisions of sections 11530 or 11557 shall be punished by imprisonment in the county jail for not more than one year or in the state prison for not more than 10 years.

"If such person has been previously convicted of any offense described in this division or has been previously convicted of any offense under the laws of any other state or of the United States which if committed in this State would have been punishable as an offense described in this division, the previous conviction shall be charged in the indictment or information and if found to be true by the jury, upon a jury trial, or if found to be true by the court, upon a court trial, or is admitted by the defendant, he shall be imprisoned in the state prison for not less than two years nor more than 20 years." (sec. 11712.)

Where a defendant was convicted of possession of narcotics and had admitted a charge of prior conviction of violating section 11500 of the Health and Safety Code the court struck out the allegation of prior conviction and sentenced the defendant to the county jail, the order and sentence were sustained (People v. Burke, 47 Cal. 2d 45).

Penalty for Selling, Furnishing, Transporting

"Any person convicted under this division for transporting, selling, furnishing or giving away, or offering to transport, sell, furnish, or give away, any narcotic shall be punished by imprisonment in the county jail for not more than one year, or in the state prison from five years to life.

"If such person has been previously convicted of any offense described in this division or has been previously convicted of any offense under the laws of any other state or of the United States which if committed in this State would have been punishable as an offense described in this division, the previous conviction shall be charged in the indictment or information and if found to be true by the jury, upon a jury trial, or if found to be true by the court, upon a court trial, or is admitted by the defendant, he shall be imprisoned in the state prison from ten years to life." (sec. 11713.)

"Sale," "Transport" Defined

" 'Sale,' as used in this division, includes barter, exchange or gift, or offer thereof, and each such transaction made by nished or given to any person and then sells, delivers, furnishes, transports, administers or gives or offers, arranges or negotiates to have sold, delivered, transported, furnished, administered, or given to any person any other liquid, substance, or material in lieu of any narcotic shall be punished by imprisonment in the county jail for not more than one any person whether as principal, proprietor, agent, servant or employee." (sec. 11008.)

Agreeing, Consenting, Offering, etc. to Sell,

" 'Transport' as used in this division, with reference to narcotics, includes 'conceal,' 'convey' or 'carry'." (sec. 11012.)

"Every person who agrees, consents, or in any manner offers to unlawfully sell, furnish, transport, administer, or give any narcotic to any person, or offers, arranges, negotiates to

Furnish, Transport, etc. Substance in Lieu of Narcotic

have any narcotic unlawfully sold, delivered, transported, fur-year, or in the state prison for not more than 10 years." (sec. 11502.)

"Offering"

While there has been no judicial determination of what is necessary to constitute the offense of offering to sell, barter, exchange or give a prohibited narcotic, the principle is indicated by the interpretations given to the statutes punishing the offering of a bribe whereby it has been decided that to constitute an offer it is not necessary that any particular language be used to convey the offer and that it is sufficient if the language and conduct, viewed in the light of the circumstances, warrant the conclusion that such an offer is being made, that it is not necessary to an offer that an actual tender of the narcotic be made, and that it need not be proved that the accused in fact had such narcotic in his possession. (See People v. Ford, 81 Cal. App. 449.)

Exceptions

The exceptions referred to in section 11500 are the legal furnishing of a narcotic through a legitimate prescription of a physician, dentist, chiropodist or veterinarian in the regular practice of their respective professions (sections 11161 to 11451) and the legitimate sale to the members of the above professions by retailers, jobbers, wholesalers and manufacturers and sales between such dealers (sections 11570 to 11576) all of which transactions are strictly regulated and limited by the statutes. It is specially provided that no person shall prescribe for or administer a narcotic to an addict or to any person representing himself as such (sec. 11164) and physicians are prohibited from furnishing or prescribing narcotics in order to satisfy the narcotic addiction of a user of narcotics (sec. 11331) and no person may be treated for narcotic addiction except in an institution approved by the Board of Medical Examiners and where the patient is kept under restraint and control or in a state hospital or in a jail or prison (sec. 11391) and no person may prescribe, administer or furnish a narcotic to himself. (sec. 11167.)

While the possession of a narcotic is lawful if the possessor has a lawful prescription therefor, it is unlawful to possess a narcotic which was sold to another person on a prescription (People v. Wallace, 109 Cal. App. 2d 676; People v. Ard, 25 Cal. App. 2d 630). The fact that a narcotic was sold originally on a legal prescription does not legalize the possession of that narcotic by any person other than the one for whom it was prescribed or a person such as a nurse or doctor having custody of the narcotic for the purpose of administering the same to the person for whom it was prescribed.

"Addict"

The term "addict", as used in Division 10 of the Health and Safety Code, "means a person who unlawfully uses, or is addicted to the unlawful use of, narcotics."(sec. 11009.)

Negativing Exceptions

It is not necessary, in a prosecution under the narcotic law, for the prosecution to negative any of the exceptions in the statute and the burden of proving such exceptions is upon the defendant. (In re Lord, 199 Cal. 773; People v. Harmon, 89 Cal. App. 2d 55; People v. Martinez, 117 Cal. App. 2d 701.)

Sale of Narcotics

The sale, barter, exchange or gift or offer thereof, all included under the term sale (sec. 11008) involves no specific intent and, unless the act comes within an exception in Division 10, this portion of the statute may be violated whether the accused was lawfully in possession of the narcotic or not. Thus a sale by a physician would be as much a violation of the law as a similar sale by any other person. (People v. Kinsley, 118 Cal. App. 593; see also In re Lord, 199 Cal. 773.) The provision of section 1558 of the Civil Code that it is essential to the validity of a contract, that it should be possible to identify the parties, applies to executory contracts and does not apply to an executed contract, a sale by defendant to an unnamed informer (People v. Bradford, 130 Cal. App. 2d. 606).

It is not a defense for a pharmacist, who sells narcotics without a prescription, that a doctor had telephoned him to sell the narcotics and that he would later send over a prescription (People v. Gelardi, 77 Cal. App. 2d 467).

Evidence that marked money was given by an officer to an operator who over an hour later returned to the officer and handed him a paper containing heroin and that thereafter the marked money was found in the possession of the defendant is not sufficient to convict a defendant of selling narcotics even though the defendant was unable to state where he got the marked money found among other currency in his pocket (People v. Barnett, 118 Cal. App. 2d 336).

Possession of Narcotics—Intent—Knowledge

The crime of possession of narcotics does not include as an essential ingredient a specific intent (People v. Gory, 25 Cal. 2d 450; People v. Lapin, 138 Cal. App. 2d 251). The corpus delicti of this offense may be proven by circumstantial evidence (People v. Robarge, 151 Cal. App. 2d ......; People v. Flores, 155 Cal. App. 2d.........).

A person is in possession of a narcotic when it is under his dominion and control and, to his knowledge, either is carried on his person or is in his presence and custody or, if not on his person or in his presence, the possession thereof is immediate, accessible and exclusive to him, provided, however, that two or more persons may have joint possession of a narcotic if jointly and knowingly they have such dominion, control and exclusive possession and the possession may be individual, through an agent or joint with another (People v. Bigelow, 104 Cal. App. 2d 380, 388).

The statute does not require proof of possession at the very time of arrest nor is it necessary to prove that the accused had the unlawful article on his person (People v. Brickman, 119 Cal. App. 2d 253, and cases cited).

The mere possession of one of the prohibited narcotics is a violation of the law, (People v. Randolph, 133 Cal. App. 192; People v. Le Baron, 92 Cal. App. 550) and the corpus delicti of the offense of possession of a narcotic drug does not include any specific intent nor knowledge on the part of the accused of the nature of the drug possessed (People v. Randolph, 133 Cal. App. 192; People v. Le Baron, 92 Cal. App. 550; People v. Johnson, 66 Cal. App. 2d 164; People v. Sweeney, 66 Cal App. 2d 855; People v. Gory, 28 Cal. 2d 450; People v. Bledsoe, 75 Cal. App. 2d 862; People v. Martin, 76 Cal. App. 2d 317) the mere possession of the narcotic drug being substantial evidence to sustain the finding that the possessor knew the nature of that which he possessed (People v. Carlton, 83 Cal. App. 2d 475; People v. Physioc, 86 Cal. App. 2d 650) and it need not be proved that the drug in question was habit-forming or that it was pure and not a compounded preparation. (People v. Bill, 140 Cal. App. 389.) It has, however, been held that it is essential to the proof of possession of a narcotic not only that the defendant knowingly had possession thereof but that he must have knowledge that the article is a narcotic (People v. Cole, 113 Cal. App. 2d. 253; People v. Perez, 128 Cal. App. 2d. 750, which also held, as did People v. Candiotta, 128 Cal. App. 2d. 750 and People v. Prez, 128 Cal. App. 2d. 750, that the refusal of such instruction on knowledge is not prejudicial where it is apparent that the defendant must have known the nature of the narcotic. Note:—The illustrations of innocent possession stated in the opinion are instances of honest ignorance or mistake of fact, defendable under section 26, subd. 4, of the Penal Code. The better reasoning would be that, where a person knowingly has in his possession what is in fact a narcotic, it is logical to draw the inference that he knew that it was a narcotic and that the burden is upon him to prove his defense under section 26 as is the law in cases coming within the scope of section 26). In People v. Gory, 28 Cal. 2d 450, the trial judge had withdrawn from the jury's consideratin an instruction to the effect that to constitute the offense the defendant must have knowledge of the ''character'' of the narcotic involved and it was held (p. 455) ''knowledge of the presence of the object'' is ''the essence of the offense'' but that ''Knowledge of the character of the object and the unlawfulness of possession thereof'' is immaterial. (See also cases cited therein and People v. Garcia, 124 Cal. App. 2d 822). Later, in reviewing the Gory case the court in People v. Winston, 46 Cal. 2d 151, disapproves the position that mere possession of the narcotics without knowledge of their nature would sustain a conviction but, in view of the fact that the defendant obviously knew the nature of the narcotic involved, the refusal of an instruction, that knowledge of the narcotic character of the thing possessed is an essential ingredient of the offense, was not ground for a reversal. In People v. Candiotto, 128 Cal. App. 2d 347 and People v. Perez, 128 Cal. App. 2d 750, the Cole case is followed but the refusal of an instruction that knowledge of the narcotic character of the thing possessed is an essential element of the offense of possession was held not prejudicial the defendant being familiar with the narcotic in question when he saw it. Knowledge of the illegal nature of the contraband is sufficiently shown by the conduct of the defendant in attempting to conceal the narcotic (People v. Tennyson, 127 Cal. App. 2d 243). The resistance of a lawfully arrested person to a lawful search of his person and his refusal to deliver the package of narcotics found on his person to his captors justifies the finder of facts in finding that he knew the package contained narcotics and his wilful possession thereof and a prisoner's secret knowledge of the character of the narcotics in his possession is shown by an attempt on his part to secrete or dispose of them and a finding of knowledge of the presence of narcotics in the clothing of the defendant encompasses a finding that he knew the nature of the object and its uses (People v. MacCagnan, 129 Cal. App. 2d. 100). It is, however, essential that it be shown by the evidence that the defendant had possession of the narcotic knowingly for there can be no possession of an article without knowledge of its existence and presence. (People v. Gory, 28 Cal. 2d. 450; People v. Bledsoe, 75 Cal. App. 2d. 862; People v. Martin, 76 Cal. App. 2d. 317. The statement in People v. Gorg, 45 Cal. 2d 776, that awareness that the substance which the defendant is charged with planting and cultivating, marihuana, was a narcotic is not sustained by any citation of authority and is in conflict with People v. Gory, supra). "To show such knowing possession, the conduct of the parties, admissions or contradictory statements and explanations are frequently sufficient" (People v. Gory, 28 Cal. 2d. 456; People v. Foster, 115 Cal. App. 2d. 866 and cases cited) but where three defendants were riding in a car from which a narcotic was thrown there is not, in the absence of further evidence, sufficient proof as to which of the three possessed the narcotic (People v. Foster, supra).

To show knowing possession, the conduct of the parties, admissions or contradictory statements and explanations are frequently sufficient (People v. Foster, 115 Cal. App. 2d 866, 868; People v. Brickman, 119 Cal. App. 2d 253, 263) and evidence of other similar acts are admissible to show knowledge (People v. Torres, 98 Cal. App. 2d 189, 192) as is evidence that the defendant had been convicted of possession of narcotics and was on parole and had recently associated with a person trafficking in narcotics and the narcotic was found in his room (People v. Denne, 141 Cal. App. 2d 499) or that it was found in the defendant's purse (People v. Douglass, 141 Cal. App. 2d 33).

Those cases in which the evidence shows that the narcotic was found upon the person of the defendant or concealed in his clothing (People v. Randolph, 133 Cal. App. 192) present little difficulty so far as the element of possession is concerned for in such cases the essentials to possession, dominion and control and power of disposition over the drug are obviously present, and the same is true in those cases where the evidence shows that the defendant dropped the drug as the means of passing it to another or threw it away upon the approach of officers of the law. (People v. Belli, 127 Cal. App. 269; People v. Rodriguez, 25 Cal. App. 2d 393; People v. Herbert, 59 Cal. App. 158; People v. Sinclair, 129 Cal. App. 320; People v. Hamm, 145 Cal. App. 2d 242). It is not necessary, however, to constitute possession that the drug be upon the person of the accused. (People v. Sinclair, 129 Cal. App. 320). In the case last cited the defendant, having agreed to sell morphine to a police informer, drove the latter in his automobile to a place where he picked up another man. Shortly thereafter they were stopped by a police officer, whereupon defendant shouted to the man he had picked up, "throw them out" and the latter then threw out of the car a matchbox containing cubes of morphine. The court held that the disposition and control and dominion over the drug being in the defendant and it being subject to his order as to what should be done with it, the possession in another under such circumstances was a constructive possession sufficient to sustain defendant's conviction of possession of the morphine. (People v. Sinclair, 129 Cal. App. 320; see also People v. Gallagher, 12 Cal. App. 2d 434). In such a case the conviction could also be sustained on the theory that defendant, by reason of aiding and abetting or advising and encouraging, was a principal in the unlawful possession by the other person. Where three defendants were riding in an automobile which one of them had had in his possession for several weeks and four marihuana cigarettes in perfect condition were found neatly rolled under a blanket which covered the front seat and defendants told conflicting stories as to whether other persons had ridden in the car on the same evening it was held that possession of the cigarettes by the defendants had been sufficiently established (People v. Torres, 98 Cal. App 2d 189). Where the officers found two bindles of heroin, two spoons blackened by fire with cotton filters saturated with heroin in the apartment of a husband and wife, the evidence was held sufficient to support the finding of joint possession of the defendants (People v. Crews, 110 Cal. App. 2d 218). Where morphine was found under the floor mat in an automobile in front of the seat where the defendant had just been sitting the evidence was held sufficient to sustain a conviction (People v.

Brown, 102 Cal. App. 2d 60). In a case in which a quantity of heroin was thrown from a moving automobile but there was no direct evidence, as to which of the three occupants of the car had thrown the narcotic, and each of them denied any knowledge thereof, a conviction of one of the occupants, who had falsely testified that the window, from which the evidence showed the narcotic was thrown was closed, was sustained (People v. Foster, 115 Cal. App. 2d 866). Where the defendant and his fiancee were riding in an automobile and the narcotics were found on the person of the woman and the defendent stated that the narcotics were his, the conviction was sustained. (People v. Gonzales, 116 Cal. App. 2d 843). The possession of as little as two milligrams of morphine recovered from a hypodermic outfit by a chemist is sufficient to establish probable cause in a prosecution for possession (People v. Hyden, 118 Cal. App. 2d 744). The open display on a table in a bedroom of bindles of heroin and other articles used in the preparation and use of heroin and the finding of a hypodermic needle on the person of the defendant, one of two men found in the room, was held sufficient to establish possession of the narcotic by the defendant (People v. Williams, 121 Cal. App. 2d. 679). Evidence that the defendant, when the officers entered the room, was seated at a table on which were two packages of marihuana and a package of wheat straw cigarette papers and stated that he had recognized the material as marihuana and was just helping his companion to manicure it and get it ready to roll is sufficient to sustain a conviction of possession of narcotics (People v. Cuevas, 131 Cal. App. 2d. 393). Where the defendant on a dark night walked over to a tree in front of his house and reached down to the base of a tree where a package of heroin capsules was located, such evidence supports the inference that he knew of the existence of the narcotic and was sufficient to establish the corpus delicti of the possession of narcotics (People v. Rodriguez, 133 Cal. App. 2d. 49). The finding of a package of regular cigarettes containing marihuana cigarettes in the crotch of defendant's overalls is prima facie evidence of possession (People v. Mc-Cagnan, 129 Cal. App. 2d. 1000 and defendant's effort to conceal the cigarettes and resistance to the search sufficiently shows his knowledge of the illegal character of the narcotics (id). To show knowing possession, the conduct of the parties, admissions or contradictory statements and explanations are frequently sufficient (People v. Foster, 115 Cal. App. 2d. 886; People v. Stanciell, 121 Cal. App. 2d. 798). Where the officers found two boxes of narcotics on the person of a man who occupied a hotel room with the defendant who thereafter told the officers that they had all of the narcotics and that she knew that her companion had the narcotics on his person and that she had narcotics on her person when she and the man came to Stockton from Los Angeles and had used what she had brought, the jury could reasonably infer a joint possession (People v. Basco, 121 Cal. App. 2d. 794).

Where the defendant rented a room, signing the name of one D. H. as well as his own, paid the rent and occupied the room for over a month the joint occupancy of the room would not necessarily exonerate the defendant and the fact that defendant was a narcotic addict and under the influence of narcotics at the time of arrest, there being no testimony as to the mythical D. H. or that the latter was an addict or peddler, coupled with other facts, justified the inference that the defendant had possession of the narcotics for his own use (People v. Ross, 149 Cal. App. 2d 287).

When narcotics are found concealed in or about an automobile in the possession of the owner or his entrustee knowledge may be inferred (People v. Dewson, 150 Cal. App. 2d 119).

(For illustrations of cases of constructive possession see People v. Mac Arthur, 126 Cal. App. 2d. 232, and cases cited.)

When Found in Building

Where one or more of the prohibited narcotics is found in an occupied building, room or office this is sufficient to establish the crime of unlawful possession of such drug by someone (People v. Marquis, 140 Cal. App. 73; People v. Gallagher, 12 Cal. App. 2d 434) and this evidence supplemented by proof as to the identity of the possessor will sustain a conviction. (People v. Marquis, 140 Cal. App. 72, and illustrations following:— drug found in the rooming house of defendant and proof that she had recently made several sales of the same drug, People v. Torres, 5 Cal. App. 2d 580; drug found in the room of defendant, People v. Quong, 5 Cal. App. 2d 137; People v. Contreras, 23 Cal. App. 2d 547; People v. Ng King, 60 Cal. App. 2d 239; drug found in a valise under a desk in defendant's office, People v. Gin Shue, 58 Cal. App. 2d 625; found in a light well, People v. Bassett, 68 Cal. App. 2d 241; People v. Eberhard, 114 Cal. App. 2d 113; among a female defendant's wearing apparel in a dresser People v. Hoff, 84 Cal. App. 2d. 398). Where defendant had placed the narcotics in a vase outside the door of his room the court said that "a person has possession of a chattel who has physical control with the intent to exercise such control, or having had such physical control, has not abandoned it and no other person has obtained possession." (People v. Noland, 61 Cal. App. 2d. 364.) Where a defendant was found in sole occupancy of business premises with the key to a locked room on his person and admits being in the room the day before and narcotics are found therein, a jury may fairly draw the inference that he knowingly possessed the narcotics (People v. Neal, 122 Cal. App. 2d. 749). The presence of the narcotics in the defendant's room, in his shirt pocket and among his personal papers is sufficient evidence of possession by him and justifies an inference that he had knowledge that the narcotics were there (People v. Millum, 42 Cal. 2d. 524).

The mere fact that narcotics were found in the apartment of the defendant, there being no evidence that the defendant knew of their presence, that he had ever used narcotics or that narcotics had been used in the apartment, but there was evidence that guests of the defendant, present at the time of the arrest, were narcotic users, the narcotics being found where such persons could have placed them, will not support a conviction (People v. Savage, 128 Cal. App. 2d. 123; People v. Antista, 129 Cal. App. 2d. 47).

Constructive Possession—Joint Possession

The possession "need not be a personal one it being sufficient if such possession is constructive so long as it is immediate and exclusive and under the dominion and control of the violator." (People v. Gallagher, 12 Cal. App. 2d 434, 436.) But exclusive possession need not be shown to be in any one person where two or more persons are jointly charged. (People v. Rodriguez, 25 Cal. App. 2d 393; see also People v. Le Baron, 92 Cal. App. 550.) "The possession may be individual, through an agent, or joint with another . . . one may aid and abet another in the possession of a narcotic and . . . one who is not present may advise and encourage another in the commission" (People v. Bigelow, 104 Cal. App. 2d. 380). Where the evidence showed that officers entered the room of defendant and found 13 grams of heroin in a tub under the bed and with defendant was one H, a companion of defendant with a record of narcotic violations, who testified that he had brought the narcotics to the apartment and showed them to the defendant who handed them back and, when the officers rang the door buzzer he threw the narcotics into the tub, and the officers testified that H had denied ownership of the narcotics, that defendant and H were drug addicts and that the defendant had offered no explanation of the presence of the narcotics and defendant did not testify at the trial, the evidence was sufficient to sustain a conviction of possession of narcotics by defendant (People v. Lama, 129 Cal. App. 2d. 391).

Where appellant W had left money with his roommate C for the purchase of a capsule of heroin from H and C purchased the capsule and placed it in a box on the dresser, the evidence showed a conspiracy between W, H and C to violate the statute prohibiting the purchase, sale and possession of narcotics and that the possession of C was the possession of appellant and C's knowledge of the character of the capsule was in legal contemplation the knowledge of appellant (People v. Conover, 155 Cal. App. 2d ......).

For illustrations of constructive possession see People v. MacArthur, 126 Cal. App. 2d 232.

Lawful Possession May Become Unlawful

A person in lawful possession of one of the listed narcotics becomes a violator of the statute if the possession ceases to be lawful. If a registered nurse is in lawful possession of narcotics for use in the care of her patient, such right will cease upon the death of the patient and by keeping them in her possession she becomes guilty of unlawful possession. (People v. Ard, 25 Cal. App. 2d 630.)

Possession in Jail, Prison, etc.

Section 4573 of the Penal Code, making it a felony for "any person" to have possession of a narcotic in any jail, prison or place where prisoners are under the custody of the sheriff, applies to prisoners and inmates (People v. Trout, 137 Cal. App. 2d 794).

Employing Minor to Handle Narcotic—
Furnishing Narcotic to Minor.

"Every person who hires, employs, or uses a minor in unlawfully transporting, carrying, selling, giving away, preparing for sale or peddling any narcotic, or who unlawfully sells, furnishes, administers, gives, or offers to sell, furnish, administer, or give any narcotic to a minor is guilty of a felony punishable by imprisonment in the state prison for not less than five years.

"If such a person has been previously convicted of any offense described in this division or has been previously convicted of any offense under the laws of any other state or of the United States which if committed in this State would have been punishable as an offense described in this division, the previous conviction shall be charged in the indictment or information and if found to be true by the jury, upon a jury trial, or if found to be true by the court, upon a court trial, or is admitted by the defendant, he shall be imprisoned in the state prison for not less than 10 years." (sec. 11714).

Evidence that two adults picked up a minor, all three being narcotic addicts, and drove to a place where defendant gave the minor $5 which she handed to W who purchased two bindles of narcotics which he gave to the minor and all three then drove to a place where they intended to inject the heroin, and the minor testified that the narcotic was purchased for her by the defendant, was held to sustain a conviction of using a minor to transport heroin (People v. De Paula, 43 Cal. 2d. 643). Where the defendant handed a marihuana cigarette to M, an adult, who lit it and passed it to a minor who took several "drags" out of it and handed it back to M and the cigarette was then passed around the group which included three other minors each of whom took several "drags" and finally defendant finished the cigarette and, during the incident, defendant told the others to keep the cigarette hidden, a conviction of furnishing narcotics to a minor was sustained (People v. Sykes, 44 Cal. 2d 166; see also People v. Winston, 46 Cal. 2d 151).

Soliciting, Encouraging, Inducing or Intimidating a Minor

"Every person who in any voluntary manner solicits, induces, encourages or intimidates any minor with the intent that said minor shall violate any provision of this division shall be punished by imprisonment in the State prison for not less than five years" (sec. 11501).

The word "induce" means to lead on; to influence; to prevail on; to move by persuasion or influence. The word "encourage" means to give courage to; to inspire with courage, spirit or hope; to raise the confidence of; to animate; hearten (People v. Drake, 151 Cal. App. 2d ...... A.C.A. 27).

Furnishing Narcotics

The corpus delicti of the offense of furnishing narcotics to another may be proved by circumstantial evidence and it is not necessary that the narcotic involved be produced in court or that its nature be proved by the expert testimony of a chemist (People v. Candalaria, 121 Cal. App. 2d. 686, nature of the narcotic proved by the testimony of the person to whom it was furnished by the defendant and who was familiar with its use and effects).

Forging Prescription, etc.

"Every person who forges or alters a prescription, or who issues or utters an altered prescription or who issues or utters a prescription bearing a forged or fictitious signature for any narcotic, or who obtains any narcotic by any forged, fictitious, or altered prescription, or who has in possession any narcotic secured by such forged, fictitious or altered prescription, shall for the first offense be punished by imprisonment in the county jail for not less than six months nor more than one year, or in the State prison for not more than six years, and for each subsequent offense shall be imprisoned in the State prison for not more than 10 years." (sec. 11715.)

Intent To Defraud Not Essential

This section, while punishing the forgery of a prescription for narcotics, bears only a partial resemblance to the crime of forgery under section 470 of the Penal Code, for the forgery of such a prescription if prosecuted under this section of the Health and Safety Code does not involve, as an element of the offense, the intent to defraud. (People v. Beesly, 119 Cal. App. 82.)

The section also makes it a felony for anyone to obtain any narcotic by means of a prescription which is either forged, fictitious or altered or to possess a narcotic obtained by such a prescription. This offense differs from that of uttering a forgery (Penal Code, sec. 470) in that it does not require that the act be done with intent to defraud or with knowledge that the prescription was forged, fictitious or altered.

Transportation—Knowledge—Intent

Section 11500 of the Health and Safety Code makes it a crime to transport or offer to transport or attempt to transport a narcotic except upon a legal prescription and the penalty is the same as that provided for selling such narcotic. The word "transport' includes "conceal," "convey" or "carry" (sec. 11012). Possession of the narcotic may be a circumstance tending to prove the transportation but is not an essential element of the offense of transportation any more than an "offer to transport" or an "attempt to transport." Knowledge of the presence of the object, with intent to exercise, individually or jointly, control over it is an element of the offense but knowledge of the exact character of the object or a specific intent to violate the law are not essential (People v. Watkins, 96 Cal. App. 2d 74; see also Possession of Narcotics—Intent—Knowledge, supra).

Where, after being stopped by officers, defendant fled in his car and, when apprehended, narcotics were found in his car, this was sufficient to sustain a charge of transportation (People v. Dewson, 150 Cal. App. 2d 119).

Administering Narcotic to Commit Crime

"Every person guilty of administering to another any chloroform, ether, laudanum, narcotic, anaesthetic, or intoxicating agent, with intent thereby to enable or assist himself or any other person to commit a felony, is guilty of a felony." (Penal Code, sec. 222.) The penalty for this offense is imprisonment in the state prison for not less than six months and not exceeding five years. (Penal Code, secs. 18, 18a.)

The term "intoxicating agent" includes any drug, substance or compound which, when introduced into the human system, produces a serious disturbance of the physical and mental equilibrium by causing sleep, stupor, unconsciousness or semi-unconsciousness together with impairment of the power of self control (People v. Cline, 138 Cal. App. 184, luminal used to commit grand theft from the person); causing a person to inhale chloroform is "administering" chloroform (People v. Tinnen, 49 Cal. App. 18).

Illegal Prescription

"No person shall write, issue, fill, compound or dispense a prescription that does not conform to this division." (sec. 11162.)

"An order purporting to be a prescription issued to an addict or habitual user of narcotics, not in the course of professional treatment but for the purpose of providing the user with narcotics sufficient to keep him comfortable by maintaining his customary use, is not a prescription within the meaning and intent of this division; and the person filling such an order as well as the person issuing it, may be charged with violation of the law." (sec. 11162.5.)

"Except in the regular practice of his profession, no person shall prescribe, administer or furnish a narcotic to or for any person who is not under his treatment for a pathology or condition other than narcotic addiction, except as provided in this division." (sec. 11163).

"No person shall prescribe for or administer or dispense a narcotic to an addict, or to any person representing himself as such except as permitted by this division." (sec. 11164.)

The law includes the prescribing for a fictitious person. A conviction of a doctor for prescribing and furnishing narcotics for a person not under his treatment was sustained where the doctor had delivered narcotics to a person who had represented that his wife needed narcotics when in fact that statement was false and the name he gave and that of the purported wife were fictitious, the court holding that the purpose of the statute was not to protect persons under a physician's treatment but to regulate the conduct of persons who in their professions have legitimate access to narcotics and the prescription of narcotics for legitimate medical purposes (People v. Braddock, 41 Cal. 2d. 794).

Where a state narcotic inspector went to the office of the defendant, an osteopathic physician, gave an assumed name and address and stated that he was using heroin and the defendant wrote him a prescription for sixty one-tenth grain tablets of dilaudid, a narcotic, and the inspector paid him $20 therefor and the defendant filled out a patient's card listing migraine headache and the diagnosis "Narcotic addiction" and at intervals of a week gave the inspector three other prescriptions for dilaudid, defendant at no time making any physical examination nor did the inspector ever tell the defendant that he had any ailment other than narcotics addiction, the court held that the evidence amply showed that the defendant had on four separate occasions violated sections 11163 and 11164 of the Health and Safety Code and that section 11330 (providing that a physician may prescribe narcotics only when in good faith he believes the disease, ailment, injury or infirmity of the patient requires) are constitutional (People v. Nunn, 46 cal. 2d 460).

Penalties. Secs. 11162; 11162.5; 11163; 11163.5; 11164.

The punishment for a violation of these sections is by imprisonment in the county jail for not less than six months or in the state prison for not more than six years (sec. 111715.7).

Taking Narcotics Into Jail or Prison

"Any person, not authorized by law, who brings into any state prison or prison road camp, prison forestry camp or other prison camp or farm or other place where prisoners of the state are located under the custody of prison officials, officers or employees or into any county, city and county or city jail, road camp, farm or other place where prisoners or inmates are located under the sheriff, chief of police, probation officer or employees, or within the grounds belonging to any such institution, any narcotic the possession of which is prohibited by Division 10 of the Health and Safety Code is guilty of a felony." (Penal Code, sec. 4573) . The penalty for this offense is imprisonment in the state prison for not less than six months nor more than five years. (Penal Code, sec. 18, 18a.) (see also Penal Code, sec. 4573.5).

Barbiturates and Veronal

The possession and sale of veronal and barbiturates except as authorized by law is a misdemeanor (secs. 29001, 29023, Health and Safety Code; see People v. Brac, 73 Cal. App. 2d 629).

Obtaining Narcotics by Fraud

"1. No person shall obtain or attempt to obtain narcotics, or procure or attempt to procure the administration of or prescription for narcotics, (a) by fraud, deceit, misrepresentation, or subterfuge; or (b) by concealment of a material fact.

2. No person shall make a false statement in any prescription, order, report or record required by this division.

3. No person shall, for the purpose of obtaining narcotics, falsely assume the title of, or represent himself to be, a manufacturer, wholesaler, pharmacist, physician, dentist, veterinarian or other authorized person.

4. No person shall affix any false or forged label to a package or receptacle containing narcotics." (sec. 11170 H & S Code.) (People v. Henry, 86 Cal. App. 2d 785).

False Name and Address

"No person shall, in connection with the prescribing, furnishing, administering or dispensing of a narcotic, give a false name or address." (H & S Code, sec. 11170.5). Both the giver and the receiver of a prescription are within the scope of this section. It is not a defense in a prosecution of the receiver that the doctor who gave the prescription would have done so just as readily if the true name and address of the receiver had been given (People v. Oviedo, 106 Cal. App. 2d 690). Evidence that the defendant had previously been known by another name and that there was no such address as that given by him to the doctor from whom he obtained the prescription for morphine and that he had the prescription filled by a pharmacist establishes the offense (People v. Wood, 127 Cal. App. 2d. 770).

Penalties. Secs. 11170 and 11170.5

A violation of sections 11170 and 11170.5 is punishable by imprisonment in a county jail for not less than six months or in the state prison for not more than six years (H & S Code, sec. 11715.7).

Immunity

"All duly authorized peace officers, while investigating violations of this division, in the performance of their official duties, and any person working under their immediate direction, supervision or instruction, are immune from prosecution under this division." (H & S Code, sec. 11710).

Where a narcotic inspector, in securing a narcotic prescription from a physician, used a fictitious name and address upon the direction of his superior officer, he was immune from prosecution and his acts in so doing were not illegal (People v. Nunn, 46 Cal. 2d 460).

CHAPTER XXXIII

FORMER JEOPARDY

The Constitution of the United States provides that "no person shall be . . subject, for the same offense, to be twice put in jeopardy", and the Constitution of California (Art. 1, Sec. 13) contains the similar provision, "No person shall be twice put in jeopardy for the same offense." This rule has been carried into section 687 of the Penal Code in the following language, "No person can be subjected to a second prosecution for a public offense for which he has once been prosecuted and convicted or acquitted."

Acts Punishable by Different Code Sections or Statutes of Another State

"An act or omission which is made punishable in different ways by different provisions of this code may be punished under either of such provisions, but in no case can it be punished under more than one; an acquittal or conviction and sentence under either one bars a prosecution for the same act or omission under any other." (Penal Code, Section 654.)

"Section 654 prohibits double punishment for the commission of a single act (Citations) but it does not prohibit convictions of different offenses arising out of a single act unless one is necessarily included within the other (citations)" (People v. Smith, 36 Cal. 2d 444, 448; People v. Moore, 143 Cal. App. 2d 333).

"If any single act is charged as the basis of the multiple convictions only one conviction can be affirmed notwithstanding that the offenses are not necessarily included offenses." Thus where the act constitutes both robbery and kidnaping under section 209 of the Penal Code and the defendant was convicted of both offenses it was held that but one of the convictions could stand and the conviction for kidnaping was affirmed and the robbery conviction reversed (People v. Knowles, 35 Cal. 2d 175). (see also subhead, infra:—Offenses Connected in Their Commission).

"When an offense is within the jurisdiction of two or more courts, a conviction or acquittal thereof in one court is a bar to a prosecution or indictment therefor in another." (Penal Code, Sec.794.)

"Whenever on the trial of an accused person it appears that upon a criminal prosecution under the laws of another state, government, or country, founded upon the act or omission in respect to which he is on trial, he has been acquitted or convicted, it is a sufficient defense." (Penal Code, sec. 656). Where the defendant was convicted in the Federal Court of the robbery of a national bank and was prosecuted thereafter in the state court for the same robbery, the prior conviction was a sufficient defense by plea of former conviction (People v. Candelaria, 139 Cal. App. 2d 432).

"When an act charged as a public offense is within the jurisdiction of another state or country, as well as of this state, a conviction or acquittal thereof in the former is a bar to the prosecution or indictment therefor in this state." (Penal Code, sec. 793.) (Coumas v. Sup. Ct., 31 Cal. 2d 682, conviction in a foreign country).

"When the defendant is convicted or acquitted, or has been once placed in jeopardy upon an accusatory pleading, the conviction, acquittal or jeopardy is a bar to another accusatory pleading for the offense charged in the former, or for an attempt to commit the same, or for an offense necessarily included therein, of which he might have been convicted under that accusatory pleading." (Penal Code, sec. 1023.)

Basic Principle of Jeopardy

The basic principle in the law of former jeopardy is that a person who has committed a criminal act shall be subject to but one prosecution for that act and that when that prosecution has resulted in a final judgment of conviction or if the defendant has been acquitted or, even if there be no formal verdict or finding that the accused is not guilty, the cause has proceeded to a stage equivalent in law to an acquittal, no further prosecution of such defendant can be had for such act.

A conviction by plea of guilty is as much a conviction which will bar a second prosecution as if the case in which such plea was entered had been tried and had resulted in a finding that the accused was guilty (People v. Goldstein, 32 Cal. 432) and the law of former jeopardy applies to all crimes, misdemeanors as well as felonies. (In re Herron, 191 Cal. 457.)

One Act Chargeable Under Several Theories

Where a statute provides that any one of a number of methods of committing an act shall constitute the crime such crime may be charged under each of the tenable theories but, since there is but one act, but one crime is committed and jeopardy resulting from a prosecution under one theory will bar another prosecution for the same act. Thus the crime of rape may be committed under two or more of the conditions specified in the definition of that offense: "but one punishable offense of rape results from a single act of intercourse." (People v. Craig, 17 Cal. 2d 453; People v. Scott, 24 Cal. 2d 774.)

When Jeopardy Attaches

"When a party is once placed upon his trial for a public offense, on a valid indictment, before a competent court, with a competent jury, duly empanelled, sworn and charged with the case, he has then reached and is placed in jeopardy . . . and after jeopardy has once so attached, a discharge of the jury, without consent of the defendant, for any cause within the control of the court, before they have rendered a verdict, is equivalent to a verdict of acquittal." (People v. Webb, 38 Cal. 467; People v. Hinshaw, 194 Cal. 1; Jackson v. Superior Court, 10 Cal. 2d 350; People v. Hess, 107 Cal. App. 2d 407.) Where alternate jurors are ordered the jury is not considered complete and jeopardy does not attach until not only the original twelve but also the alternate or alternates have been sworn to try the case (People v. Burns, 84 Cal. App. 2d 18). If the trial is commenced before the court without a jury, jeopardy attaches when the trial has commenced by the swearing of the first witness for the prosecution. (See:—In re Herron, 191 Cal. 457). Where it is proposed that a cause will be submitted upon the evidence taken at the preliminary examination, jeopardy does not attach prior to the commencement of the trial (People v. Blau, 140 Cal. App. 2d 193).

Competent Court

One prerequisite to jeopardy is that the court in which the prosecution is had must be a competent court having jurisdiction of the offense and the accused. (People v. Hamberg, 84 Cal. 468; People v. Hinshaw, 194 Cal. 1.) Unless the court has jurisdiction a trial, conviction or acquittal therein is void and cannot be made the basis of a plea of former jeopardy, former acquittal or former conviction. (People v. Hamberg, 84 Cal. 468; People v. Woods, 84 Cal. 441; People v. Zadro, 20 Cal. App. 2d 320.)

Valid Charge

There can be no jeopardy unless the indictment, information, accusation or complaint is sufficient in form to charge a criminal offense and sustain a conviction. (People v. Giminiani, 70

Cal. App. 195; People v. Clark, 67 Cal. 99; People v. Larson, 68 Cal. 18; People v. Ammerman, 118 Cal. 23; People v. Lee Look, 137 Cal. 590, 143 Cal. 216; People v. Terrill, 133 Cal. 120; People v. Eppinger, 109 Cal. 294) but "Whenever the defendant is acquitted on the merits, he is acquitted of the same offense, notwithstanding any defect in form or substance in the accusatory pleading on which the trial was had." (Penal Code, sec. 1022.)

Judgment Not Necessary

Where a prior conviction has been suffered it is a bar to a second prosecution for the same offense even though no judgment and sentence were pronounced on the conviction. (People v. Goldstein, 32 Cal. 432.)

Effect of Rule

It is the effect of the application of the law of former jeopardy that when a person has been placed on trial under a valid complaint, indictment, information or accusation, before a competent court having jurisdiction of the offense charged and the trial has resulted in a conviction which has become final, in an acquittal, or the equivalent of an acquittal, the defendant cannot be prosecuted a second time for either the identical offense involved in the first trial or for another offense based upon the act constituting the offense charged in the first trial, nor can he be prosecuted a second time upon a charge of an attempt to commit such offense nor for any offense necessarily included therein nor for an offense in which such offense is necessarily included. (See: Jackson v. Superior Court, 10 Cal. 2d 350.)

Identity of Offense the Test

The bar to a second prosecution created by former jeopardy depends upon the identity of the offense and not upon the action of the accused which constitutes an unlawful act (People v. Mehra, 73 Cal. App. 162), for a person may by one act or action commit two or more separate and distinct crimes. Thus if A shoots at B with intent to kill him but misses and the bullet kills C he is guilty not only of the murder of C but also of the crime involved in his attempt to kill B (People v. Brannon, 70 Cal. App. 225) and may be convicted of both offenses and the result of the trial of one charge can have no effect upon his trial for the other charge, and the same rule applies where in the perpetration of a robbery two persons are killed (People v. Majors, 2 Cal. Unrep. 264, 65 Cal. 138) or where two persons are kidnaped at the same time. (People v. Johnson, 140 Cal. App. 729.)

Identity of Evidence Not the Test

The mere fact that the same evidence is used at the subsequent trial as was received at the first trial on a different charge does not establish a basis for jeopardy since the same evidence may establish two entirely separate and distinct offenses. (See: People v. Mehra, 73 Cal. App. 162; People v. Alibez, 49 Cal. 452; People v. Majors, 65 Cal. 138; People v. McFarlane, 126 Cal. App. 777; People v. Johnson, 82 Cal. App. 41; People v. Nelson, 70 Cal. App. 476; In re O'Connor, 80 Cal. App. 647.) Thus a person who has been convicted of carrying a concealed deadly weapon may thereafter be convicted of illegal possession of the same weapon under the Dangerous Weapons Control Law Act even though the evidence used in the first prosecution is also used in the second. (People v. McFarlane, 126 Cal. App. 777.) "Where the two offenses are entirely separate and distinct and the one is not necessarily included in the other, a prosecution for the one is no bar to a prosecution for the other even though the same testimony may be applicable to both" (People v. Coltrin, 5 Cal. 2d. 649, 660; see also cases in next paragraph).

Offenses Connected in Their Commission

Where a defendant in pursuance of his criminal design commits successive offenses such crimes are separate from each other and an acquittal or conviction of one of such offenses will not bar a prosecution for any other of such offenses even though the evidence used upon the several trials is the same. (People v. Majors, 65 Cal. 138; People v. Deolin, 143 Cal. 128; People v. Kerrick, 144 Cal. 46; People v. Ciulla, 44 Cal. App. 725; In re O'Connor, 80 Cal. App. 647; People v. Snyder, 74 Cal. App. 138; In re Mullin, 75 Cal. App. 150; People v. Sheasby, 82 Cal. App. 454.) Thus a conviction of burglary will not bar a subsequent prosecution upon the charge of receiving stolen property, such property being the fruits of such burglary (In re Kinney, 71 Cal. App. 490) or for the larceny of such property (People v. Snyder, 74 Cal. App. 138) or for a robbery committed after the unlawful entry. (People v. Brain, 75 Cal. App. 109.) A conviction of unlawful possession of intoxicating liquor will not bar a prosecution for maintaining a nuisance in keeping such liquor and a conviction of unlawful possession of intoxicating liquor will not bar a procecution for transportation, selling or manufacturing such liquor (People v. Mehra, 73 Cal. App. 162; People v. Arnarez, 68 Cal. App. 645) and a conviction of possessing and manufacturing intoxicating liquor will not prevent a prosecution for possession of a still. (People v. Painetti, 210 Cal. 476.)   While robbery ordinarily includes an assault and a conviction of robbery will bar a subsequent prosecution for such assault still where, in addition to the assault which is an element of the robbery, there is a further and additional assault after the robbery is consummated there can be a conviction of both the robbery and such assault. (People v. Van Every, 133 Cal. App. 354; People v. James, 20 Cal. App. 2d 88; see also: People v. Pickens, 61 Cal. App. 405; People v. Bentley, 77 Cal. 7.)   An acquittal of receiving stolen property is not a bar to a conviction of the burglary and robbery in which such property was stolen. (People v. Derenzo, 46 Cal. App. 2d 411.)   Where the defendant was charged in three counts with conspiracy to commit robbery, the consummated robbery and murder, connected in their commission, he may be convicted of all three offenses.   (People v. Hoyt, 20 Cal. 2d 306.)   Soliciting a person to commit perjury and subornation of perjury are separate offenses and the perpetrator may be convicted of both. (People v. Gray, 52 Cal. App. 2d 620.)   A conviction of forcible rape and of an assault by means of force likely to cause great bodily injury, both offenses forming a part of the same transaction, may properly be had where such assault was over and above the assault necessarily involved in the rape.   (People v. McIlvain, 55 Cal. App. 2d 322.)   An acquittal of the charge of abortion is not a bar to a prosecution on the same evidence for practicing medicine without a license.   (People v. Johnson, 82 Cal. App. 411; see also: In re O'Connor, 80 Cal. App. 647.)   A conviction in one county for being a member of an organization in violation of the Criminal Syndicalism Act is not a bar to a prosecution in another county for his being a member of that organization in that county.   (People v. Johansen, 66 Cal. App. 343.) The conviction or acquittal of a defendant of an offense in which a deadly weapon was used does not bar a prosecution for the unlawful possession of such weapon.   (People v. Warren, 16 Cal. 2d 103; People v. McFarland, 126 Cal. App. 777.) A conviction of drunkenness will not prevent a prosecution for driving an automobile while under the influence of intoxicating liquor (People v. Burkhardt, 5 Cal. 2d 641) and a conviction of reckless driving will not bar a prosecution for manslaughter.

People v. Herbert, 6 Cal. 2d 541.) A defendant may be convicted of both robbery and kidnaping for the purpose of robbery connected therewith (People v. Simpson, 66 Cal. App. 2d 319; People v. Tanner, 77 Cal. App. 2d 181), but where both charges are based upon the same act, as where the kidnaping is an incident in the perpetration of the robbery, there can be a conviction of but one of these offenses and if the defendant is convicted of both offenses, one of the convictions, generally that of the lesser crime, will be reversed on appeal (People v. Knowles, 35 Cal. 2d 175). Violations of two separate statutes in the same transaction constitute the commission of two separate offenses (People v. Gelardi, 77 Cal. App. 2d 467; People v. Palaccio, 86 Cal. App. 2d 778). Where the defendant is charged and convicted of two crimes and the commission of the greater necessarily includes the lesser as a matter of law (see LESSOR OFFENSES) only the conviction of the greater can stand (People v. Greer, 30 Cal. 2d 589; People v. Chapman, 81 Cal. App. 2d 857; People v. Esposti, 82 Cal. App. 2d 763. and this is the law where by one act two separate statutes are violated and both offenses are charged in which case the conviction of the greater offense will be sustained and the other reversed (People v. Knowles, 35 Cal. 2d 175), but where both counts are based on separate acts and neither is necessarily included in the other the defendant may be convicted of both offenses (People v. Slobodion, 31 Cal. 2d 555). Two separate attempts at abortion to relieve a woman of the same pregnancy constitutes two offenses (People v. Rhoades, 93 Cal. App. 2d 448; People v. Mullendorf, 110 Cal. App. 2d 286).

Illustrative Cases

Other illustrations of cases in which where more than one offense is committed and the offenses are connected in their commission and the perpetrator may be convicted of all the offenses committed are:—rape and violation of section 288 of the Penal Code (People v. O'Donnell, 11 Cal. 2d 666; People v. Parker, 74 Cal. App. 540); statutory rape and contributing to the delinquency of a minor (Rodriquez v. Sup. Court, 27 Cal. 2d 500); incest and violation of section 288 of the Penal Code (People v. McAfee, 82 Cal. App. 389); robbery and attempted murder (People v. Hanna, 41 Cal. App. 2d 252; arson and destroying insured property (People v. Miller, 41 Cal. App. 2d 252); attempted robbery and the violation of section 503 of the Vehicle Code (People v. Pearson, 41 Cal. App. 2d 614); attempted murder and malicious use of explosives (People

v. Kynette, 15 Cal. 2d 731); robbery and burglary (People v. Brain, 75 Cal. App. 109; People v. Case, 77 Cal. App. 477; People v. Shaffer, 81 Cal. App. 558; People v. Sharp, 58 Cal. App. 637; People v. Marzek, 108 Cal. App. 264); injuring two or more persons by the same criminal act (People v. Brannon, 70 Cal. App. 225; People v. Shiek, 75 Cal. App. 421); abortion and murder of the same woman (People v. Coltrin, 5 Cal. 2d 649); conspiracy to commit a crime and the consummated crime (People v. Eiseman, 78 Cal. App. 223; People v. Martin, 114 Cal. App. 392; People v. Menne, 4 Cal. App. 2d 91; People v. McMullen, 218 Cal. 655; People v. Dukes, 2 Cal. App. 2d 698; People v. Sharpe, 96 Cal. App. 2d 943); manslaughter and violation of section 480 of the Vehicle Code (People v. McKee, 80 Cal. App. 200); false advertisement and larceny by trick and device (In re O'Connor, 81 Cal. App. 506); robbery and kidnaping (People v. Sheasby, 82 Cal. App. 459; People v. Bruno, 140 Cal. App. 460; People v. Johnson, 140 Cal. App. 729); burglary and theft (People v. DeHoog, 100 Cal. App. 235; People v. Devlin, 143 Cal. 128); kidnaping two persons at the same time (People v. Johnson, 140 Cal. App. 729); forgery and preparing false evidence (People v. Glab, 3 Cal. App. 2d 528); theft of an automobile and the violation of section 503 of the Vehicle Code (People v. Cuevas, 18 Cal. App. 2d 151), the violation of section 503 being on a day subsequent to the theft, but where the theft and the violation of section 503 are committed at the same time, the defendant can be convicted of only one of the offenses (People v. Kehoe, 33 Cal. 2d 711), grand larceny of a calf and altering the brand on the same calf (People v. Kerrick, 144 Cal. 46; forging two separate instruments at the same time (People v. Gayle, 202 Cal. 159; People v. Cline, 79 Cal. App. 2d 11); theft from the person and administering a narcotic to commit the theft (People v. Cline, 138 Cal. App. 184); forgery, filing a false will, offering a false will in evidence and preparing a false will have been held to be separate offenses (In re Horowitz, 33 Cal. 2d 534). Where a check without funds or credit (Penal Code, sec. 476a) is issued and property obtained therewith, the separate crime of theft is also committed (People v. Freedman, 111 Cal. App. 611). The possession of three different narcotics, heroin, opium, morphine and cocaine), though contained in one package, constitutes three separate offenses. (People v. Mandell, 90 Cal. App. 2d 93). Where defendants, life convicts in the state prison, assaulted another prisoner with deadly weapons and murdered him, convictions of assault by life convict (Penal Code, sec. 4500) and first degree murder, both carrying the death penalty, were sustained (People v. Smith, 36 A. C. 395, 36 Cal. 2d 444). It has been held that each of the subdivisions of section 337a of the Penal Code constitutes a separate offense (People v. Bryant, 147 Cal. App. 2d 259) but it may be that a conviction under subdivision 1 may include a violation of one or more of the other subdivisions.

Act Prosecutable under Several Sections

Where a person commits a single unlawful act which may be prosecuted under two or more sections of the law the jeopardy which attaches in a prosecution under one of such sections constitutes a bar to a subsequent prosecution under any one of the other sections. (Penal Code, sec. 654.) When there is but one criminal act but one corpus delicti can be carved out of the facts and there can be but one prosecution and when the single unlawful act is charged in separate counts of an indictment or information as different statements of the same offense the accused can be convicted under but one count. Thus a conviction of a felonious assault will bar a subsequent prosecution for mayhem involved in the assault. (People v. De Foor, 100 Cal. 150.) On charges of grand theft, extortion and robbery, all based on one act of taking the property in question, the accused could be convicted of but one of the offenses and a conviction of one would bar a prosecution for the others. (People v. Sigel, 55 Cal. App. 2d 279.) And where a defendant is charged with robbery and kidnapping for the purpose of robbery, both charges being based upon the same act, he can be convicted of only one of these offenses and, if convicted of both, one of the convictions will be reversed on appeal (People v. Knowles, 35 Cal. 2d 175; People v. Kennedy, 101 Cal. App. 2d 709).

Separate Similar Offenses Against Same Victim

The fact that the defendant was tried and convicted, or acquitted, of one offense committed upon the person of another is in no degree a bar for the prosecution of the defendant for an offense of the same character committed upon the same person on a different occasion. (People v. Lachuk, 5 Cal. App. 2d 729; People v. Sanders, 103 Cal. App. 2d 200). Where, however, the defendant was tried on four counts of grand theft and acquitted, each of the counts alleging the offenses as having been committed "or or about" certain days in June and July of 1950 and thereafter a new indictment was returned charging the defendant with five counts of grand theft

alleged to have been committed "on or about" certain days
in August and September of 1949, both indictments being
based upon the theory that the defendant, pursuant to the
same general plan, had obtained from the complainant four
hundred dollars a week by means of the same misrepresentation, and the proof upon the first trial included all of the
transactions between the defendant and the complainant, the
court held that the plea of former jeopardy as to the second
prosecution was good since the court trying the first case had
instructed the jury that it was immaterial on what dates the
offenses charged were committed and that the jury could
convict if they believed that the offenses charged had been
committed at any time within three years preceding the indictment and that, under this instruction, the jury in the first
case might have convicted the defendant for those acts, of
earlier date, set forth in the second indictment (People v.
Bechtel, 41 Cal. 2d. 441).

One Act With Several Victims

Though there be but one act or action and one intent but
more than one victim of the crime there are instances in which
there are as many crimes committed as there are victims. Thus
where by the same act two persons are unlawfully killed there
are two homicides (People v. Majors, 65 Cal. 138; People v
De Casaus, 150 Cal. App. 2d 274, six offenses of manslaughter
where six people were killed by defendant's unlawful driving
of an automobile; People v. Holman, 72 Cal. App. 2d 25); 22
homicides where 22 people were burned to death in the setting
fire to a hotel; where one shot is fired at A and B is killed
thereby the assailant may be convicted of both the assault on
A and the killing of B (People v. Brannon, 70 Cal. App. 225)
and where in one robbery two persons are deprived of their
property there are two robberies (People v. Lagomarsino, 97
Cal. App. 2d 92).

Prosecution for Included Offense Barred

A final determination by a former trial bars not only another prosecution for the same offense, either under the same
or another section of the law but also will bar a subsequent
prosecution for any offense of which the defendant might have
been convicted in the first prosecution. (In re Getzoff, 104
Cal. App. 261; In re Berman, 104 Cal. App. 259.) In other
words the former trial bars not only another prosecution for the
offense there charged but also bars a prosecution for any lesser

offense necessarily included therein. (See: Penal Code, sec. 1023; In re O'Connor, 80 Cal. App. 647; People v. McDaniels, 137 Cal. 192; People v. Ny Sam Ching, 94 Cal. 304.)

Compound Act Constituting But One Offense

There are some offenses in which though the unlawful act involves more than one item as the subject matter but one offense is committed and in such a case a conviction or acquittal based on one item is a bar to another prosecution for the same offense but involving another item. Thus an acquittal of the charge of receiving stolen property is a bar to another prosecution for receiving stolen property where the property involved in the two cases, though not the same, was received by the defendant at the same time. (People v. Willard, 92 Cal. 482; People v. Smith, 26 Cal. 2d 854.) The passing or uttering of a number of forged checks at the same time (People v. Ryan, 74 Cal. App. 125) or the unlawful possession of two revolvers by an ex-convict or alien (People v. Pupillo, 100 Cal. App. 559) constitute but one offense for which there can be but one prosecution. A conviction for libel will bar another prosecution for libel based on another libelous statement in the same newspaper article as that upon which the conviction was based there being but one offense under such article. (People v. Stephens, 79 Cal. 428.) A defendant charged with statutory rape and a violation of section 288 of the Penal Code can not be convicted of both offenses where the charges are both based on the act of sexual intercourse, and in the act of removing the clothing of the prosecutrix would not constitute an act separate and apart from the act of rape as would also permit a conviction under section 288 (People v. Greer, 30 Cal. 2d 589). The possession of three different narcotics—morphine, opium and cocaine,—though contained in one package, constitutes three separate offenses of possession, but, when the only possession shown is that involved in the transportation of the narcotics, but one conviction, either for possession or for transportation, can be had (People v. Mandell, 90 Cal. App. 2d 93).

Conviction or Acquittal of Lesser Offense

A conviction or acquittal will bar a subsequent prosecution for a greater offense which necessarily includes the offense for which such conviction or acquittal was had (People v. Greer, 30 Cal. 2d 589). Thus a conviction of assault and battery is a bar to a prosecution for assault with a deadly weapon

with intent to murder based on the same assault (People
v. McDaniels, 137 Cal. 192), a conviction of assault with
a deadly weapon is a bar to a subsequent prosecution for
an assault with a deadly weapon with intent to commit murder (People v. Gordon, 88 Cal. 422; People v. Gordon, 99 Cal.
227); a conviction of simple assault would bar a subsequent
prosecution for a felonious assault (People v. Apgar, 35 Cal.
389; see also: In re O'Connor, 80 Cal. App. 647; People v. De-
foor, 100 Cal. 150) and a conviction of "being drunk in an automobile upon a public highway" in violation of a county ordinance will bar a prosecution for driving an automobile upon
a public highway while under the influence of intoxicating liquor. (People v. Burkhardt, 5 Cal. 2d 641.) (See also People
v. Krupa, 64 Cal. App. 2d 592.)

After Conviction of Lesser Offense

Where a defendant, charged with assault with a deadly
weapon, is convicted of simple assault and a new trial is granted, he cannot thereafter be convicted or tried for other than the
simple assault. (People v. Apgar, 35 Cal. 389.) Under a
charge of assault with a deadly weapon with intent to commit
murder a conviction of assault with a deadly weapon will, upon
a new trial, bar a conviction of any offense greater than assault with a deadly weapon. (People v. Gordon, 88 Cal. 422,
99 Cal. 227; see also: People v. McDaniels, 137 Cal. 192; People
v. Frank, 134 Cal. App. 61, 211.) Where upon a trial upon the
charge of murder the defendant is convicted of the lesser offense of manslaughter and a new trial is granted the defendant
may be tried again for the homicide but cannot be convicted
of any offense other than manslaughter since the verdict upon
the first trial has the effect of acquitting him of the charge of
murder. (People v. McFarlane, 138 Cal. 481; People v. Muh-
ler, 115 Cal. 303; People v. Smith, 134 Cal. 453; People v. Gil-
man, 4 Cal. 380; People v. Backus, 5 Cal. 278; People v. Huntington, 8 Cal. App. 612.)

Where the defendant plead guilty to petty theft in the
Municipal Court and, upon motion of the district attorney,
the court set aside the plea of guilty and held a preliminary
examination on a complaint charging petty theft after a prior
conviction of petty theft, both charges being based upon the
same taking of property, and held the defendant to answer,
it was held that the entry of the plea of guilty to the misdemeanor had placed the defendant once in jeopardy and that
the provision of section 1429 of the Penal Code (that in the

case of a misdemeanor triable in an inferior court the court may "before pronouncing judgment" examine witnesses and, if it appear that a higher offense has been committed, hold the defendant to answer any complaint or indictment for such higher offense at any time before judgment) is unconstitutional as contrary to the constitutional provisions as to former Jeopardy (People v. Mims, 136 Cal. App. 2d 828).

After Conviction of Lower Degree of Offense

The rule just stated is limited to cases wherein a defendant charged with one offense is convicted of a lesser included but different offense. Where, however, upon a trial of an offense divided into degrees a defendant is convicted of less than the first degree of such offense, he is still convicted of the offense charged, the degree element being merely a matter of penalty, and, if a new trial be granted, he may at the ensuing trial be convicted of such offense in any of its degrees. Thus a defendant convicted of murder in the second degree may upon a new trial be convicted of murder in the first degree (People v. Keefer, 65 Cal. 232; People v. Carty, 77 Cal. 216; People v. Dye. 130 Cal. App. 522; People v. McNeer, 14 Cal. App. 2d 22) and the same rule applies to other offenses which are divided into degrees. (In re Moore and Smith, 29 Cal. App. 2d 56, burglary).

Discharge of Jury

"Except as provided by law, the jury cannot be discharged after the cause is submitted to them until they have agreed upon their verdict and rendered it in open court, unless by consent of both parties, entered upon the minutes, or unless, at the expiration of such time as the court may deem proper, it satisfactorily appears that there is no reasonable probability that the jury can agree." (Penal Code, sec. 1140).

"In all cases where a jury is discharged or presented from giving a verdict by reason of an accident or other cause, except where the defendant is discharged during the progress of the trial, or after the cause is submitted to them, the cause may be tried again." (Penal Code. sec. 1141.)

"If before the jury has returned its verdict into court, a juror becomes sick or upon other good cause shown to the court is unable to perform his duty, the court may order him to be discharged. If any alternate jurors have been selected as provided by law, one of them shall then be designated by the court to take the place of the juror so discharged. If, after all alternate jurors have been made regular jurors, or if there be no alternate juror, a juror becomes sick or otherwise unable to perform his duty and has been discharged by the court as provided herein, the jury shall be discharged and a new jury then or afterwards impanelled, and the cause may be again tried.'' (Penal Code, sec. 1123).

Where the trial court is warranted in concluding that there is no reasonable probability of an agreement of the jurors the section applies and the discharge of the jury is proper and there has been no jeopardy and it is not necessary that all the jurors declare that an agreement is impossible (People v. Sullivan, 101 Cal. App. 2d 322; People v. Westwood, 154 Cal. App. 2d ......).

''When the jury have agreed upon their verdict, they must be conducted into court by the officer having them in charge. Their names must then be called, and if all do not appear, the rest must be discharged without giving a verdict. In that case the action may be tried again.'' (Penal Code, sec. 1147.)

The jeopardy which will bar a subsequent prosecution arises and attaches as soon as the jury is sworn to try the case and the discharge of the jury before it has returned a verdict will as effectively bar another prosecution for the same offense as would an acquittal or a conviction unless such discharge becomes necessary because the jury cannot agree upon a verdict, or where, by reason of the death or illness of a juror he is unable to continue his duties or by reason of any other cause, accident or overruling necessity, a verdict cannot be rendered. (People v. Webb, 38 Cal. 467; People v. Cage, 48 Cal. 323; People v. Hunckeler, 48 Cal. 334; People v. Higgins. 59 Cal. 359; People v. Horn, 70 Cal. 17; Jackson v. Superior Court, 10 Cal. 2d 350.)

Where the court, having ruled that there was no reasonable cause for the defendant's arrest, dismissed the information and discharged the jury, defendant had been once in jeopardy and could not be tried again and jeopardy was not waived by accepting the benefits of the dismissal and not objecting thereto (People v. Valenti, 49 Cal. 2d ......).

When Not a Bar

The discharge of a jury because of illness of a juror (People v. Ross, 85 Cal. 383) or because of inability of the jury to agree (People v. Cage, 48 Cal. 323; People v. Smalling, 94 Cal. 112; People v. James, 97 Cal. 400; People v. Greene, 100 Cal. 140; Ex parte McLaughlin, 41 Cal. 211; People v. Lavine, 115 Cal.

App. 289) even though such inability to agree exists after the court has advised an acquittal (People v. James, 97 Cal. 400) or because the defendant fled during the course of the trial (People v. Higgins, 59 Cal. 357) or because the information was found to be fatally defective (People v. Larson, 68 Cal. 18) would permit the discharge of the jury and remove the effect of the jeopardy which had theretofore arisen and would not bar a retrial of the case. The effect of such a discharge is not affected by the fact that it occurs on a Sunday or legal holiday. (People v. Lightner, 49 Cal. 226.) Where a defendant though charged with the crime of extortion was tried and the case submitted to the jury on the theory that he was guilty of an attempt to commit extortion but the jury was discharged because of its inability to agree upon a verdict the defendant can not upon a second trial predicate any claim of former jeopardy upon the theory under which the first trial was had since the issues are determined by the pleadings and not the theory of the trial. (People v. Lavine, 115 Cal. App. 289.)

Where, on the second day of the trial, one of the jurors did not appear, he having been arrested on a felony charge on his way to court, and, when he later appeared, he stated that he could not impartially discharge his duties as a juror and requested that he be relieved of his duties as a juror and the court dismissed him and the rest of the jurors, it was held that the jury was discharged for "good cause" and that the case might again be tried (In re Devlin, 139 Cal. App. 2d 810).

Consent of Defendant

Where the defendant consents or requests, or the parties agree to, the discharge of the jury before the verdict, the bar of jeopardy is removed and the defendant may again be prosecuted for the same transaction. (Penal Code, sec. 1140; People v. Curtis, 76 Cal. 57; People v. Nash, 15 Cal. App. 320; People v. Kelly, 132 Cal. App. 118, 444; People v. Baillie, 133 Cal. App. 508.)

Mistrial on Motion of Defendant

Where the court, on motion of defendant, granted a motion for a mistrial, the consent inherent in such a motion precludes a later claim of double jeopardy (People v. Mills, 148 Cal. App. 2d 392).

Discharge Which is a Bar

Where a jury is discharged, without the consent of the defendant, before it arrives at a verdict, and such discharge is not due to unavoidable necessity, such a discharge operates as an acquittal and as a bar to another prosecution. (People v. Webb, 38 Cal. 467; People v. Horn, 70 Cal. 17; People v. Curtis, 76 Cal. 57; People v. Arnett, 129 Cal. 306; People v. Kelly, 132 Cal. App. 118, 444; People v. Garcia, 120 Cal. App. 767.)

Where upon a trial of a defendant upon the charge of manslaughter the court, without the consent of the defendant, discharged the jury so that an indictment for murder could be returned, the discharge would bar a subsequent prosecution for the homicide. (People v. Hunckeler, 48 Cal. 331.) Where, upon a trial for murder the jury came into court with a verdict finding the defendant not guilty of murder, but informed the court that they had considered the guilt of the defendant of the included offense of manslaughter but were in disagreement as to whether the defendant was guilty of manslaughter, and the court accepted the verdict and discharged the jury and reset the case for trial on the charge of manslaughter, it was held that the defendant stood acquitted of murder and the prosecution for manslaughter was barred by reason of the discharge of the jury. (Menjou v. Superior Court, 128 Cal. App. 117.) If the court dismisses an indictment and discharges the jury during the trial upon the ground that the indictment fails to charge a criminal offense, but the indictment is in fact good, the defendant will be immune from further prosecution for the matters covered by the indictment. (People v. Superior Court, 214 Cal. 513.) Where the court, after the jury had been sworn to try the cause, allowed the prosecution to excuse a juror by a peremptory challenge, this had the effect of discharging the jury and it was held that the defendant could not again be prosecuted for the same offense. (People v. Young, 100 Cal. App. 18.) The discharge of a jury, which had been unable to agree upon a verdict, without calling the jury into court has been held to have the same effect. (People v. Cage, 48 Cal. 323.) The declaring of a mistrial and the discharge of the jury, on motion of the prosecutor and without the consent of the defendant, upon the ground of error of the court in compelling the defense to exercise the first peremptory challenge is a bar to another prosecution for the same offense as the error in the empanelling of the jury was not such as would prevent jeopardy from arising. (Jackson v. Superior Court, 10 Cal. 2d 350.) The dismissal of a prosecution for petit larceny, at the conclusion of the evidence for the prosecution, to permit the filing of a charge of grand larceny based on the same evidence is a bar to any subsequent prosecution for such larceny. (People v. Ny Sam Chung, 94 Cal. 304.)

Defective Verdict

Where the jury returns a verdict which, though apparently an effort on the part of the jury to find the defendant guilty, falls short of being a valid verdict of conviction as a matter of law and the verdict is recorded and the jury discharged there is no legal verdict and the defendant can successfully plead former jeopardy in a subsequent prosecution for the same offense. Thus, where a defendant was charged and tried for receiving stolen property, a verdict finding the defendant "guilty of receiving stolen property" was held fatally defective because the verdict was without the words "as charged" or words to the effect that the receiving was found by the jury to have been such as would constitute a crime and, the accused having been in jeopardy, he could not again be tried for the offense. (People v. Tilley, 135 Cal. 61; see also: People v. Small, 1 Cal. App. 320.) Where the verdict finds the defendant guilty of an offense other than that charged and not included therein the verdict is void and the discharge of the jury has the same effect as if the jury had been discharged without returning any verdict and the defendant can successfully claim former jeopardy if again prosecuted for the offense charged. (People v. Arnarez, 68 Cal. App. 645; People v. Arnett, 129 Cal. 306; People v. Curtis, 76 Cal. 57.)

Incomplete Verdict

Where, however, the verdict of the jury clearly and unmistakably finds the defendant guilty of the offense charged but is not sufficiently complete to permit a judgment to be entered thereon and the defendant fails to have the verdict corrected before the jury is discharged, he is considered as having consented to the verdict as returned and as waiving any objection, including the plea of former jeopardy, to being put again on trial for the same charge. (In re Colford, 68 Cal. App. 308.) Thus, where the crime charged is one divided by law into degrees, and the indictment or information merely charges the offense generally without pleading that the offense is of a particular degree (a common and proper form of pleading such an offense) a verdict which finds the defendant guilty of the offense charged, but fails to fix the degree of the offense, is so defective that judgment and sentence can not be pronounced and where the jury has been discharged so that it can not correct the defect, the case may be retried and the defective verdict cannot be made the basis of a plea of former jeopardy or former conviction. (People v. Travers, 73 Cal. 580; In re Colford, 68 Cal. App. 308.) The same rule applies to a case in which the jury, which finds the defendant guilty, is charged with the further duty of fixing the penalty (as in the crime of first degree murder, statutory rape, or kidnaping), but returns a verdict which finds the defendant guilty but is silent as to the penalty. (People v. Sachau, 78 Cal. App. 702.)

If, however, in charging an offense divided into degrees the pleading specifically charges the degree of the crime (first degree burglary in the case cited) the jury can only return a verdict of acquittal or a verdict finding the defendant guilty of the offense in the degree charged and a verdict finding the defendant guilty of another degree of such offense is a nullity and the equivalent of an acquittal and the defendant is entitled to his discharge and cannot again be prosecuted for the same offense. (People v. Smith, 136 Cal. 207.)

Where a defendant is found guilty but the jury fails to find a separate verdict or any verdict as to his plea of former jeopardy no judgment can be pronounced and a new trial must be granted but there is no jeopardy. (People v. Tucker, 117 Cal. 229.)

Defective Indictment or Information

Where a defendant is convicted of the offense charged but the indictment or information is legally insufficient to charge such offense though it is sufficient to charge an offense necessarily included therein, the defendant is entitled to an arrest of judgment or a reversal of the judgment on appeal but the case may be retried for there is no jeopardy. (People v. Ham Tong, 155 Cal. 579, the court saying: "If it be the doctrine of People v. Arnett, 129 Cal. 306; People v. Smith, 136 Cal. 207; People v. Tilley, 135 Cal. 61, and People v. Curtis, 76 Cal. 57, that the defendant has been once in jeopardy in every case wherein a verdict of guilty of a crime not strictly within the pleading has been returned and the jury has been discharged without consent, then those cases should be overruled".)

Directed Acquittal

While the trial court has the power to advise but not the power to direct the jury to return a verdict of acquittal still, if the court exceeds its authority and directs the jury to acquit the defendant, the return of such a verdict is as much a bar to another prosecution as an acquittal by the jury of its own volition and without such direction (People v. Horn, 70 Cal. 17; People v. Roberts, 114 Cal. 67; People v. Stoll, 143 Cal. 689; People v. Hill, 146 Cal. 145) and this is the rule even though such direction was the product of an erroneous ruling of the trial judge in excluding competent prosecution evidence. (People v. Webb, 38 Cal. 467) or an erroneous opinion of the judge that the information failed to charge a criminal offense. (People v. Newell, 192 Cal. 659.)

Effect of Granting New Trial

"The granting of a new trial places the parties in the same position as if no trial had been had. All the testimony must be produced anew, and the former verdict cannot be used or referred to, either in evidence or in argument, or be pleaded in bar of any conviction which might have been had under the new indictment." (Penal Code, sec. 1180.)

Where a new trial is granted by the trial court (People v. Baza, 53 Cal. 690) or is ordered as the result of an appeal by the defendant he may again be tried for the offense of which he was convicted upon the first trial. (People v. Olwell, 28 Cal. 456; People v. Hardisson, 61 Cal. 378; People v. Travers, 77 Cal. 176; People v. Frank, 75 Cal. App. 74; People v. Stratton, 136 Cal. App. 201; People v. d'A Philippo, 140 Cal. App. 236.)

While section 1180 of the Penal Code declares that "the granting of a new trial places the parties in the same position as if no trial had been had" this is not the effect of the granting of a new trial where the case is one in which the defendant was convicted of a lesser and necessarily included offense for in such a case the effect of granting a new trial is only to grant a new trial as to the offense of which the defendant was convicted. Notwithstanding the language of section 1180 the conviction of a defendant of a lesser offense than that with which he was charged and placed on trial is in effect an acquittal of all greater offenses included in the crime charged; the verdict of conviction of the lesser offense eliminates from the case for the purpose of future verdict all elements of the corpus delicti of any greater offense which is not an element of the corpus delicti of the offense of which the accused was convicted. And this is true even though, as a matter of law the defendant, if guilty at all, is guilty of the greater offense.

Plea of Guilty Set Aside

Where a plea of guilty is set aside on coram nobis both the People and the defendant are restored to their original positions on all counts of the information as they existed immediately before the entry of the plea (People v. Gilbert, 25 Cal. 2d 422, 440). Where such plea is entered after the trial has commenced this rule should be equally applicable for, even though the jury was discharged after the plea was entered, the discharge was for cause and the result of the action of the defendant and the case, if the plea of not guilty be restored, may be tried again. (Penal Code, sec. 1141).

Dismissal, Effect of

An order for the dismissal of the action as provided in Chapter VIII, Part 2 of the Penal Code, is not a bar if the offense is a felony but is a bar to any other prosecution for the same offense if it is a misdemeanor unless the order is explicitly made for the purpose of amending the complaint in such action, in which instance it is not a bar to a prosecution upon such amended complaint. (Penal Code, sec. 1387; see also: People v. Kerrick, 144 Cal. 46; Patterson v. Coulan, 123 Cal. 453; People v. Schmidt, 64 Cal. 263.) Where a misdemeanor complaint is dismissed, not for the purpose of amending the complaint but because of the filing of a new action based on the same offense, the dismissal is a bar to the prosecution of the new charge (People v. Aiken, 108 Cal. App. 2d 343).

It must be noted that the order of dismissal which is not a bar in the case of a felony is, "An order for the dismissal of the action **as provided in this chapter.**" (Penal Code, Sec. 1387.) Thus, in case of a dismissal by the court, under Section 1385 of the Penal Code, "of its own motion or upon the application of the district attorney and in furtherance of justice," it is required that, "The reasons of the dismissal must be set forth in an order entered upon the minutes"; and, if the order of dismissal does not recite the grounds upon which it is based, the dismissal is a bar to another prosecution for the same offense. (People v. Desperati, 11 Cal. App. 469, 474.)

The dismissal of a prosecution on motion of the defendant, made after the jury has been sworn, waives the right of the defendant to plead former jeopardy in a subsequent prosecution (People v. Finch, 119 Cal. App. 2d 892).

Where there is pending against a defendant an indictment and an information, each charging the same offense, the defendant cannot complain if the information is dismissed and he is convicted under the indictment (People v. MacCagnan, 129 Cal. App. 2d. 100).

Dismissal of One Count During Trial

While the dismissal of one count of an indictment or information during the trial will operate as an acquittal of that offense it has no effect upon other offenses charged in other counts. (People v. Moon, 7 Cal. App. 2d 96; People v. Clensy, 97 Cal. App. 71; People v. Schofield, 203 Cal. 703; People v. Derenzo, 46 Cal. App. 2d 411; People v. Kearney, 20 Cal. 2d 435; People v. Dreyer, 71 Cal. App. 2d 181; People v. Carothers, 77 Cal. App. 252). Where the defendant was charged in one count with the crime of assault with intent to commit rape and in another count with attempted rape of the same woman, based on the same act, and during the trial the latter count was dismissed, it was held that, whether the counts charged different statements of the same offense or two offenses of the same class, the dismissal of the one count was not tantamount to an acquittal of the other (People v. Nye, 37 Cal. 2d 34).

Dismissal of Misdemeanor To Charge Felony

Where a prosecution for a misdemeanor is pending and thereafter a felony charge based upon the same act is filed and the misdemeanor charge is then dismissed, such dismissal is not a bar to the felony prosecution (People v. Brown, 42 Cal. App. 462; People v. Hinshaw, 194 Cal. 1); and the rule would be the same were the dismissal of the misdemeanor to precede the filing of the felony charge. (People v. Smith, 143 Cal. 597.)

Failure To File or Try in Time

The dismissal of a prosecution because of the failure to file an information or to bring the defendant to trial within the time provided by statute does not bar another prosecution for the same offense or any offense involved in the act forming the basis of the first prosecution. (In re Bergerow, 136 Cal. 293; People v. Dawson, 210 Cal. 366; People v. Godlewski, 22 Cal. 2d 677.)

Dismissal To Use One Defendent As a Witness

Sections 1099 and 1100 of the Penal Code provide that, when two or more persons are included in the same charge, the court may in certain instances discharge any defendant upon application of the district attorney that he may be called as a witness for the people or of the court's own motion tnat he may be a witness for his co-defendant. Such discharge has the effect of an acquittal of the defendant so discharged and is a bar to his further prosecution for the same offense. (Penal Code, Sec. 1101; People v. Bruzzo, 24 Cal. 41.) But the dismissal of a charge against a defendant in order to permit him to be a witness at a preliminary examination is not a bar. (People v. Indian Peter, 48 Cal. 250.)

After Compromise of Misdemeanor

The compromise of a misdemeanor charge in accordance with the provisions of Section 1377, 1378 and 1379 of the Penal Code is a bar to another prosecution for the same offense. (Penal Code, Sec. 1378.)

Second Prosecution—When for an Offense Not Consummated At Time of Former Prosecution

The conviction, acquittal or prosecution of a person is not a bar to the subsequent prosecution of such person for an offense which did not have an existence at the time of the former trial. Thus, where a defendant has committed an act of violence which in its immediate results amounts to a misdemeanor but which in its after consequences upon the victim of violence becomes a felonious homicide through the death of the victim, a conviction, acquittal or trial of such person for the misdemeanor will not bar a prosecution for murder or manslaughter based upon the death of the victim subsequent to such prior prosecution. (People v. Wilson, 193 Cal. 512.)

Prior Conviction Procured by the Accused

It is an essential part of the basis of the rule of former jeopardy that a person shall not be compelled to submit to more than one prosecution for the same offense, but does not contemplate a case wherein the accused has endeavored, by his own act, to create a former jeopardy to prevent a bona fide prosecution for his wrongful act. If a person committed a felonious assault and procured his own prosecution for a simple assault as a means of preventing a prosecution for a felony, there would be no jeopardy. As stated by our Supreme Court, "Of course, if the former conviction was procured by the fraud, connivance or collusion of the defendant, this fact vitiates it and it is no bar to a subsequent prosecution." (People v. McDaniels, 137 Cal. 192.)

Arrest of Judgment

Ordinarily an order granting a motion in arrest of judgment in a superior court does not bar a subsequent prosecution as its effect is "to place the defendant in the same position in which he was before the indictment was found or information filed; in any other court the effect is to place the defendant in a situation in which he was before the trial was had"; (Penal Code, Sec. 1187), but "if no evidence appears sufficient to charge him with any offense . . . the arrest of judgment shall operate as an acquittal of the charge upon which the indictment or information was founded." (Penal Code, Sec. 1188; see also: People v. Eppinger, 109 Cal. 294; People v. Indian Peter, 48 Cal. 250.)

What Is Not a Former Acquittal—Variance

"If a defendant was formerly acquitted on the ground of variance between the indictment or information and the proof, or the indictment was dismissed upon an objection to its form or substance, or in order to hold the defendant for a higher offense without a judgment of acquittal, it is not an acquittal of the same offense." (Penal Code, Sec. 1021.)

Material Variance

Where there is a material variance between the allegations of the indictment or information and the proof offered in support thereof, an acquittal or conviction will not bar a subsequent prosecution for the same offense. (People v. Hughes, 41 Cal. 234; People v. McNealy, 17 Cal. 332; People v. Oreileus, 79 Cal. 178; People v. Castilla, 28 Cal. App. 190; People v. Nelson, 70 Cal. App. 476; People v. Allan, 80 Cal. App. 709.) But where the jury at the instance of the court returns a verdict of not guilty upon the ground of variance, such verdict is a bar to another prosecution for the same offense where no material variance did in fact exist. (People v. Hughes, 41 Cal. 234; People v. Terrill, 132 Cal. 497; 133 Cal. 120; People v. Newell, 192 Cal. 659.)

Conviction Where Evidence Only Shows
Offense Not Charged

Where a defendant is convicted but the offense established by the evidence is a crime other than and not included in the offense charged or where in such a case the defendant is acquitted the bar of jeopardy will not apply to the offense shown by the evidence. Under such circumstances the defendant could not legally be convicted of the offense shown by the evidence since that offense was not within the scope of the charge and, therefore, the defendant never was in jeopardy for the offense proved. Such a case is not one of a mere variance as to an incidental fact but is a total failure to prove the offense charged and the evidence showing a crime not within the issues is immaterial and irrelevant. Where a defendant was charged with the embezzlement of money but the evidence, while failing to prove that offense, showed that he had embezzled jewelry, an acquittal will not support a claim of former jeopardy in a subsequent prosecution for the embezzlement of the jewelry. (People v. Nelson, 70 Cal. App. 476, the court saying: "It has repeatedly been held that one test applicable to determine the identity of the offense is to ascertain if the evidence which is necessary to support the second information was admissible under the former, and was sufficient if believed by the jury to have warranted a conviction of that crime. It is obvious that the evidence offered in the case in which this defendant was convicted would not have stood this test as applied to the prosecution of the case in which the jury found the defendant not guilty. . . . It follows, therefore that appellant was not tried in the first instance for the same offense with which he was charged in this case; and since the offenses were not the same, his plea of having formerly been in jeopardy is without merit.") A similar conclusion was reached where, in the first trial, the check proved materially varied from the check pleaded. (People v. Allan, 80 Cal. App. 709.)

What Is Not Former Jeopardy

A second indictment is not barred by reason of a former indictment for the same offense where no trial has been had under the first indictment (People v. Hatfield, 129 Cal. 162) or where the first indictment was set aside (Penal Code, sec. 999; People v. Varnum, 53 Cal. 630; Kalloch v. Superior Court, 56 Cal. 229; People v. Campbell, 59 Cal. 243; People v. Breen, 130 Cal. 72) or where the case was reversed on appeal because the indictment was defective. (People v. Schmidt, 64 Cal. 260.) Forfeiture of a prisoner's credits because of his escape will not bar his prosecution for the crime of escape. (People v. Conson, 72 Cal. App. 509.) The allegation and proof that the defendant has previously suffered a conviction of a felony is not affected by the rule of former jeopardy. (People v. Frank, 134 Cal. App. 211; People v. Schneider, 107 Cal. App. 555; People v. Di

Michele, 149 Cal. App. 2d 277). The fact that evidence of the
commission by the defendant of a crime other than that for
which he is on trial is received against him does not prevent
his subsequent prosecution for such other crime since he could
not have been convicted of such other crime in the first trial.
(People v. Wilson, 79 Cal. 709; People v. Rogers, 112 Cal. App.
615). The substitution of an alternate juror for a juror who
had become too ill to continue his duties furnishes no basis for
a claim of former jeopardy. (People v. Von Bodenthal, 8 Cal.
App. 2d 404). A verdict finding a defendant not guilty by
reasons of insanity as to one offense will not bar a prosecution
for a separate offense committed at the same time as the offense of which he was acquitted. (People v. Perry, 99 Cal.
App. 90). The release of a defendant on habeas corpus for
insufficiency of the evidence to sustain his commitment upon
a preliminary examination does not in any way prevent his
being held to answer on the same charge at a subsequent preliminary examination (In re Heinze, 116 Cal. App. 286) and a
discharge upon a preliminary examination is not a bar to the
holding of another preliminary examination for the same offense before the same or another magistrate. (Ex parte Fen-
ton, 77 Cal. 183; People v. Hejack, 85 Cal. App. 301; Patterson
v. Carlson, 123 Cal. 453.) A defendant sentenced to the state
prison, his sentence being later erroneously changed to a sentence in the county jail, cannot object to his resentence to the
state prison upon the ground that he has already been in
jeopardy. (In re Wilson, 196 Cal. 515.) The failure of the
grand jury to return an indictment has no effect upon any
subsequent prosecution. (Ex parte Cahill, 52 Cal. 463; Ex
parte Clarke, 54 Cal. 412; Kalloch v. Superior Court, 56 Cal.
235.)

Juvenile Court Proceedings, Effect of

Where a defendant was charged under section 700 of the
Welfare and Institutions Code as a minor who had violated
the law of this state by committing a burglary and was committed to the Youth Authority by the Juvenile Court, that proceeding, not being criminal in nature, does not constitute a
bar to a subsequent prosecuton and conviction of the defendant under an information charging him with the same burglary after his certification by the Youth Authority as an
improper person for handling by the Authority (People v.
Silverstein, 121 Cal. App. 2d. 140).

CHAPTER XXXIV

RES JUDICATA

The doctrine of res judicata applies in criminal as well as in civil cases and may be invoked where a jeopardy plea would not be available (People v. Beltran, 94 Cal. App. 2d. 197 and cases cited; People v. Joseph, 153 Cal. App. 2d ......). The court having, in the first prosecution, decided that the defendant was deprived of his right to counsel at his preliminary examination, that matter was held res judicata in a subsequent prosecution for the same offense (People v. Mora, 120 Cal. App. 2d 896). Upon the first trial of the defendant for two counts of robbery and one count of kidnapping for the purpose of robbery the jury disagreed as to the robberies but acquitted him of the kidnapping charge and upon a retrial of the robbery charges the defendant was convicted of both robberies and raised the point that the acquittal on the kidnapping charge, it being an incident in the robberies, was res judicata which precluded his conviction of the robberies but the court held that the acquittal on the kidnapping charge did not constitute res judicata as it did not amount to a finding inconsistent with the robbery convictions (People v. Beltran, 94 Cal. App. 2d 197). Where, upon a trial for conspiracy to commit thefts, the sole overt acts alleged were also pleaded as separate offenses of theft and the jury disagreed as to the charge of conspiracy but acquitted as to all of the theft counts, such latter finding was res judicata and there could not be a retrial of the conspiracy charge since, in effect the verdicts constituted findings that the overt acts had not been committed (Oliver v. Superior Court, 92 Cal. App. 94; see also California Criminal Procedure under Inconsistent Verdicts). In a prosecution for failure to provide for a minor child the court received evidence that the defendant had previously been convicted of failing to provide for the same child but excluded offered proof that the defendant was not the father of the child and it was held that the first prosecution determined the issue of parentage, that this was res judicata even though in the first case the defendant had been placed on probation and that proceeding was thereafter dismissed (People v. Majado, 22 Cal. App. 2d. 323). Where, upon motion, the information was set aside on the ground that the defendant had been deprived of counsel at the preliminary examination, this is res judicata as to the illegality of such examination and the testimony given by the defendant at such examination is inadmissible (People v. Mora, 120 Cal. App. 2d. 896).

When habeas corpus proceedings have been prosecuted in the Superior Court and that court has made findings of fact, its order is res judicata of the issues tried and decided by that court and the petitioner, if unsuccessful in the Superior Court, is estopped, in the absence of a change of circumstances, upon a petition for habeas corpus to the District Court of Appeal, from again trying the issues (In re Croze, 145 Cal. App. 2d 492).

What is Not

Where the defendant was charged by complaint with a violation of section 11500 of the Health and Safety Code and, at the conclusion of the preliminary examination, the magistrate dismissed the charge on the ground that there was no reasonable cause for defendant's arrest and, the same thing happened upon a second preliminary examination before a different magistrate, this was not res judicata and did not bar a subsequent prosecution for the same offense (People v. Joseph, 153 Cal. App. 2d ......).

INDEX

Page   Page

Page

Page